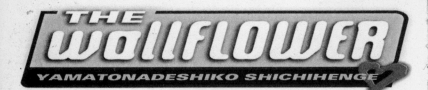

YAMATONADESHIKO SHICHIHENGE

Tomoko Hayakawa

TRANSLATED AND ADAPTED BY
David Ury

LETTERED BY
Dana Hayward

BALLANTINE BOOKS • NEW YORK

A Del Rey Trade Paperback Original

Published in the United States by Del Rey Books, an imprint of The Random House Publishing Group, a division of Random House, Inc., New York.

DEL REY is a registered trademark and the Del Rey colophon is a trademark of Random House, Inc.

Publication rights arranged through Kodansha, Ltd.

First published in Japan in 2005 by Kodansha Ltd., Tokyo, as *Yamatonadeshiko Shichihenge.*

ISBN 978-0-345-49556-3

Printed in the United States of America

www.delreymanga.com

9 8 7 6 5 4 3 2 1

Translator and adaptor—David Ury
Lettering—Dana Hayward

Contents

A Note from the Author

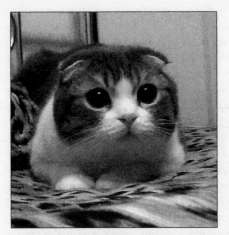

*Ten, with his eyes set on a cat toy. His eyes
and his face are both so round...*

♥ It's book 12. That means we've hit the fiftieth story mark! Thanks
so much for your support. I really mean it. ♥♥♥ I don't know how
long this series will go on for, but I hope you'll keep reading. I'll
keep doing my best.

—Tomoko Hayakawa

Honorifics Explained

Throughout the Del Rey Manga books, you will find Japanese honorifics left intact in the translations. For those not familiar with how the Japanese use honorifics and, more important, how they differ from American honorifics, we present this brief overview.

Politeness has always been a critical facet of Japanese culture. Ever since the feudal era, when Japan was a highly stratified society, use of honorifics—which can be defined as polite speech that indicates relationship or status—has played an essential role in the Japanese language. When addressing someone in Japanese, an honorific usually takes the form of a suffix attached to one's name (example: "Asuna-san"), or as a title at the end of one's name, or in place of the name itself (example: "Negi-sensei," or simply "Sensei!").

Honorifics can be expressions of respect or endearment. In the context of manga and anime, honorifics give insight into the nature of the relationship between characters. Many English translations leave out these important honorifics, and therefore distort the feel of the original Japanese. Because Japanese honorifics contain nuances that English honorifics lack, it is our policy at Del Rey not to translate them. Here, instead, is a guide to some of the honorifics you may encounter in Del Rey Manga.

-san: This is the most common honorific, and is equivalent to Mr., Miss, Ms., or Mrs. It is the all-purpose honorific and can be used in any situation where politeness is required.

-sama: This is one level higher than "-san." It is used to confer great respect.

-dono: This comes from the word "tono," which means "lord." It is an even higher level than "-sama" and confers utmost respect.

-kun: This suffix is used at the end of boys' names to express familiarity or endearment. It is also sometimes used by men among friends, or when addressing someone younger or of a lower station.

-chan: This is used to express endearment, mostly toward girls. It is also used for little boys, pets, and even among lovers. It gives a sense of childish cuteness.

Bozu: This is an informal way to refer to a boy, similar to the English term "kid" or "squirt."

Sempai/Senpai: This title suggests that the addressee is one's senior in a group or organization. It is most often used in a school setting, where underclassmen refer to their upperclassmen as "sempai." It can also be used in the workplace, such as when a newer employee addresses an employee who has seniority in the company.

Kohai: This is the opposite of "-sempai," and is used toward underclassmen in school or newcomers in the workplace. It connotes that the addressee is of a lower station.

Sensei: Literally meaning "one who has come before," this title is used for teachers, doctors, or masters of any profession or art.

-[blank]: This is usually forgotten in these lists, but it is perhaps the most significant difference between Japanese and English. The lack of honorific means that the speaker has permission to address the person in a very intimate way. Usually, only family, spouses, or very close friends have this kind of permission. Known as *yobisute*, it can be gratifying when someone who has earned the intimacy starts to call one by one's name without an honorific. But when that intimacy hasn't been earned, it can be very insulting.

THE wallFLOWER
YAMATONADESHIKO SHICHIHENGE
ヤマトナデシコ七変化♡

CONTENTS

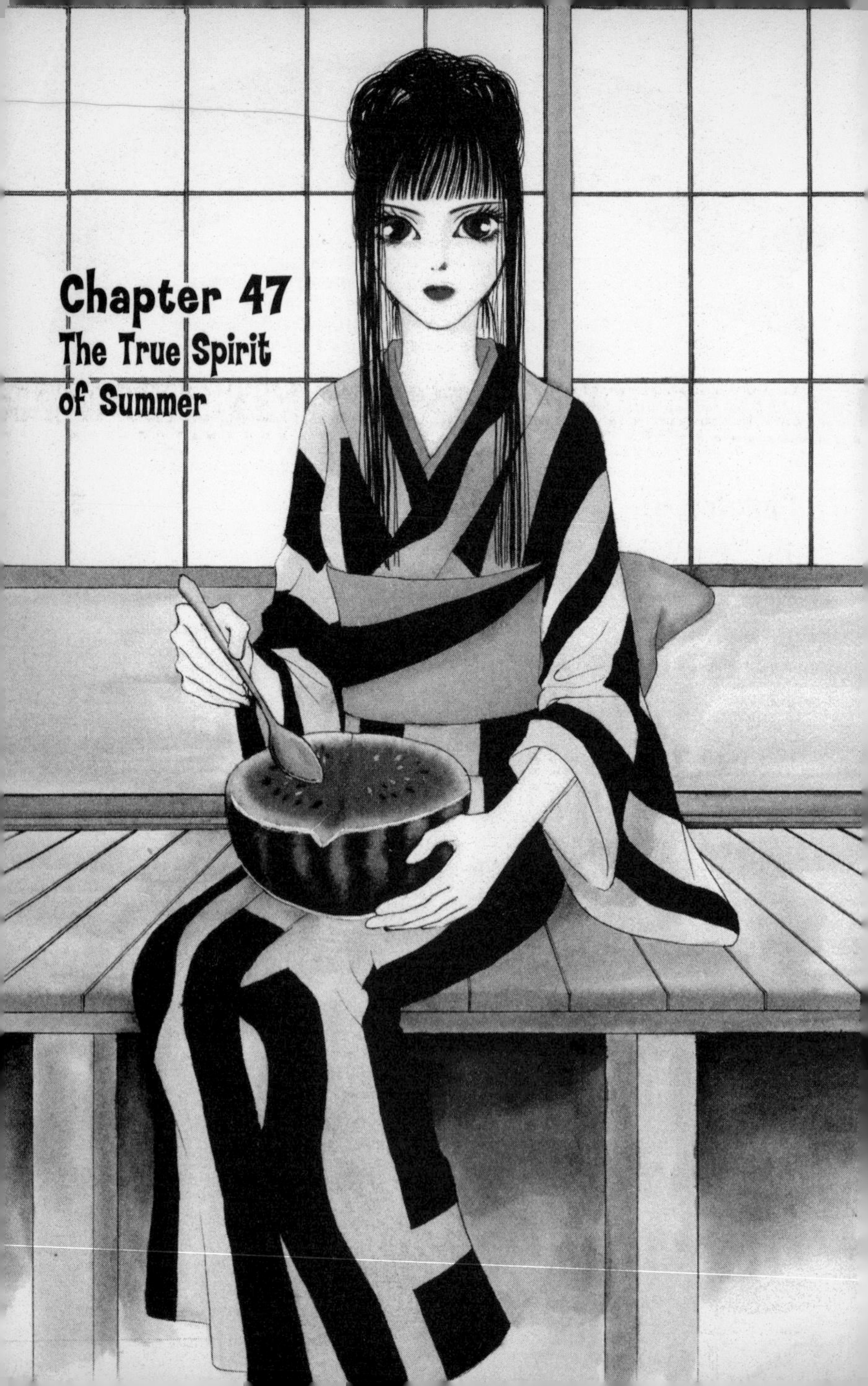

Chapter 47
The True Spirit of Summer

THE WALLFLOWER'S BEAUTIFUL CAST OF CHARACTERS (?)

SUNAKO IS A DARK LONER WHO LOVES HORROR MOVIES. WHEN HER AUNT, THE LANDLADY OF A BOARDINGHOUSE, LEAVES TOWN WITH HER BOYFRIEND, SUNAKO IS FORCED TO LIVE WITH FOUR HANDSOME GUYS. SUNAKO'S AUNT MAKES A DEAL WITH THE BOYS, WHICH CAUSES NOTHING BUT HEADACHES FOR SUNAKO: "MAKE SUNAKO INTO A LADY, AND YOU CAN LIVE RENT FREE."

SUNAKO IS ENJOYING LIFE AT HER OWN PACE, AND THE FOUR BISHONEN BOYS SEEM TO BE IN NO HURRY TO CHANGE HER.

THE WEALTHY PRINCE RANMARU HAS BEEN POISONED BY THE WORKING-CLASS ATMOSPHERE OF HIS CURRENT SURROUNDINGS. SOMETIMES RANMARU LONGS SO MUCH FOR HIS FORMER LIFE OF LUXURY THAT HE EXPLODES INTO RELAPSE.

KYOHEI TAKANO—
A STRONG FIGHTER,
"I'M THE KING."

TAKENAGA ODA—
A CARING FEMINIST

RANMARU MORII—
A TRUE LADIES' MAN

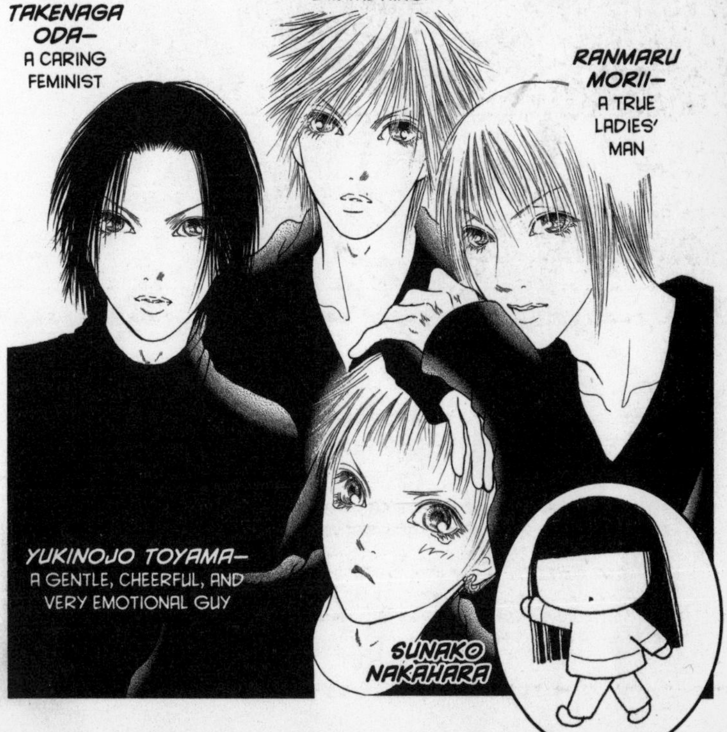
YUKINOJO TOYAMA—
A GENTLE, CHEERFUL, AND VERY EMOTIONAL GUY
SUNAKO NAKAHARA

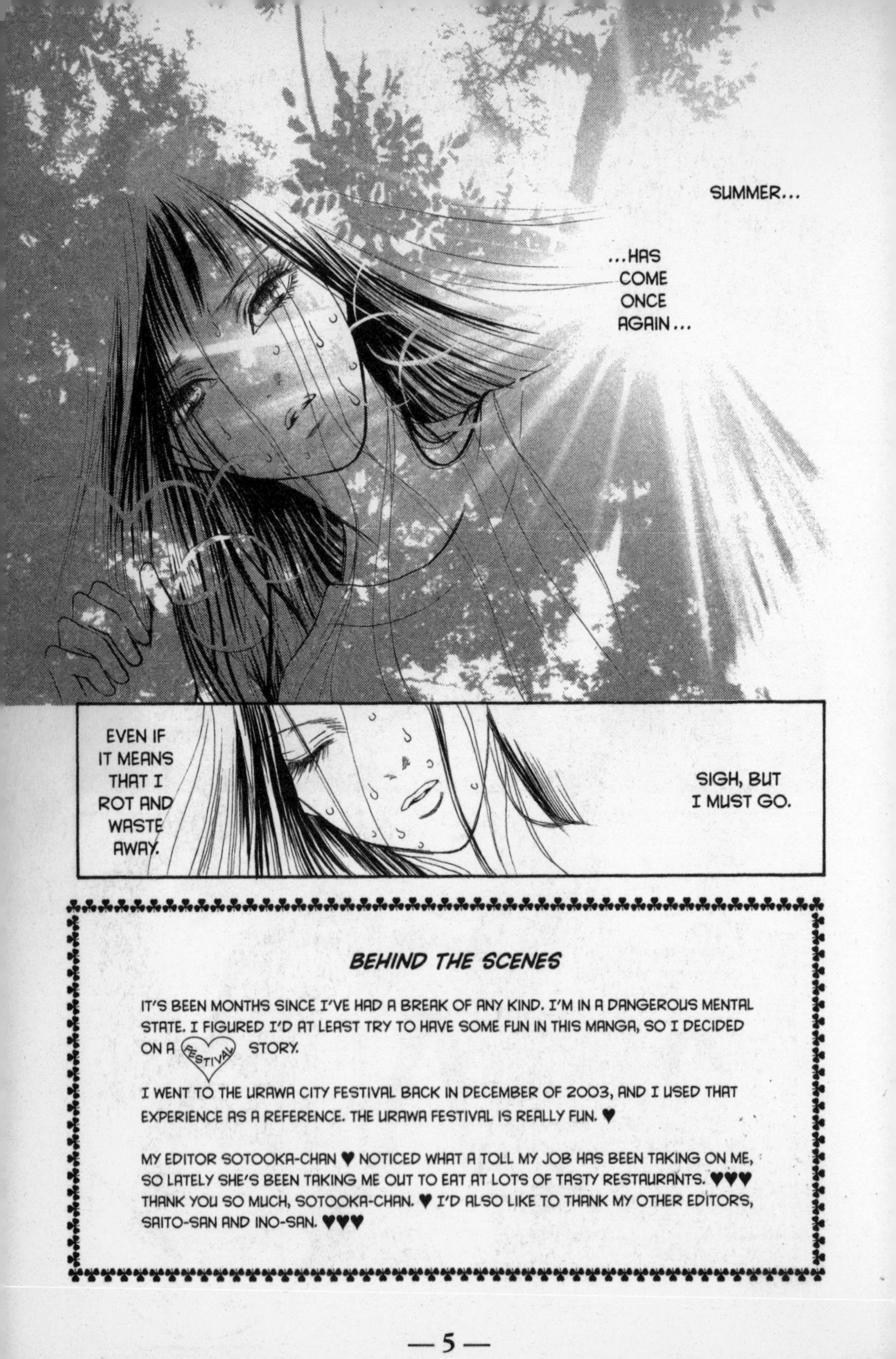
SUMMER...
...HAS COME ONCE AGAIN...
SIGH, BUT I MUST GO.
EVEN IF IT MEANS THAT I ROT AND WASTE AWAY.

BEHIND THE SCENES

IT'S BEEN MONTHS SINCE I'VE HAD A BREAK OF ANY KIND. I'M IN A DANGEROUS MENTAL STATE. I FIGURED I'D AT LEAST TRY TO HAVE SOME FUN IN THIS MANGA, SO I DECIDED ON A FESTIVAL STORY.

I WENT TO THE URAWA CITY FESTIVAL BACK IN DECEMBER OF 2003, AND I USED THAT EXPERIENCE AS A REFERENCE. THE URAWA FESTIVAL IS REALLY FUN. ♥

MY EDITOR SOTOOKA-CHAN ♥ NOTICED WHAT A TOLL MY JOB HAS BEEN TAKING ON ME, SO LATELY SHE'S BEEN TAKING ME OUT TO EAT AT LOTS OF TASTY RESTAURANTS. ♥♥♥ THANK YOU SO MUCH, SOTOOKA-CHAN. ♥ I'D ALSO LIKE TO THANK MY OTHER EDITORS, SAITO-SAN AND INO-SAN. ♥♥♥

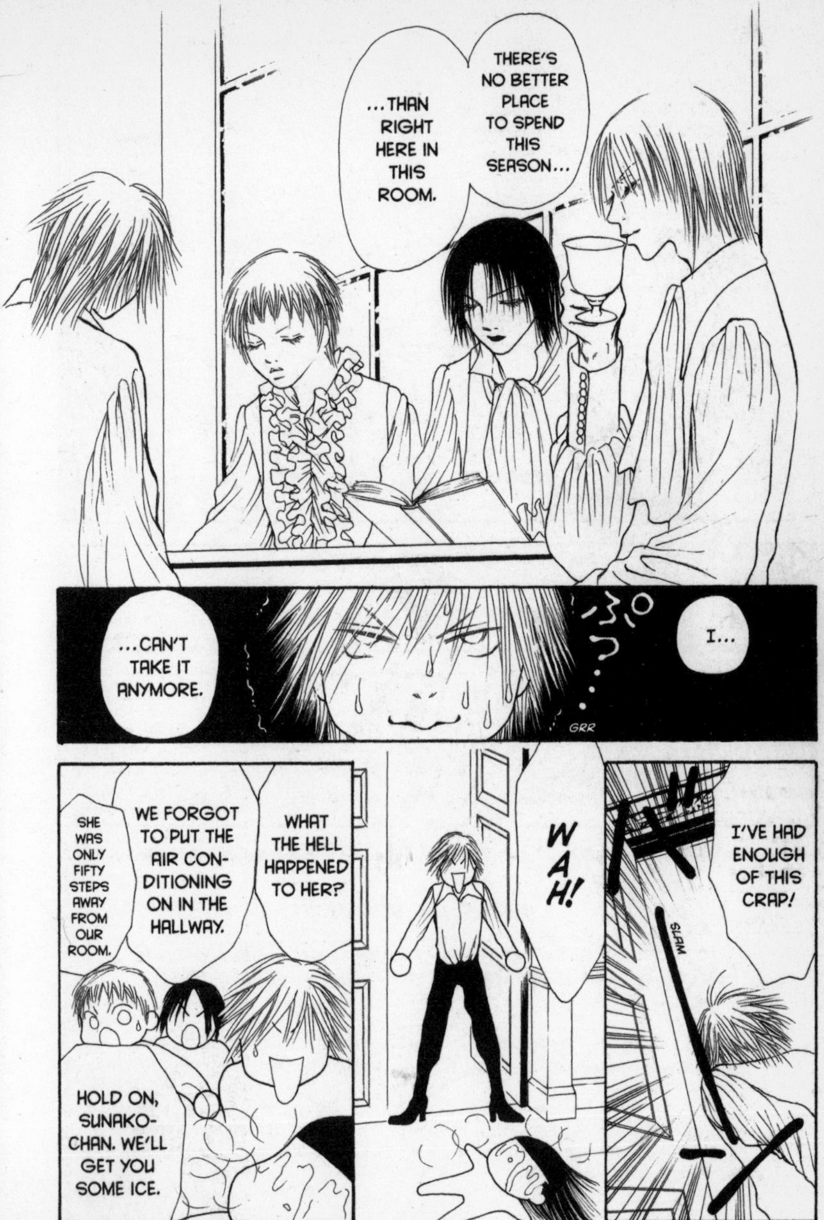
THERE'S NO BETTER PLACE TO SPEND THIS SEASON...
...THAN RIGHT HERE IN THIS ROOM.
I...
GRR
...CAN'T TAKE IT ANYMORE.
I'VE HAD ENOUGH OF THIS CRAP!
SLAM
WAH!
WHAT THE HELL HAPPENED TO HER?
WE FORGOT TO PUT THE AIR CON-DITIONING ON IN THE HALLWAY.
SHE WAS ONLY FIFTY STEPS AWAY FROM OUR ROOM.
HOLD ON, SUNAKO-CHAN. WE'LL GET YOU SOME ICE.

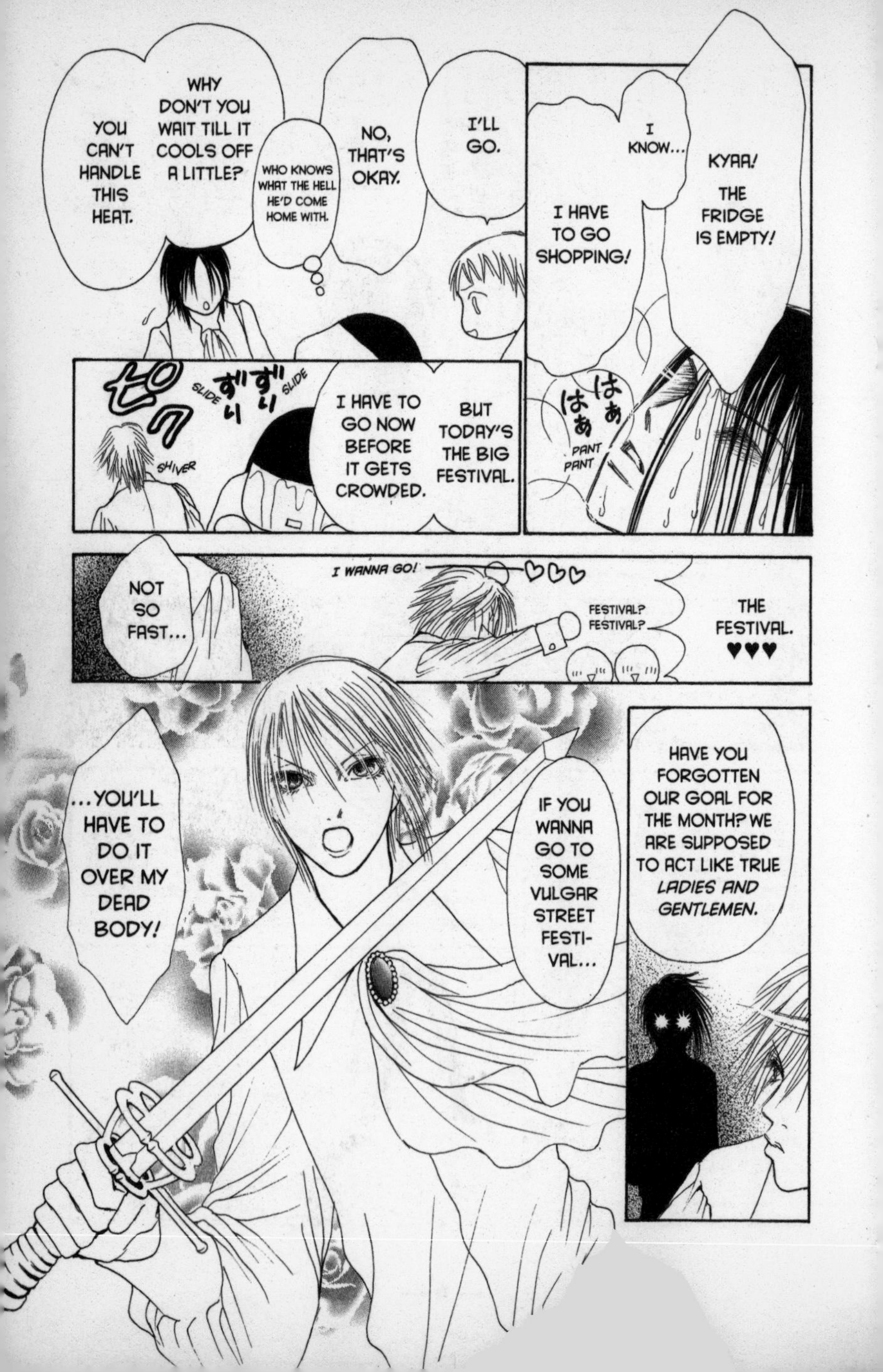
KYAA! THE FRIDGE IS EMPTY!
I KNOW...
I HAVE TO GO SHOPPING!
はぁ はぁ PANT PANT
I'LL GO.
NO, THAT'S OKAY.
WHO KNOWS WHAT THE HELL HE'D COME HOME WITH.
WHY DON'T YOU WAIT TILL IT COOLS OFF A LITTLE?
YOU CAN'T HANDLE THIS HEAT.
BUT TODAY'S THE BIG FESTIVAL.
I HAVE TO GO NOW BEFORE IT GETS CROWDED.
ずりずり SLIDE SLIDE
ピク SHIVER
THE FESTIVAL. ♥♥♥
FESTIVAL? FESTIVAL?
I WANNA GO!
NOT SO FAST...
HAVE YOU FORGOTTEN OUR GOAL FOR THE MONTH? WE ARE SUPPOSED TO ACT LIKE TRUE *LADIES AND GENTLEMEN.*
IF YOU WANNA GO TO SOME VULGAR STREET FESTI-VAL...
...YOU'LL HAVE TO DO IT OVER MY DEAD BODY!

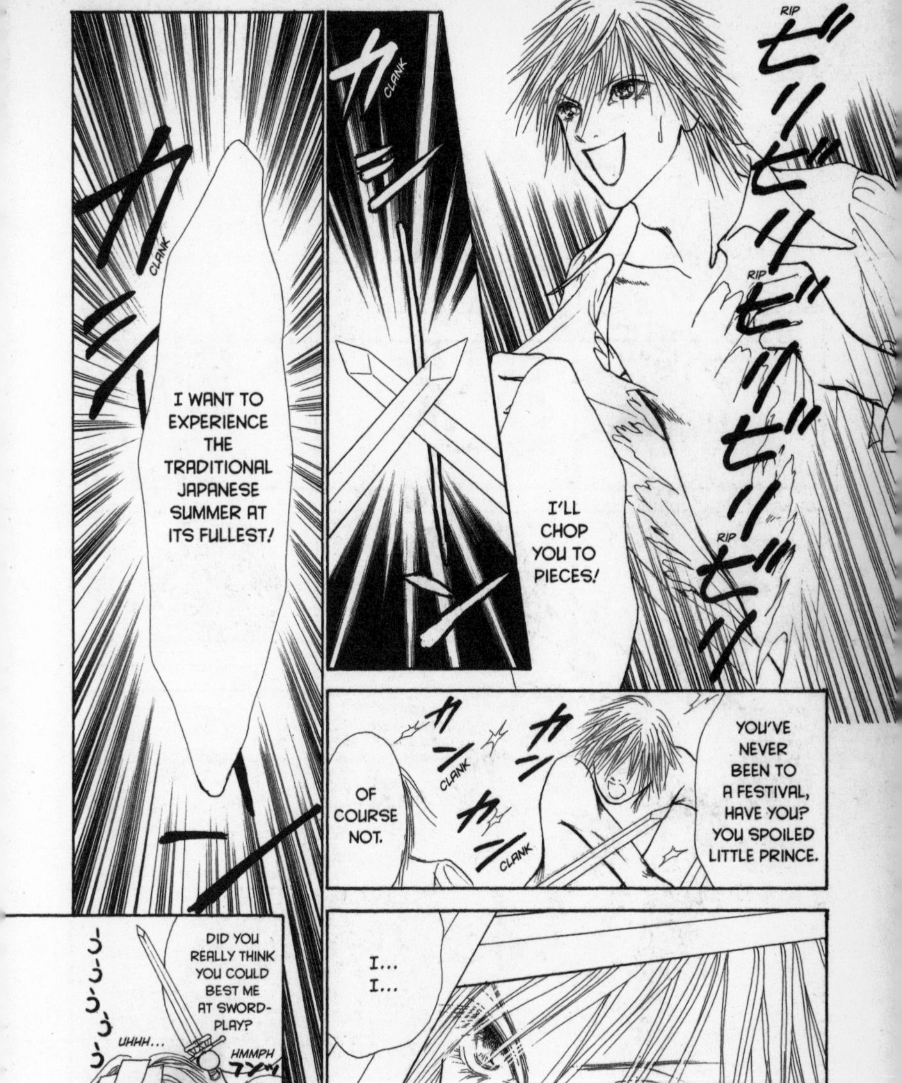
RIP
RIP
RIP
I'LL CHOP YOU TO PIECES!
CLANK
YOU'VE NEVER BEEN TO A FESTIVAL, HAVE YOU? YOU SPOILED LITTLE PRINCE.
CLANK
CLANK
OF COURSE NOT.
CLANK
I WANT TO EXPERIENCE THE TRADITIONAL JAPANESE SUMMER AT ITS FULLEST!
I...
I...
DID YOU REALLY THINK YOU COULD BEST ME AT SWORD-PLAY?
HMMPH
UHHH...

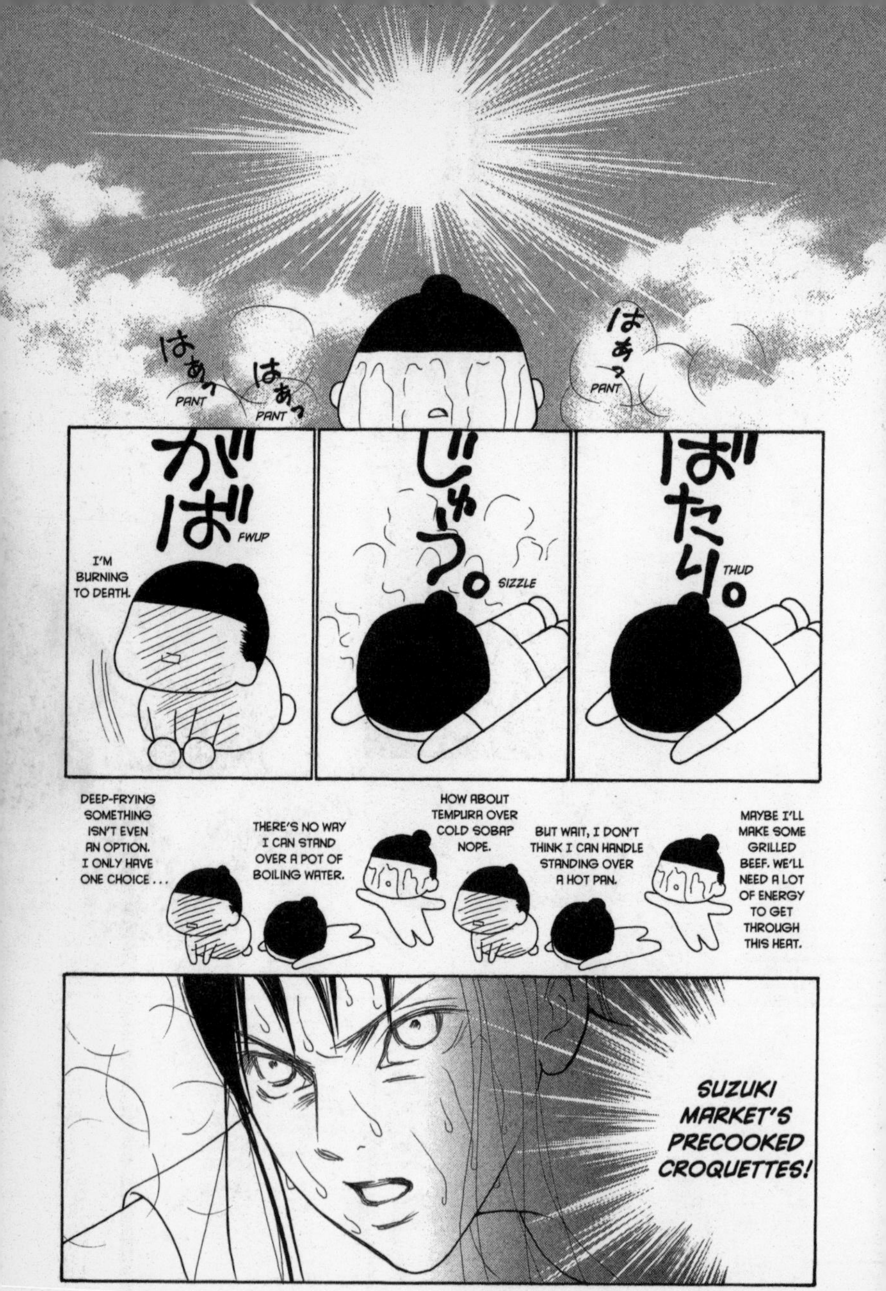
はぁっ
PANT
はあっ
PANT
はぁっ
PANT
ぱたり。
THUD
じゅう。
SIZZLE
がば
FWUP
I'M BURNING TO DEATH.
MAYBE I'LL MAKE SOME GRILLED BEEF. WE'LL NEED A LOT OF ENERGY TO GET THROUGH THIS HEAT.
BUT WAIT, I DON'T THINK I CAN HANDLE STANDING OVER A HOT PAN.
HOW ABOUT TEMPURA OVER COLD SOBA? NOPE.
THERE'S NO WAY I CAN STAND OVER A POT OF BOILING WATER.
DEEP-FRYING SOMETHING ISN'T EVEN AN OPTION. I ONLY HAVE ONE CHOICE . . .
SUZUKI MARKET'S PRECOOKED CROQUETTES!

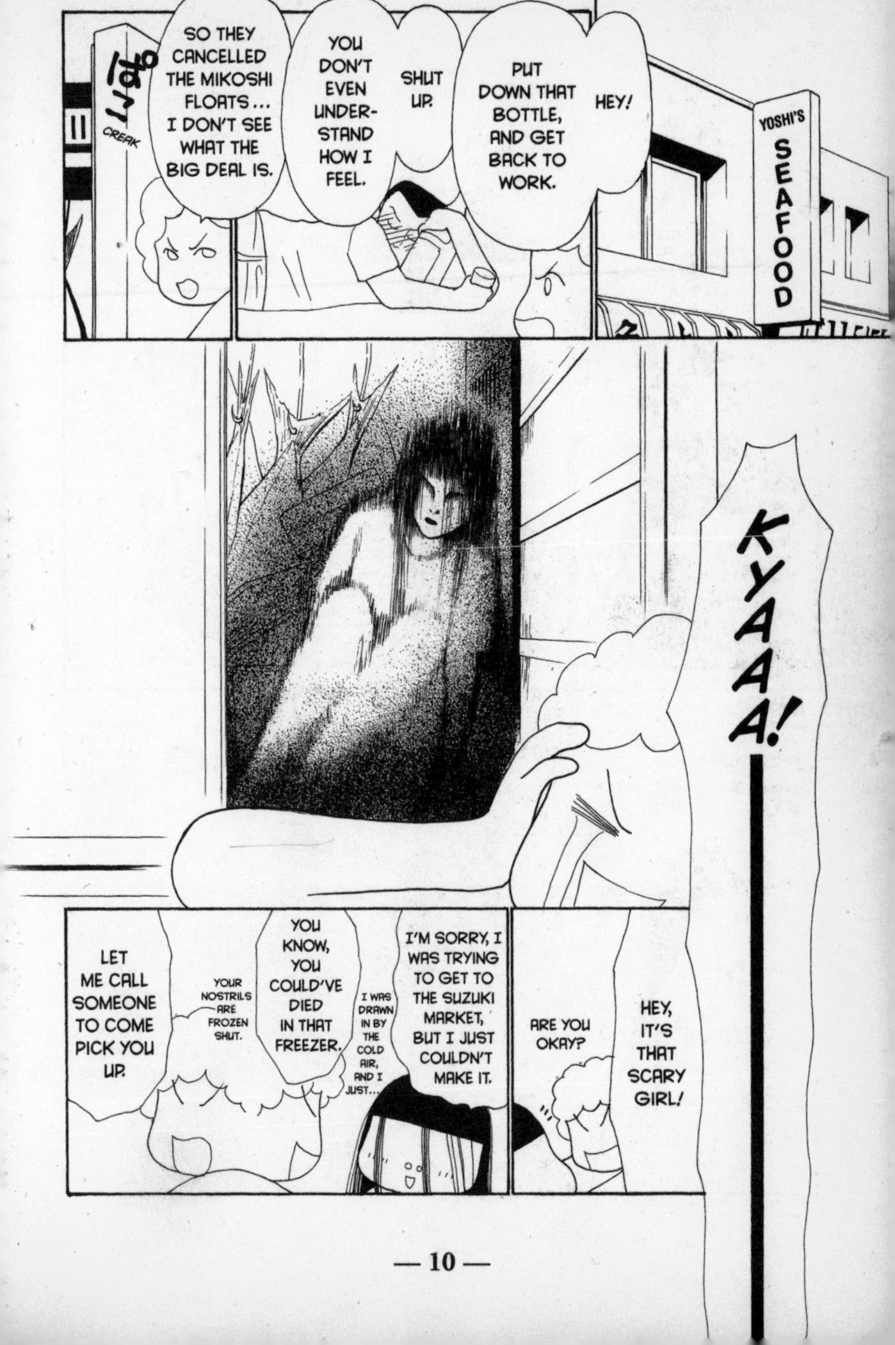
YOSHI'S SEAFOOD
HEY!
PUT DOWN THAT BOTTLE, AND GET BACK TO WORK.
SHUT UP.
YOU DON'T EVEN UNDERSTAND HOW I FEEL.
SO THEY CANCELLED THE MIKOSHI FLOATS... I DON'T SEE WHAT THE BIG DEAL IS.
CREAK
KYAAAA!
HEY, IT'S THAT SCARY GIRL!
ARE YOU OKAY?
I'M SORRY, I WAS TRYING TO GET TO THE SUZUKI MARKET, BUT I JUST COULDN'T MAKE IT.
I WAS DRAWN IN BY THE COLD AIR, AND I JUST...
YOU KNOW, YOU COULD'VE DIED IN THAT FREEZER.
YOUR NOSTRILS ARE FROZEN SHUT.
LET ME CALL SOMEONE TO COME PICK YOU UP.

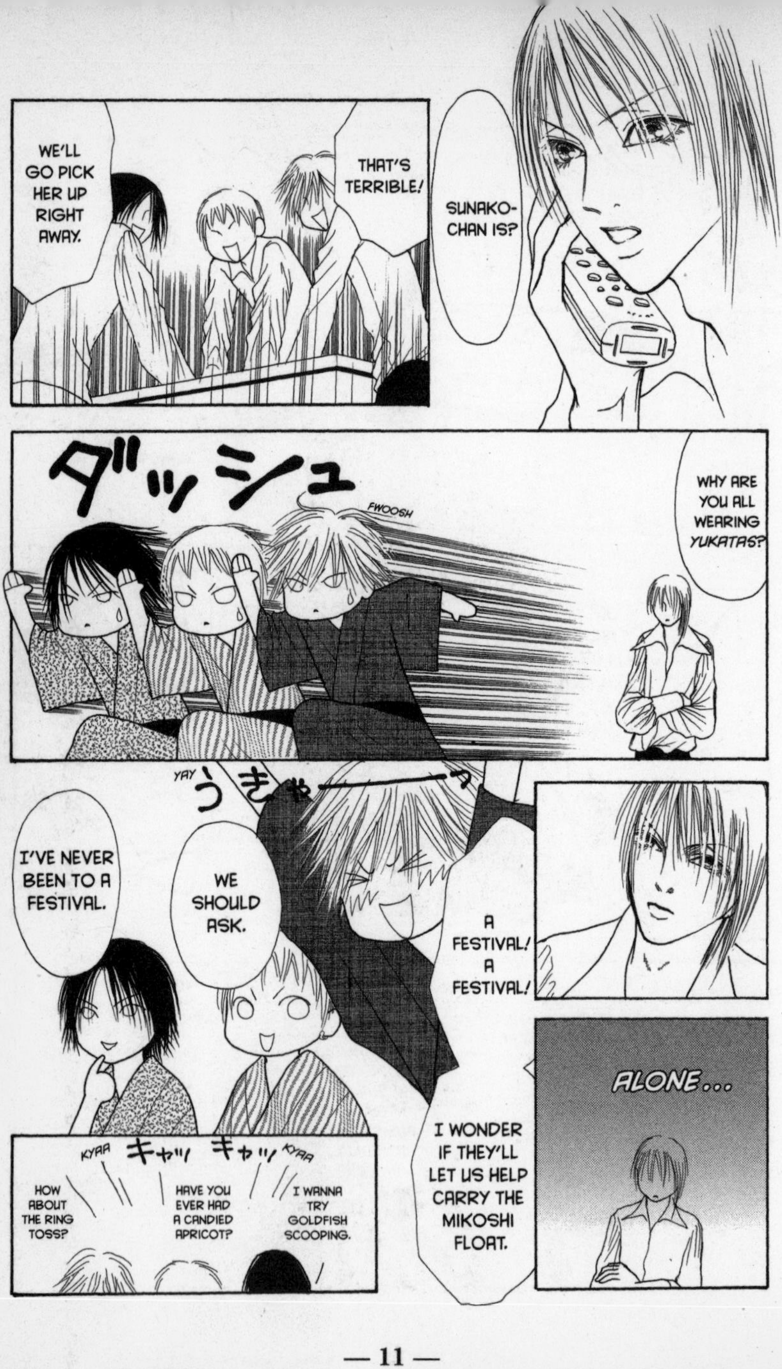
SUNAKO-CHAN IS?
THAT'S TERRIBLE!
WE'LL GO PICK HER UP RIGHT AWAY.
WHY ARE YOU ALL WEARING *YUKATAS?*
ダッシュ
FWOOSH
ALONE...
うきゃー
YAY
A FESTIVAL! A FESTIVAL!
WE SHOULD ASK.
I'VE NEVER BEEN TO A FESTIVAL.
I WONDER IF THEY'LL LET US HELP CARRY THE MIKOSHI FLOAT.
キャッ キャッ
KYAA KYAA
I WANNA TRY GOLDFISH SCOOPING.
HAVE YOU EVER HAD A CANDIED APRICOT?
HOW ABOUT THE RING TOSS?

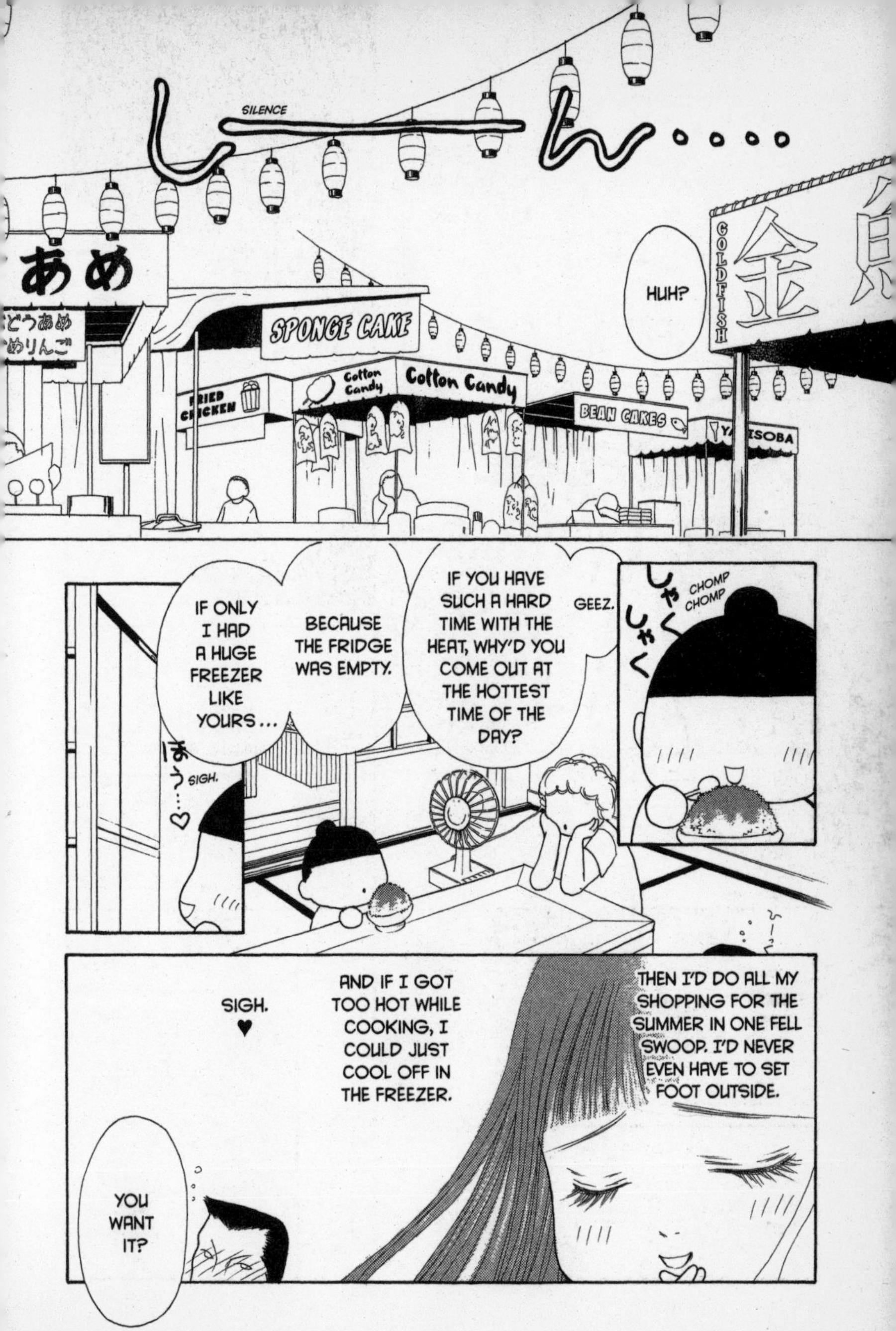
しーん....
SILENCE
HUH?
GOLDFISH
金
あめ
SPONGE CAKE
FRIED CHICKEN
Cotton Candy
Cotton Candy
BEAN CAKES
しゃくしゃく
CHOMP CHOMP
GEEZ.
IF YOU HAVE SUCH A HARD TIME WITH THE HEAT, WHY'D YOU COME OUT AT THE HOTTEST TIME OF THE DAY?
BECAUSE THE FRIDGE WAS EMPTY.
IF ONLY I HAD A HUGE FREEZER LIKE YOURS...
ほう...♡
SIGH.
THEN I'D DO ALL MY SHOPPING FOR THE SUMMER IN ONE FELL SWOOP. I'D NEVER EVEN HAVE TO SET FOOT OUTSIDE.
AND IF I GOT TOO HOT WHILE COOKING, I COULD JUST COOL OFF IN THE FREEZER.
SIGH. ♥
YOU WANT IT?

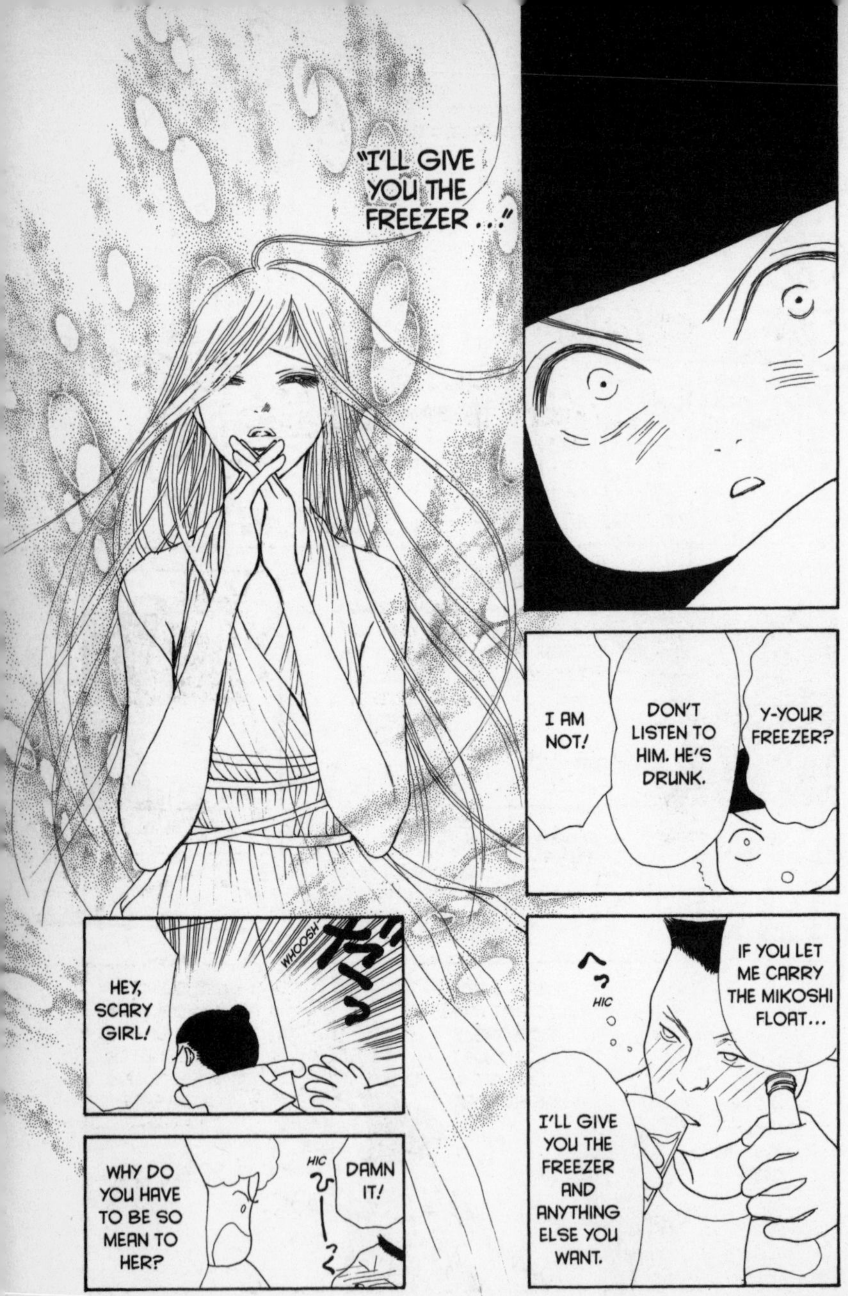

Y-YOUR FREEZER?
DON'T LISTEN TO HIM. HE'S DRUNK.
I AM NOT!
"I'LL GIVE YOU THE FREEZER..."
HIC
IF YOU LET ME CARRY THE MIKOSHI FLOAT...
I'LL GIVE YOU THE FREEZER AND ANYTHING ELSE YOU WANT.
WHOOSH
HEY, SCARY GIRL!
DAMN IT!
HIC
WHY DO YOU HAVE TO BE SO MEAN TO HER?

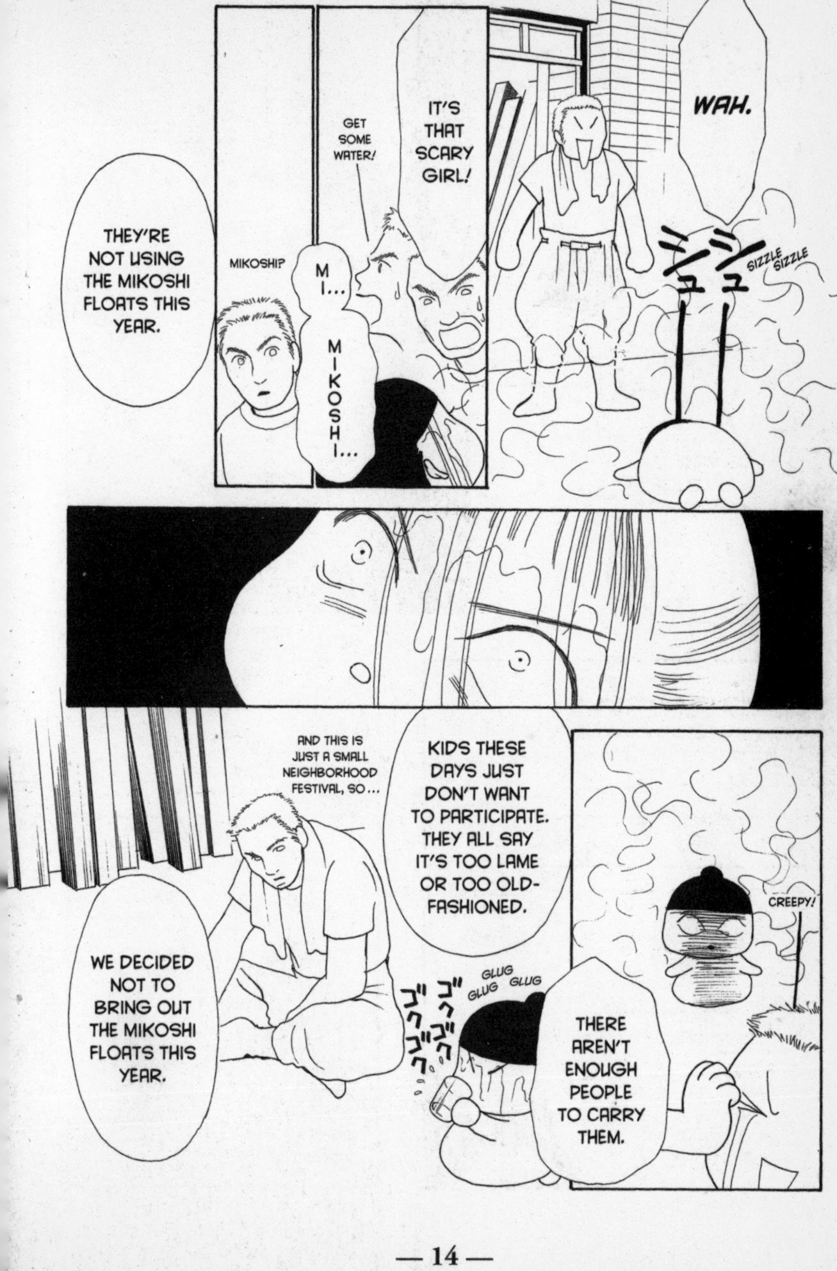
WAH.
シュ シュ
SIZZLE SIZZLE
IT'S THAT SCARY GIRL!
GET SOME WATER!
MI... MIKOSHI...
MIKOSHI?
THEY'RE NOT USING THE MIKOSHI FLOATS THIS YEAR.
CREEPY!
ゴクゴクゴクゴク
GLUG GLUG GLUG
THERE AREN'T ENOUGH PEOPLE TO CARRY THEM.
KIDS THESE DAYS JUST DON'T WANT TO PARTICIPATE. THEY ALL SAY IT'S TOO LAME OR TOO OLD-FASHIONED.
AND THIS IS JUST A SMALL NEIGHBORHOOD FESTIVAL, SO...
WE DECIDED NOT TO BRING OUT THE MIKOSHI FLOATS THIS YEAR.

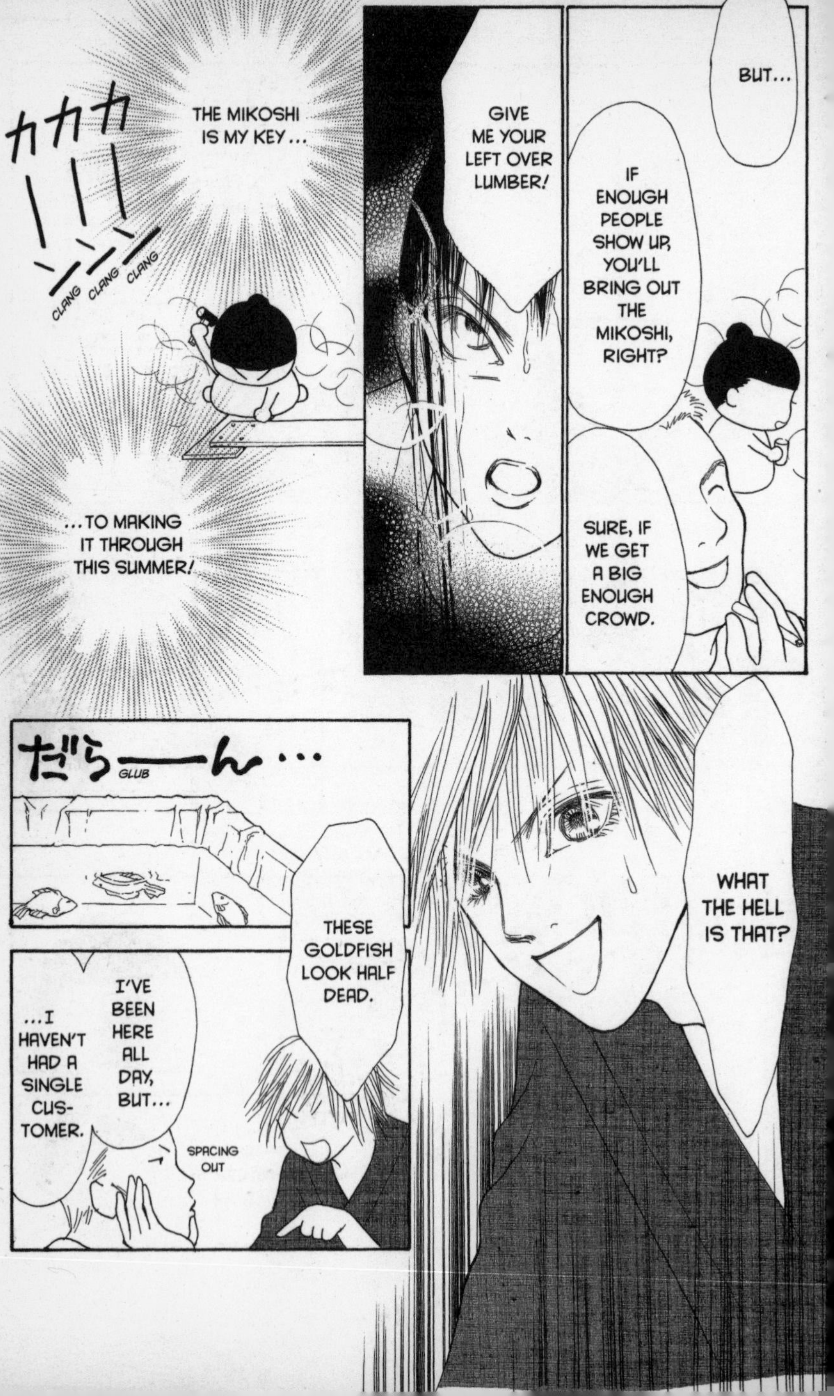
BUT...
IF ENOUGH PEOPLE SHOW UP, YOU'LL BRING OUT THE MIKOSHI, RIGHT?
SURE, IF WE GET A BIG ENOUGH CROWD.
GIVE ME YOUR LEFT OVER LUMBER!
THE MIKOSHI IS MY KEY...
CLANG CLANG CLANG
...TO MAKING IT THROUGH THIS SUMMER!
WHAT THE HELL IS THAT?
THESE GOLDFISH LOOK HALF DEAD.
だらーん…
GLUB
I'VE BEEN HERE ALL DAY, BUT...
...I HAVEN'T HAD A SINGLE CUS-TOMER.
SPACING OUT

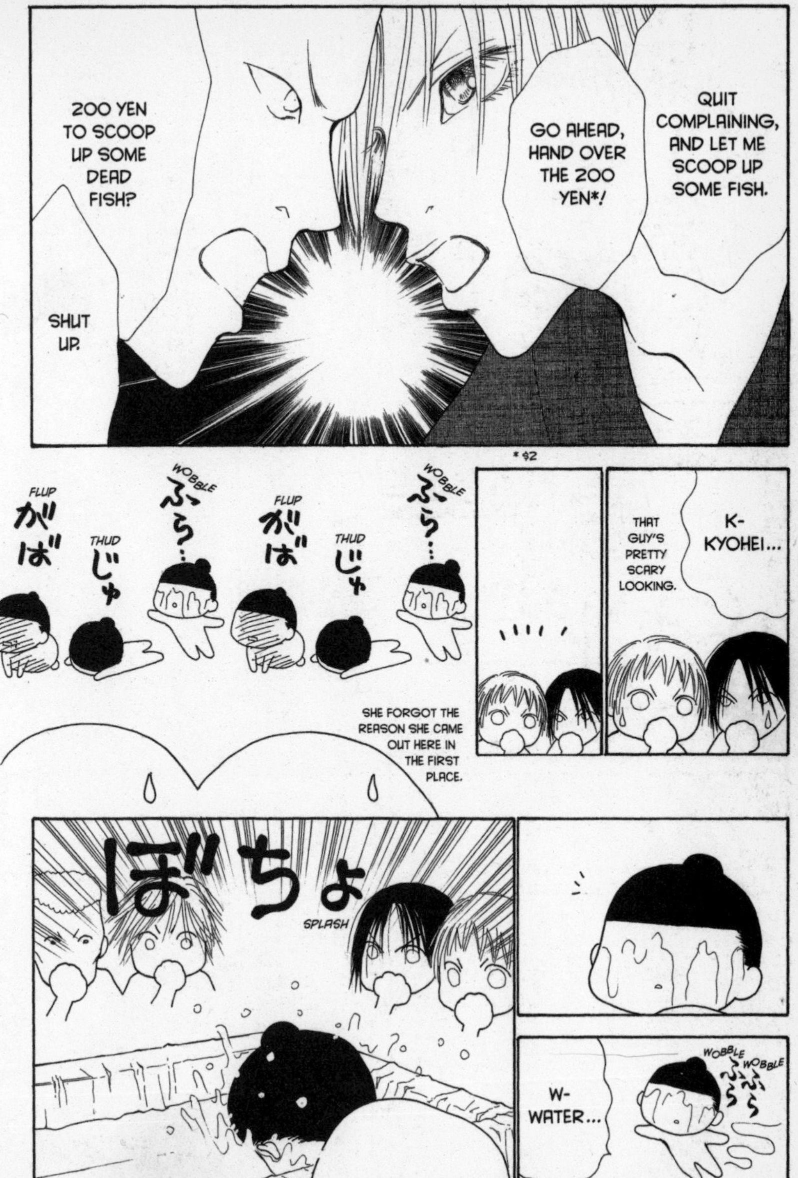
QUIT COMPLAINING, AND LET ME SCOOP UP SOME FISH.
GO AHEAD, HAND OVER THE 200 YEN*!
200 YEN TO SCOOP UP SOME DEAD FISH?
SHUT UP.
K-KYOHEI...
THAT GUY'S PRETTY SCARY LOOKING.
WOBBLE ふら...
THUD じゅ
FLUP がば
WOBBLE ふら...
THUD じゅ
FLUP がば
SHE FORGOT THE REASON SHE CAME OUT HERE IN THE FIRST PLACE.
WOBBLE WOBBLE ふらふら
W-WATER...
ぼちょ SPLASH
* $2

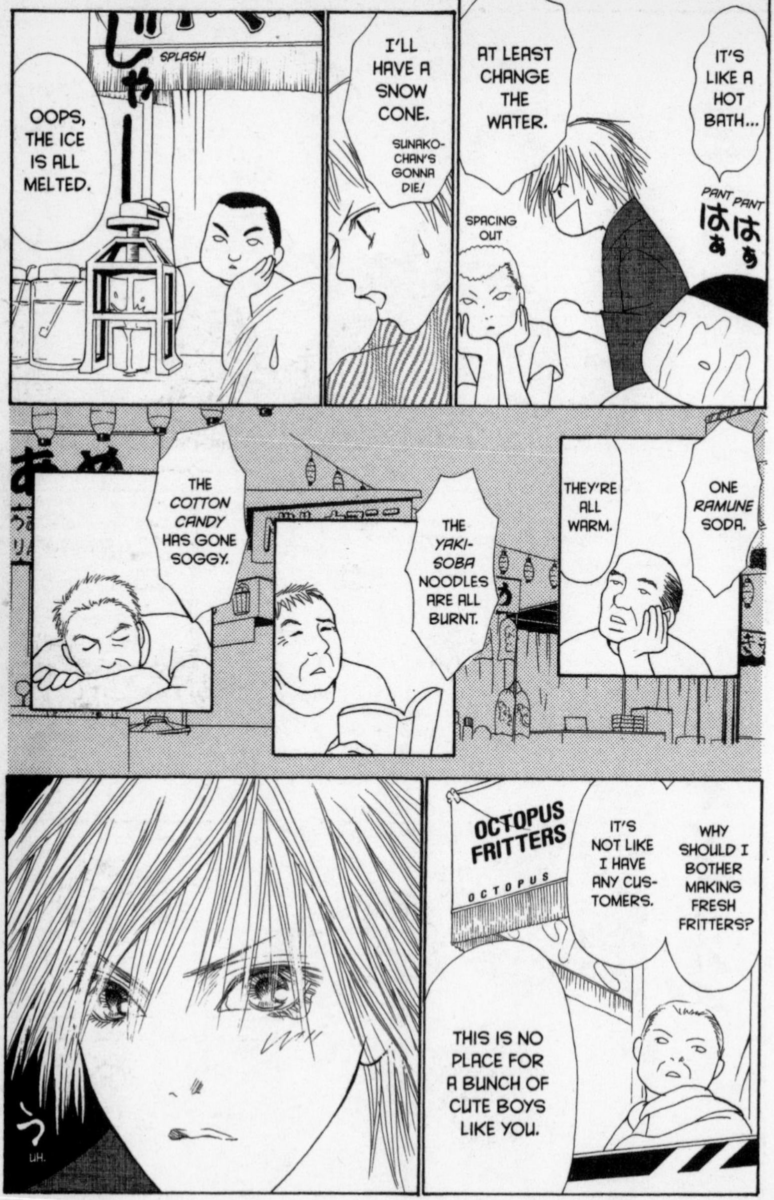
IT'S LIKE A HOT BATH...
PANT PANT
はぁはぁ
AT LEAST CHANGE THE WATER.
SPACING OUT
I'LL HAVE A SNOW CONE.
SUNAKO-CHAN'S GONNA DIE!
OOPS, THE ICE IS ALL MELTED.
SPLASH
ONE RAMUNE SODA.
THEY'RE ALL WARM.
THE YAKI-SOBA NOODLES ARE ALL BURNT.
THE COTTON CANDY HAS GONE SOGGY.
OCTOPUS FRITTERS
OCTOPUS
WHY SHOULD I BOTHER MAKING FRESH FRITTERS?
IT'S NOT LIKE I HAVE ANY CUS-TOMERS.
THIS IS NO PLACE FOR A BUNCH OF CUTE BOYS LIKE YOU.
う
UH.

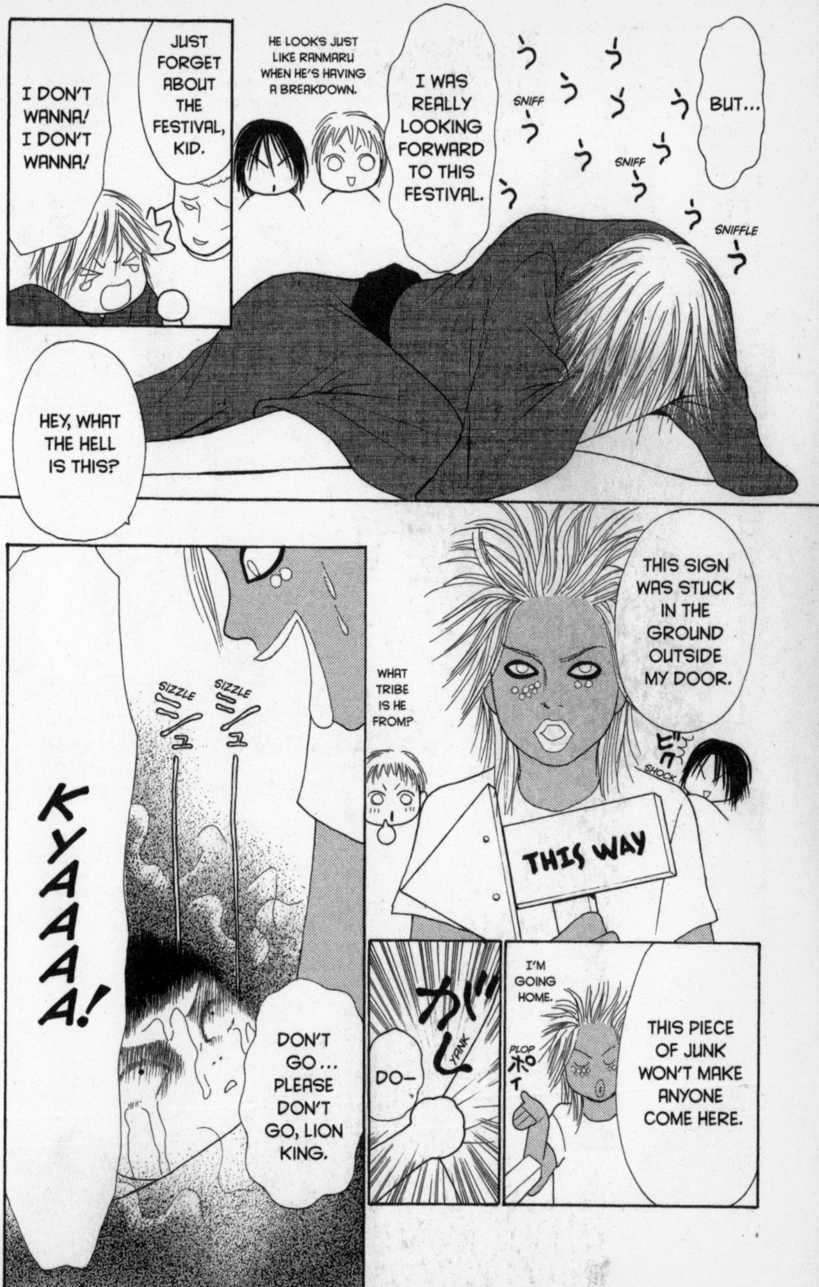
BUT...
SNIFF
SNIFF
SNIFFLE
I WAS REALLY LOOKING FORWARD TO THIS FESTIVAL.
HE LOOKS JUST LIKE RANMARU WHEN HE'S HAVING A BREAKDOWN.
JUST FORGET ABOUT THE FESTIVAL, KID.
I DON'T WANNA! I DON'T WANNA!
HEY, WHAT THE HELL IS THIS?
THIS SIGN WAS STUCK IN THE GROUND OUTSIDE MY DOOR.
SHOCK
WHAT TRIBE IS HE FROM?
THIS WAY
THIS PIECE OF JUNK WON'T MAKE ANYONE COME HERE.
I'M GOING HOME.
PLOP
YANK
DO—
SIZZLE
SIZZLE
DON'T GO... PLEASE DON'T GO, LION KING.
KYAAAAA!

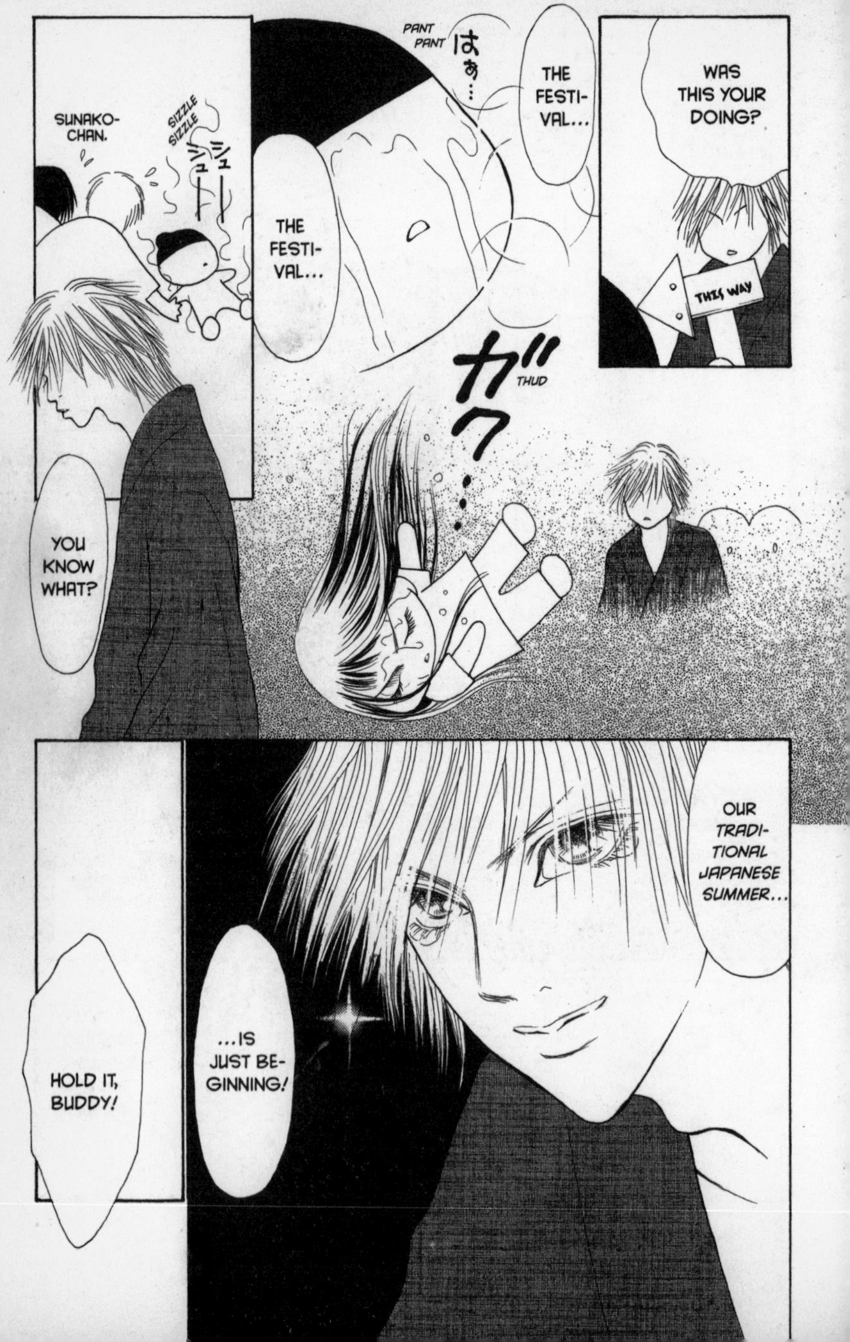
WAS THIS YOUR DOING?
THIS WAY
PANT PANT
はぁ…
THE FESTI-VAL...
THE FESTI-VAL...
SUNAKO-CHAN.
SIZZLE SIZZLE
シュー
シュー
ガク
THUD
YOU KNOW WHAT?
OUR TRADI-TIONAL JAPANESE SUMMER...
...IS JUST BE-GINNING!
HOLD IT, BUDDY!

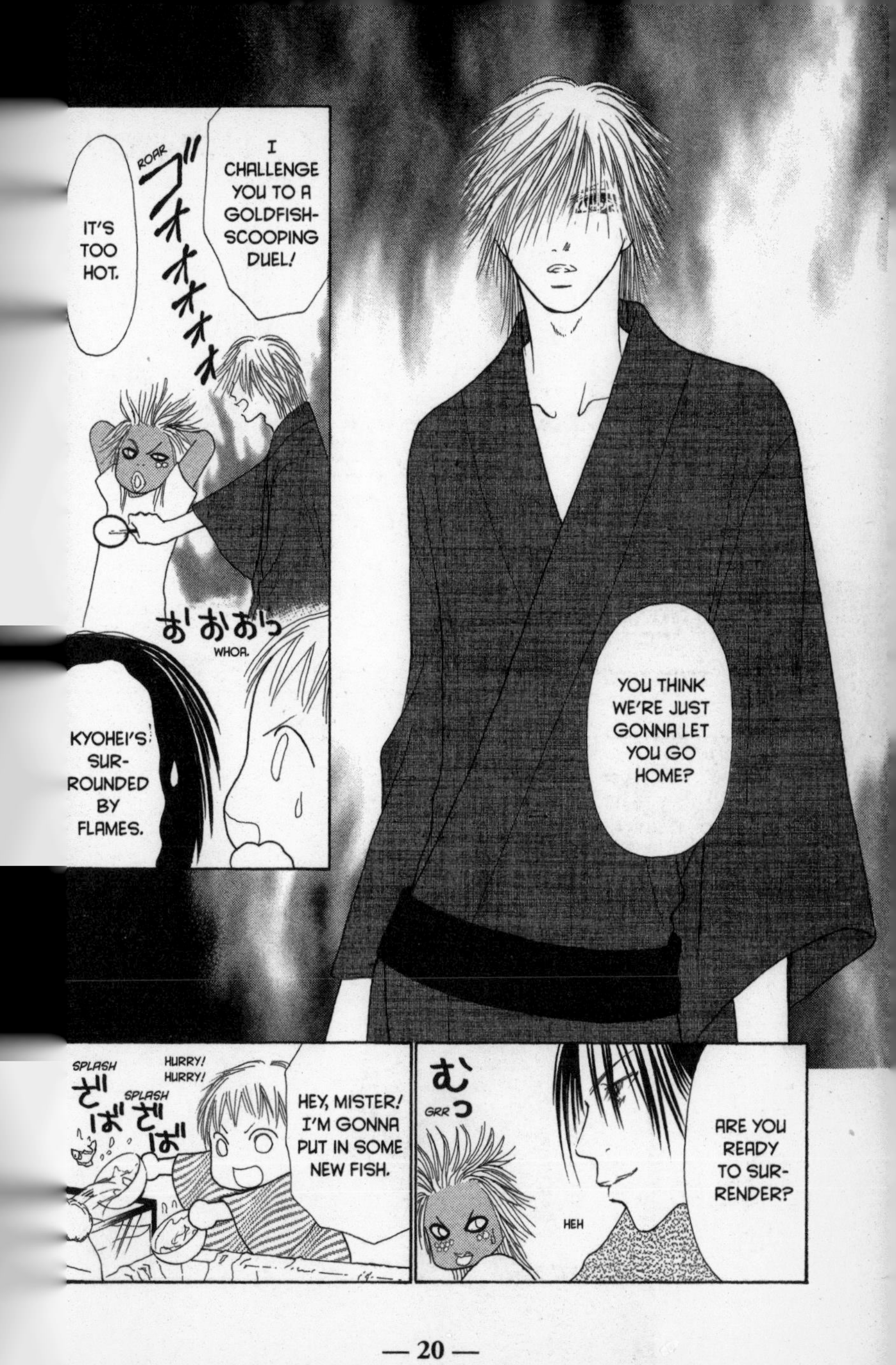
YOU THINK WE'RE JUST GONNA LET YOU GO HOME?
I CHALLENGE YOU TO A GOLDFISH-SCOOPING DUEL!
ゴオオオオオ
ROAR
IT'S TOO HOT.
おおおっ
WHOA.
KYOHEI'S SURROUNDED BY FLAMES.
ARE YOU READY TO SURRENDER?
むっ
GRR
HEH
HEY, MISTER! I'M GONNA PUT IN SOME NEW FISH.
HURRY! HURRY!
ざばざば
SPLASH
SPLASH

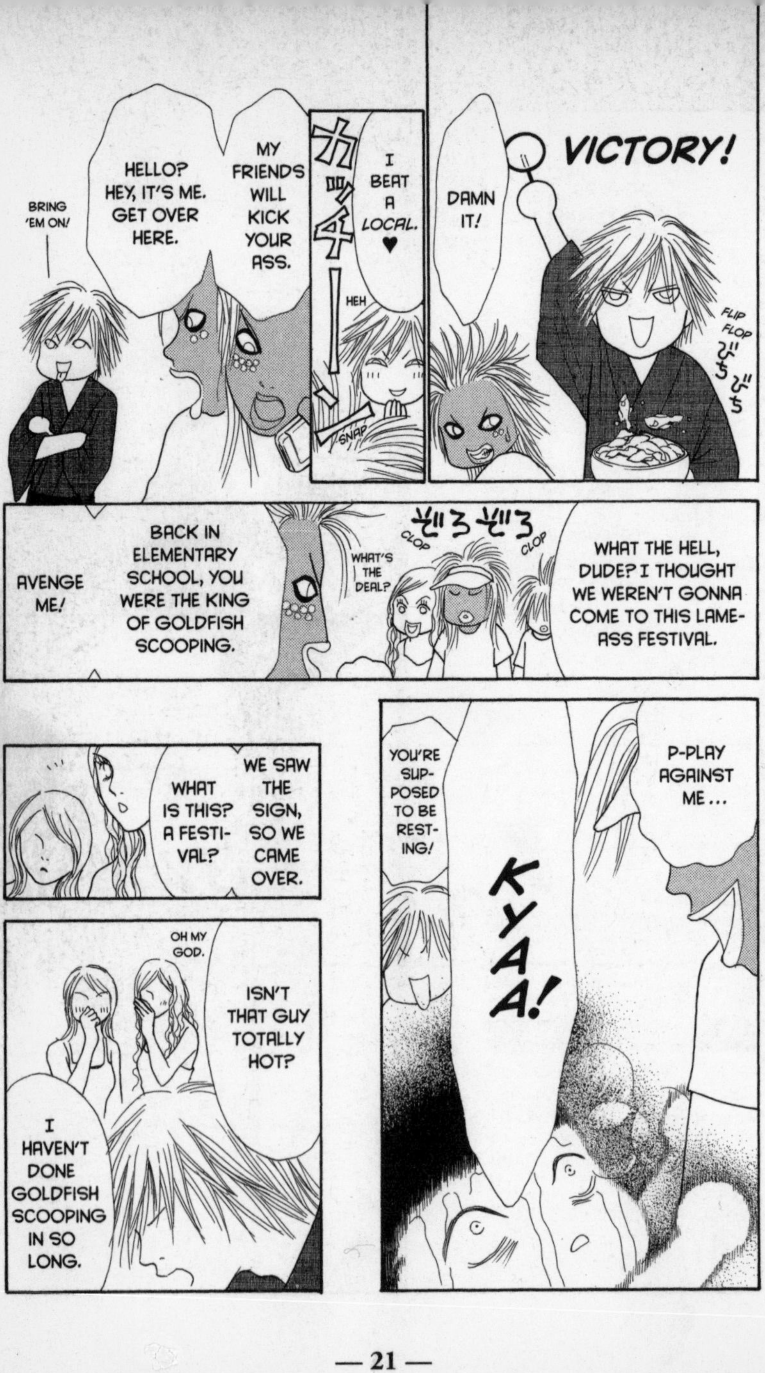
VICTORY!
DAMN IT!
FLIP FLOP
びちびち
カッチーン
I BEAT A LOCAL. ♥
HEH
SNAP
MY FRIENDS WILL KICK YOUR ASS.
HELLO? HEY, IT'S ME. GET OVER HERE.
BRING 'EM ON!
WHAT THE HELL, DUDE? I THOUGHT WE WEREN'T GONNA COME TO THIS LAME-ASS FESTIVAL.
CLOP
ぞろぞろ
CLOP
WHAT'S THE DEAL?
BACK IN ELEMENTARY SCHOOL, YOU WERE THE KING OF GOLDFISH SCOOPING.
AVENGE ME!
P-PLAY AGAINST ME...
KYAA!
YOU'RE SUP-POSED TO BE REST-ING!
WE SAW THE SIGN, SO WE CAME OVER.
WHAT IS THIS? A FESTI-VAL?
OH MY GOD.
ISN'T THAT GUY TOTALLY HOT?
I HAVEN'T DONE GOLDFISH SCOOPING IN SO LONG.

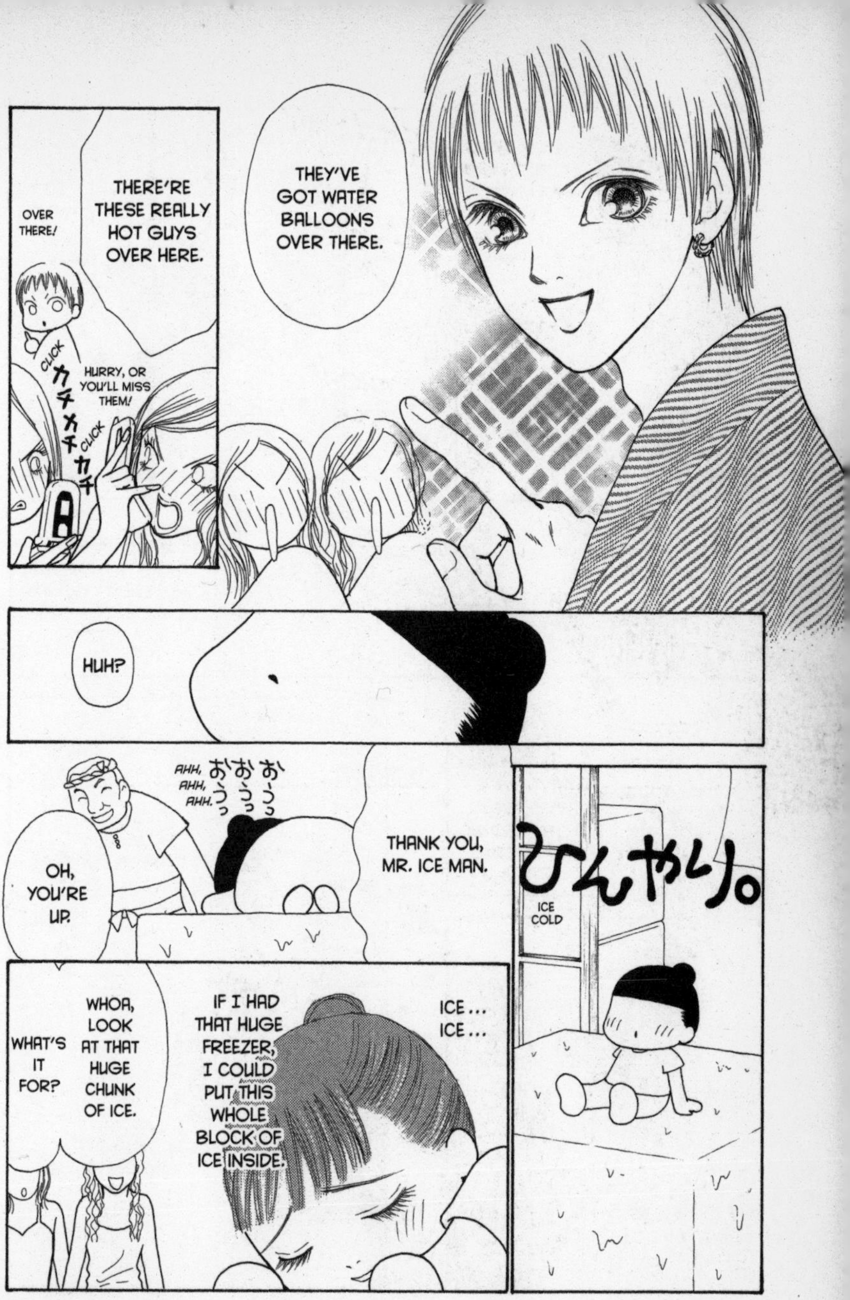
THEY'VE GOT WATER BALLOONS OVER THERE.
THERE'RE THESE REALLY HOT GUYS OVER HERE.
OVER THERE!
HURRY, OR YOU'LL MISS THEM!
CLICK カチ
CLICK カチ
カチ
HUH?
ひんやり。
ICE COLD
THANK YOU, MR. ICE MAN.
おおお
AHH, AHH, AHH.
うっうっうっ
OH, YOU'RE UP.
ICE... ICE...
IF I HAD THAT HUGE FREEZER, I COULD PUT THIS WHOLE BLOCK OF ICE INSIDE.
WHOA, LOOK AT THAT HUGE CHUNK OF ICE.
WHAT'S IT FOR?

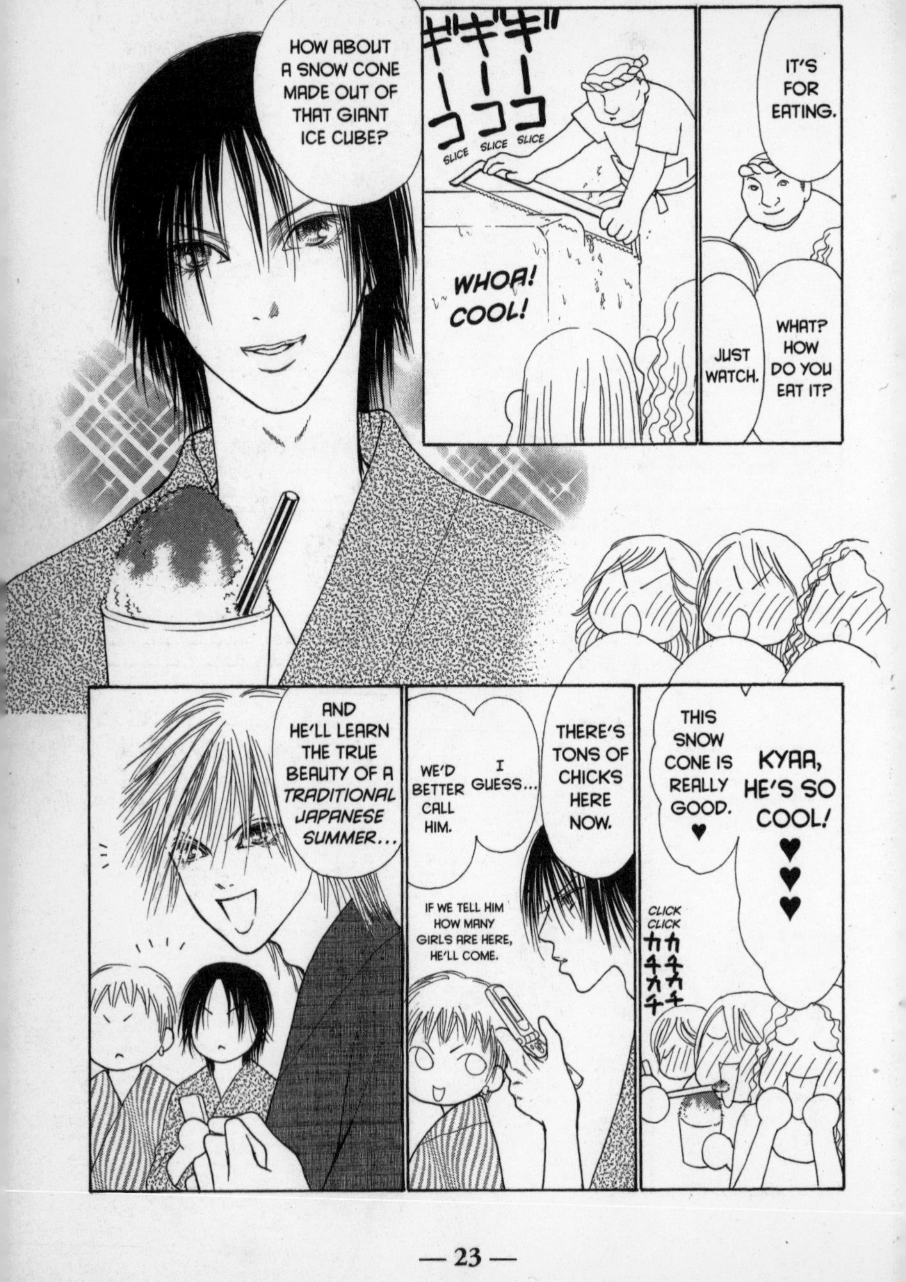
IT'S FOR EATING.
WHAT? HOW DO YOU EAT IT?
JUST WATCH.
ギーコギーコギーコ
SLICE SLICE SLICE
WHOA! COOL!
HOW ABOUT A SNOW CONE MADE OUT OF THAT GIANT ICE CUBE?
KYAA, HE'S SO COOL! ♥♥♥
THIS SNOW CONE IS REALLY GOOD. ♥
CLICK CLICK
カチカチカチ
THERE'S TONS OF CHICKS HERE NOW.
I GUESS...
WE'D BETTER CALL HIM.
IF WE TELL HIM HOW MANY GIRLS ARE HERE, HE'LL COME.
AND HE'LL LEARN THE TRUE BEAUTY OF A *TRADITIONAL JAPANESE* SUMMER...

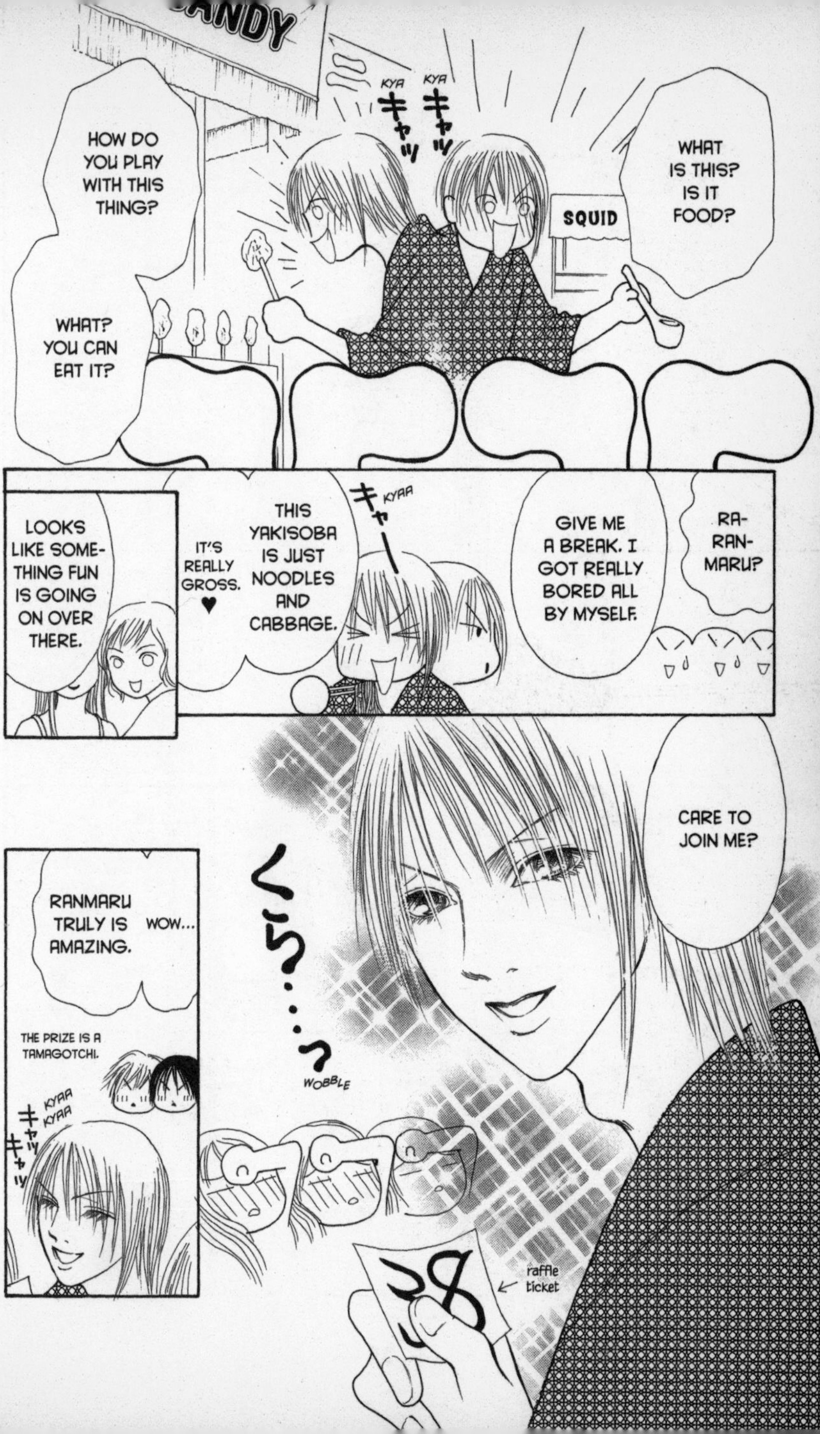
WHAT IS THIS? IS IT FOOD?
SQUID
キャッ KYA
キャッ KYA
HOW DO YOU PLAY WITH THIS THING?
ANDY
WHAT? YOU CAN EAT IT?
RA- RAN- MARU?
GIVE ME A BREAK. I GOT REALLY BORED ALL BY MYSELF.
キャー KYAA
THIS YAKISOBA IS JUST NOODLES AND CABBAGE.
IT'S REALLY GROSS. ♥
LOOKS LIKE SOME- THING FUN IS GOING ON OVER THERE.
CARE TO JOIN ME?
くら…っ WOBBLE
28
raffle ticket
WOW...
RANMARU TRULY IS AMAZING.
THE PRIZE IS A TAMAGOTCHI.
キャッ キャッ KYAA KYAA

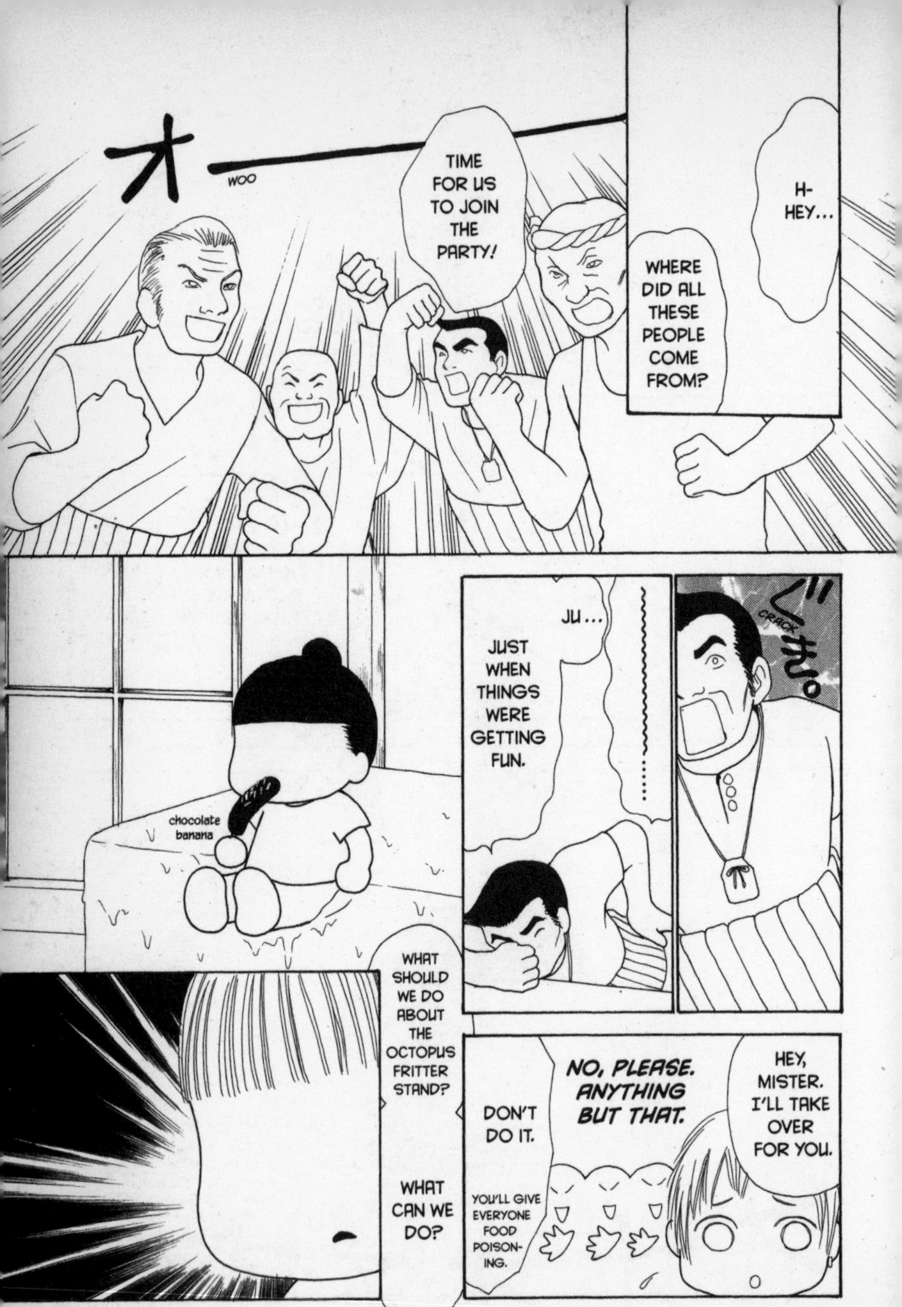
H-
HEY...
WHERE DID ALL THESE PEOPLE COME FROM?
TIME FOR US TO JOIN THE PARTY!
オー
WOO
ぐき。
CRACK
JU...
JUST WHEN THINGS WERE GETTING FUN.
chocolate banana
HEY, MISTER. I'LL TAKE OVER FOR YOU.
NO, PLEASE. ANYTHING BUT THAT.
DON'T DO IT.
YOU'LL GIVE EVERYONE FOOD POISON-ING.
WHAT SHOULD WE DO ABOUT THE OCTOPUS FRITTER STAND?
WHAT CAN WE DO?

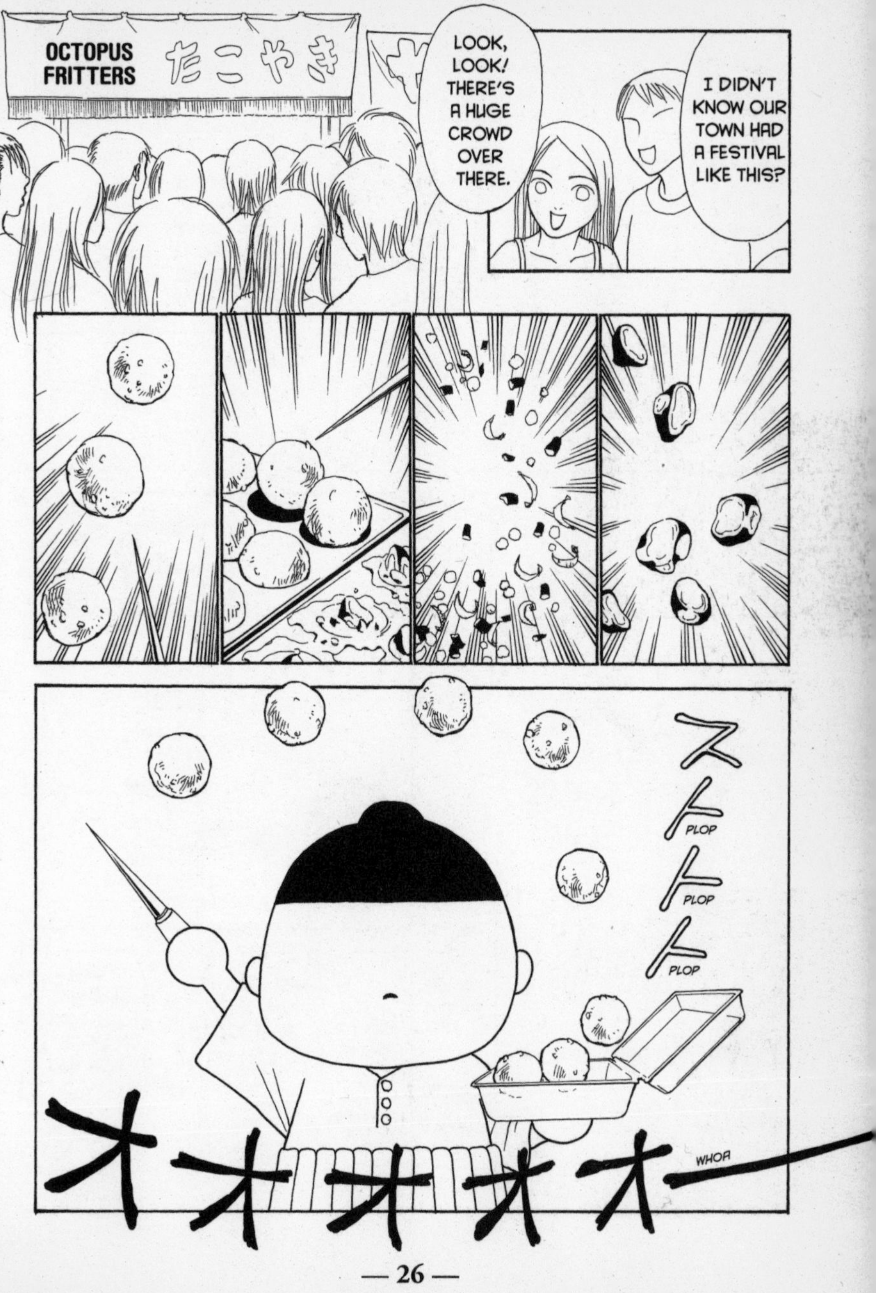

I DIDN'T KNOW OUR TOWN HAD A FESTIVAL LIKE THIS?
LOOK, LOOK! THERE'S A HUGE CROWD OVER THERE.
OCTOPUS FRITTERS
たこやき
スト PLOP
ト PLOP
ト PLOP
オオオオオー
WHOA

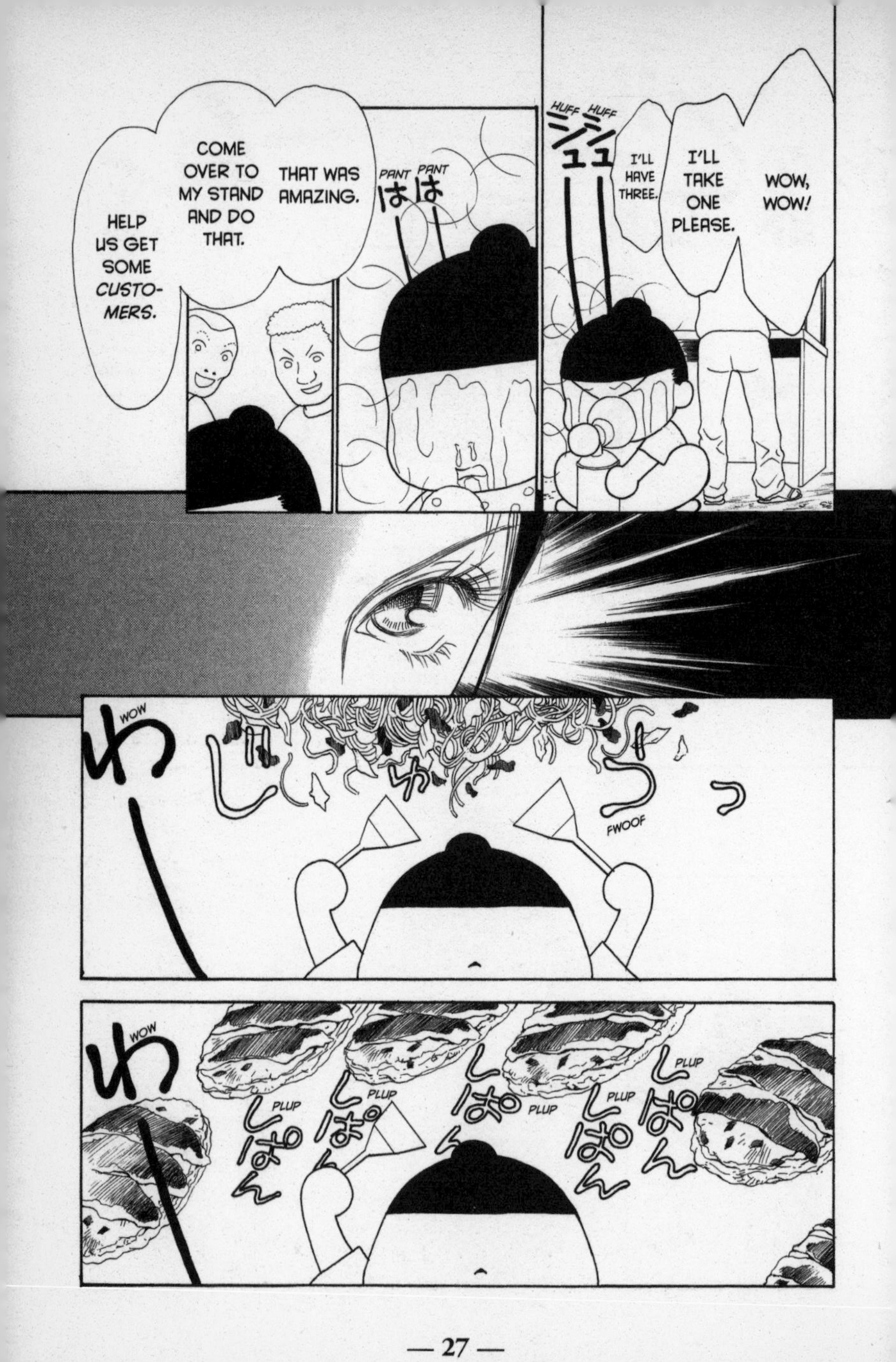
WOW, WOW!
I'LL TAKE ONE PLEASE.
I'LL HAVE THREE.
HUFF HUFF
ジュ
PANT PANT
はは
THAT WAS AMAZING.
COME OVER TO MY STAND AND DO THAT.
HELP US GET SOME *CUSTOMERS.*
わー
WOW
じゅうっ
FWOOF
わー
WOW
ぱん
PLUP
ぱん
PLUP
ぱん
PLUP
ぱん
PLUP
ぱん
PLUP

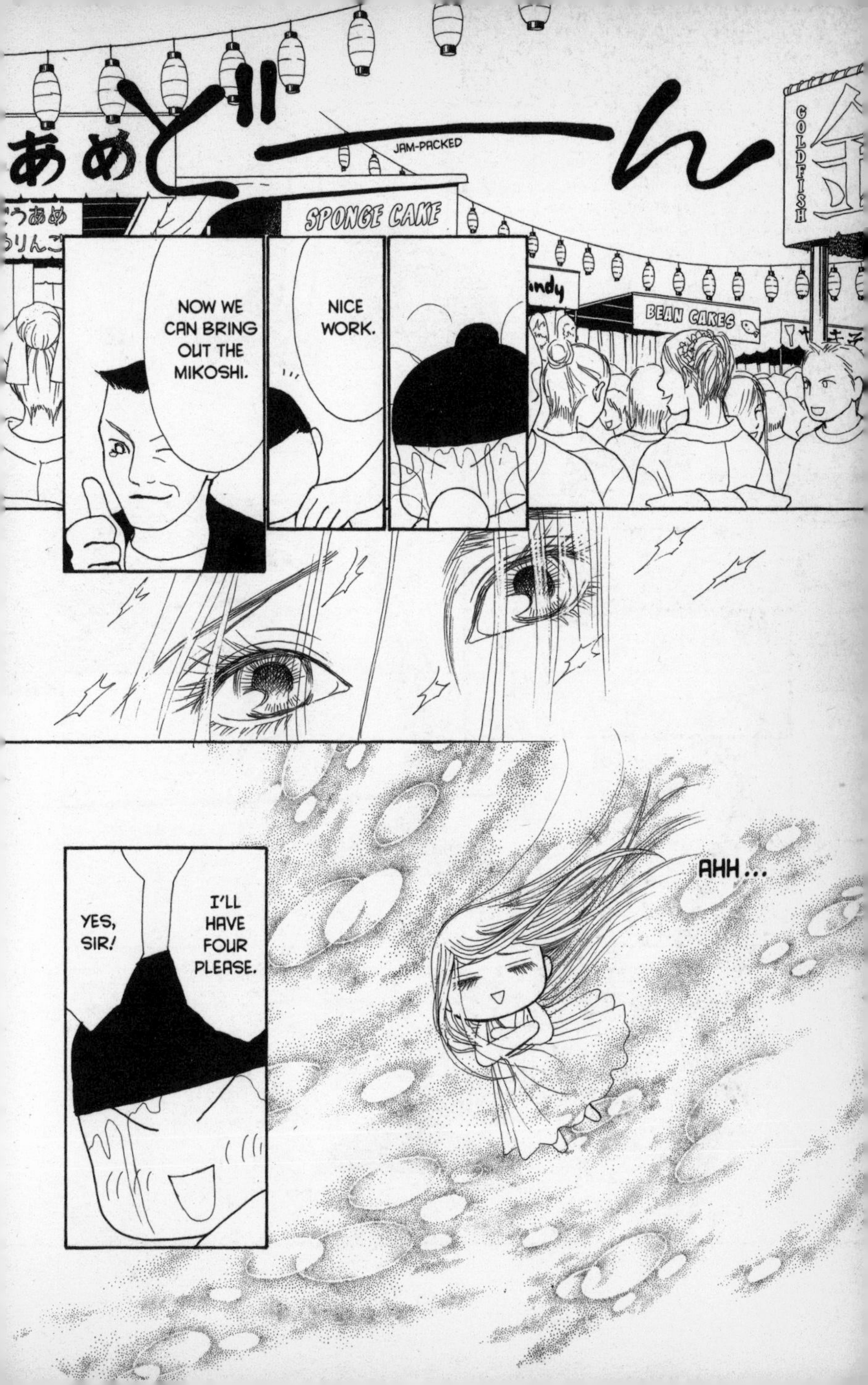
どーん
JAM-PACKED
あめ
SPONGE CAKE
GOLDFISH
BEAN CAKES
NICE WORK.
NOW WE CAN BRING OUT THE MIKOSHI.
AHH...
I'LL HAVE FOUR PLEASE.
YES, SIR!

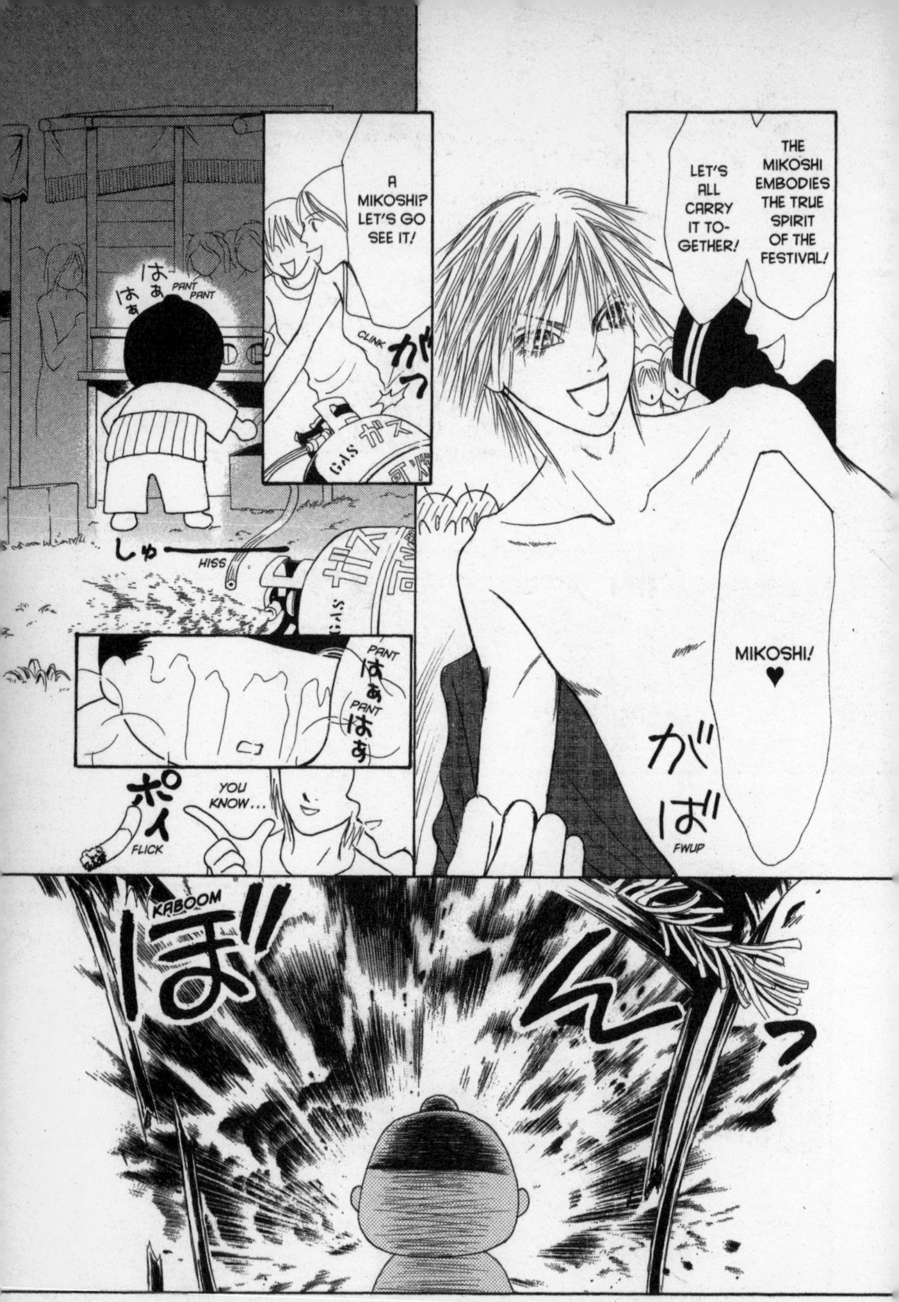
THE MIKOSHI EMBODIES THE TRUE SPIRIT OF THE FESTIVAL!
LET'S ALL CARRY IT TO-GETHER!
MIKOSHI! ♥
がば
FWUP
A MIKOSHI? LET'S GO SEE IT!
がっ
CLINK
はぁ はぁ
PANT PANT
しゅー
HISS
はぁ
PANT
はぁ
PANT
YOU KNOW...
ポイ
FLICK
ぼーんっ
KABOOM

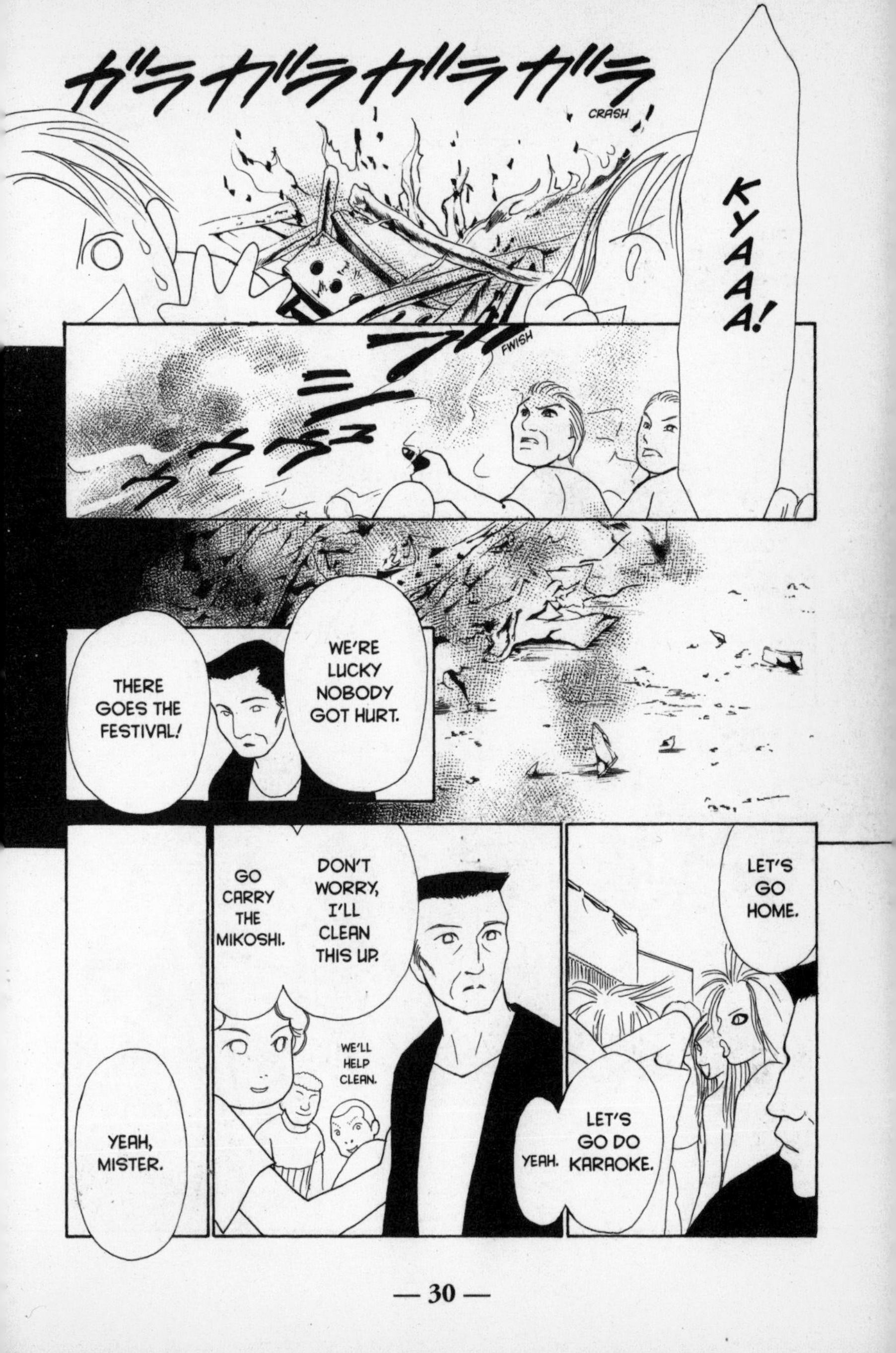
KYAAAA!
CRASH
ガラガラガラガラ
FWISH
WE'RE LUCKY NOBODY GOT HURT.
THERE GOES THE FESTIVAL!
LET'S GO HOME.
LET'S GO DO KARAOKE.
YEAH.
DON'T WORRY, I'LL CLEAN THIS UP.
GO CARRY THE MIKOSHI.
WE'LL HELP CLEAN.
YEAH, MISTER.

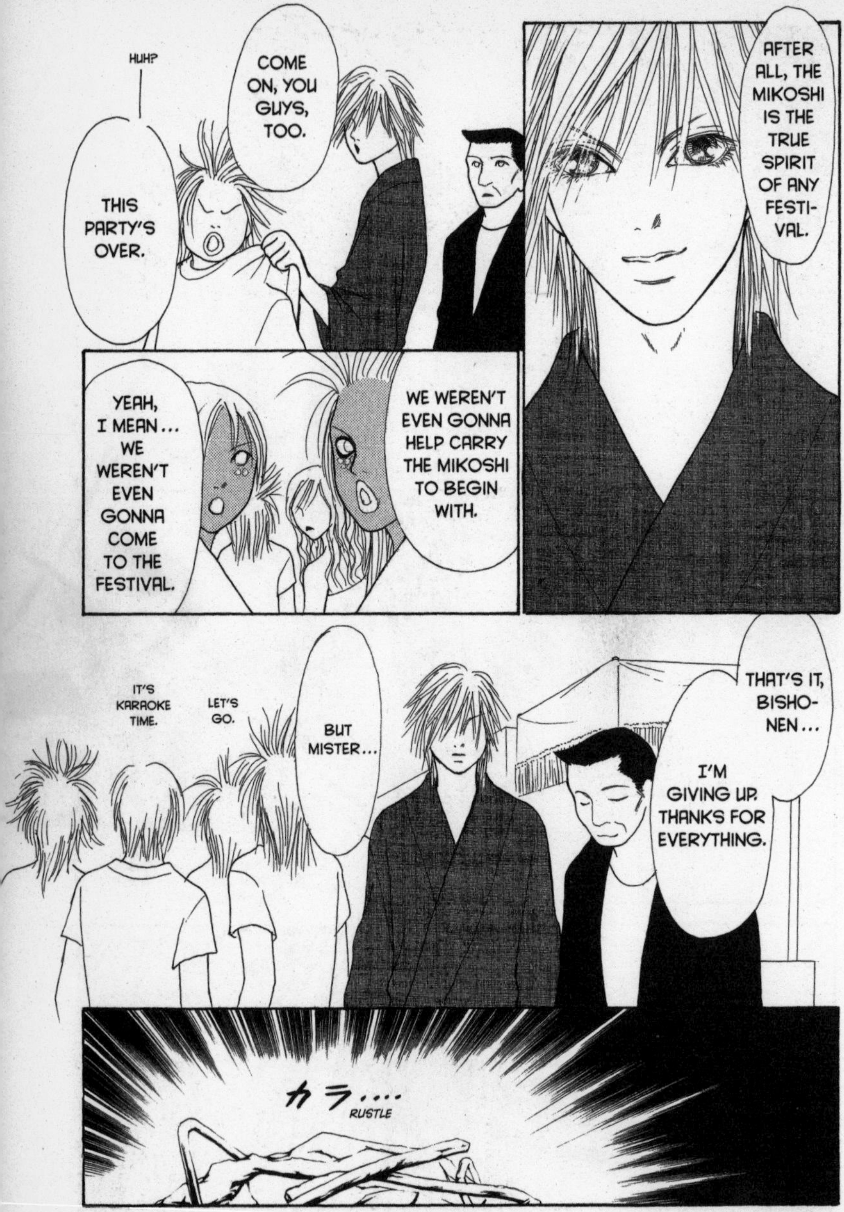
AFTER ALL, THE MIKOSHI IS THE TRUE SPIRIT OF ANY FESTI-VAL.
COME ON, YOU GUYS, TOO.
HUH?
THIS PARTY'S OVER.
WE WEREN'T EVEN GONNA HELP CARRY THE MIKOSHI TO BEGIN WITH.
YEAH, I MEAN... WE WEREN'T EVEN GONNA COME TO THE FESTIVAL.
THAT'S IT, BISHO-NEN...
I'M GIVING UP. THANKS FOR EVERYTHING.
BUT MISTER...
LET'S GO.
IT'S KARAOKE TIME.
カラ....
RUSTLE

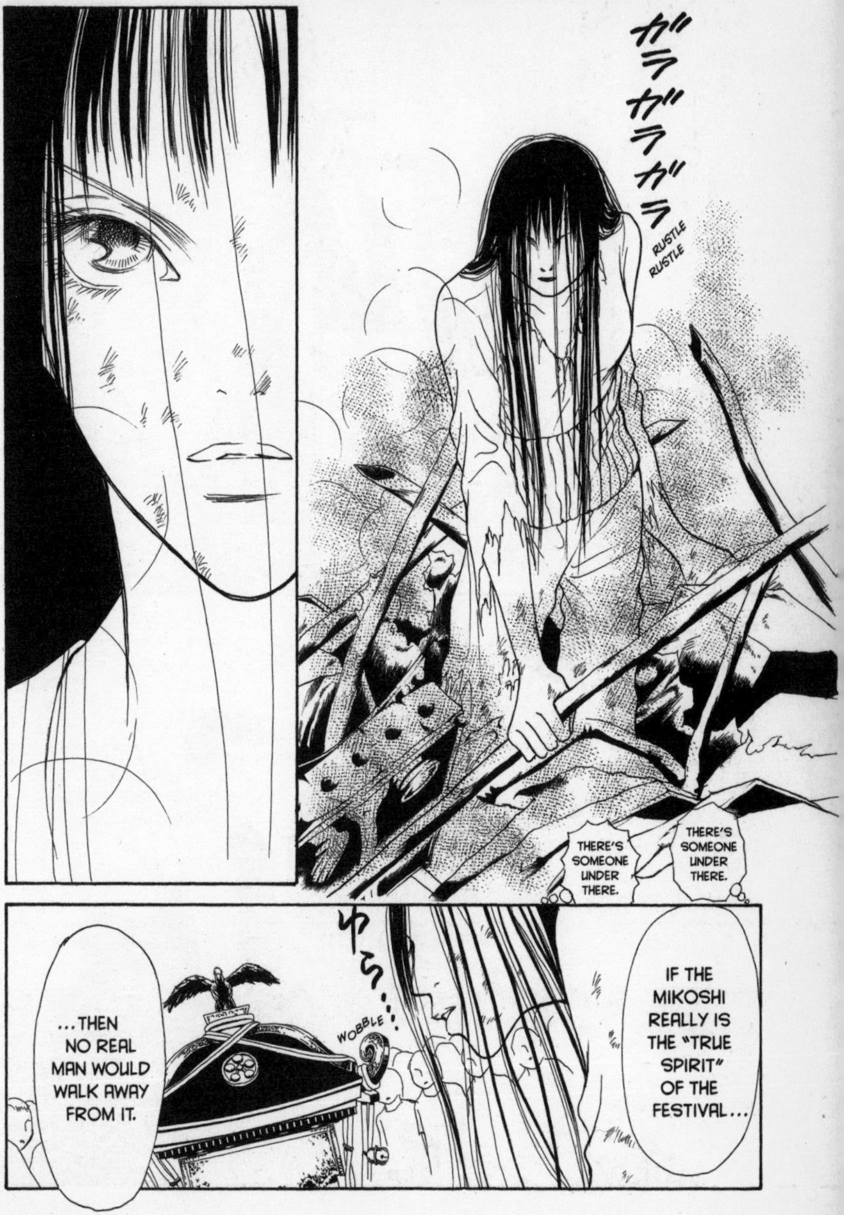
ガラガラガラ
RUSTLE RUSTLE
THERE'S SOMEONE UNDER THERE.
THERE'S SOMEONE UNDER THERE.
IF THE MIKOSHI REALLY IS THE "TRUE SPIRIT" OF THE FESTIVAL...
ゆら…
WOBBLE
...THEN NO REAL MAN WOULD WALK AWAY FROM IT.

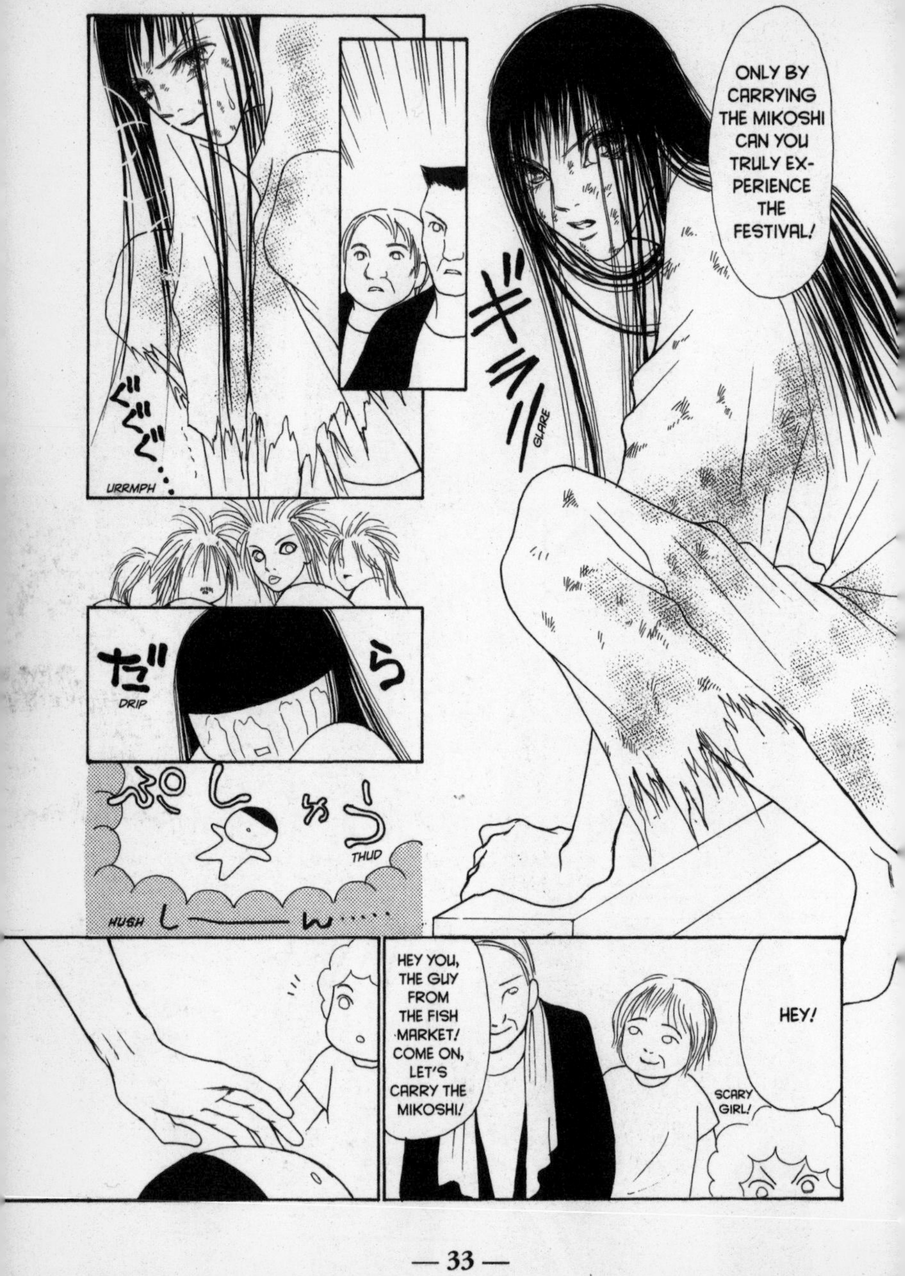
ONLY BY CARRYING THE MIKOSHI CAN YOU TRULY EXPERIENCE THE FESTIVAL!
ギラ
GLARE
ぐぐぐ…
URRMPH
だら
DRIP
ぷしゅう
THUD
しーん……
HUSH
HEY!
SCARY GIRL!
HEY YOU, THE GUY FROM THE FISH MARKET! COME ON, LET'S CARRY THE MIKOSHI!

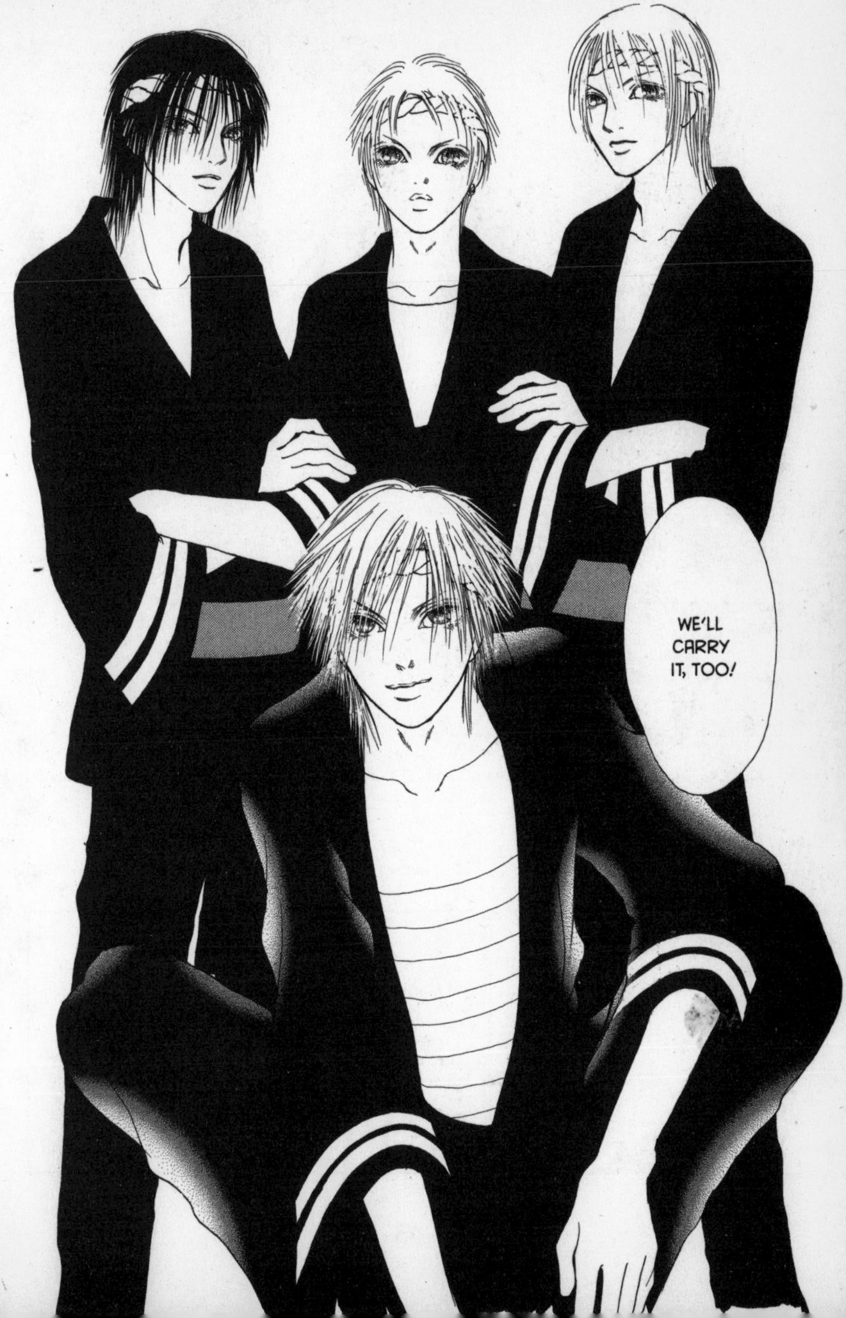
WE'LL CARRY IT, TOO!

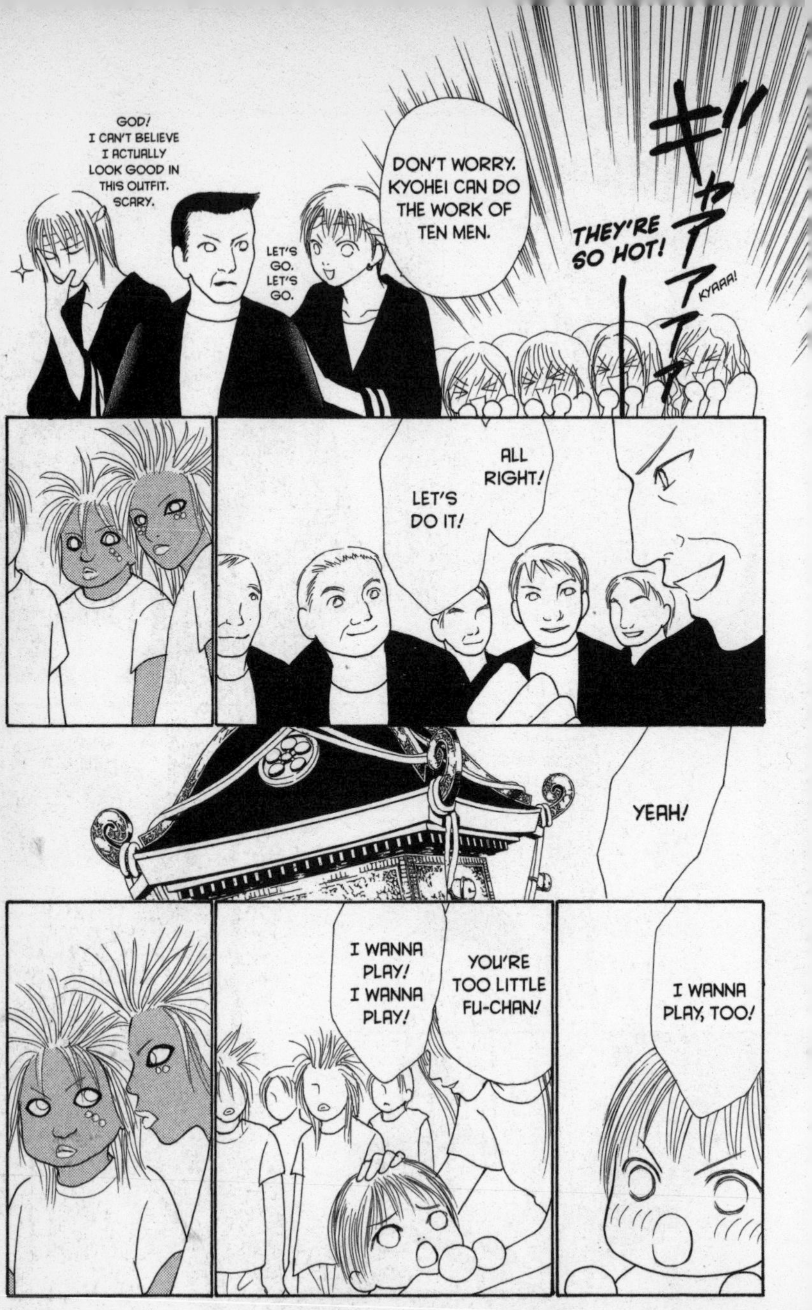
ギャアアアァ
THEY'RE SO HOT!
KYAAA!
DON'T WORRY. KYOHEI CAN DO THE WORK OF TEN MEN.
LET'S GO. LET'S GO.
GOD! I CAN'T BELIEVE I ACTUALLY LOOK GOOD IN THIS OUTFIT. SCARY.
ALL RIGHT!
LET'S DO IT!
YEAH!
I WANNA PLAY, TOO!
YOU'RE TOO LITTLE FU-CHAN!
I WANNA PLAY! I WANNA PLAY!

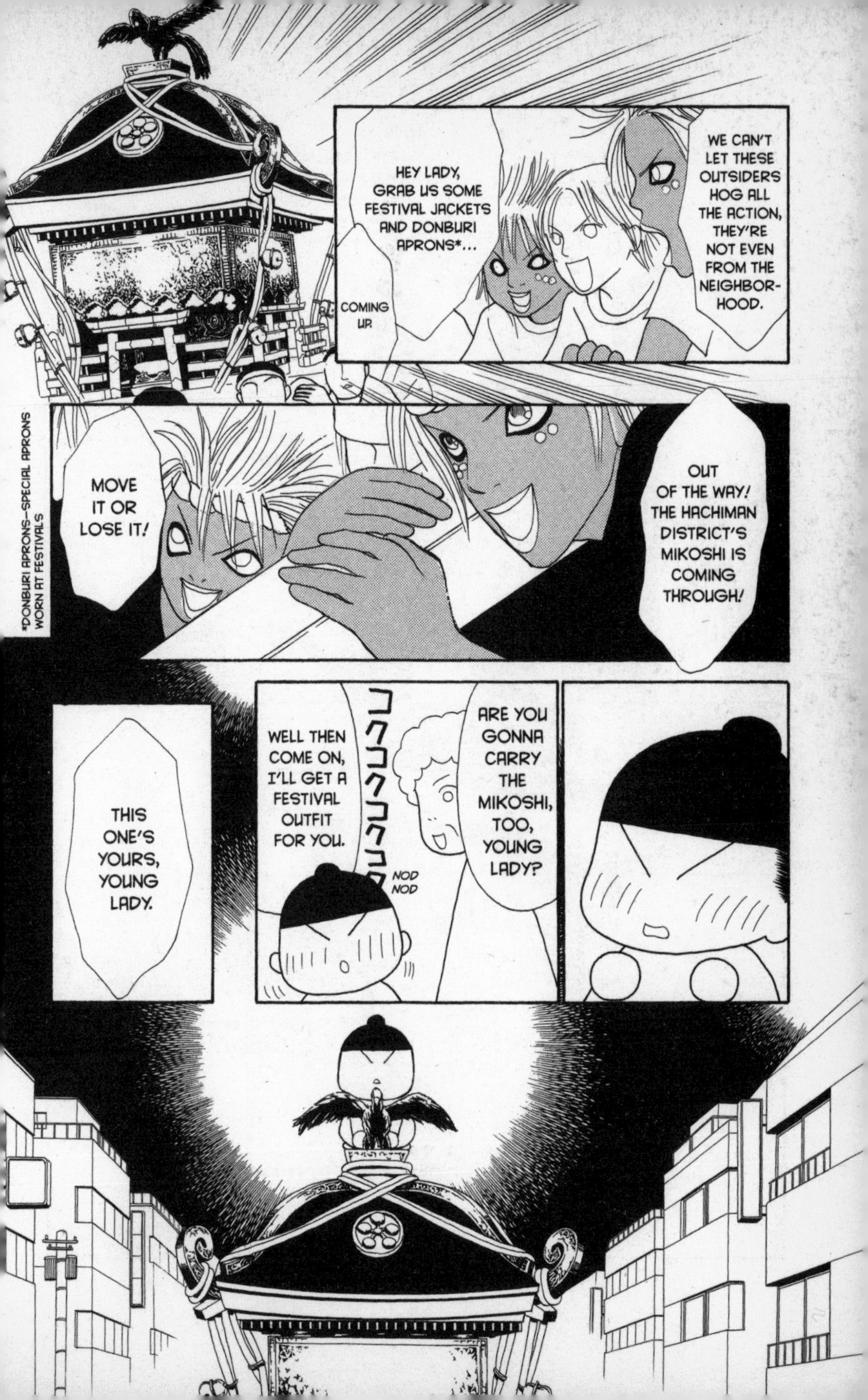
WE CAN'T LET THESE OUTSIDERS HOG ALL THE ACTION, THEY'RE NOT EVEN FROM THE NEIGHBOR-HOOD.
HEY LADY, GRAB US SOME FESTIVAL JACKETS AND DONBURI APRONS*...
COMING UP.
OUT OF THE WAY! THE HACHIMAN DISTRICT'S MIKOSHI IS COMING THROUGH!
MOVE IT OR LOSE IT!
ARE YOU GONNA CARRY THE MIKOSHI, TOO, YOUNG LADY?
NOD NOD
WELL THEN COME ON, I'LL GET A FESTIVAL OUTFIT FOR YOU.
THIS ONE'S YOURS, YOUNG LADY.

*DONBURI APRONS—SPECIAL APRONS WORN AT FESTIVALS

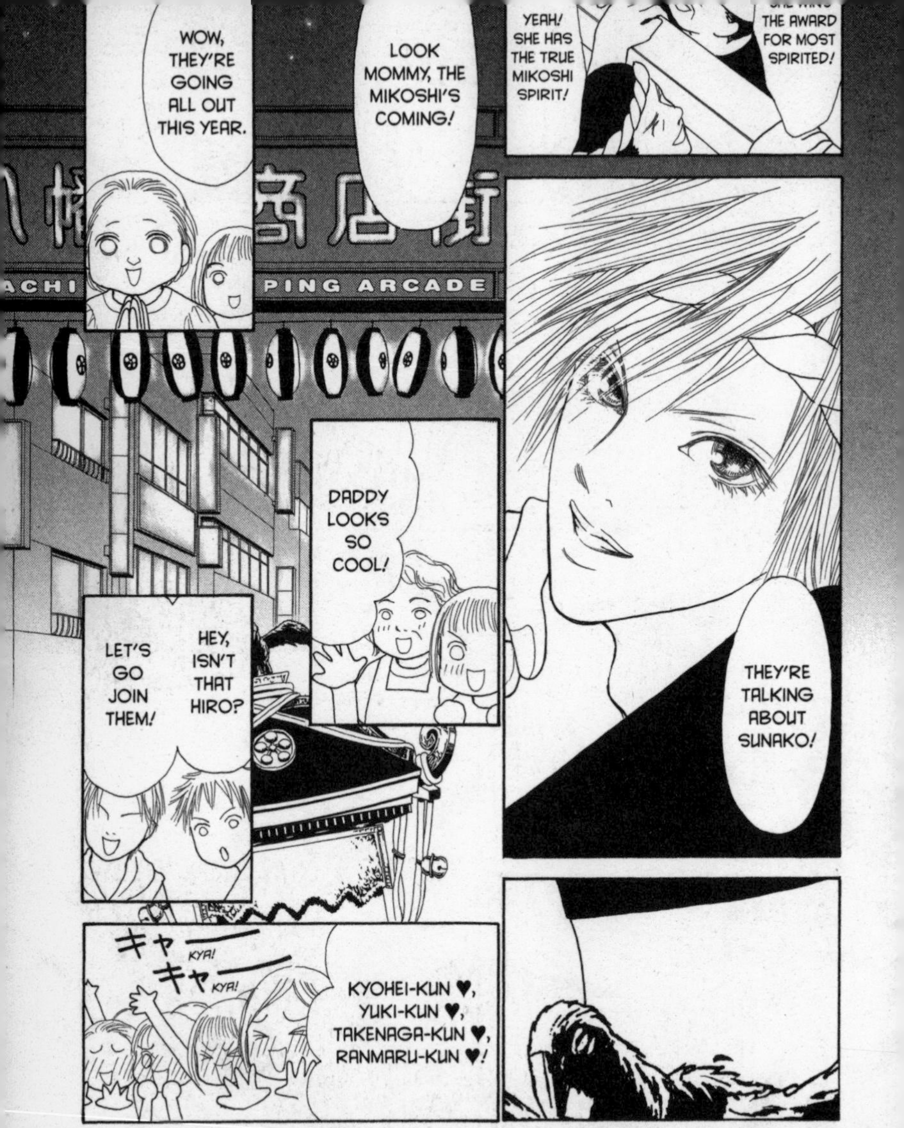
THE AWARD FOR MOST SPIRITED!
YEAH! SHE HAS THE TRUE MIKOSHI SPIRIT!
THEY'RE TALKING ABOUT SUNAKO!
LOOK MOMMY, THE MIKOSHI'S COMING!
WOW, THEY'RE GOING ALL OUT THIS YEAR.
PING ARCADE
DADDY LOOKS SO COOL!
HEY, ISN'T THAT HIRO?
LET'S GO JOIN THEM!
KYOHEI-KUN ♥, YUKI-KUN ♥, TAKENAGA-KUN ♥, RANMARU-KUN ♥!
キャー KYA!
キャー KYA!

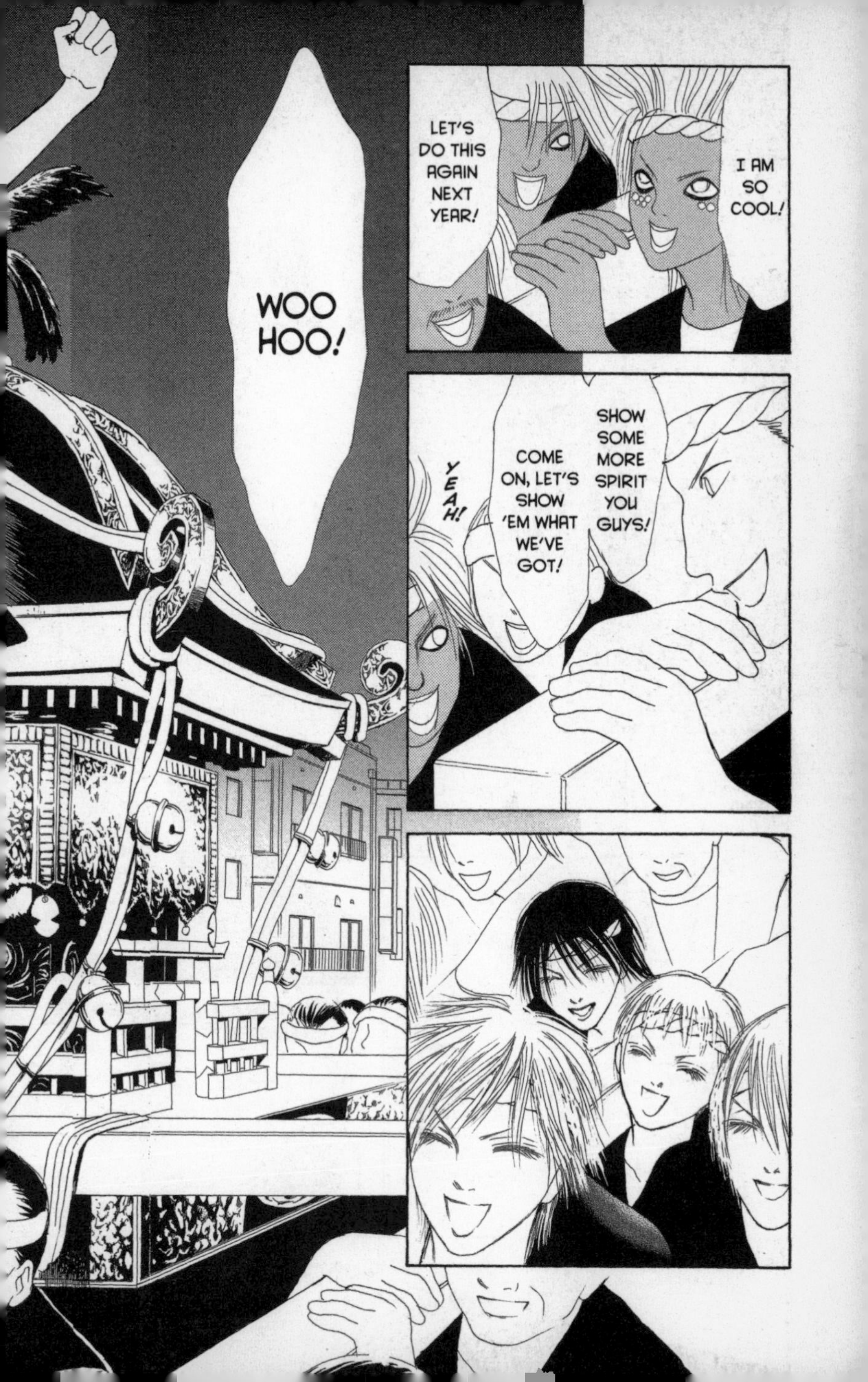

I AM SO COOL!
LET'S DO THIS AGAIN NEXT YEAR!
SHOW SOME MORE SPIRIT YOU GUYS!
COME ON, LET'S SHOW 'EM WHAT WE'VE GOT!
YEAH!
WOO HOO!

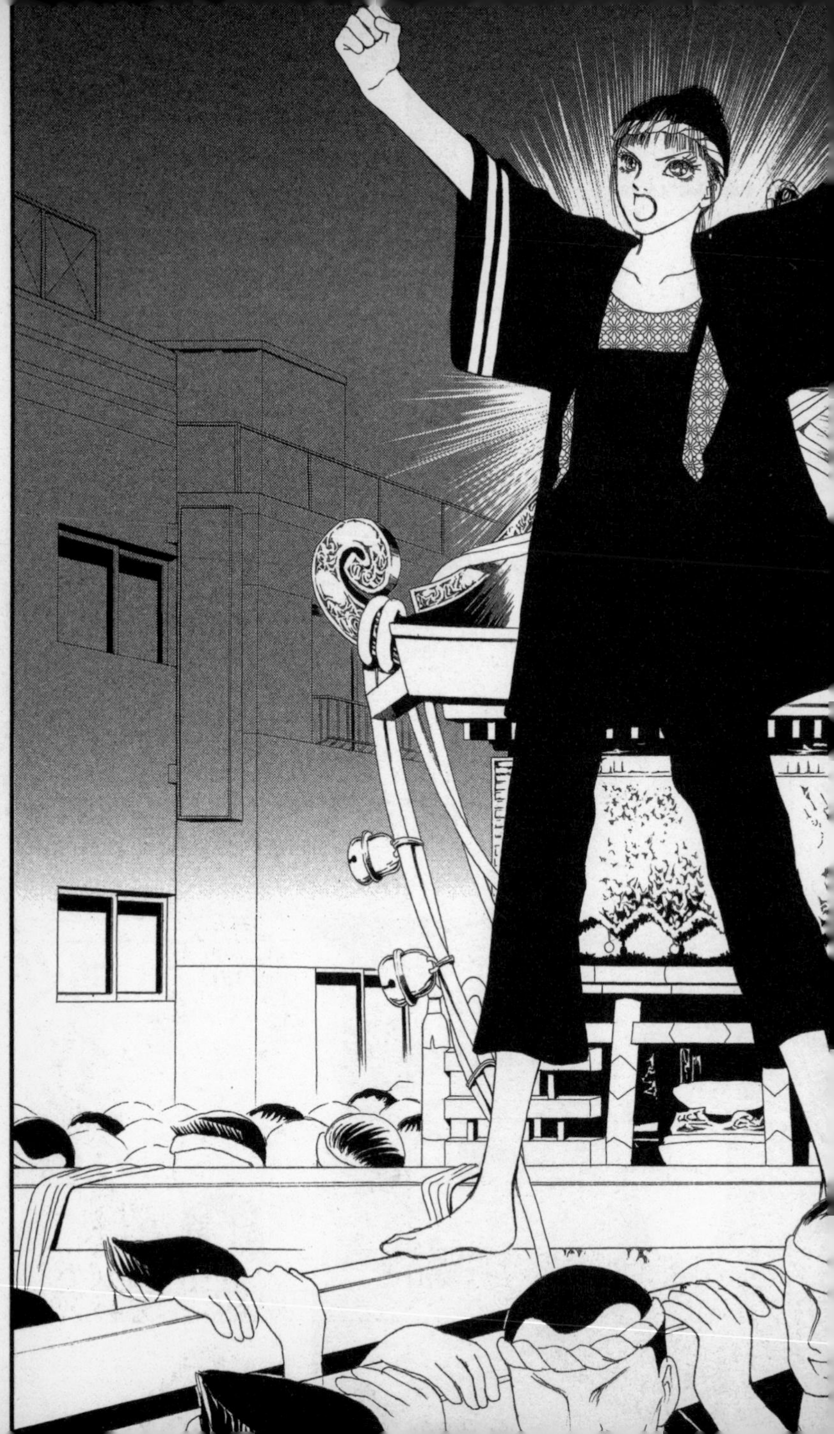

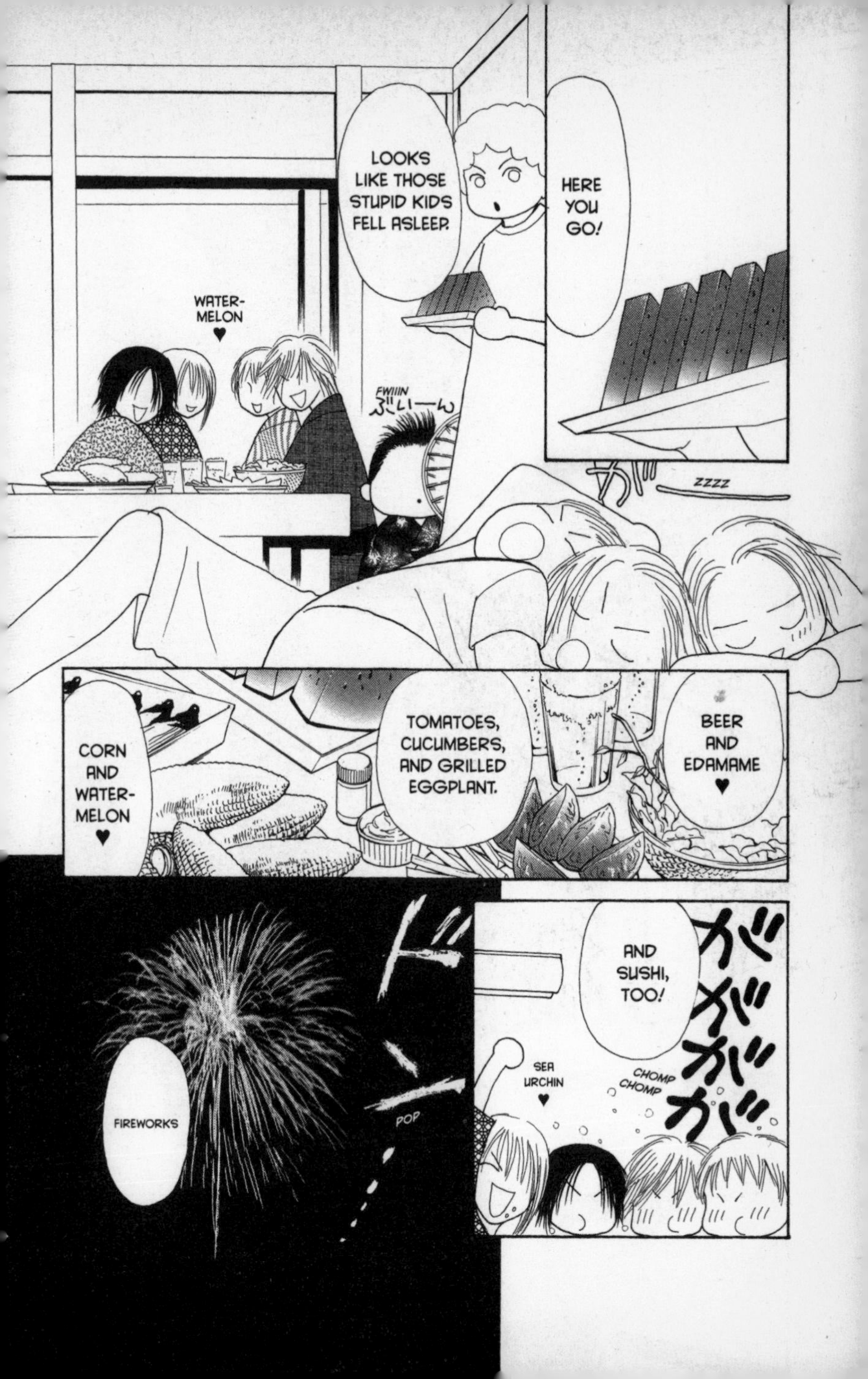
HERE YOU GO!
LOOKS LIKE THOSE STUPID KIDS FELL ASLEEP.
WATER-MELON ♥
FWIIIN
ぶいーん
ZZZZ
BEER AND EDAMAME ♥
TOMATOES, CUCUMBERS, AND GRILLED EGGPLANT.
CORN AND WATER-MELON ♥
AND SUSHI, TOO!
がががが
CHOMP CHOMP
SEA URCHIN ♥
ド
POP
FIREWORKS

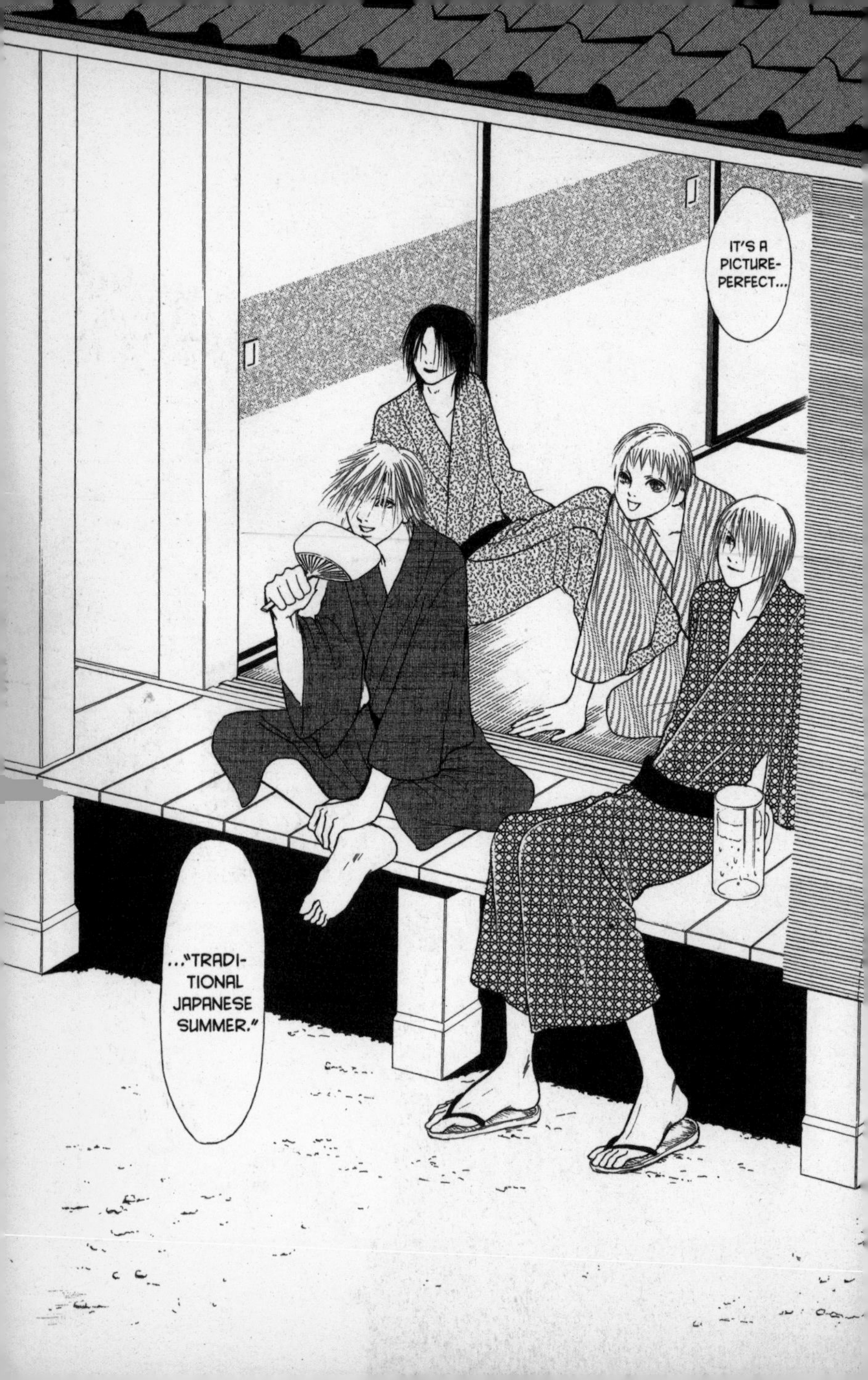
IT'S A PICTURE-PERFECT...
..."TRADITIONAL JAPANESE SUMMER."

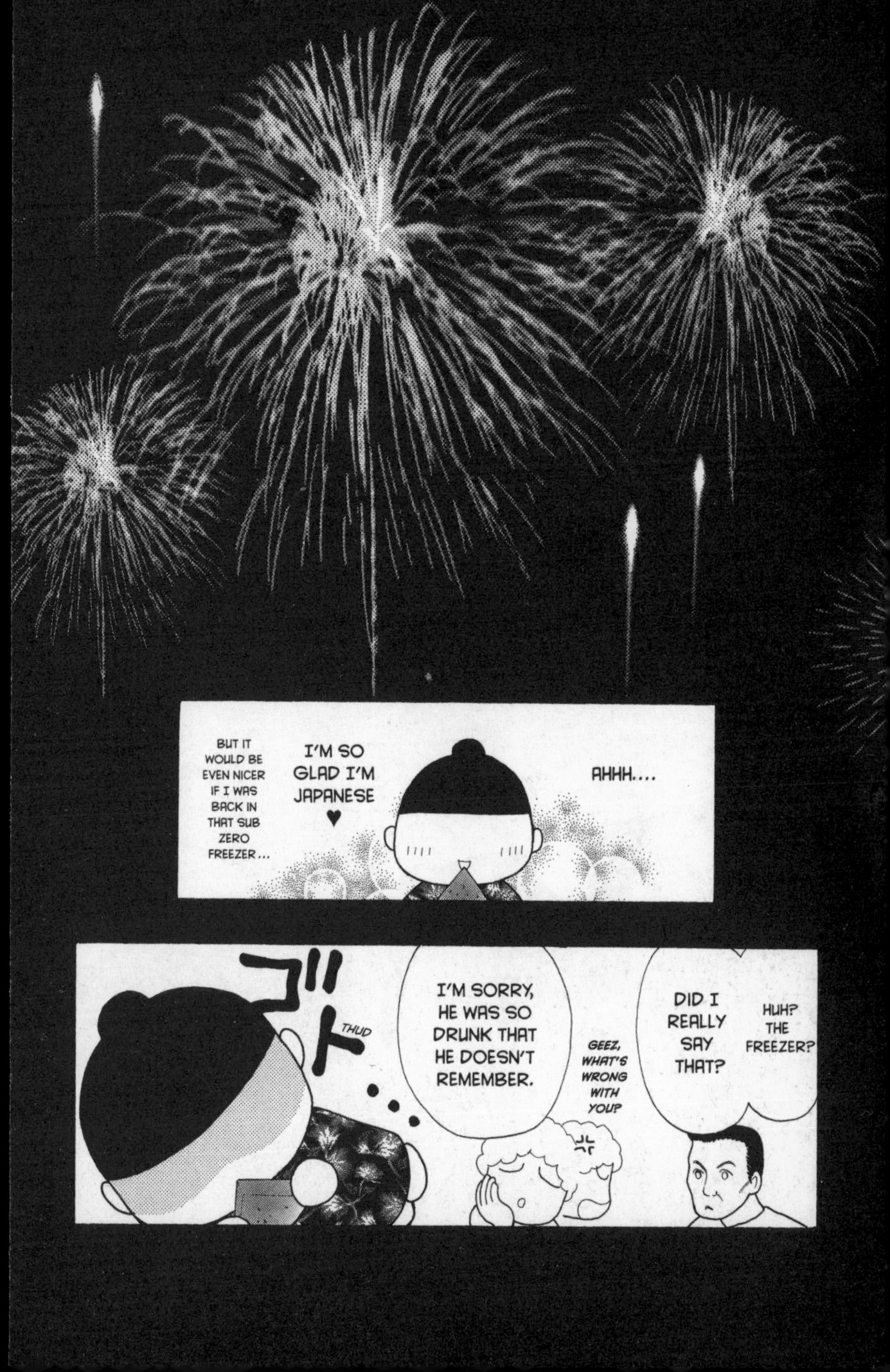
AHHH....
I'M SO GLAD I'M JAPANESE ♥
BUT IT WOULD BE EVEN NICER IF I WAS BACK IN THAT SUB ZERO FREEZER...
HUH? THE FREEZER?
DID I REALLY SAY THAT?
GEEZ, WHAT'S WRONG WITH YOU?
I'M SORRY, HE WAS SO DRUNK THAT HE DOESN'T REMEMBER.
ゴト
THUD

もりもり
CHOMP CHOMP
Haagen Daccho

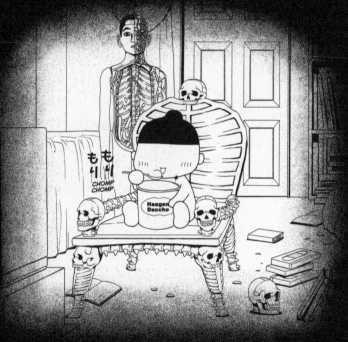

Chapter 48
The Summer Vacation of Love

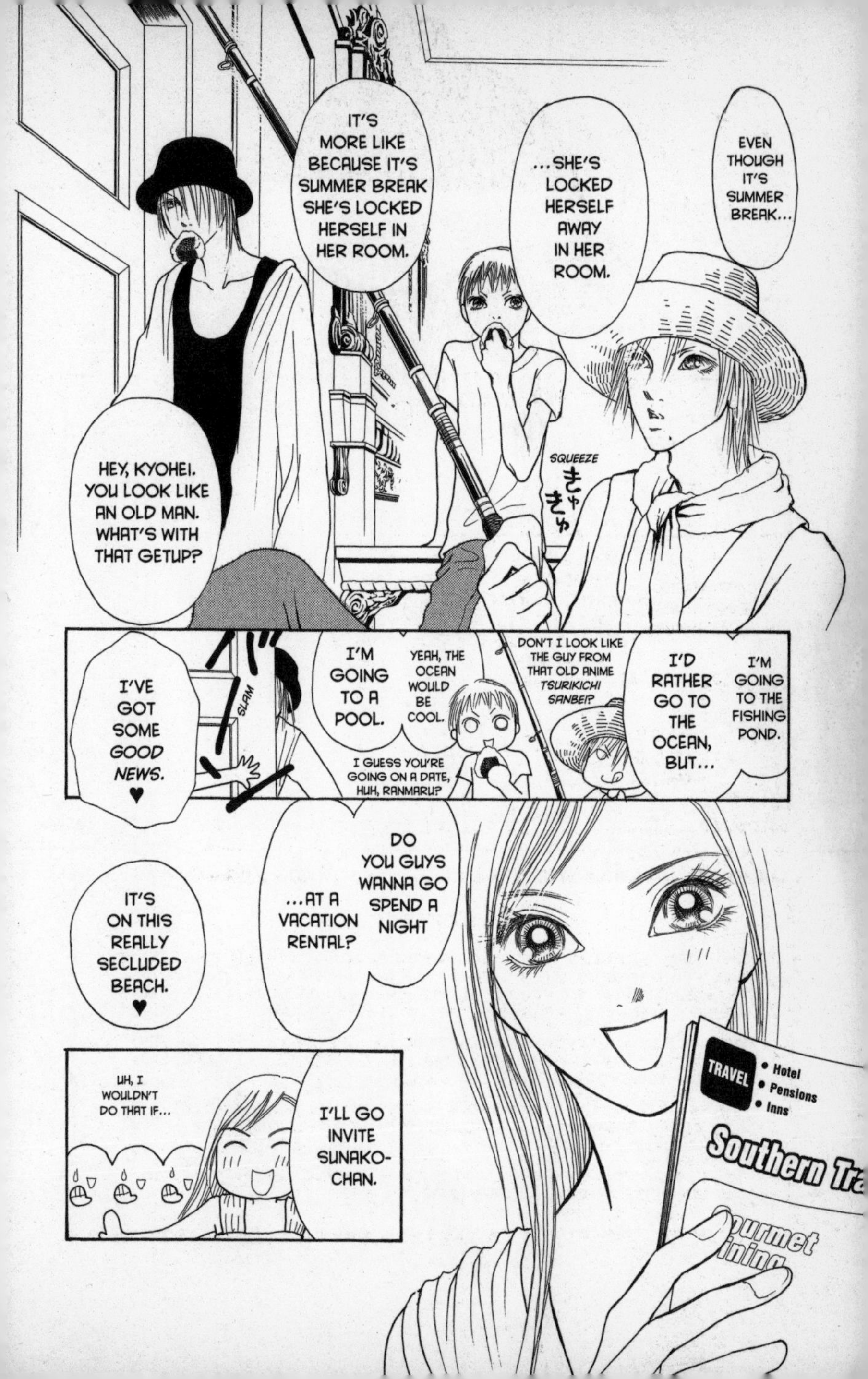
EVEN THOUGH IT'S SUMMER BREAK...
...SHE'S LOCKED HERSELF AWAY IN HER ROOM.
IT'S MORE LIKE BECAUSE IT'S SUMMER BREAK SHE'S LOCKED HERSELF IN HER ROOM.
SQUEEZE
HEY, KYOHEI. YOU LOOK LIKE AN OLD MAN. WHAT'S WITH THAT GETUP?
I'M GOING TO THE FISHING POND.
I'D RATHER GO TO THE OCEAN, BUT...
DON'T I LOOK LIKE THE GUY FROM THAT OLD ANIME *TSURIKICHI SANBEI*?
YEAH, THE OCEAN WOULD BE COOL.
I'M GOING TO A POOL.
I GUESS YOU'RE GOING ON A DATE, HUH, RANMARU?
SLAM
I'VE GOT SOME *GOOD NEWS*. ♥
DO YOU GUYS WANNA GO SPEND A NIGHT
...AT A VACATION RENTAL?
IT'S ON THIS REALLY SECLUDED BEACH. ♥
TRAVEL
• Hotel
• Pensions
• Inns
I'LL GO INVITE SUNAKO-CHAN.
UH, I WOULDN'T DO THAT IF...

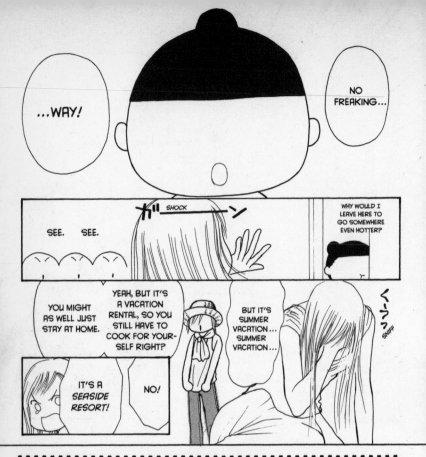

NO FREAKING...
...WAY!
WHY WOULD I LEAVE HERE TO GO SOMEWHERE EVEN HOTTER?
SHOCK
SEE. SEE.
SNIFF
BUT IT'S SUMMER VACATION... SUMMER VACATION...
YEAH, BUT IT'S A VACATION RENTAL, SO YOU STILL HAVE TO COOK FOR YOURSELF RIGHT?
YOU MIGHT AS WELL JUST STAY AT HOME.
NO!
IT'S A *SEASIDE* RESORT!

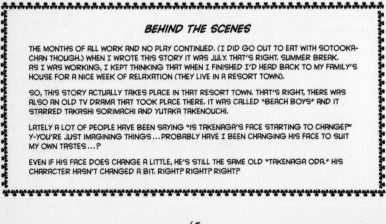

BEHIND THE SCENES

THE MONTHS OF ALL WORK AND NO PLAY CONTINUED. (I DID GO OUT TO EAT WITH SOTOOKA-CHAN THOUGH.) WHEN I WROTE THIS STORY IT WAS JULY. THAT'S RIGHT. SUMMER BREAK. AS I WAS WORKING, I KEPT THINKING THAT WHEN I FINISHED I'D HEAD BACK TO MY FAMILY'S HOUSE FOR A NICE WEEK OF RELAXATION (THEY LIVE IN A RESORT TOWN).

SO, THIS STORY ACTUALLY TAKES PLACE IN THAT RESORT TOWN. THAT'S RIGHT, THERE WAS ALSO AN OLD TV DRAMA THAT TOOK PLACE THERE. IT WAS CALLED "BEACH BOYS" AND IT STARRED TAKASHI SORIMACHI AND YUTAKA TAKENOUCHI.

LATELY A LOT OF PEOPLE HAVE BEEN SAYING "IS TAKENAGA'S FACE STARTING TO CHANGE?" Y-YOU'RE JUST IMAGINING THINGS...PROBABLY HAVE I BEEN CHANGING HIS FACE TO SUIT MY OWN TASTES...?

EVEN IF HIS FACE DOES CHANGE A LITTLE, HE'S STILL THE SAME OLD "TAKENAGA ODA." HIS CHARACTER HASN'T CHANGED A BIT. RIGHT? RIGHT? RIGHT?

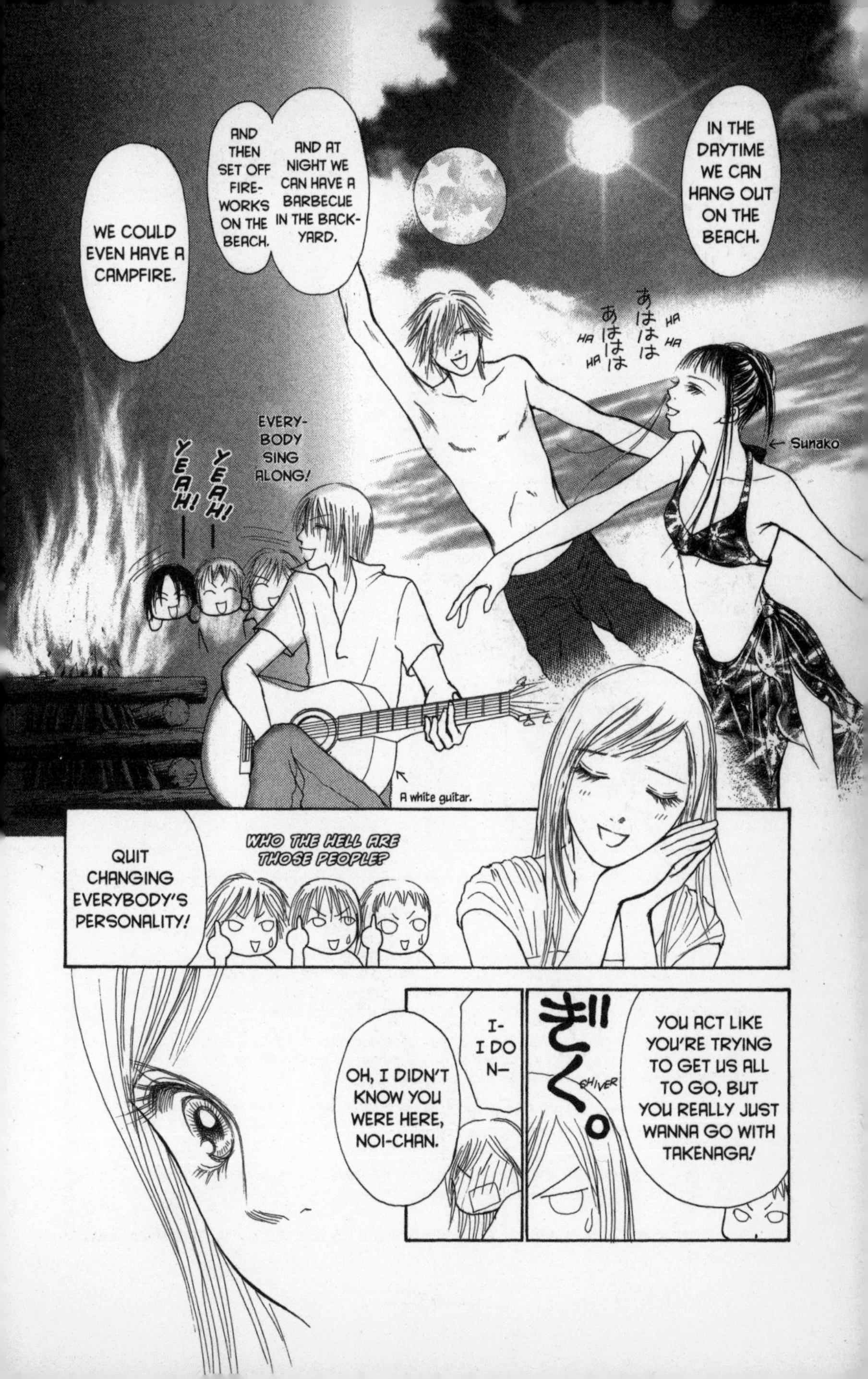
IN THE DAYTIME WE CAN HANG OUT ON THE BEACH.
AND AT NIGHT WE CAN HAVE A BARBECUE IN THE BACK-YARD.
AND THEN SET OFF FIRE-WORKS ON THE BEACH.
WE COULD EVEN HAVE A CAMPFIRE.
あははは
あははは
HA HA HA HA
Sunako
EVERY-BODY SING ALONG!
YEAH!
YEAH!
A white guitar.
WHO THE HELL ARE THOSE PEOPLE?
QUIT CHANGING EVERYBODY'S PERSONALITY!
YOU ACT LIKE YOU'RE TRYING TO GET US ALL TO GO, BUT YOU REALLY JUST WANNA GO WITH TAKENAGA!
ぞく。
SHIVER
I- I DO N—
OH, I DIDN'T KNOW YOU WERE HERE, NOI-CHAN.

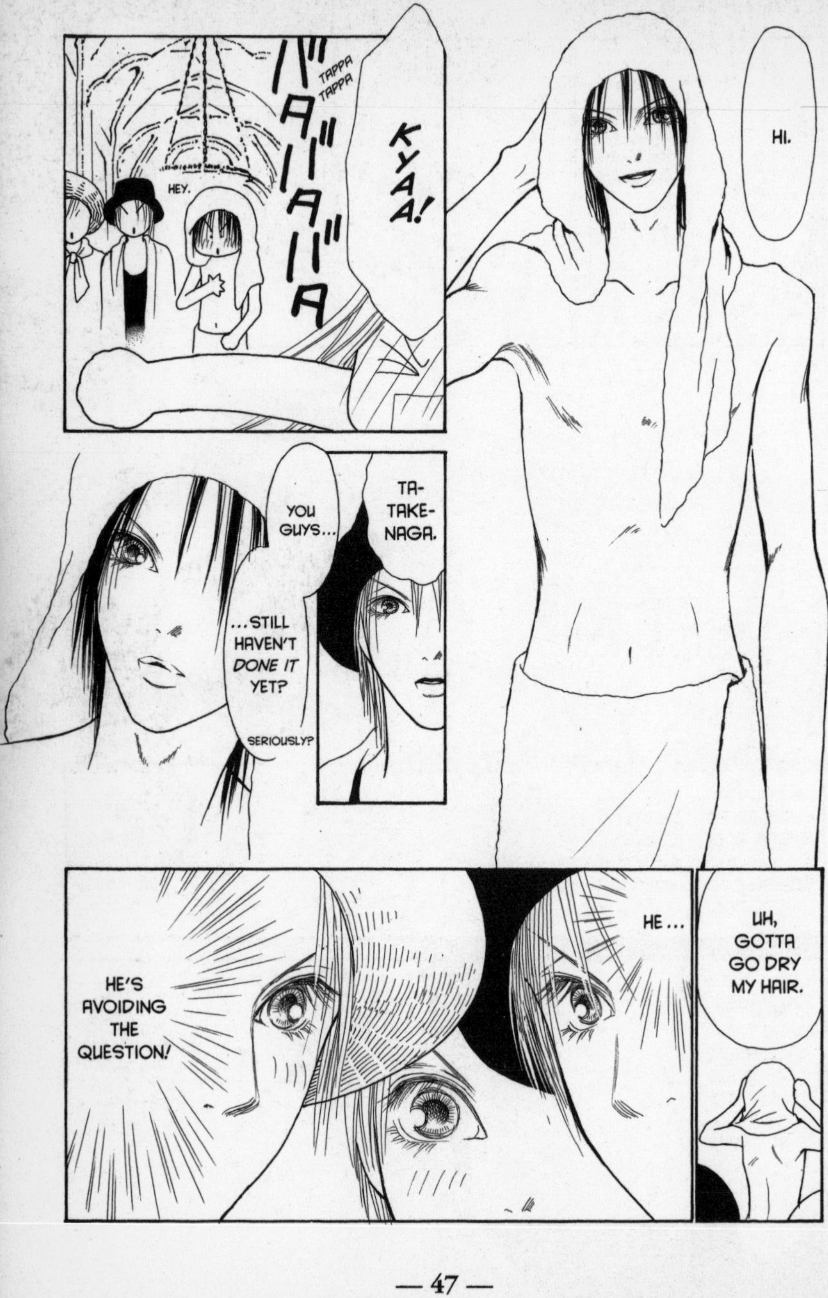
HI.
KYAA!
TAPPA TAPPA
バタバタバタ
HEY.
TA-TAKE-NAGA.
YOU GUYS...
...STILL HAVEN'T *DONE IT* YET?
SERIOUSLY?
UH, GOTTA GO DRY MY HAIR.
HE...
HE'S AVOIDING THE QUESTION!

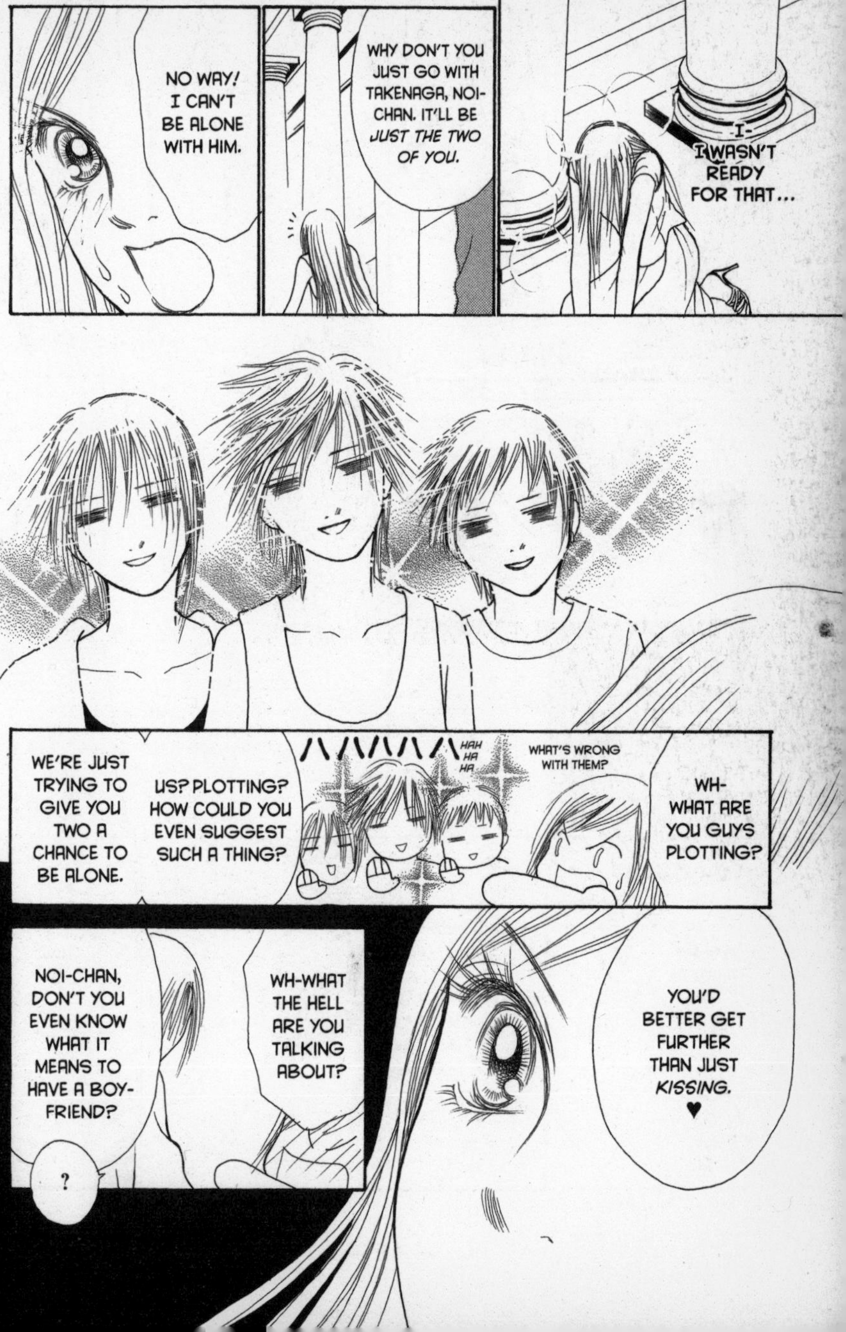
I- I WASN'T READY FOR THAT...
WHY DON'T YOU JUST GO WITH TAKENAGA, NOI-CHAN. IT'LL BE *JUST THE TWO OF YOU.*
NO WAY! I CAN'T BE ALONE WITH HIM.
WH- WHAT ARE YOU GUYS PLOTTING?
WHAT'S WRONG WITH THEM?
HAH HA HA
US? PLOTTING? HOW COULD YOU EVEN SUGGEST SUCH A THING?
WE'RE JUST TRYING TO GIVE YOU TWO A CHANCE TO BE ALONE.
YOU'D BETTER GET FURTHER THAN JUST *KISSING.* ♥
WH-WHAT THE HELL ARE YOU TALKING ABOUT?
NOI-CHAN, DON'T YOU EVEN KNOW WHAT IT MEANS TO HAVE A BOY-FRIEND?
?

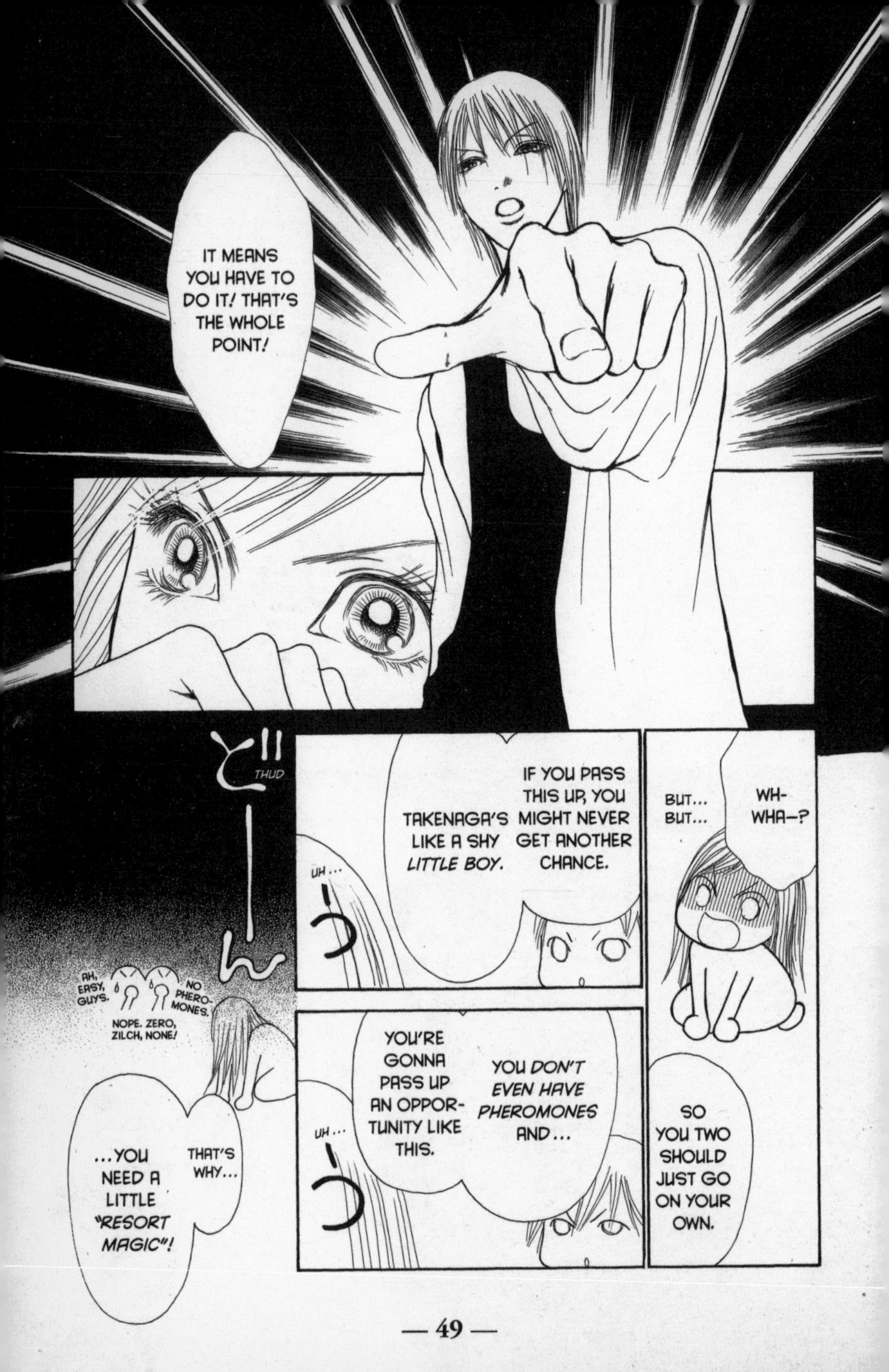
IT MEANS YOU HAVE TO DO IT! THAT'S THE WHOLE POINT!
WH- WHA-?
BUT... BUT...
SO YOU TWO SHOULD JUST GO ON YOUR OWN.
IF YOU PASS THIS UP, YOU MIGHT NEVER GET ANOTHER CHANCE.
TAKENAGA'S LIKE A SHY *LITTLE BOY.*
UH...
YOU DON'T EVEN HAVE PHEROMONES AND...
YOU'RE GONNA PASS UP AN OPPORTUNITY LIKE THIS.
UH...
THUD
NO PHEROMONES.
AH, EASY, GUYS.
NOPE. ZERO, ZILCH, NONE!
THAT'S WHY...
...YOU NEED A LITTLE *"RESORT MAGIC"*!

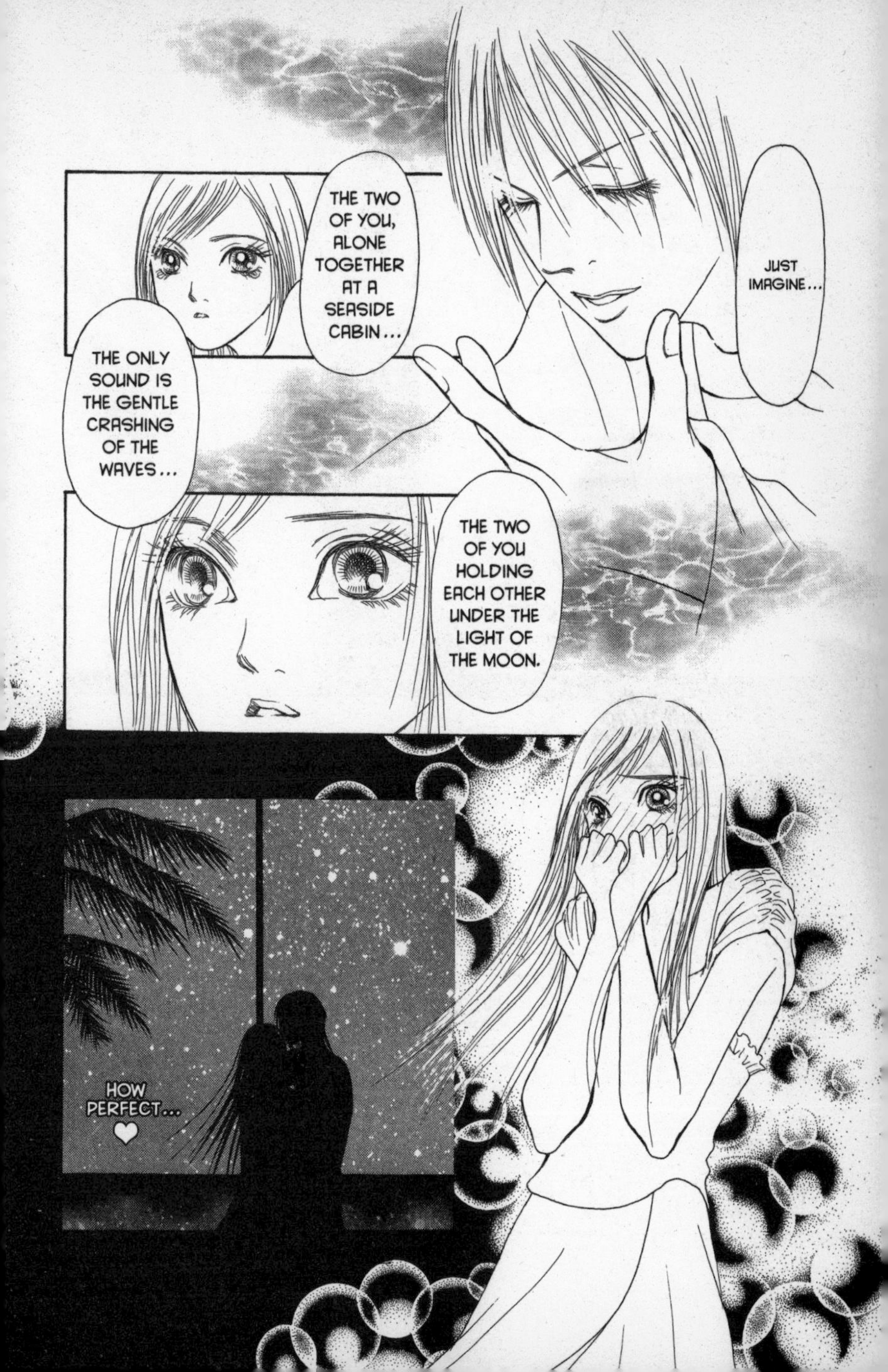
JUST IMAGINE...
THE TWO OF YOU, ALONE TOGETHER AT A SEASIDE CABIN...
THE ONLY SOUND IS THE GENTLE CRASHING OF THE WAVES...
THE TWO OF YOU HOLDING EACH OTHER UNDER THE LIGHT OF THE MOON.
HOW PERFECT... ♥

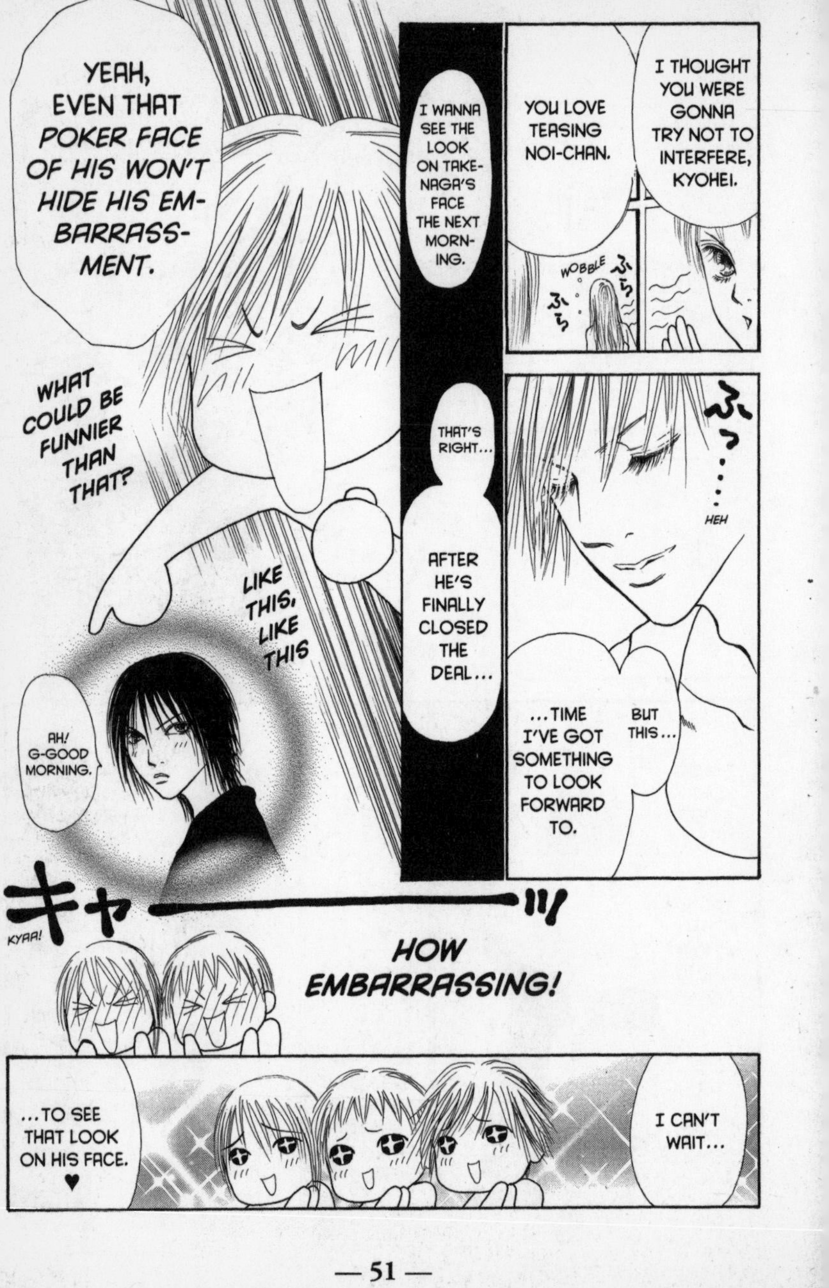
I THOUGHT YOU WERE GONNA TRY NOT TO INTERFERE, KYOHEI.
YOU LOVE TEASING NOI-CHAN.
WOBBLE
ふらふら
ふっ…
HEH
THAT'S RIGHT…
BUT THIS…
…TIME I'VE GOT SOMETHING TO LOOK FORWARD TO.
AFTER HE'S FINALLY CLOSED THE DEAL…
I WANNA SEE THE LOOK ON TAKENAGA'S FACE THE NEXT MORNING.
YEAH, EVEN THAT POKER FACE OF HIS WON'T HIDE HIS EMBARRASSMENT.
WHAT COULD BE FUNNIER THAN THAT?
LIKE THIS, LIKE THIS
AH! G-GOOD MORNING.
キャ——!!
KYAA!
HOW EMBARRASSING!
I CAN'T WAIT…
…TO SEE THAT LOOK ON HIS FACE. ♥

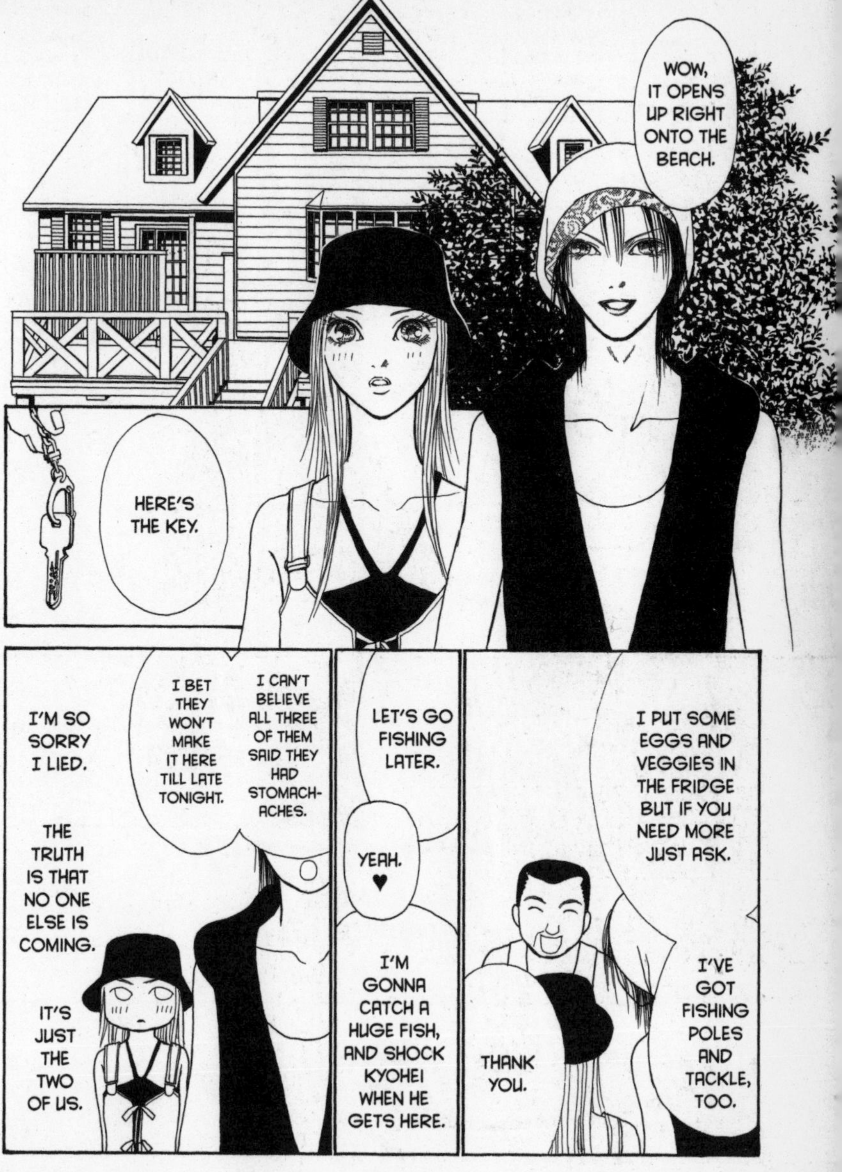
WOW, IT OPENS UP RIGHT ONTO THE BEACH.
HERE'S THE KEY.
I PUT SOME EGGS AND VEGGIES IN THE FRIDGE BUT IF YOU NEED MORE JUST ASK.
I'VE GOT FISHING POLES AND TACKLE, TOO.
THANK YOU.
LET'S GO FISHING LATER.
YEAH. ♥
I'M GONNA CATCH A HUGE FISH, AND SHOCK KYOHEI WHEN HE GETS HERE.
I CAN'T BELIEVE ALL THREE OF THEM SAID THEY HAD STOMACH-ACHES.
I BET THEY WON'T MAKE IT HERE TILL LATE TONIGHT.
I'M SO SORRY I LIED.
THE TRUTH IS THAT NO ONE ELSE IS COMING.
IT'S JUST THE TWO OF US.

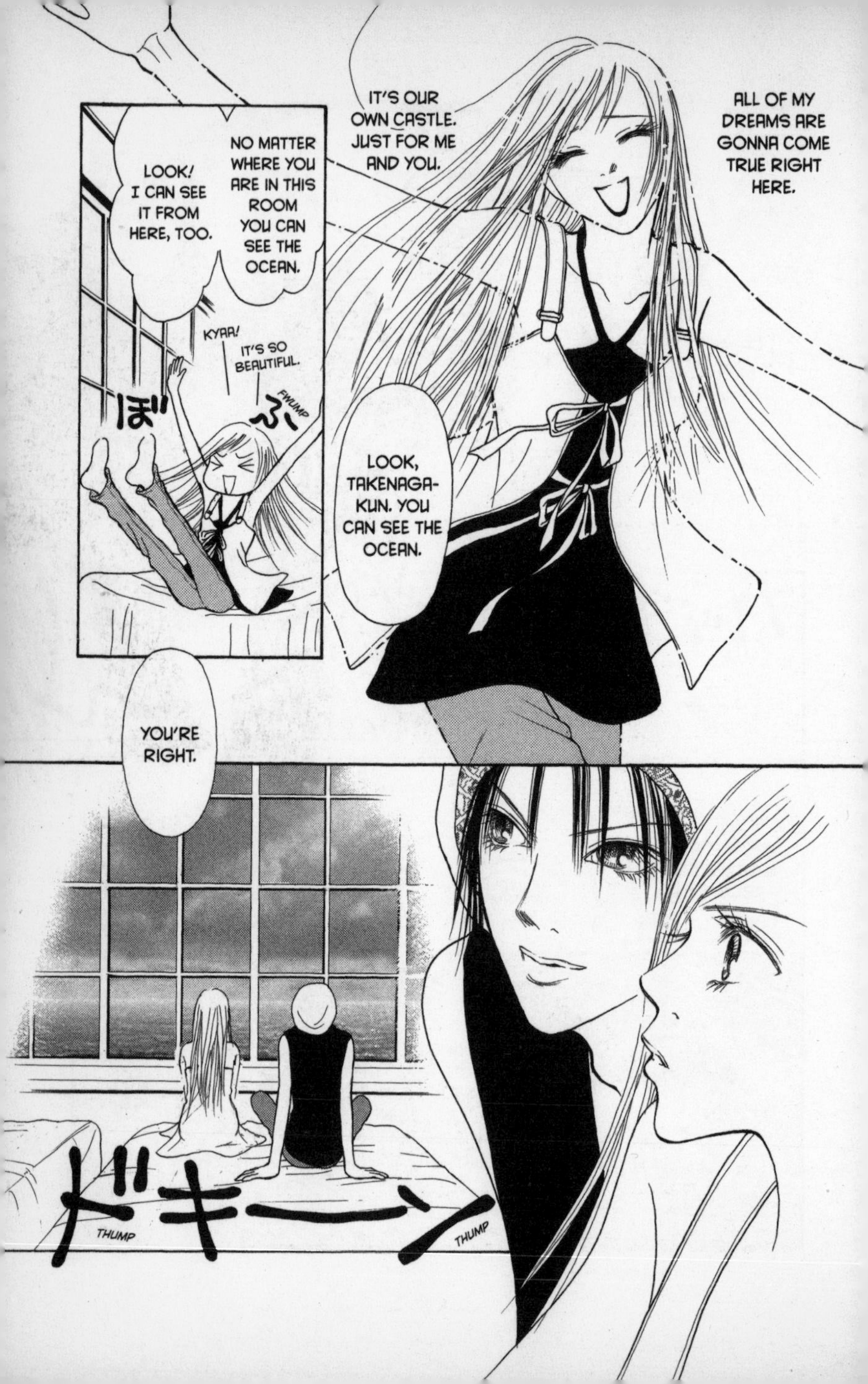
ALL OF MY DREAMS ARE GONNA COME TRUE RIGHT HERE.
IT'S OUR OWN CASTLE. JUST FOR ME AND YOU.
LOOK, TAKENAGA-KUN. YOU CAN SEE THE OCEAN.
NO MATTER WHERE YOU ARE IN THIS ROOM YOU CAN SEE THE OCEAN.
LOOK! I CAN SEE IT FROM HERE, TOO.
IT'S SO BEAUTIFUL.
KYAA!
ぼふ
FWUMP
YOU'RE RIGHT.
ドキーン
THUMP
THUMP

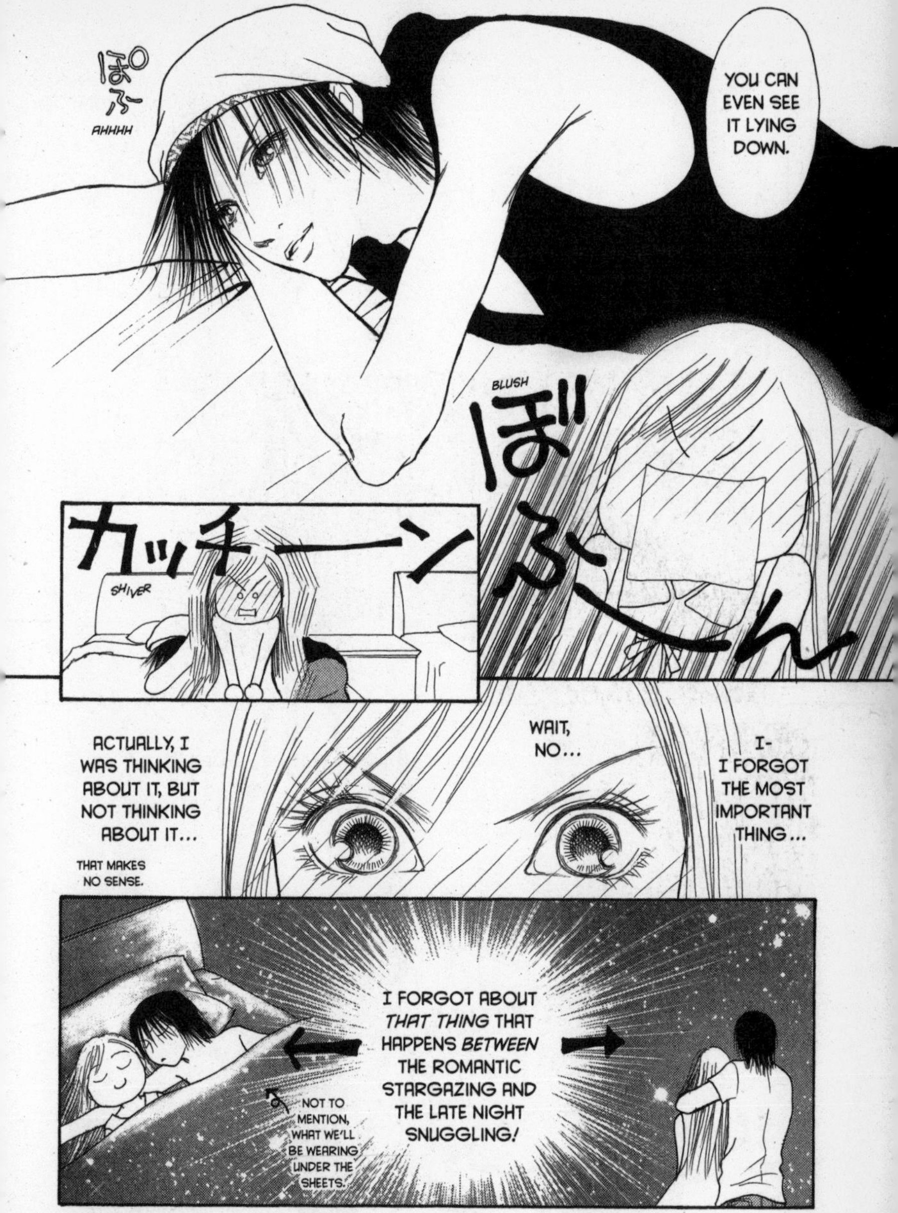
YOU CAN EVEN SEE IT LYING DOWN.
ぽふ
AHHHH
BLUSH
ぼふーん
カッチーン
SHIVER
I- I FORGOT THE MOST IMPORTANT THING...
WAIT, NO...
ACTUALLY, I WAS THINKING ABOUT IT, BUT NOT THINKING ABOUT IT...
THAT MAKES NO SENSE.
I FORGOT ABOUT *THAT THING* THAT HAPPENS *BETWEEN* THE ROMANTIC STARGAZING AND THE LATE NIGHT SNUGGLING!
NOT TO MENTION, WHAT WE'LL BE WEARING UNDER THE SHEETS.

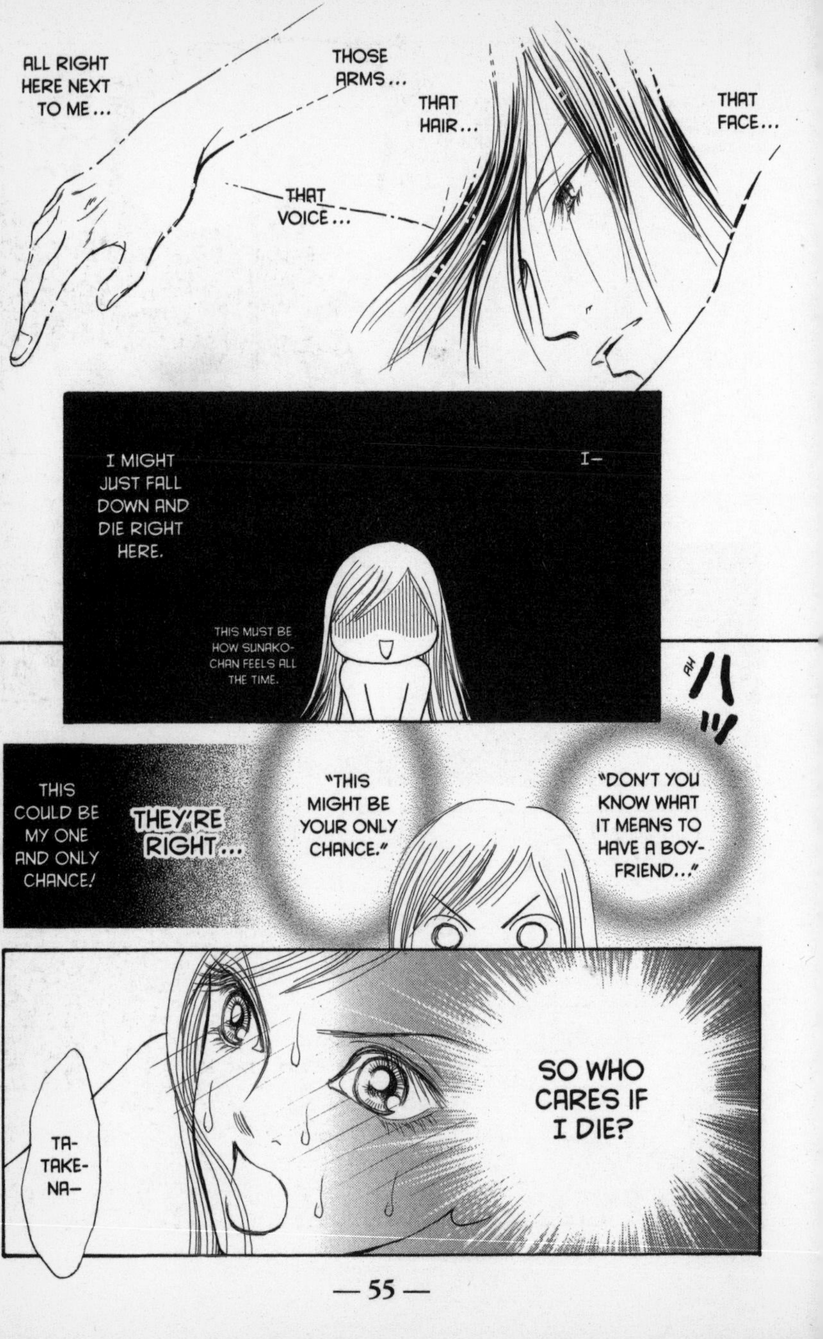
THAT FACE...
THAT HAIR...
THOSE ARMS...
THAT VOICE...
ALL RIGHT HERE NEXT TO ME...
I—
I MIGHT JUST FALL DOWN AND DIE RIGHT HERE.
THIS MUST BE HOW SUNAKO-CHAN FEELS ALL THE TIME.
AH
"DON'T YOU KNOW WHAT IT MEANS TO HAVE A BOY-FRIEND..."
"THIS MIGHT BE YOUR ONLY CHANCE."
THEY'RE RIGHT...
THIS COULD BE MY ONE AND ONLY CHANCE!
SO WHO CARES IF I DIE?
TA-TAKE-NA—

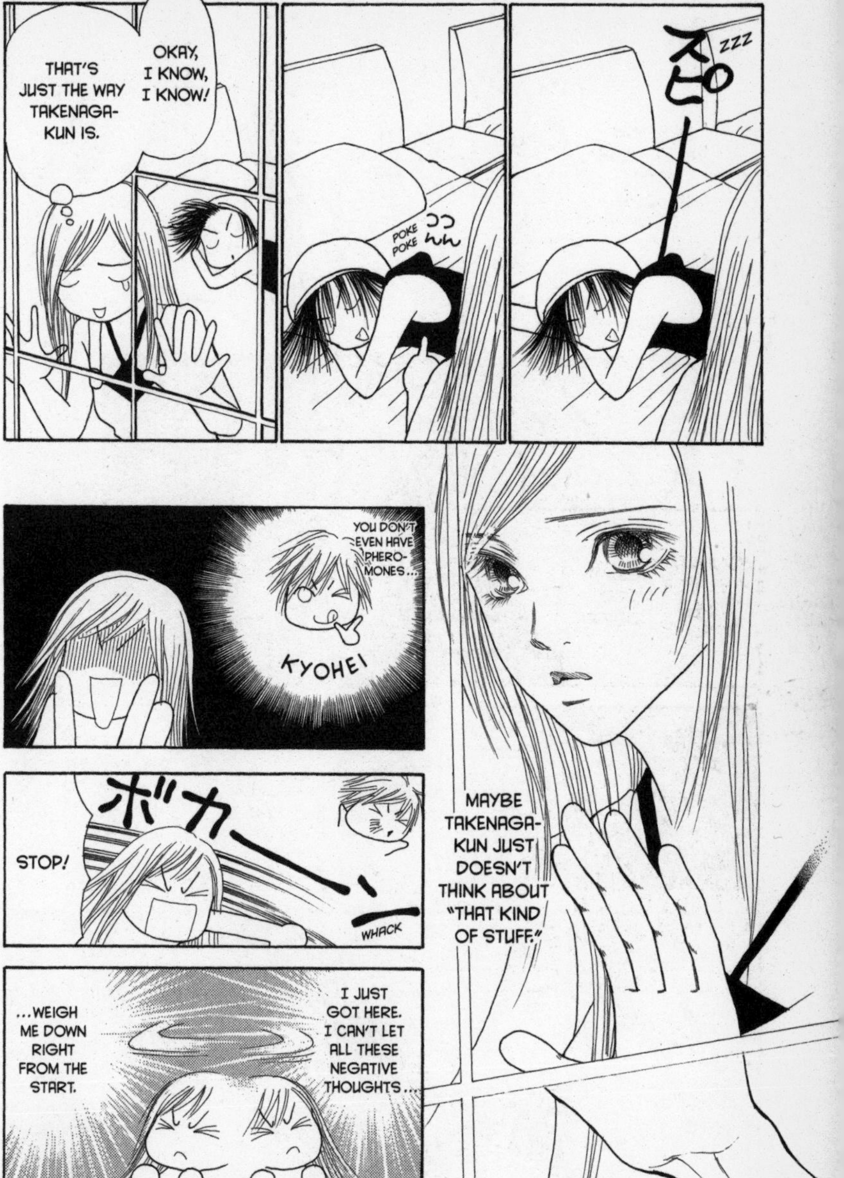
スピー
ZZZ
POKE POKE
OKAY, I KNOW, I KNOW!
THAT'S JUST THE WAY TAKENAGA-KUN IS.
MAYBE TAKENAGA-KUN JUST DOESN'T THINK ABOUT "THAT KIND OF STUFF."
YOU DON'T EVEN HAVE PHERO-MONES...
KYOHEI
ボカー
WHACK
STOP!
I JUST GOT HERE. I CAN'T LET ALL THESE NEGATIVE THOUGHTS...
...WEIGH ME DOWN RIGHT FROM THE START.

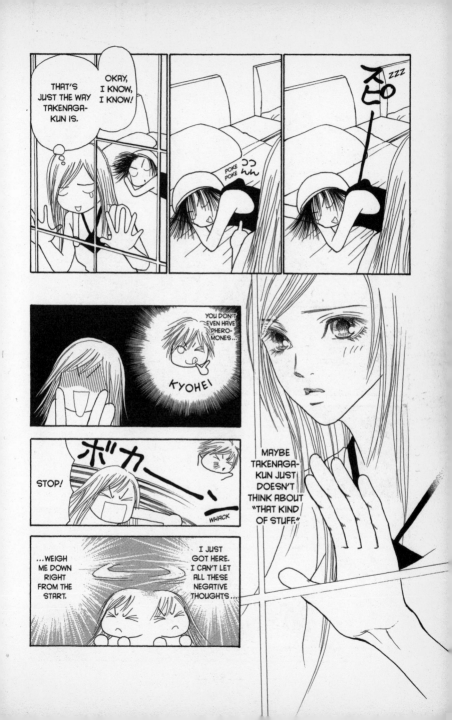

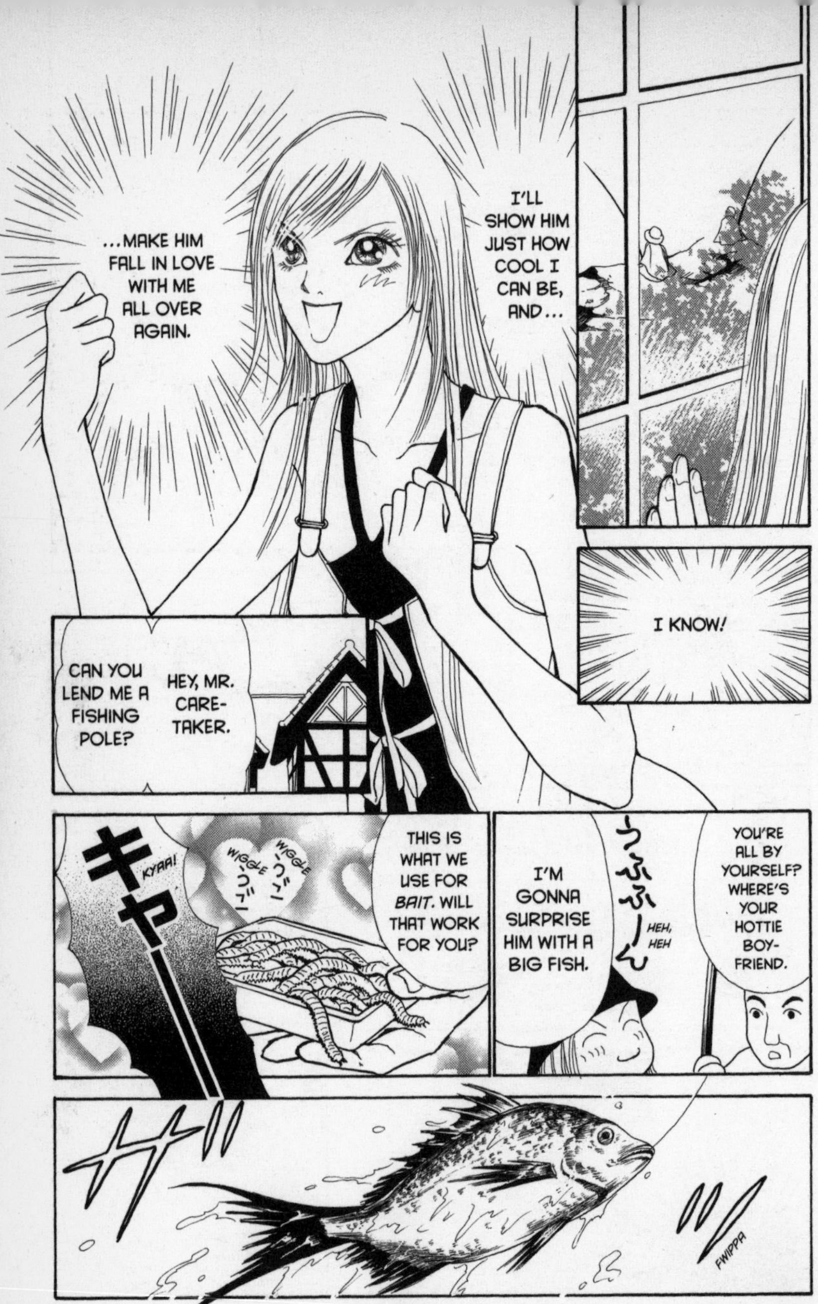
I KNOW!
I'LL SHOW HIM JUST HOW COOL I CAN BE, AND...
...MAKE HIM FALL IN LOVE WITH ME ALL OVER AGAIN.
HEY, MR. CARE-TAKER.
CAN YOU LEND ME A FISHING POLE?
YOU'RE ALL BY YOURSELF? WHERE'S YOUR HOTTIE BOY-FRIEND.
うふふーん
HEH, HEH
I'M GONNA SURPRISE HIM WITH A BIG FISH.
THIS IS WHAT WE USE FOR *BAIT*. WILL THAT WORK FOR YOU?
WIGGLE
WIGGLE
キャー
KYAA!
FWIPPA

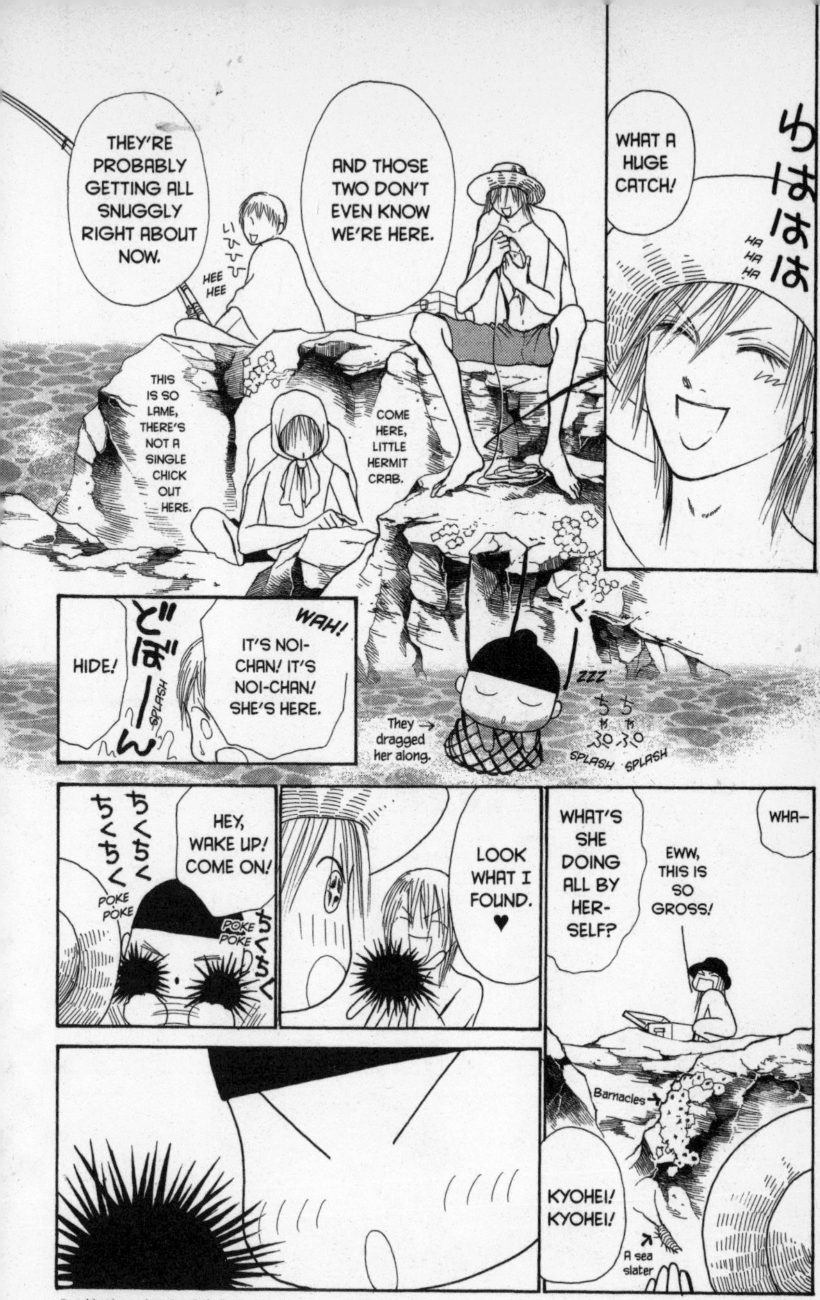
WHAT A HUGE CATCH!
わははは
HA HA HA
AND THOSE TWO DON'T EVEN KNOW WE'RE HERE.
THEY'RE PROBABLY GETTING ALL SNUGGLY RIGHT ABOUT NOW.
いひひひ
HEE HEE
COME HERE, LITTLE HERMIT CRAB.
THIS IS SO LAME, THERE'S NOT A SINGLE CHICK OUT HERE.
くー
ZZZ
ちゃぷちゃぷ
SPLASH SPLASH
They dragged her along.
WAH!
IT'S NOI-CHAN! IT'S NOI-CHAN! SHE'S HERE.
HIDE!
どぼーん
SPLASH
WHA-
EWW, THIS IS SO GROSS!
WHAT'S SHE DOING ALL BY HER-SELF?
LOOK WHAT I FOUND. ♥
HEY, WAKE UP! COME ON!
ちくちく ちくちく
POKE POKE
POKE POKE
ちくちく
KYOHEI! KYOHEI!
Barnacles
A sea slater

Poaching is a crime. Don't do it. You must have a commercial license to collect sea urchins.

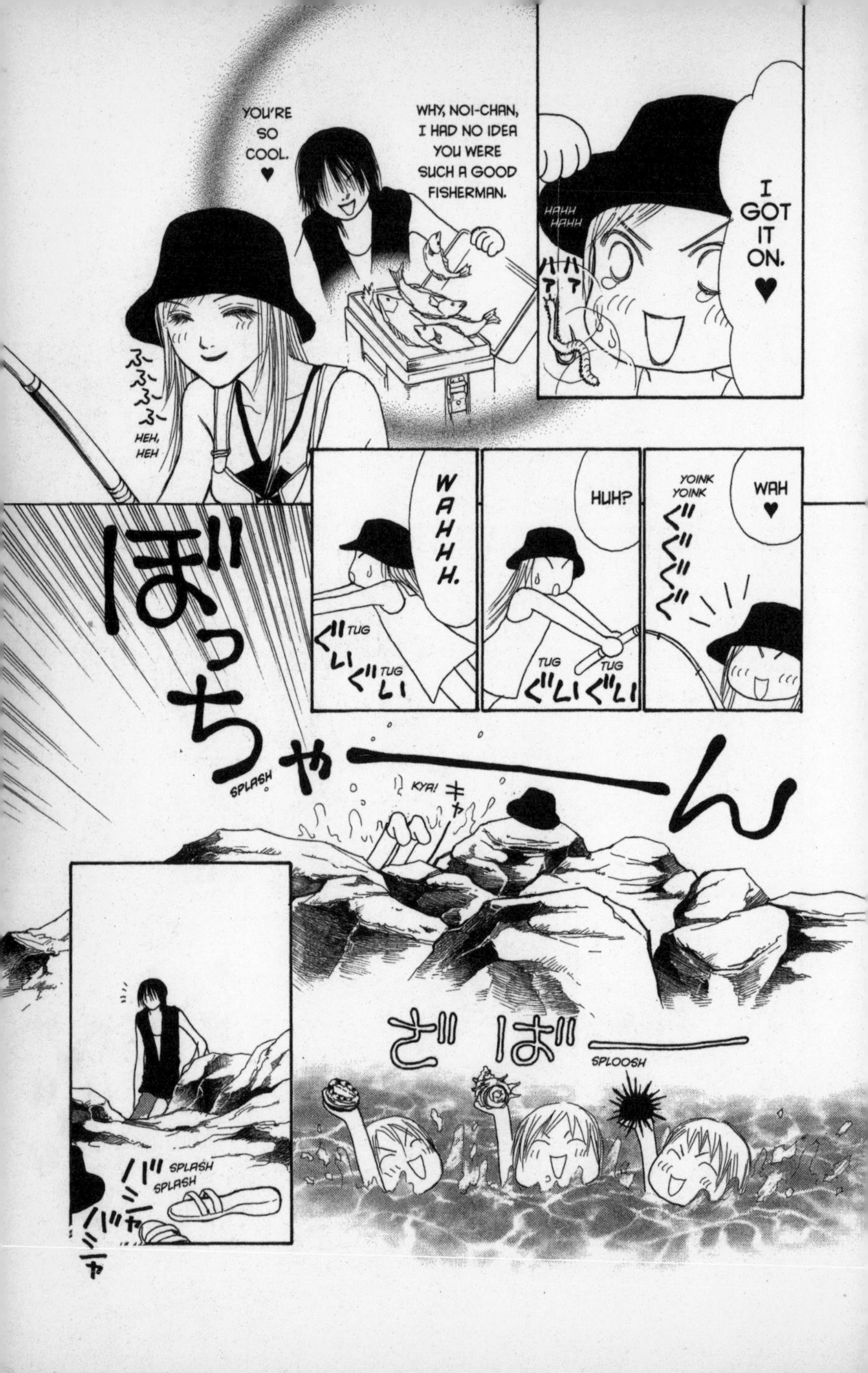

I GOT IT ON. ♥
HAHH HAHH
ハァハァ
WHY, NOI-CHAN, I HAD NO IDEA YOU WERE SUCH A GOOD FISHERMAN.
YOU'RE SO COOL. ♥
ふふふふ
HEH, HEH
WAH ♥
YOINK YOINK
ぐぐぐぐ
HUH?
TUG TUG
ぐいぐい
WAHHH.
ぐいぐい
TUG TUG
ぼっちゃーーん
SPLASH
KYA!
キャ
ざばーー
SPLOOSH
バシャバシャ
SPLASH SPLASH

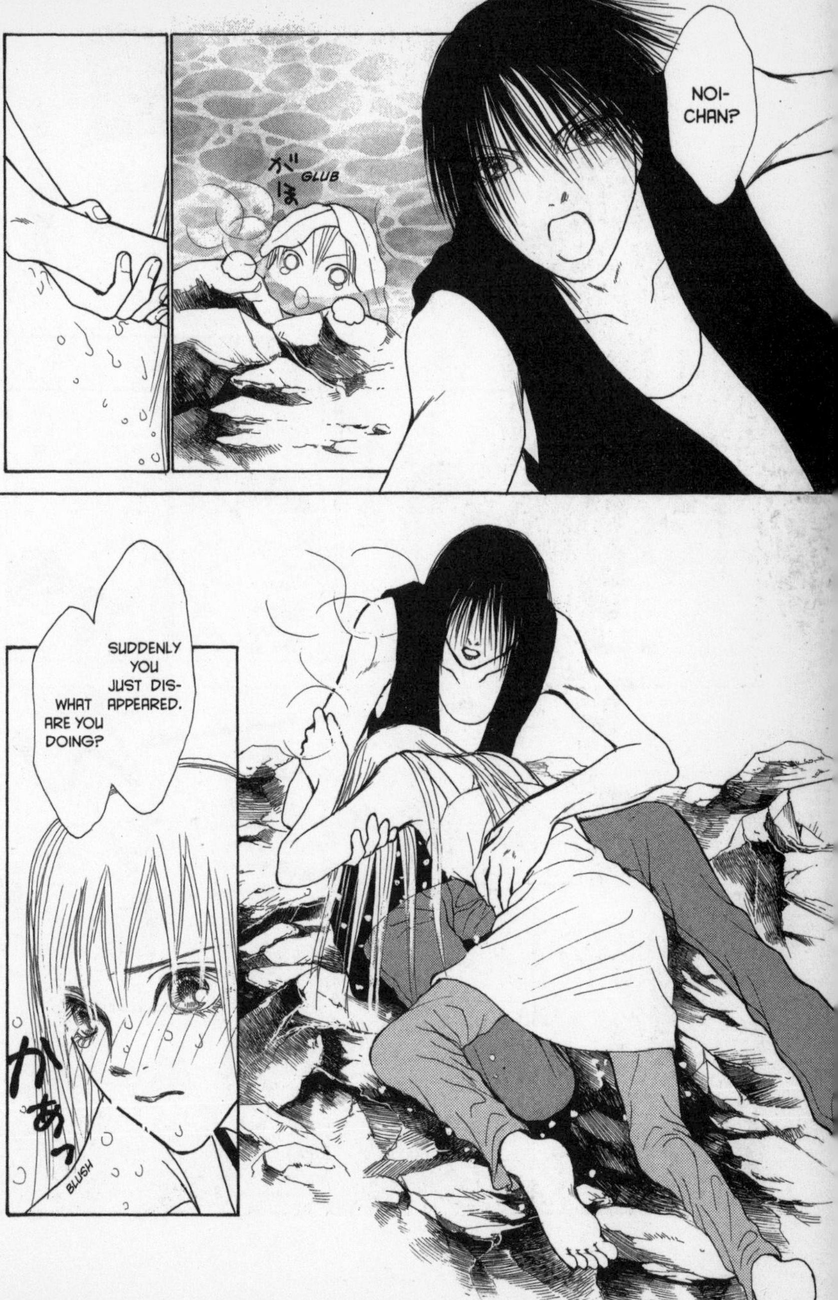
NOI-CHAN?
がほ
GLUB
SUDDENLY YOU JUST DIS-APPEARED.
WHAT ARE YOU DOING?
かあっ
BLUSH

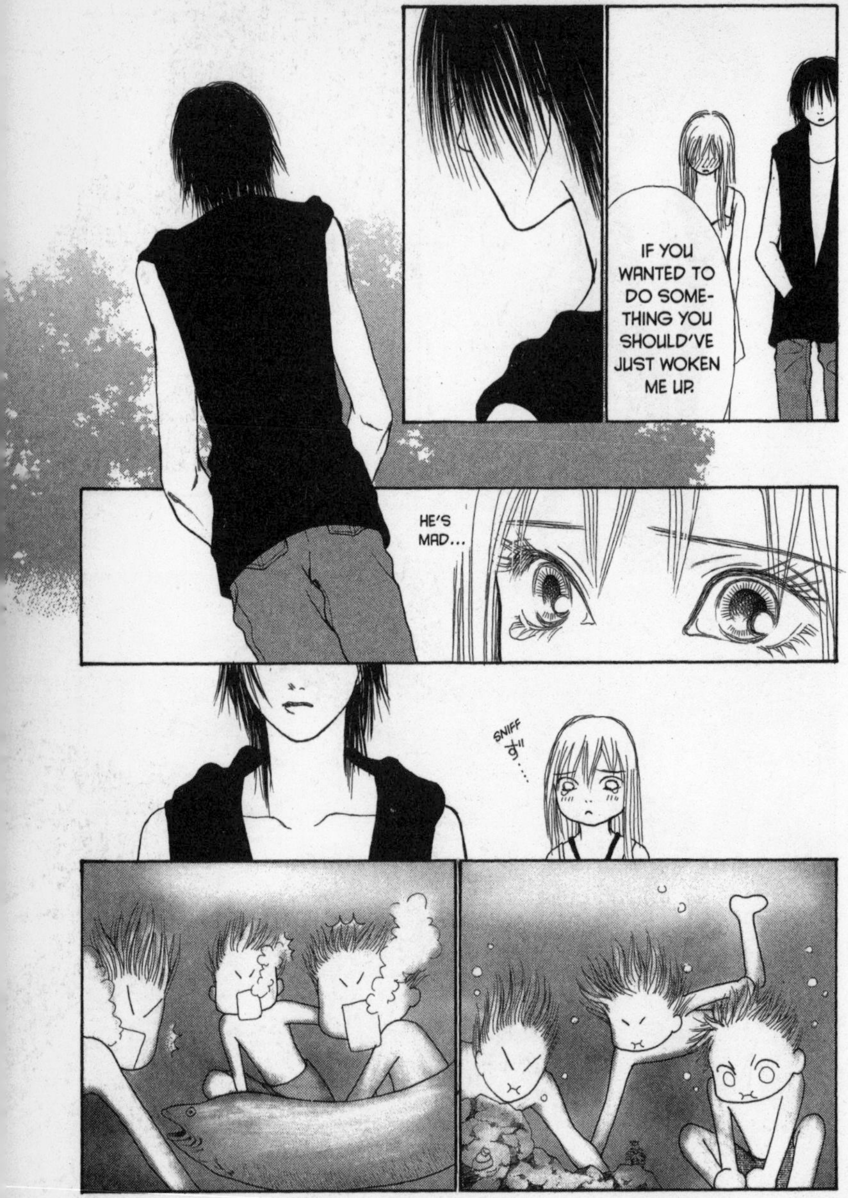
IF YOU WANTED TO DO SOMETHING YOU SHOULD'VE JUST WOKEN ME UP.
HE'S MAD...
SNIFF
ず"...

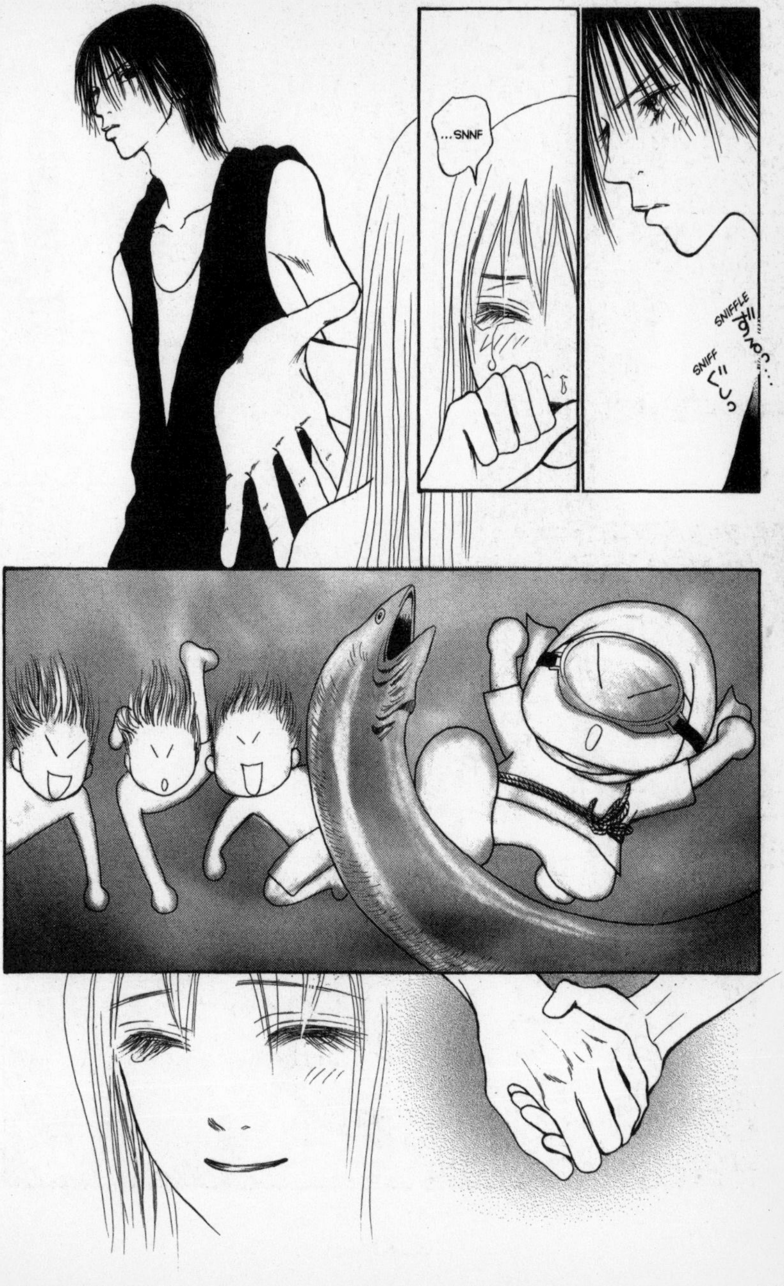

SNIFFLE
ずぅっ…
SNIFF
ぐじっ
...SNNF

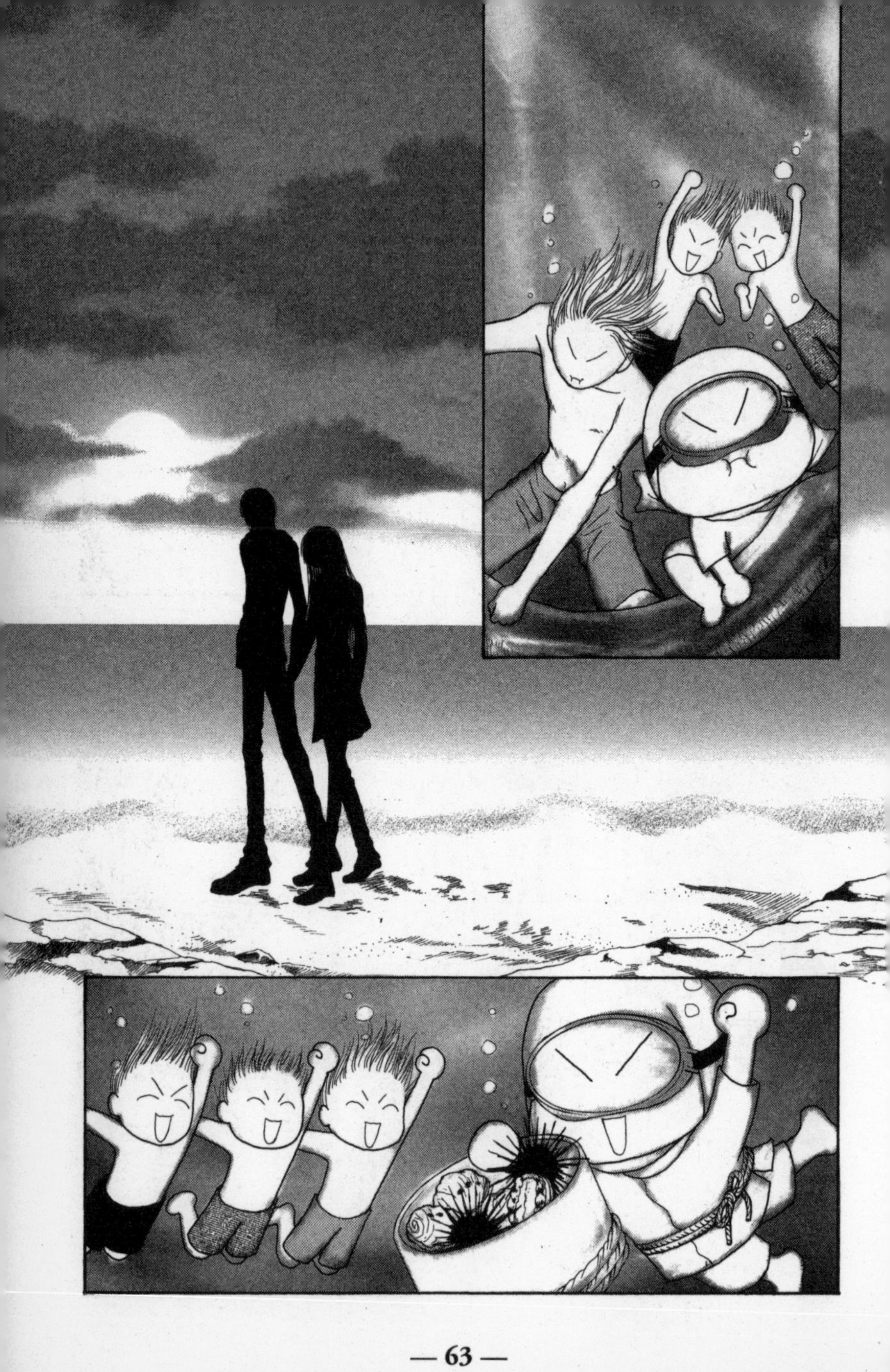

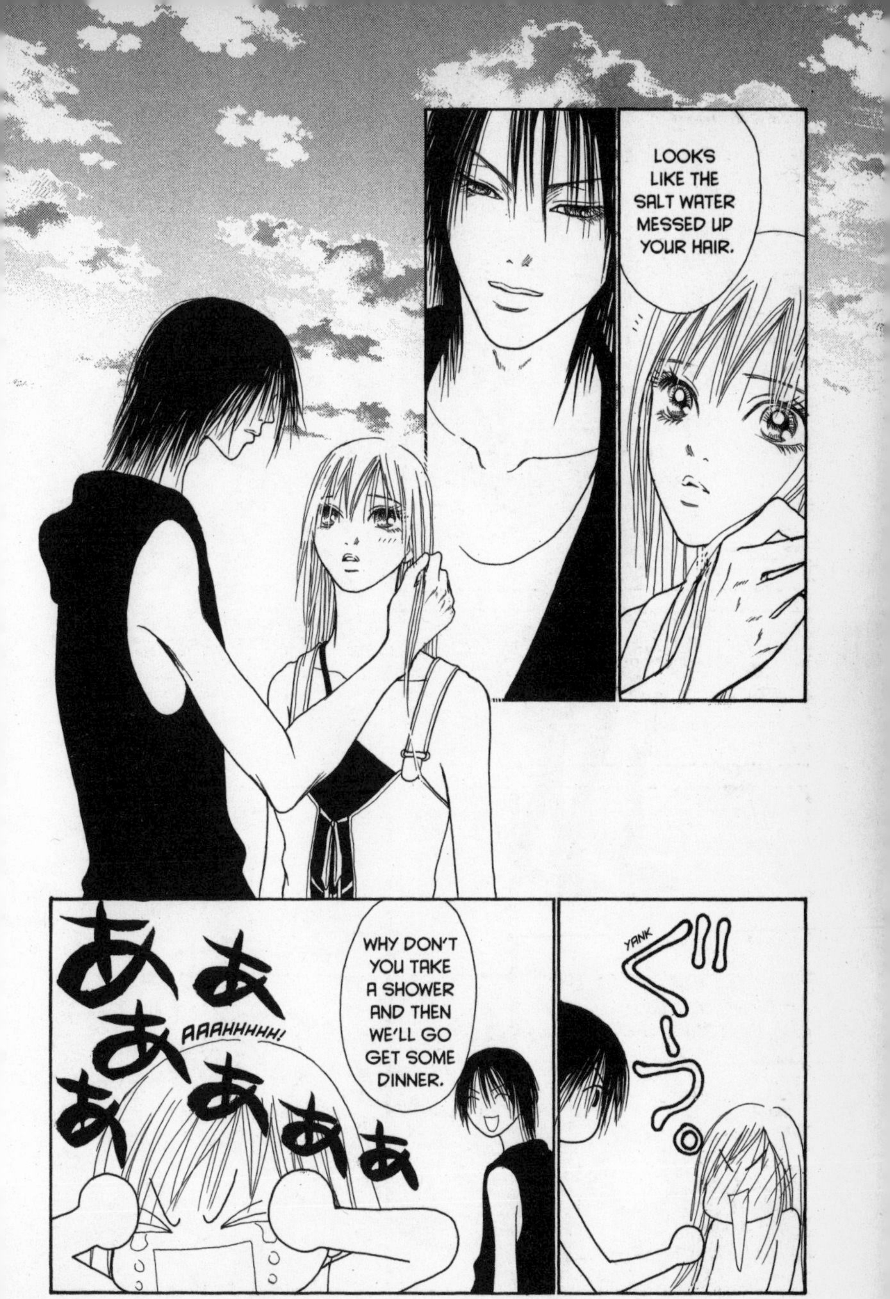
LOOKS LIKE THE SALT WATER MESSED UP YOUR HAIR.
YANK
ぐいっ。
WHY DON'T YOU TAKE A SHOWER AND THEN WE'LL GO GET SOME DINNER.
あああああああ
AAAHHHHH!

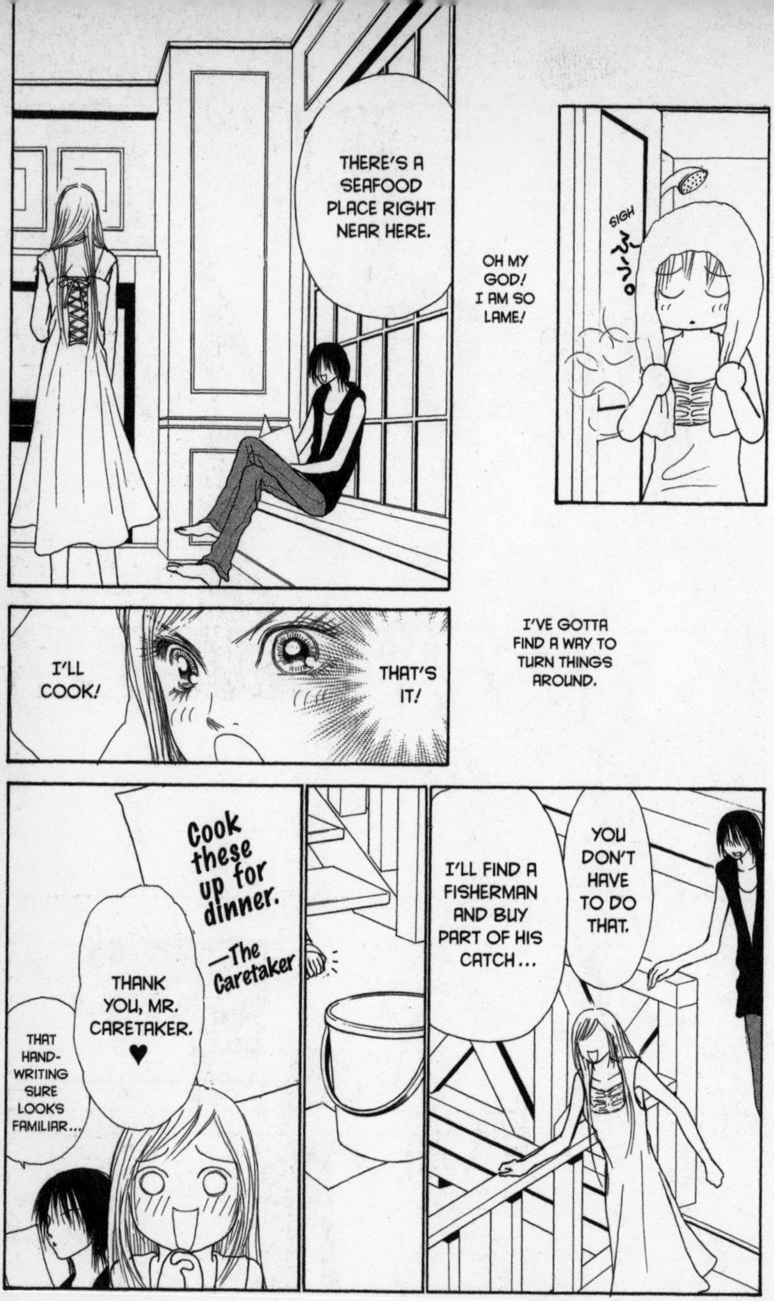
SIGH
OH MY GOD! I AM SO LAME!
THERE'S A SEAFOOD PLACE RIGHT NEAR HERE.
I'VE GOTTA FIND A WAY TO TURN THINGS AROUND.
THAT'S IT!
I'LL COOK!
I'LL FIND A FISHERMAN AND BUY PART OF HIS CATCH...
YOU DON'T HAVE TO DO THAT.
Cook these up for dinner.
—The Caretaker
THANK YOU, MR. CARETAKER. ♥
THAT HAND-WRITING SURE LOOKS FAMILIAR...

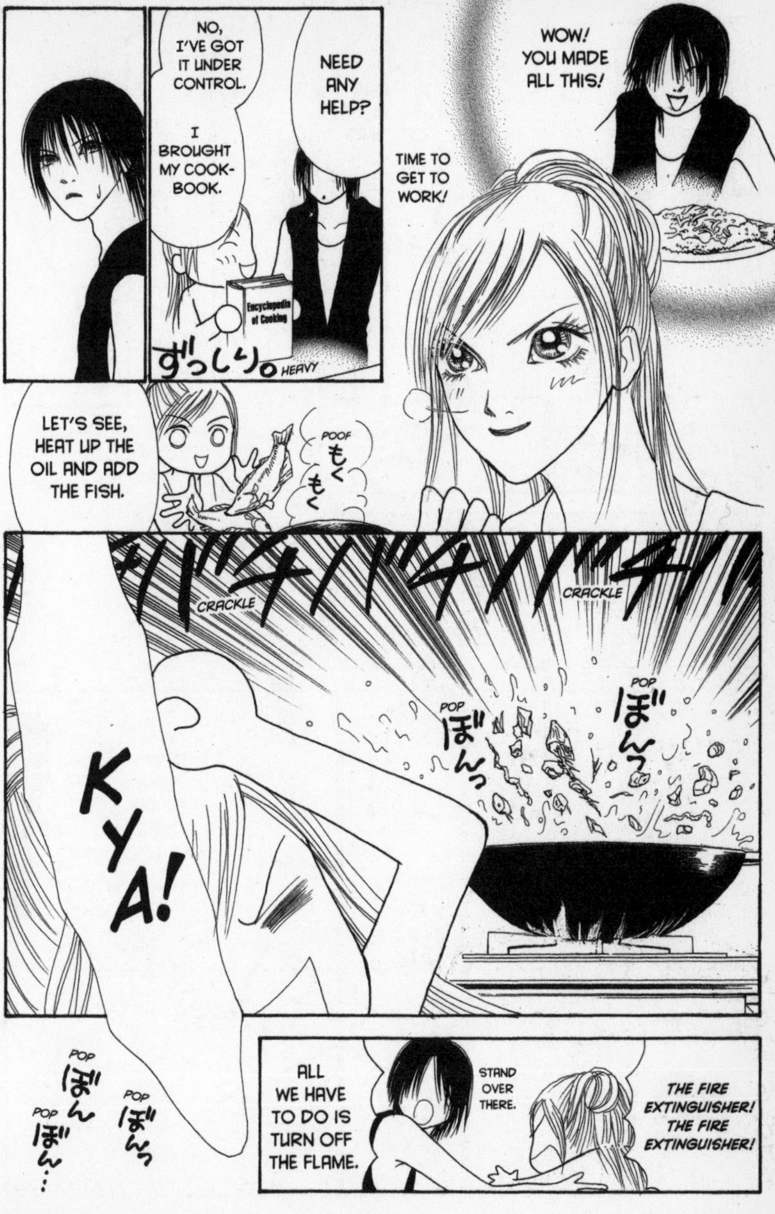

WOW! YOU MADE ALL THIS!
TIME TO GET TO WORK!
NEED ANY HELP?
NO, I'VE GOT IT UNDER CONTROL.
I BROUGHT MY COOK-BOOK.
Encyclopedia of Cooking
ずっしり。
HEAVY
POOF
もくもく
LET'S SEE, HEAT UP THE OIL AND ADD THE FISH.
バチバチバチ
CRACKLE
CRACKLE
POP
ぼんっ
POP
ぼんっ
KYA!
THE FIRE EXTINGUISHER! THE FIRE EXTINGUISHER!
STAND OVER THERE.
ALL WE HAVE TO DO IS TURN OFF THE FLAME.
POP
ぼんっ
POP
ぼん
POP
ぼん…

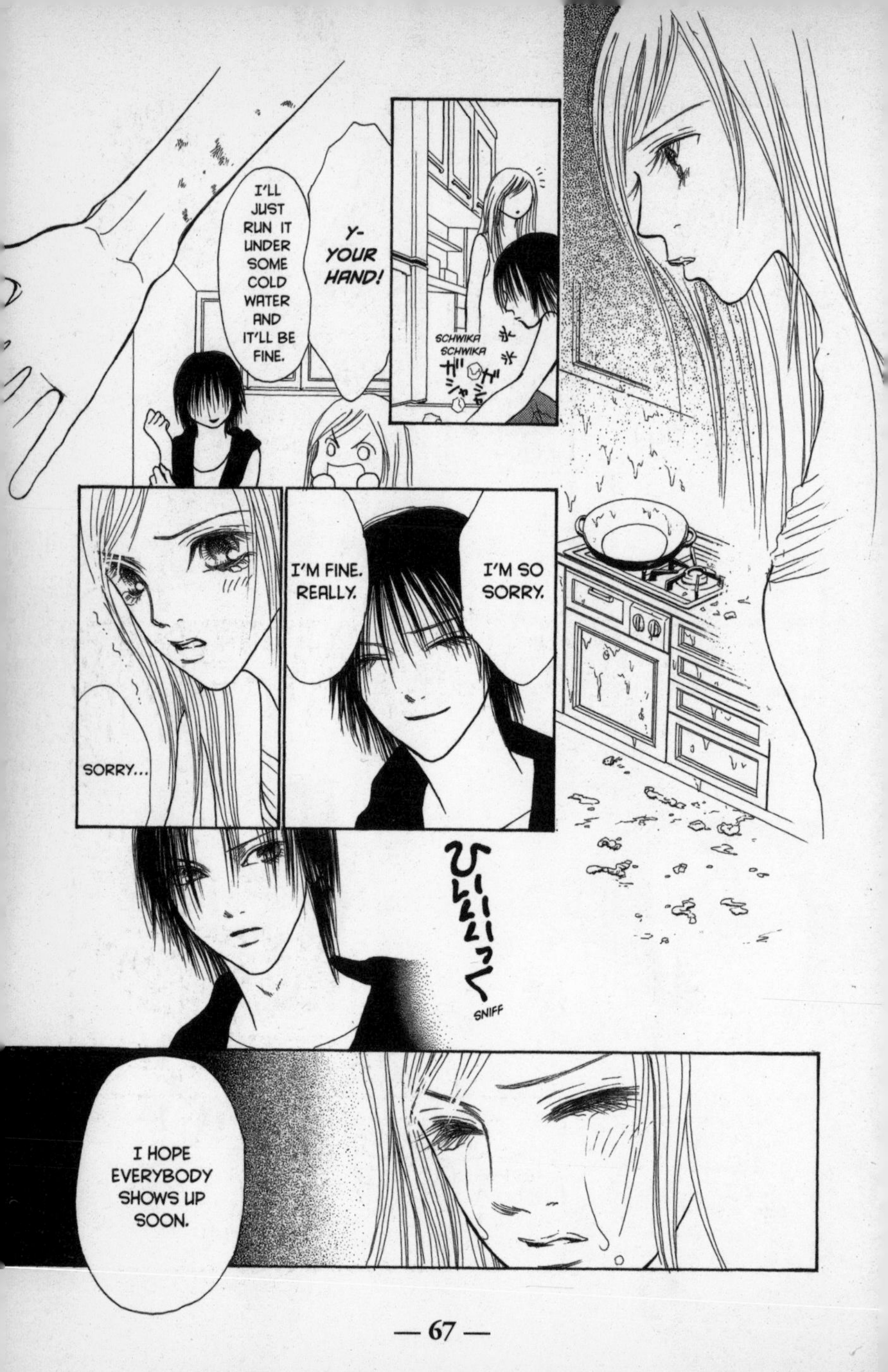
SCHWIKA SCHWIKA
Y- YOUR HAND!
I'LL JUST RUN IT UNDER SOME COLD WATER AND IT'LL BE FINE.
I'M SO SORRY.
I'M FINE. REALLY.
SORRY...
SNIFF
I HOPE EVERYBODY SHOWS UP SOON.

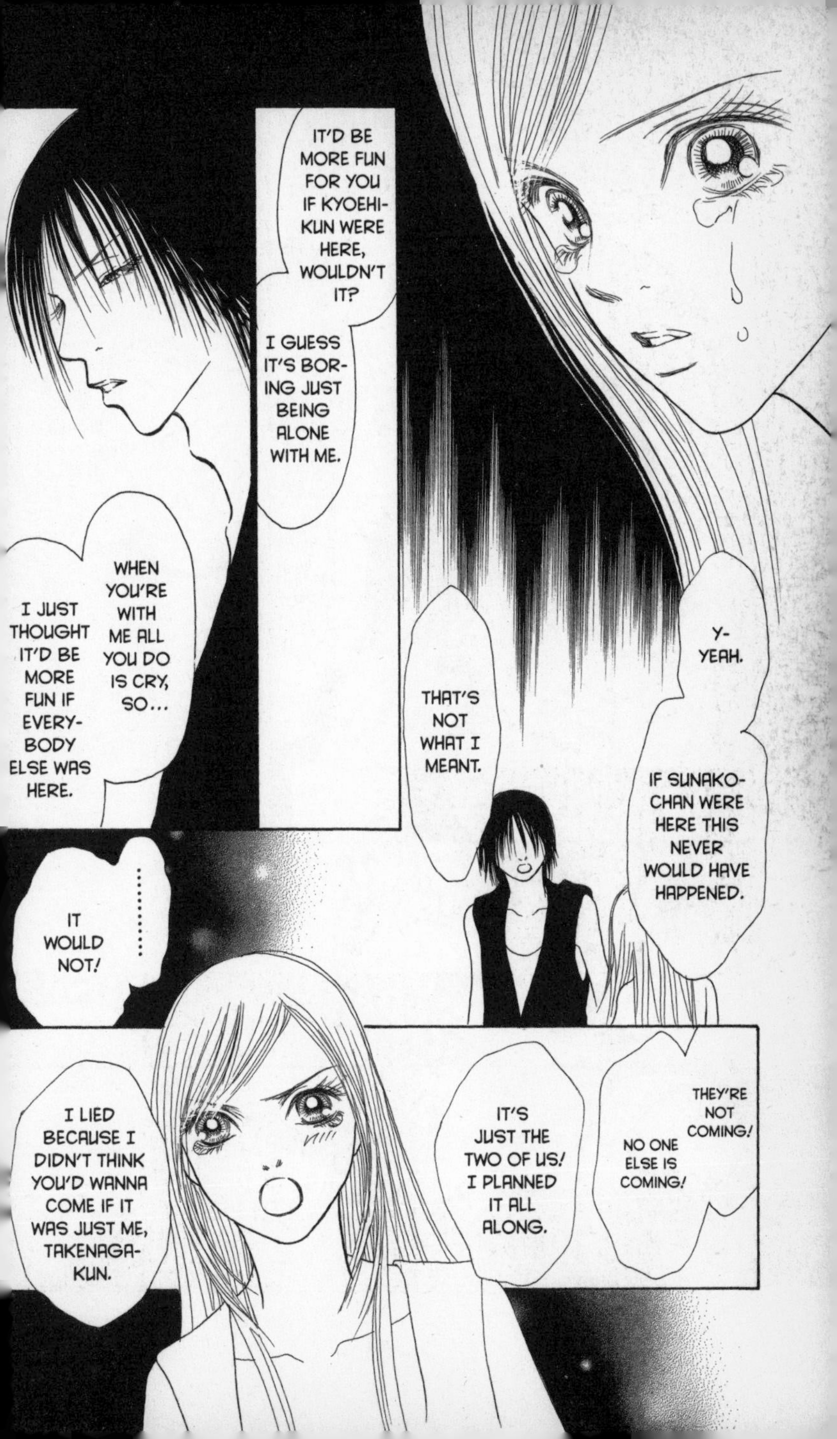
Y-YEAH.
IF SUNAKO-CHAN WERE HERE THIS NEVER WOULD HAVE HAPPENED.
THAT'S NOT WHAT I MEANT.
IT'D BE MORE FUN FOR YOU IF KYOEHI-KUN WERE HERE, WOULDN'T IT?
I GUESS IT'S BORING JUST BEING ALONE WITH ME.
WHEN YOU'RE WITH ME ALL YOU DO IS CRY, SO...
I JUST THOUGHT IT'D BE MORE FUN IF EVERYBODY ELSE WAS HERE.
......
IT WOULD NOT!
THEY'RE NOT COMING!
NO ONE ELSE IS COMING!
IT'S JUST THE TWO OF US! I PLANNED IT ALL ALONG.
I LIED BECAUSE I DIDN'T THINK YOU'D WANNA COME IF IT WAS JUST ME, TAKENAGA-KUN.

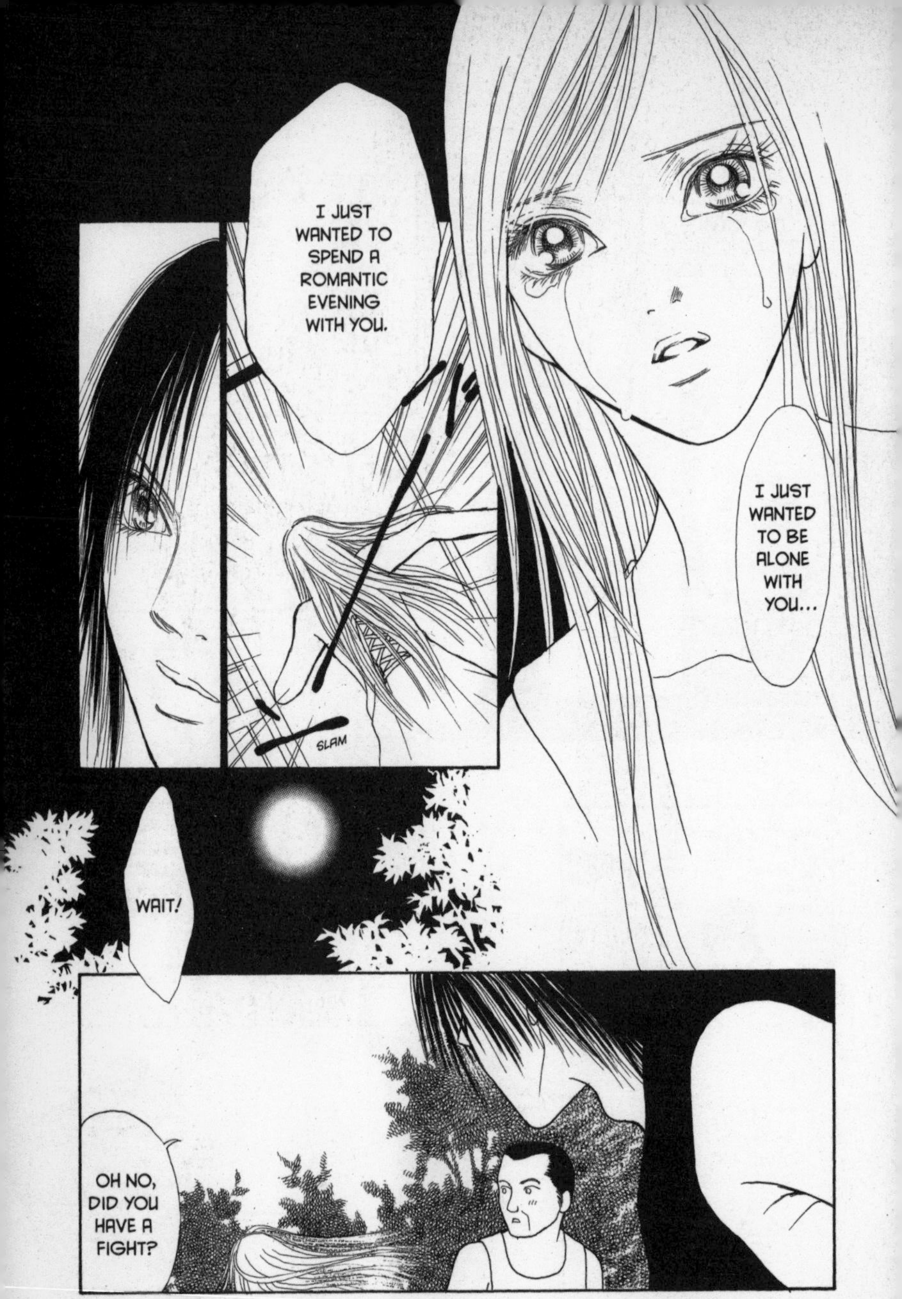
I JUST WANTED TO SPEND A ROMANTIC EVENING WITH YOU.
I JUST WANTED TO BE ALONE WITH YOU...
SLAM
WAIT!
OH NO, DID YOU HAVE A FIGHT?

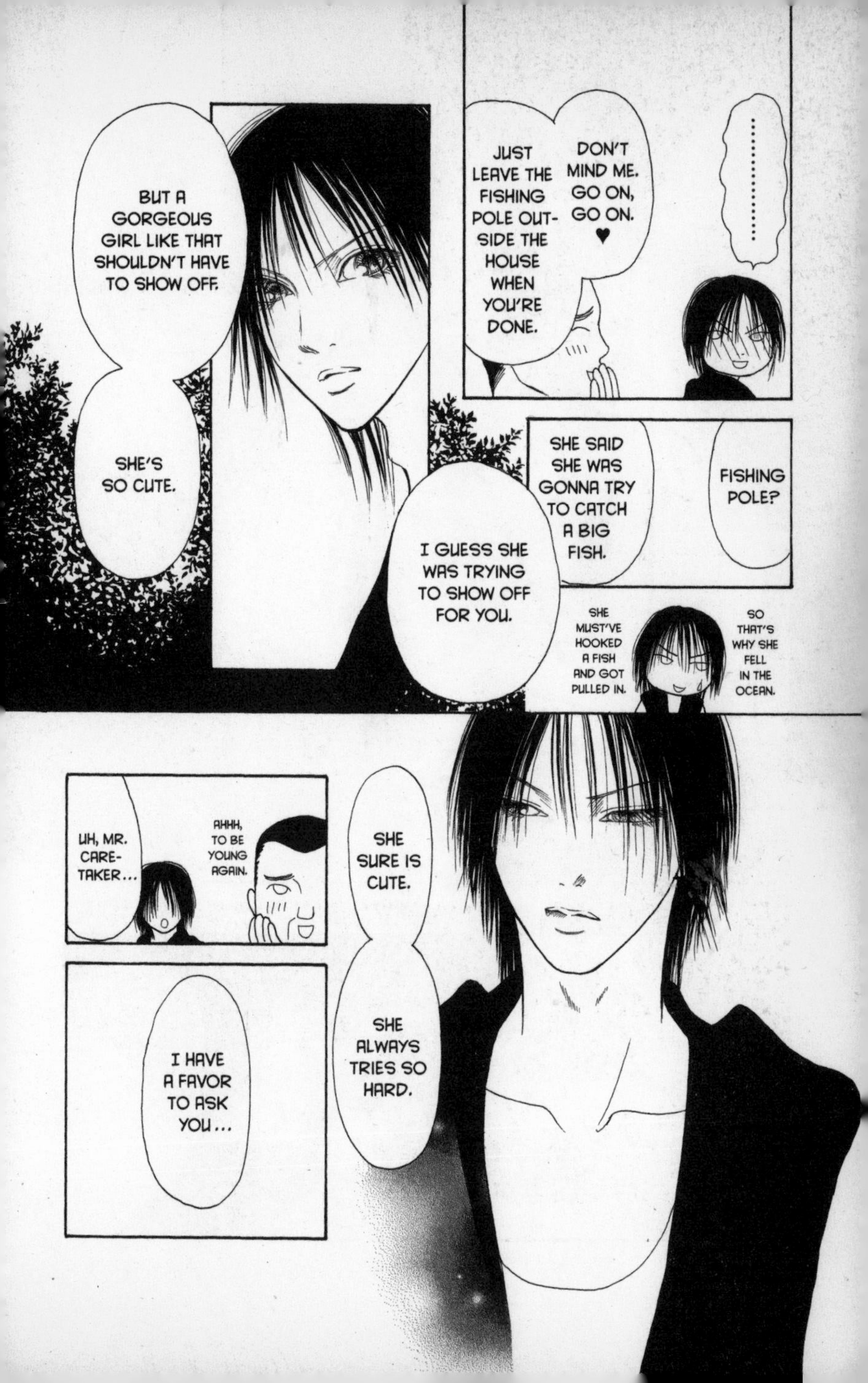
......
DON'T MIND ME. GO ON, GO ON. ♥
JUST LEAVE THE FISHING POLE OUT-SIDE THE HOUSE WHEN YOU'RE DONE.
FISHING POLE?
SHE SAID SHE WAS GONNA TRY TO CATCH A BIG FISH.
SO THAT'S WHY SHE FELL IN THE OCEAN.
SHE MUST'VE HOOKED A FISH AND GOT PULLED IN.
I GUESS SHE WAS TRYING TO SHOW OFF FOR YOU.
BUT A GORGEOUS GIRL LIKE THAT SHOULDN'T HAVE TO SHOW OFF.
SHE'S SO CUTE.
SHE SURE IS CUTE.
SHE ALWAYS TRIES SO HARD.
AHHH, TO BE YOUNG AGAIN.
UH, MR. CARE-TAKER...
I HAVE A FAVOR TO ASK YOU...

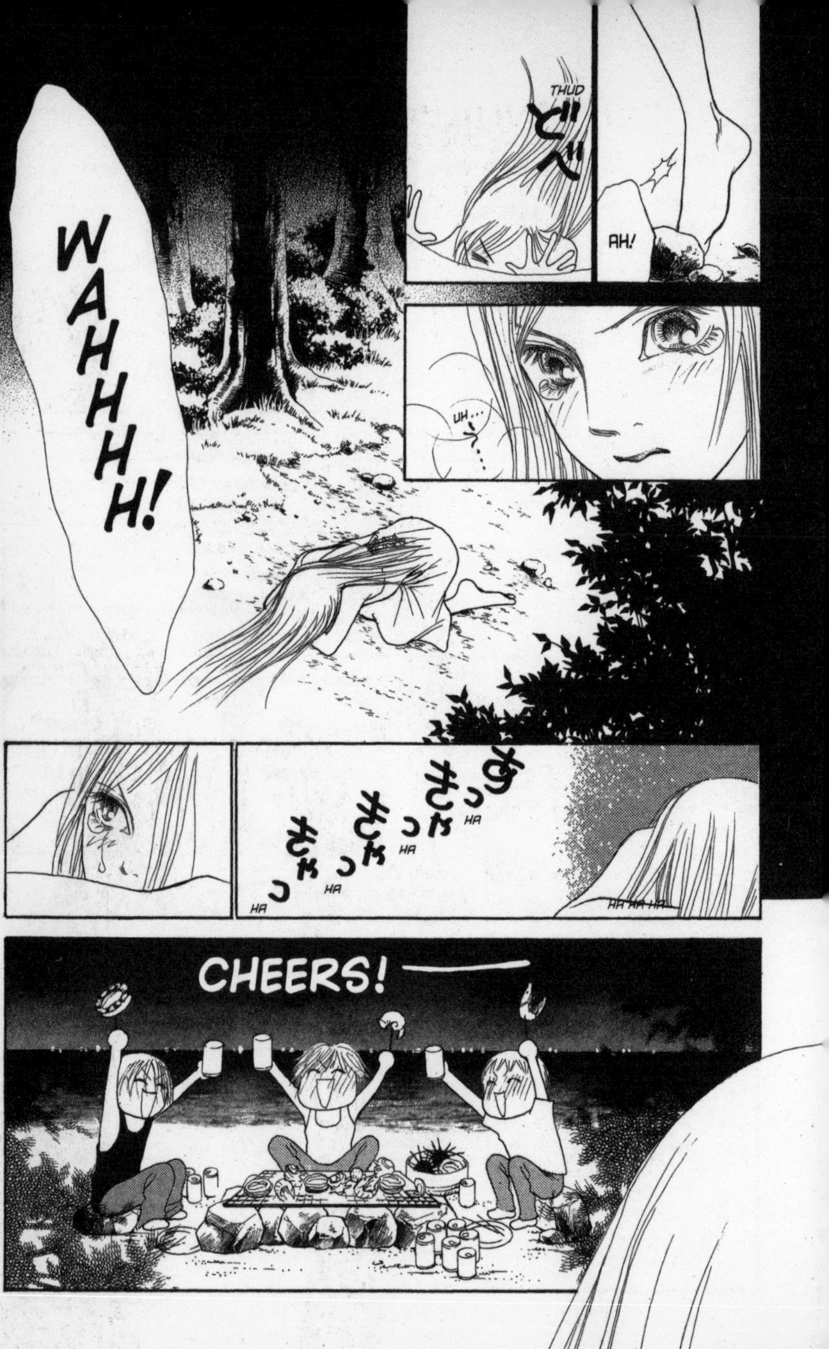
AH!
THUD
どべ
UH...
WAHHHHH!
HA HA HA
HA
HA
HA
HA
CHEERS!

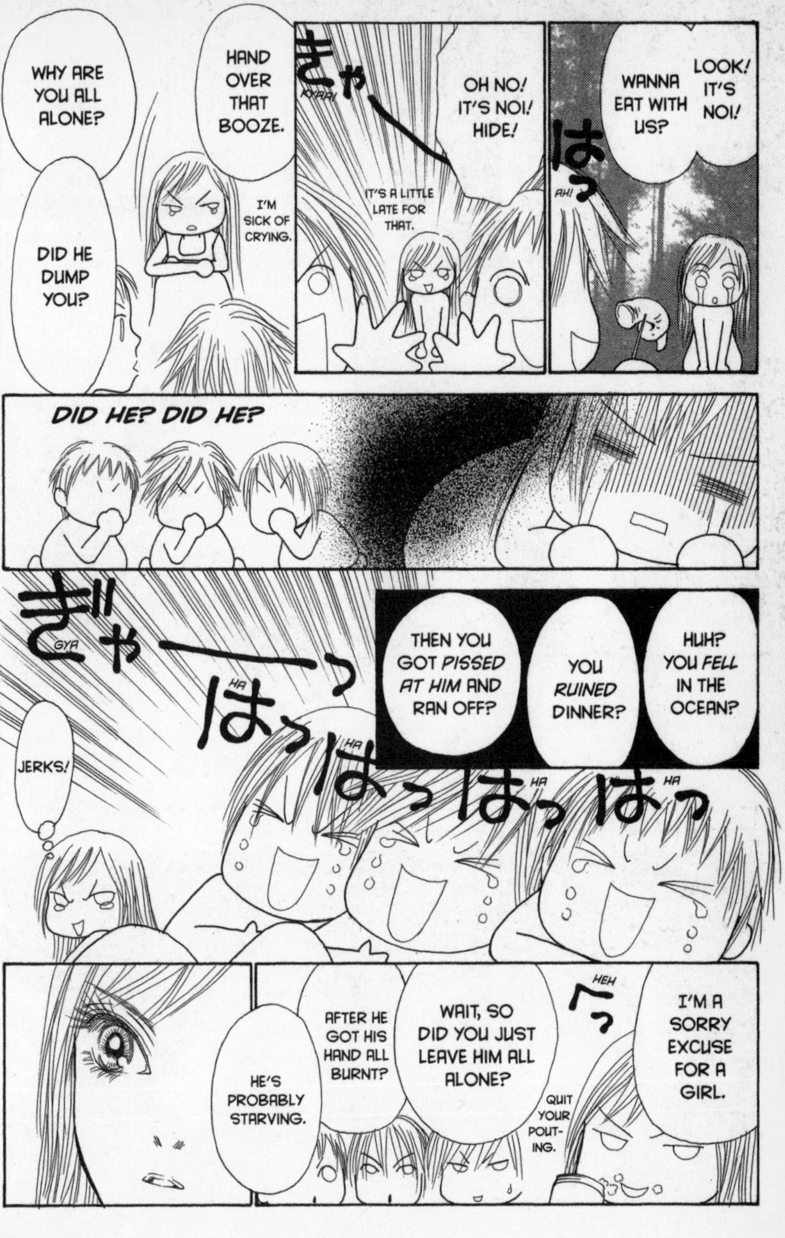
LOOK! IT'S NOI!
WANNA EAT WITH US?
はっ
AH!
OH NO! IT'S NOI! HIDE!
きゃー
KYAA!
IT'S A LITTLE LATE FOR THAT.
HAND OVER THAT BOOZE.
I'M SICK OF CRYING.
WHY ARE YOU ALL ALONE?
DID HE DUMP YOU?
DID HE? DID HE?
HUH? YOU FELL IN THE OCEAN?
YOU RUINED DINNER?
THEN YOU GOT PISSED AT HIM AND RAN OFF?
ぎゃーっ
GYA
はっはっはっはっ
HA HA HA HA
JERKS!
I'M A SORRY EXCUSE FOR A GIRL.
へっ
HEH
QUIT YOUR POUTING.
WAIT, SO DID YOU JUST LEAVE HIM ALL ALONE?
AFTER HE GOT HIS HAND ALL BURNT?
HE'S PROBABLY STARVING.

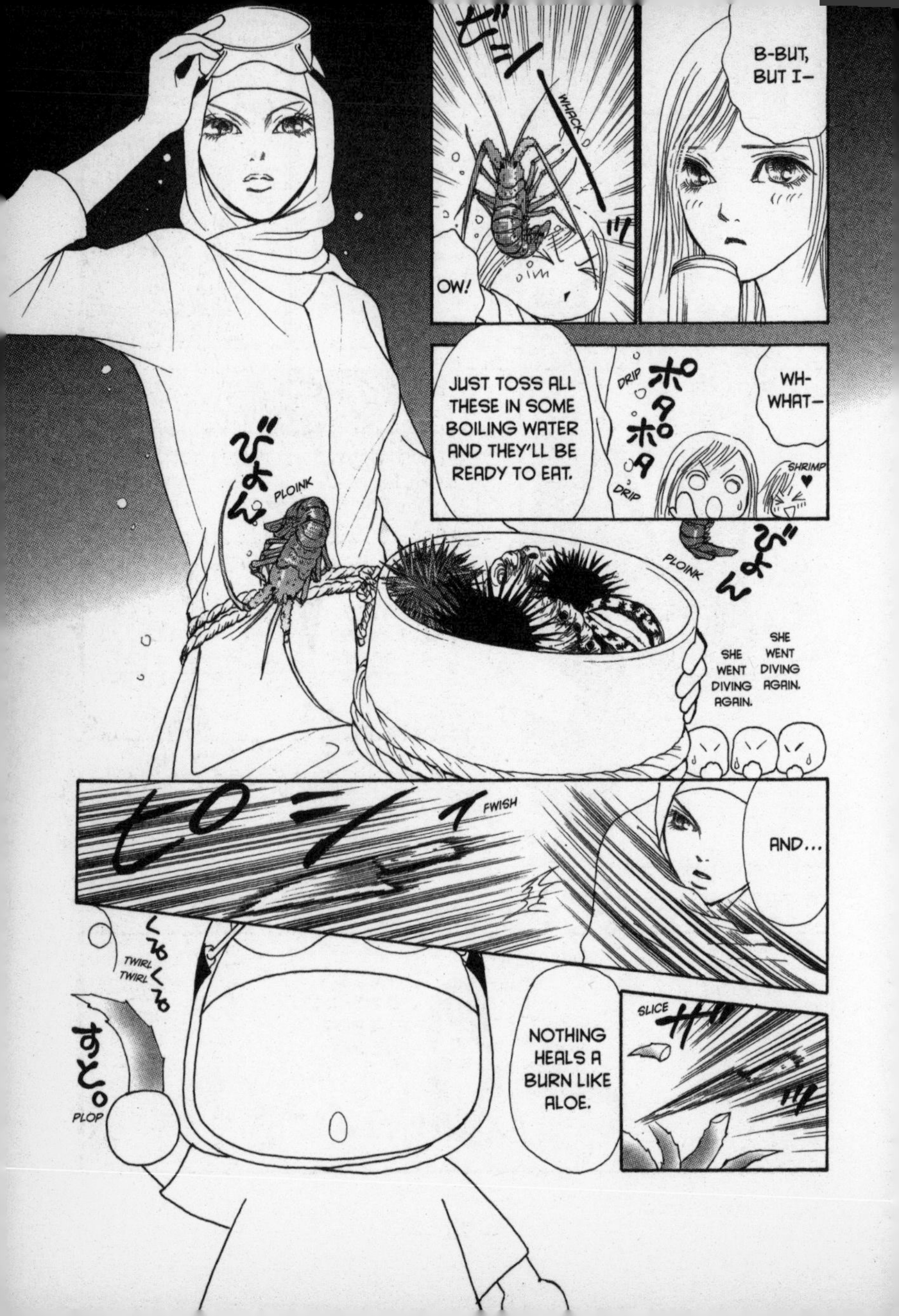
B-BUT, BUT I-
WHACK
OW!
WH- WHAT—
ポタ ポタ
DRIP
DRIP
SHRIMP ♥
JUST TOSS ALL THESE IN SOME BOILING WATER AND THEY'LL BE READY TO EAT.
ぴょん
PLOINK
ぴょん
PLOINK
SHE WENT DIVING AGAIN.
SHE WENT DIVING AGAIN.
AND...
FWISH
SLICE
NOTHING HEALS A BURN LIKE ALOE.
くるくる
TWIRL TWIRL
すとっ。
PLOP

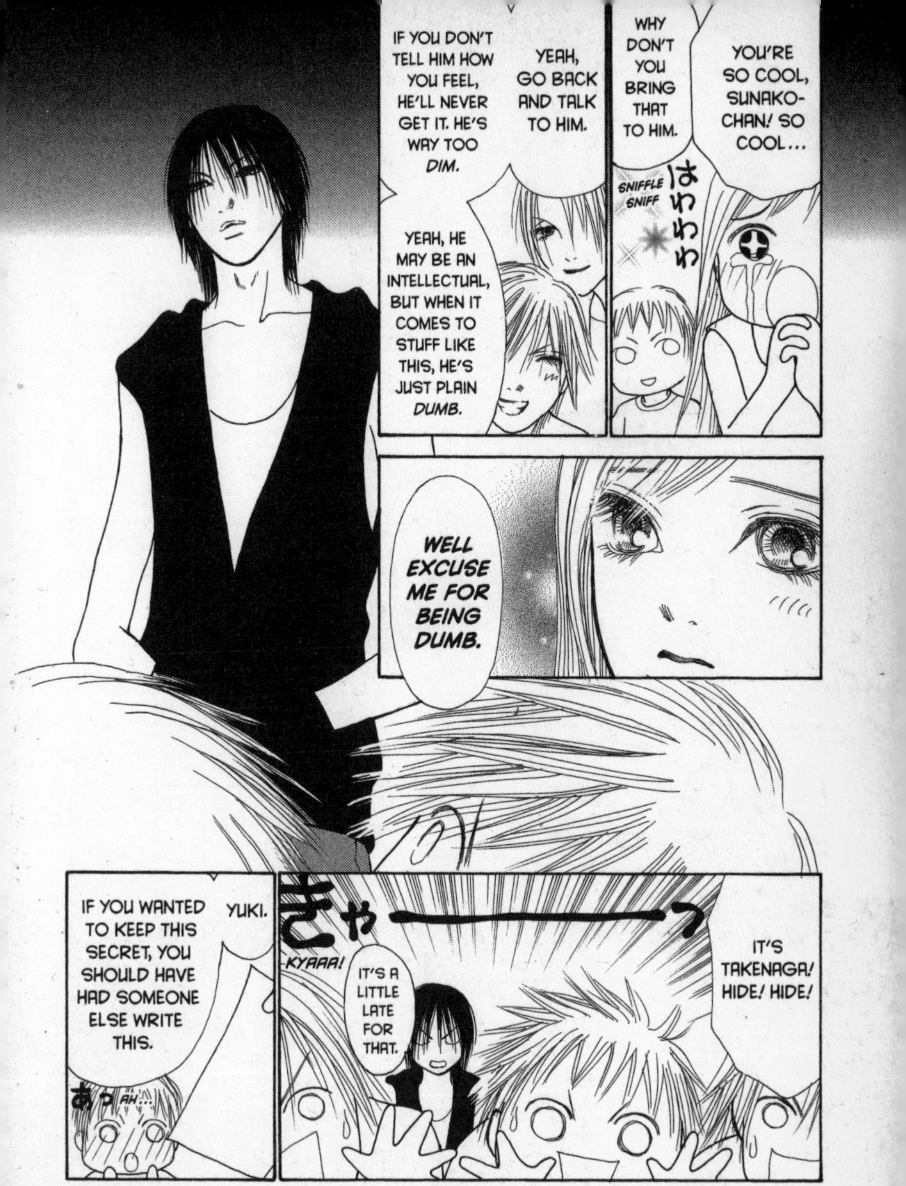

YOU'RE SO COOL, SUNAKO-CHAN! SO COOL...
WHY DON'T YOU BRING THAT TO HIM.
はわわわ
SNIFFLE SNIFF
YEAH, GO BACK AND TALK TO HIM.
IF YOU DON'T TELL HIM HOW YOU FEEL, HE'LL NEVER GET IT. HE'S WAY TOO *DIM*.
YEAH, HE MAY BE AN INTELLECTUAL, BUT WHEN IT COMES TO STUFF LIKE THIS, HE'S JUST PLAIN *DUMB*.
WELL EXCUSE ME FOR BEING DUMB.
IT'S TAKENAGA! HIDE! HIDE!
きゃーっ
KYAAA!
IT'S A LITTLE LATE FOR THAT.
YUKI.
IF YOU WANTED TO KEEP THIS SECRET, YOU SHOULD HAVE HAD SOMEONE ELSE WRITE THIS.
あっ
AH...

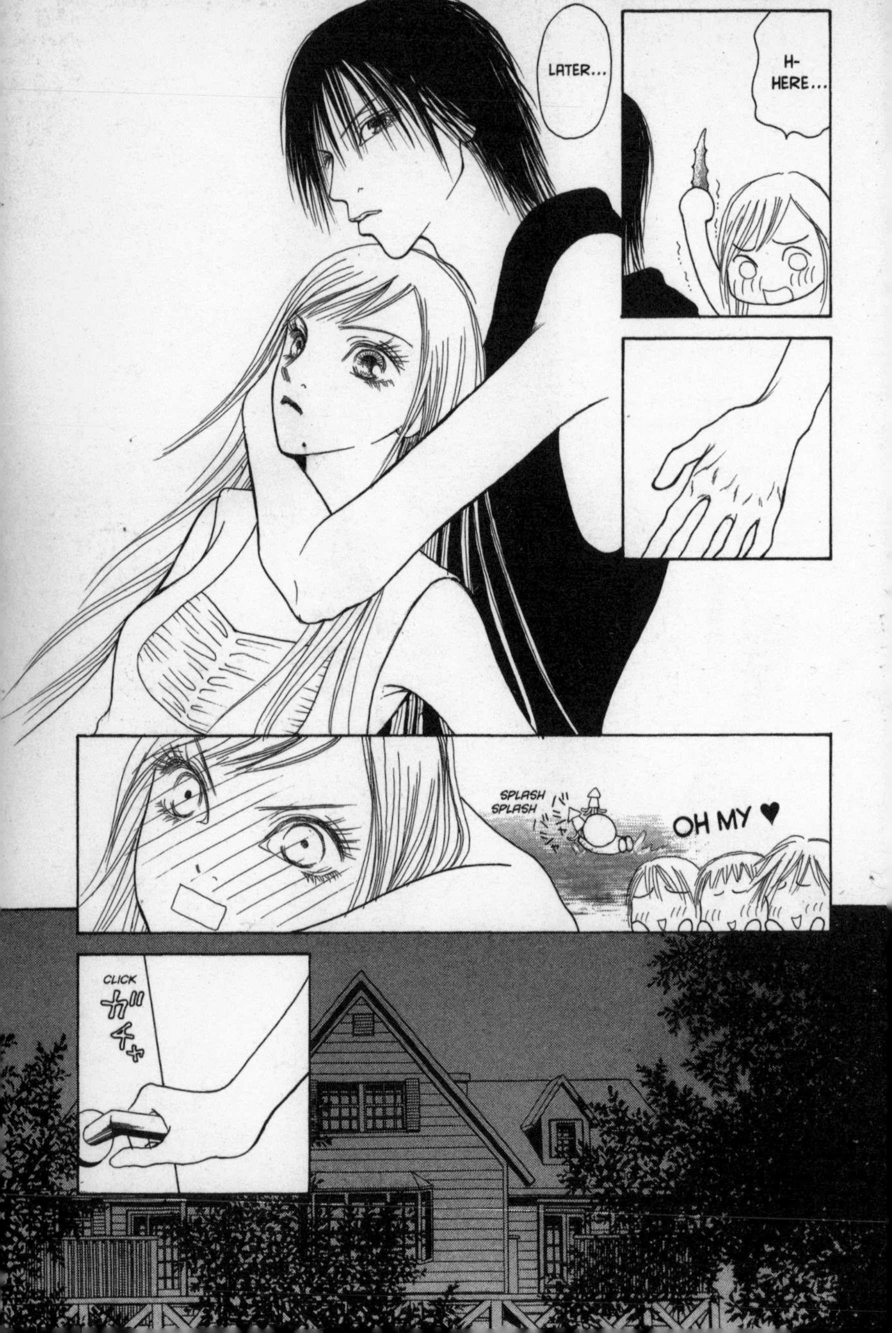
H-
HERE...
LATER...
SPLASH
SPLASH
OH MY ♥
CLICK

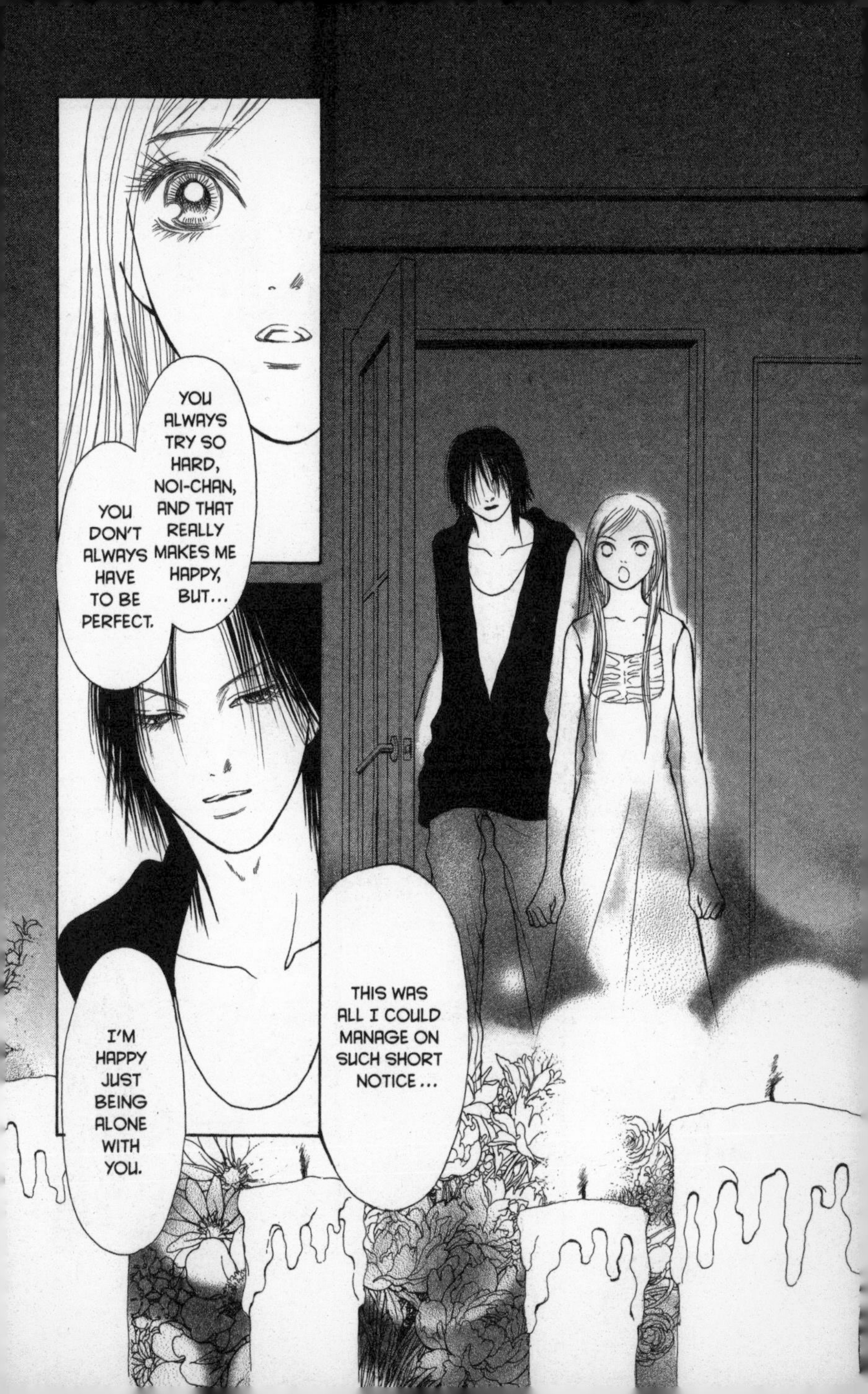
THIS WAS ALL I COULD MANAGE ON SUCH SHORT NOTICE...
YOU ALWAYS TRY SO HARD, NOI-CHAN, AND THAT REALLY MAKES ME HAPPY, BUT...
YOU DON'T ALWAYS HAVE TO BE PERFECT.
I'M HAPPY JUST BEING ALONE WITH YOU.

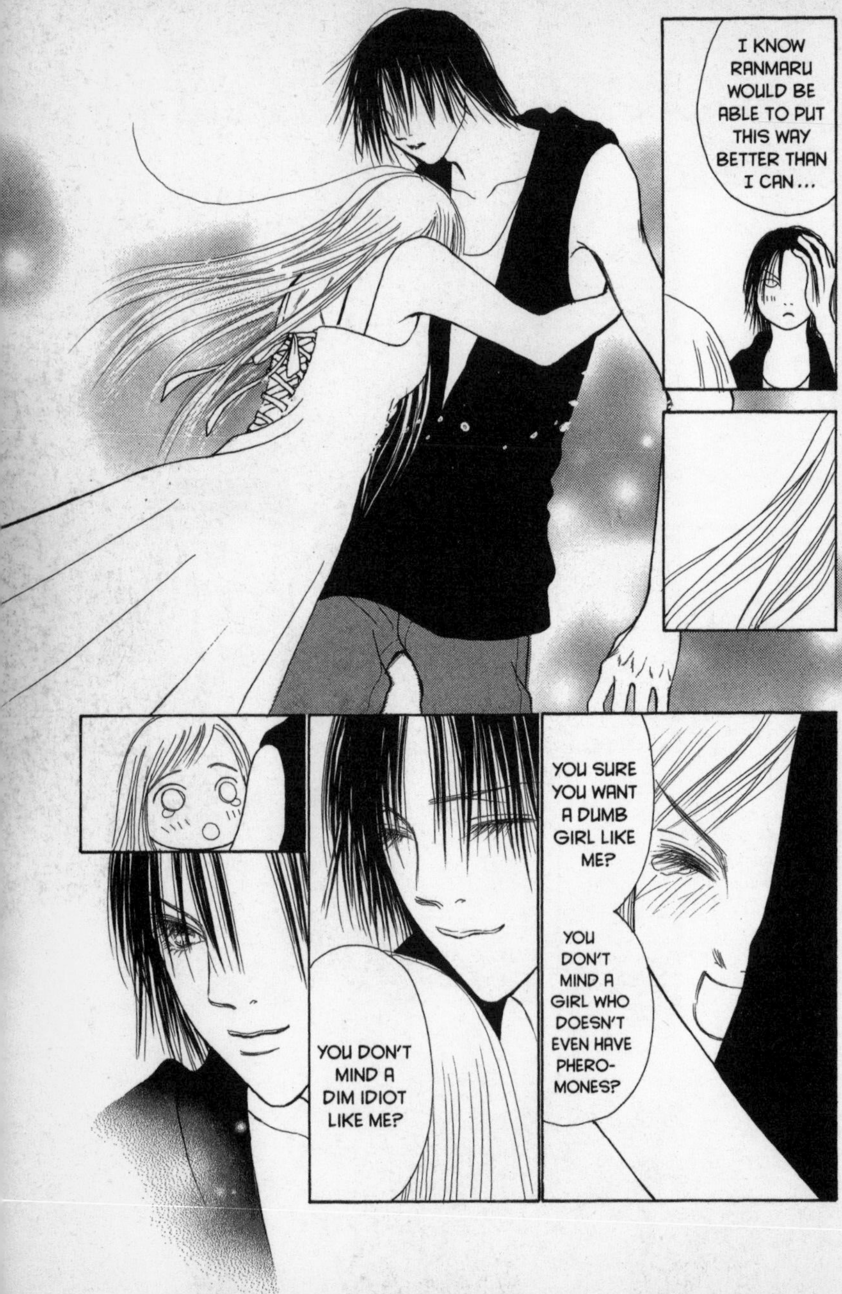
I KNOW RANMARU WOULD BE ABLE TO PUT THIS WAY BETTER THAN I CAN...
YOU SURE YOU WANT A DUMB GIRL LIKE ME?
YOU DON'T MIND A GIRL WHO DOESN'T EVEN HAVE PHERO-MONES?
YOU DON'T MIND A DIM IDIOT LIKE ME?

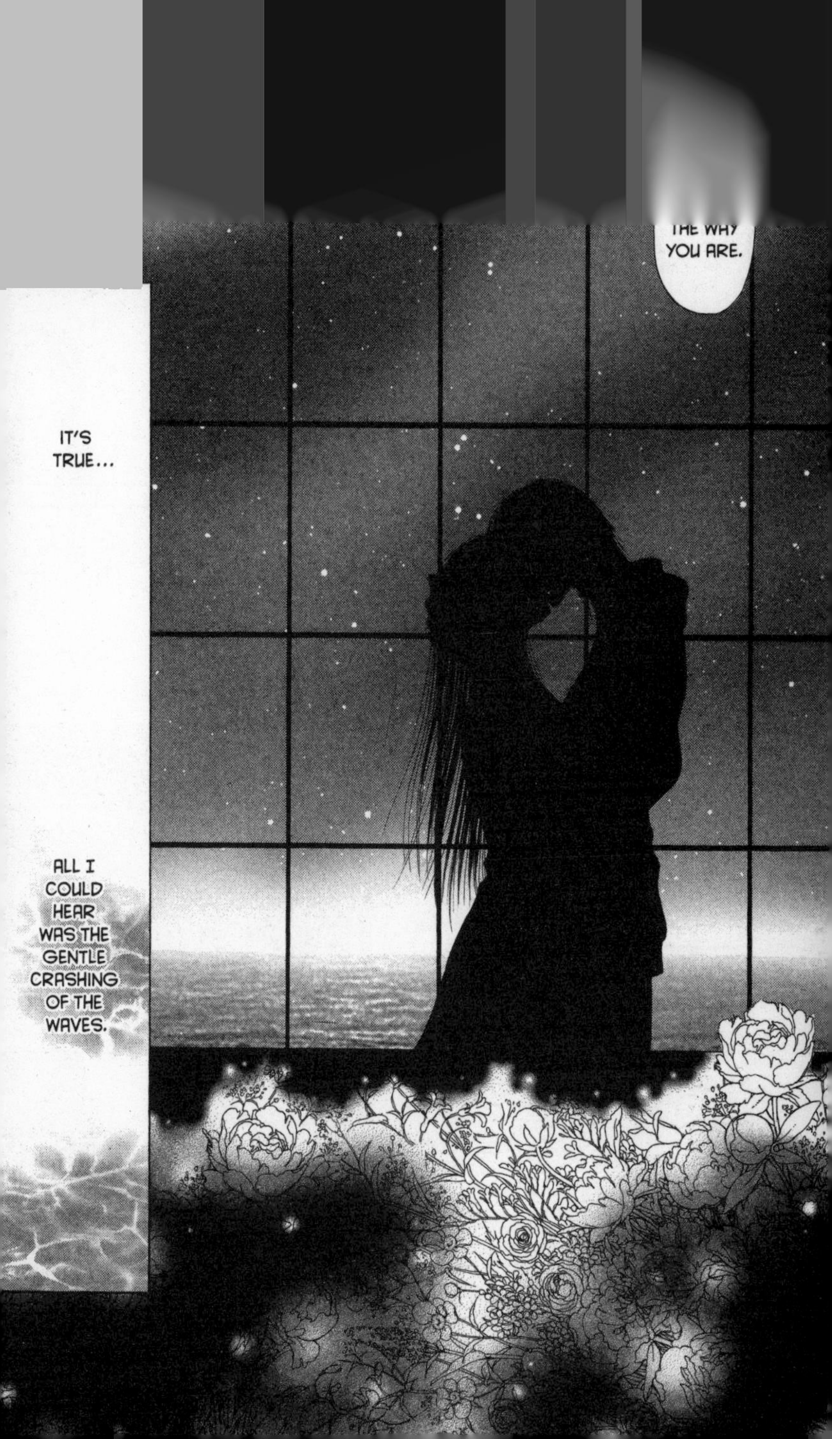
THE WAY YOU ARE.
IT'S TRUE...
ALL I COULD HEAR WAS THE GENTLE CRASHING OF THE WAVES.

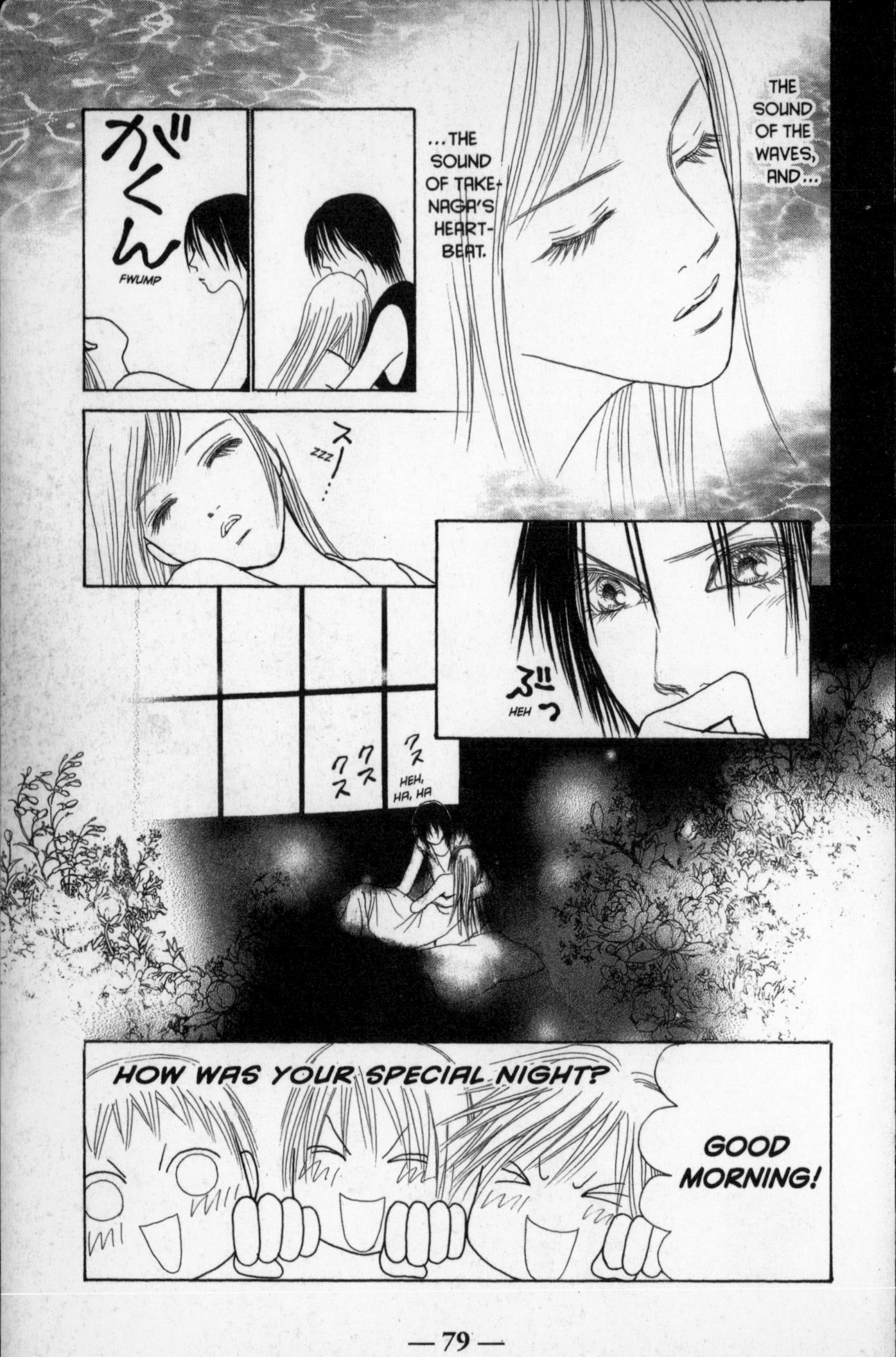
THE SOUND OF THE WAVES, AND...
...THE SOUND OF TAKE-NAGA'S HEART-BEAT.
がくん
FWUMP
スー…
zzz
ぷっ
HEH
クスクスクス
HEH, HA, HA
GOOD MORNING!
HOW WAS YOUR SPECIAL NIGHT?

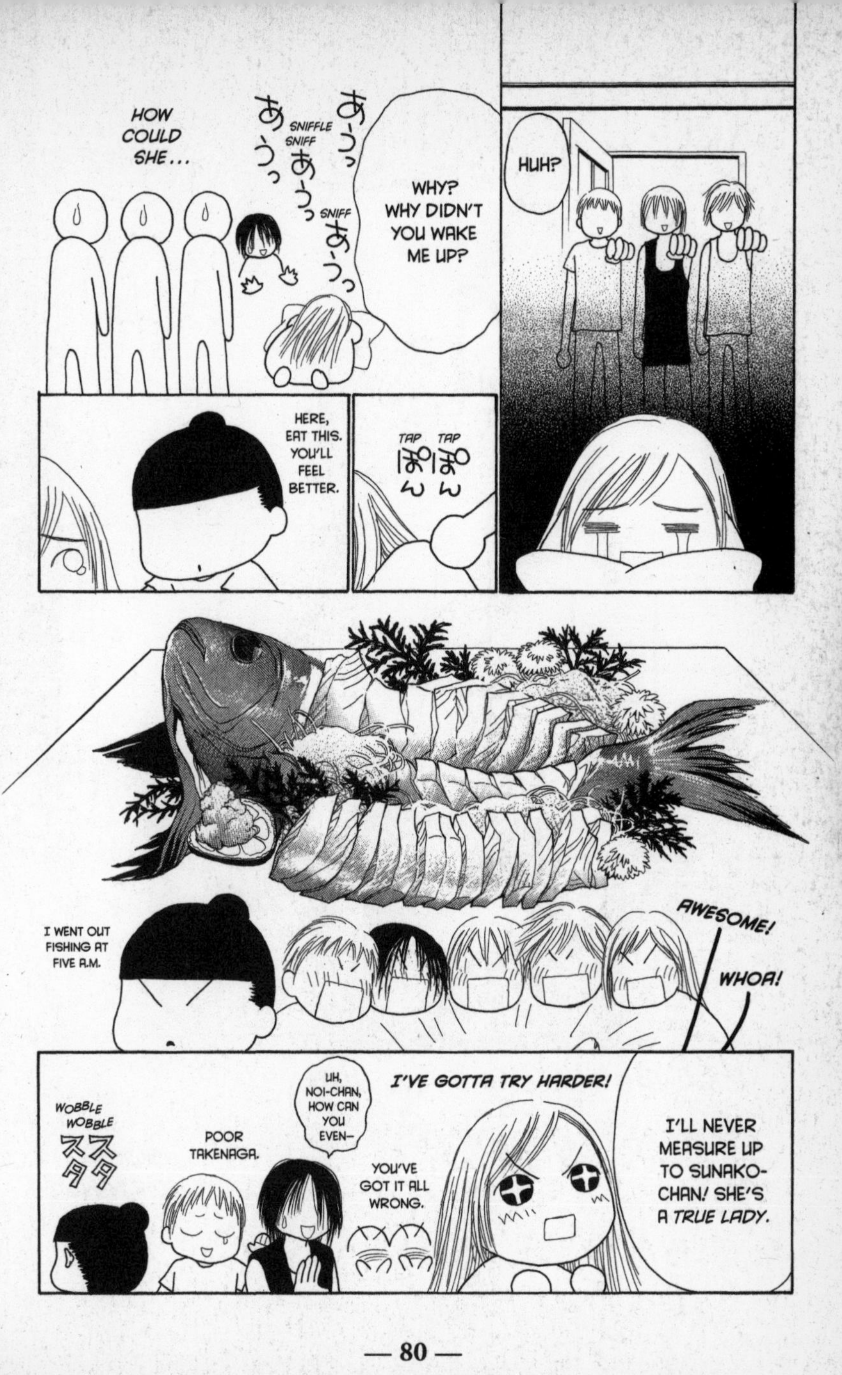
HUH?
WHY? WHY DIDN'T YOU WAKE ME UP?
あうっ
SNIFFLE
あうっ
SNIFF
あうっ
SNIFF
あうっ
HOW COULD SHE...
TAP TAP
ぽんぽん
HERE, EAT THIS. YOU'LL FEEL BETTER.
AWESOME!
WHOA!
I WENT OUT FISHING AT FIVE A.M.
I'LL NEVER MEASURE UP TO SUNAKO-CHAN! SHE'S A *TRUE LADY.*
I'VE GOTTA TRY HARDER!
YOU'VE GOT IT ALL WRONG.
UH, NOI-CHAN, HOW CAN YOU EVEN—
POOR TAKENAGA.
WOBBLE WOBBLE
スタスタ

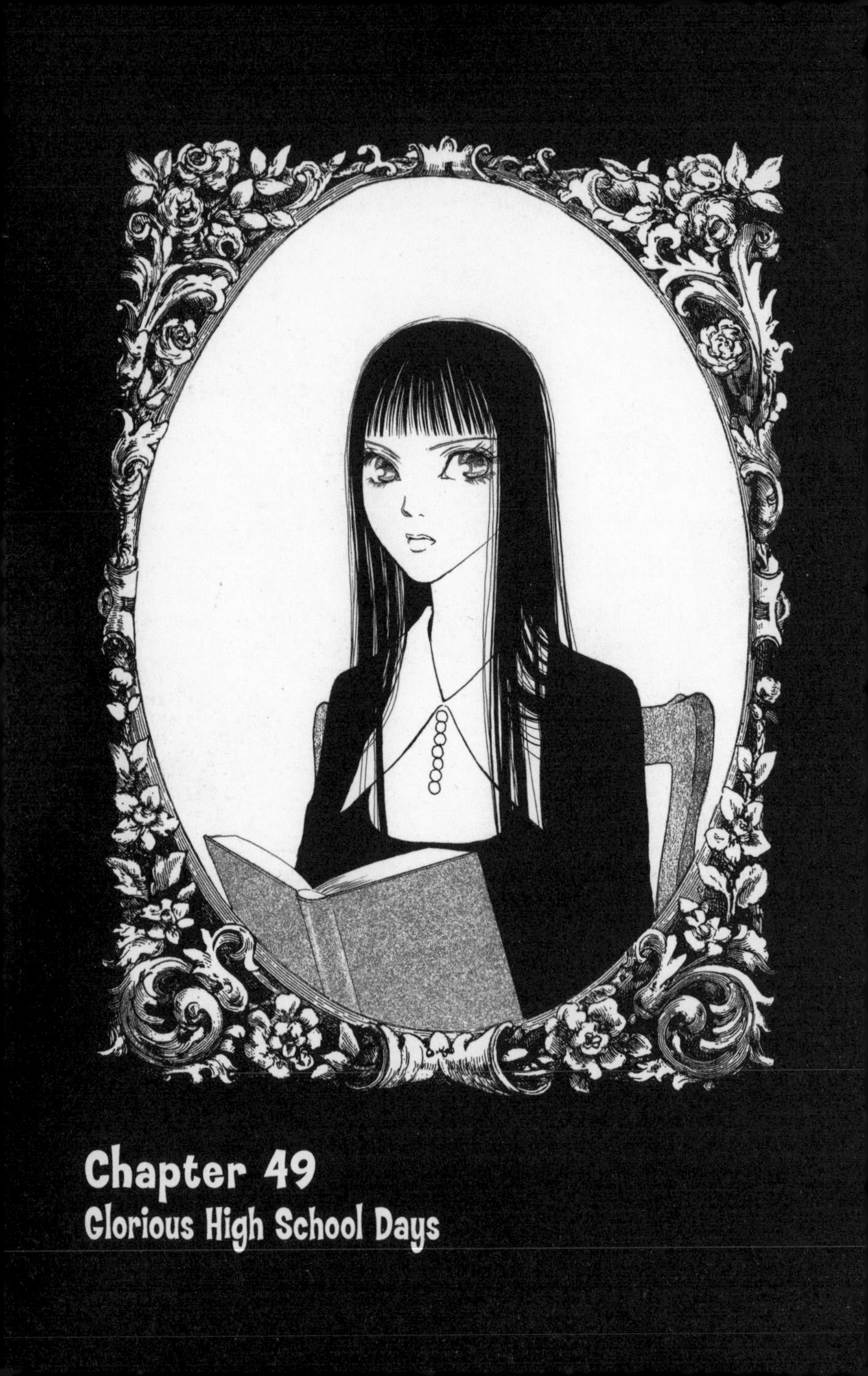

Chapter 49

Glorious High School Days

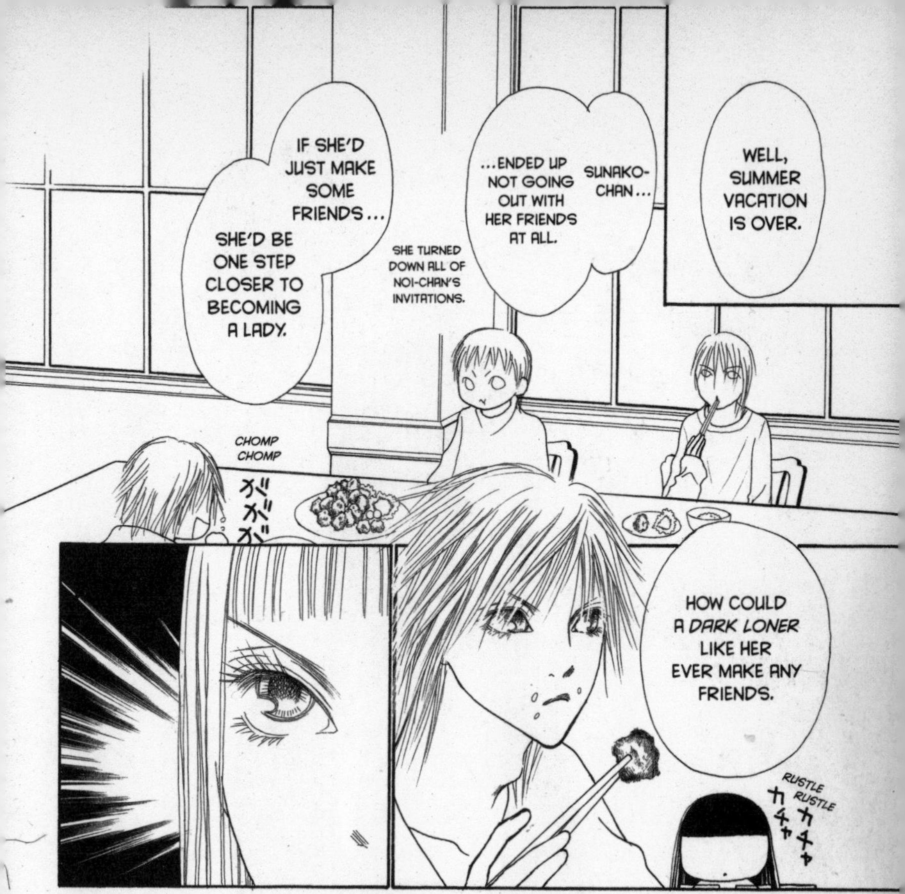
WELL, SUMMER VACATION IS OVER.
SUNAKO-CHAN...
...ENDED UP NOT GOING OUT WITH HER FRIENDS AT ALL.
SHE TURNED DOWN ALL OF NOI-CHAN'S INVITATIONS.
IF SHE'D JUST MAKE SOME FRIENDS...
SHE'D BE ONE STEP CLOSER TO BECOMING A LADY.
CHOMP CHOMP
HOW COULD A *DARK LONER* LIKE HER EVER MAKE ANY FRIENDS.
RUSTLE RUSTLE

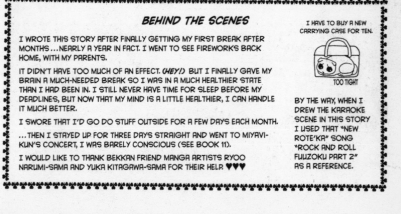

BEHIND THE SCENES

I WROTE THIS STORY AFTER FINALLY GETTING MY FIRST BREAK AFTER MONTHS...NEARLY A YEAR IN FACT. I WENT TO SEE FIREWORKS BACK HOME, WITH MY PARENTS.

IT DIDN'T HAVE TOO MUCH OF AN EFFECT. *(HEY!)* BUT I FINALLY GAVE MY BRAIN A MUCH-NEEDED BREAK SO I WAS IN A MUCH HEALTHIER STATE THAN I HAD BEEN IN. I STILL NEVER HAVE TIME FOR SLEEP BEFORE MY DEADLINES, BUT NOW THAT MY MIND IS A LITTLE HEALTHIER, I CAN HANDLE IT MUCH BETTER.

I SWORE THAT I'D GO DO STUFF OUTSIDE FOR A FEW DAYS EACH MONTH.

...THEN I STAYED UP FOR THREE DAYS STRAIGHT AND WENT TO MIYAVI-KUN'S CONCERT, I WAS BARELY CONSCIOUS (SEE BOOK 11).

I WOULD LIKE TO THANK BEKKAN FRIEND MANGA ARTISTS RYOO NARUMI-SAMA AND YUKA KITAGAWA-SAMA FOR THEIR HELP. ♥♥♥

I HAVE TO BUY A NEW CARRYING CASE FOR TEN.

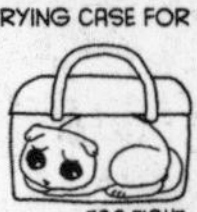

TOO TIGHT

BY THE WAY, WHEN I DREW THE KARAOKE SCENE IN THIS STORY I USED THAT "NEW ROTE'KA" SONG "ROCK AND ROLL FUUZOKU PART 2" AS A REFERENCE.

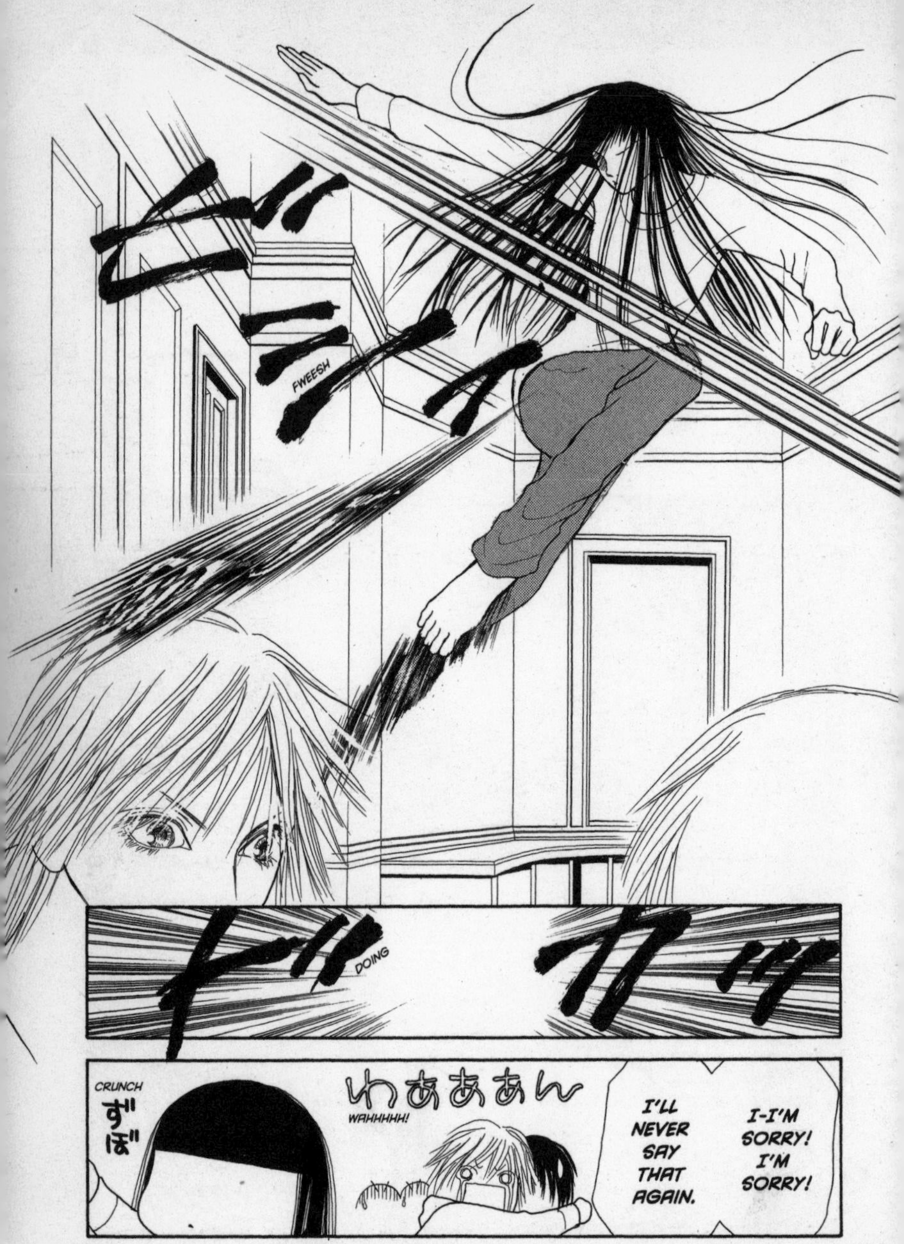
FWEESH
ドカッ
DOING
I-I'M SORRY! I'M SORRY!
I'LL NEVER SAY THAT AGAIN.
わあああん
WAHHHHH!
ずぼ
CRUNCH

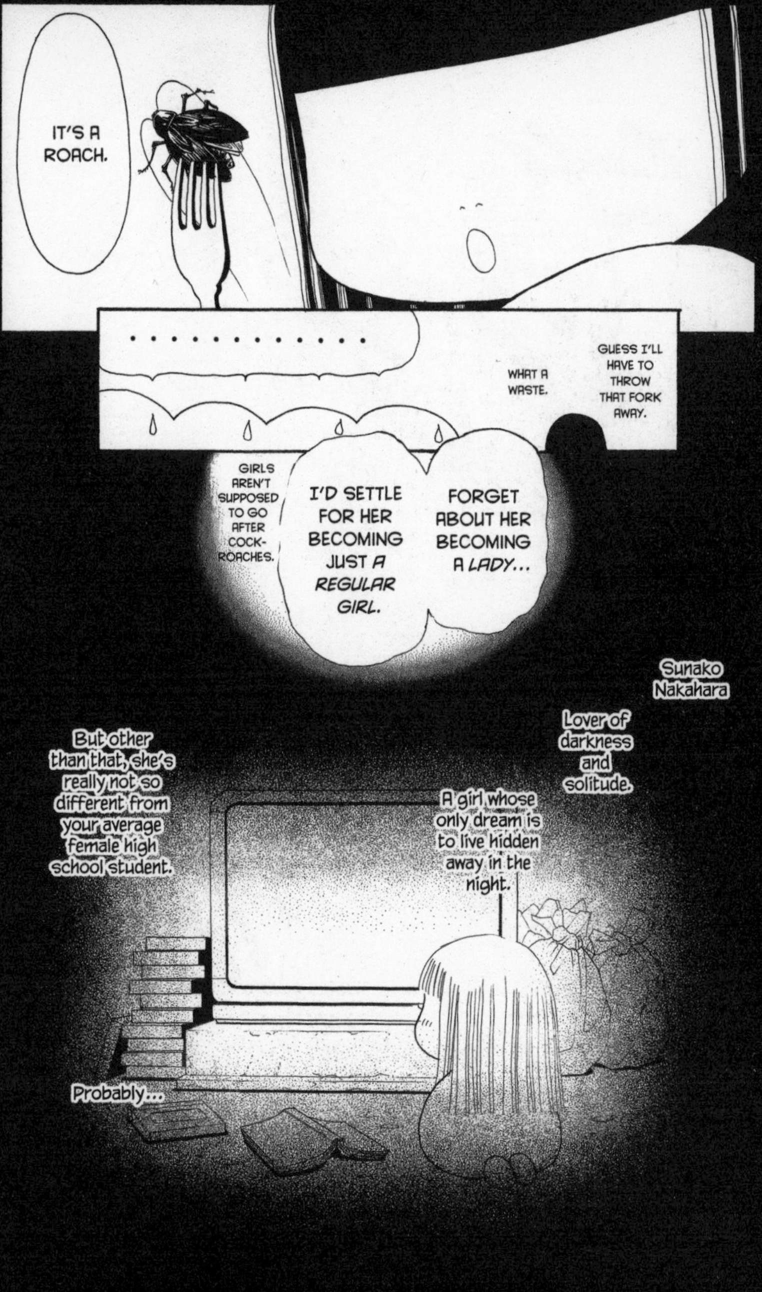
IT'S A ROACH.
GUESS I'LL HAVE TO THROW THAT FORK AWAY.
WHAT A WASTE.
. . . .
FORGET ABOUT HER BECOMING A *LADY*...
I'D SETTLE FOR HER BECOMING JUST A *REGULAR GIRL*.
GIRLS AREN'T SUPPOSED TO GO AFTER COCK-ROACHES.
Sunako Nakahara
Lover of darkness and solitude.
A girl whose only dream is to live hidden away in the night.
But other than that, she's really not so different from your average female high school student.
Probably...

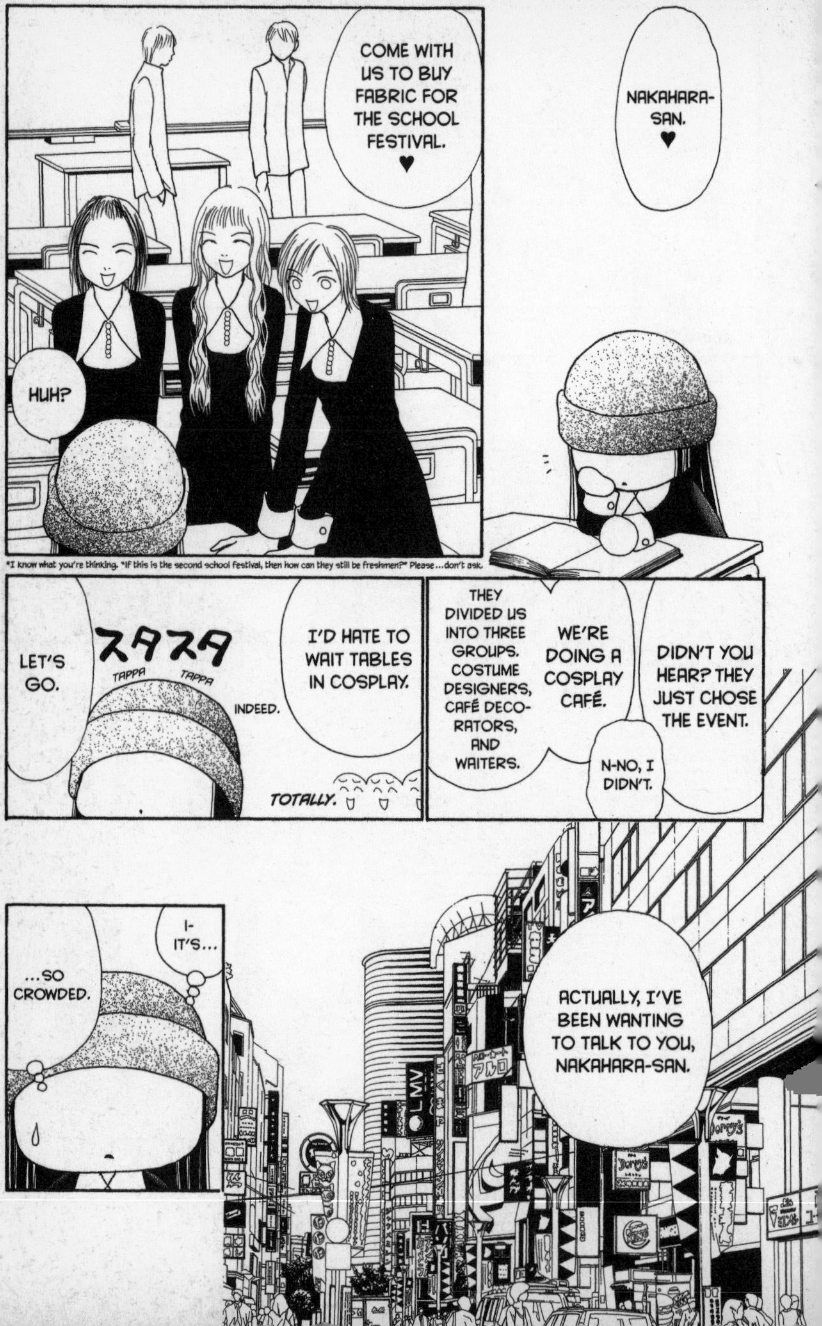
NAKAHARA-SAN. ♥
COME WITH US TO BUY FABRIC FOR THE SCHOOL FESTIVAL. ♥
HUH?
*I know what you're thinking. "If this is the second school festival, then how can they still be freshmen?" Please...don't ask.
DIDN'T YOU HEAR? THEY JUST CHOSE THE EVENT.
N-NO, I DIDN'T.
WE'RE DOING A COSPLAY CAFÉ.
THEY DIVIDED US INTO THREE GROUPS. COSTUME DESIGNERS, CAFÉ DECORATORS, AND WAITERS.
I'D HATE TO WAIT TABLES IN COSPLAY.
TOTALLY.
INDEED.
スタスタ
TAPPA TAPPA
LET'S GO.
ACTUALLY, I'VE BEEN WANTING TO TALK TO YOU, NAKAHARA-SAN.
I-IT'S...
...SO CROWDED.

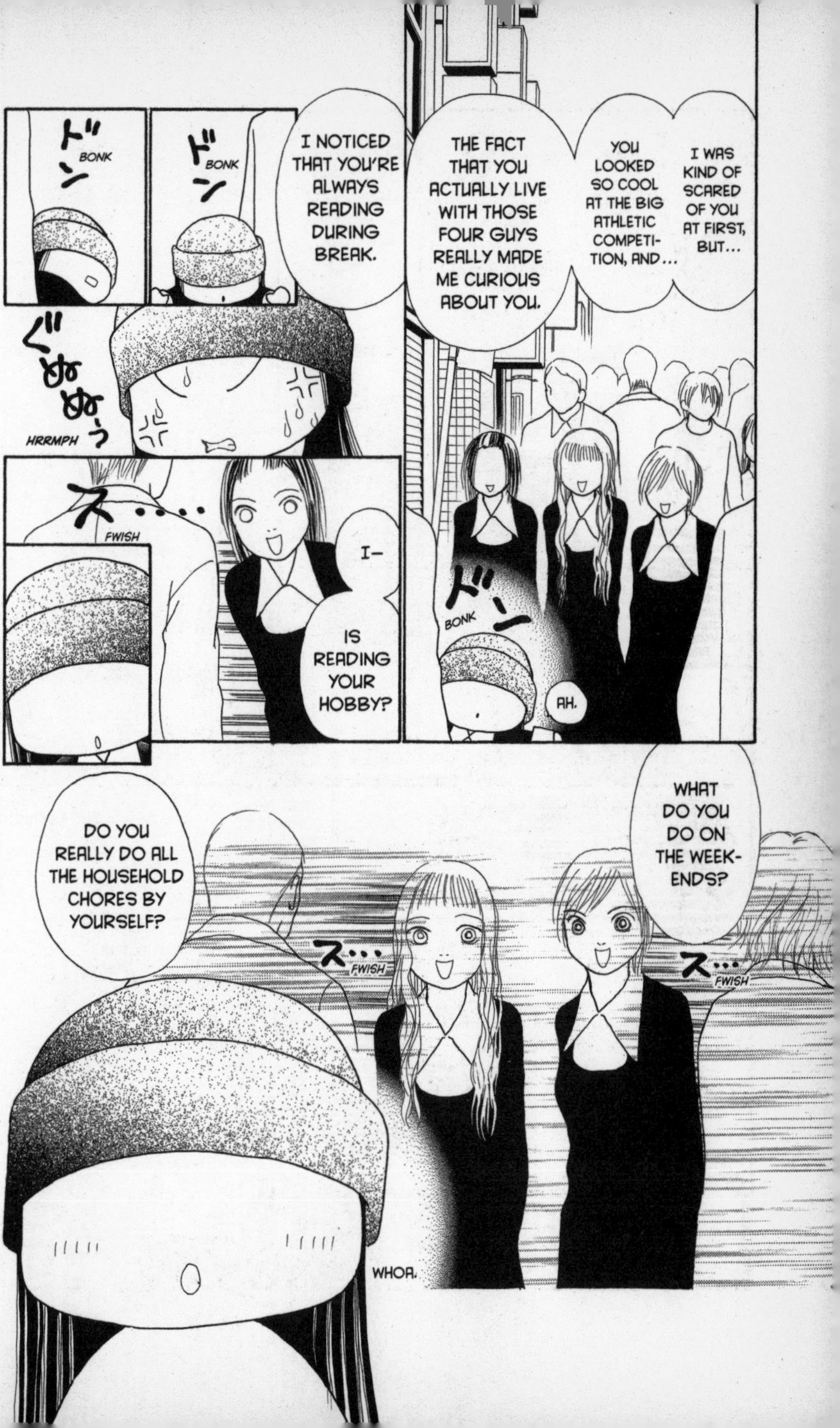

I WAS KIND OF SCARED OF YOU AT FIRST, BUT…
YOU LOOKED SO COOL AT THE BIG ATHLETIC COMPETITION, AND…
THE FACT THAT YOU ACTUALLY LIVE WITH THOSE FOUR GUYS REALLY MADE ME CURIOUS ABOUT YOU.
ドン BONK
AH.
I NOTICED THAT YOU'RE ALWAYS READING DURING BREAK.
ドン BONK
ドン BONK
ぐぬぬぅ HRRMPH
ス… FWISH
I—
IS READING YOUR HOBBY?
WHAT DO YOU DO ON THE WEEK-ENDS?
ス… FWISH
ス… FWISH
DO YOU REALLY DO ALL THE HOUSEHOLD CHORES BY YOURSELF?
WHOA.

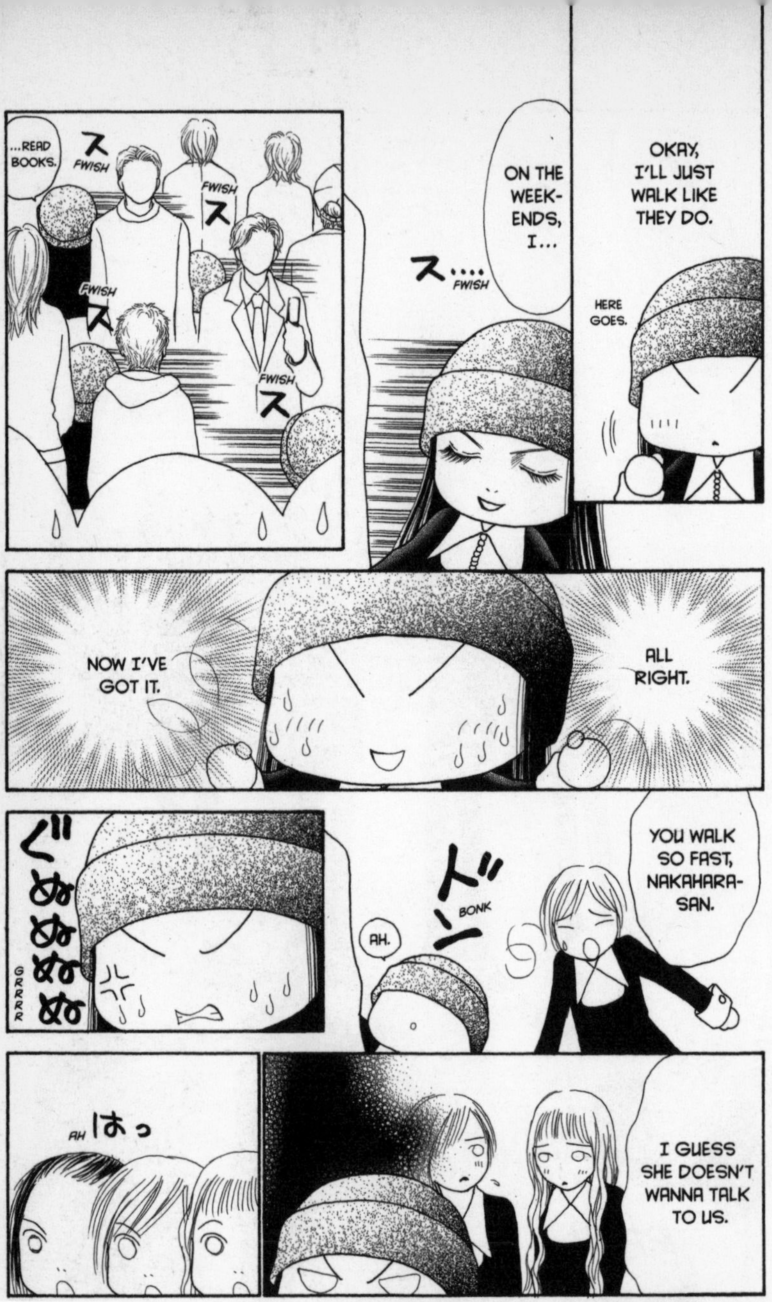
OKAY, I'LL JUST WALK LIKE THEY DO.
HERE GOES.
ON THE WEEK-ENDS, I...
ス.... FWISH
...READ BOOKS.
ス FWISH
FWISH ス
FWISH ス
FWISH ス
ALL RIGHT.
NOW I'VE GOT IT.
YOU WALK SO FAST, NAKAHARA-SAN.
ドン BONK
AH.
ぐぬぬぬぬぬ GRRRR
I GUESS SHE DOESN'T WANNA TALK TO US.
AH はっ

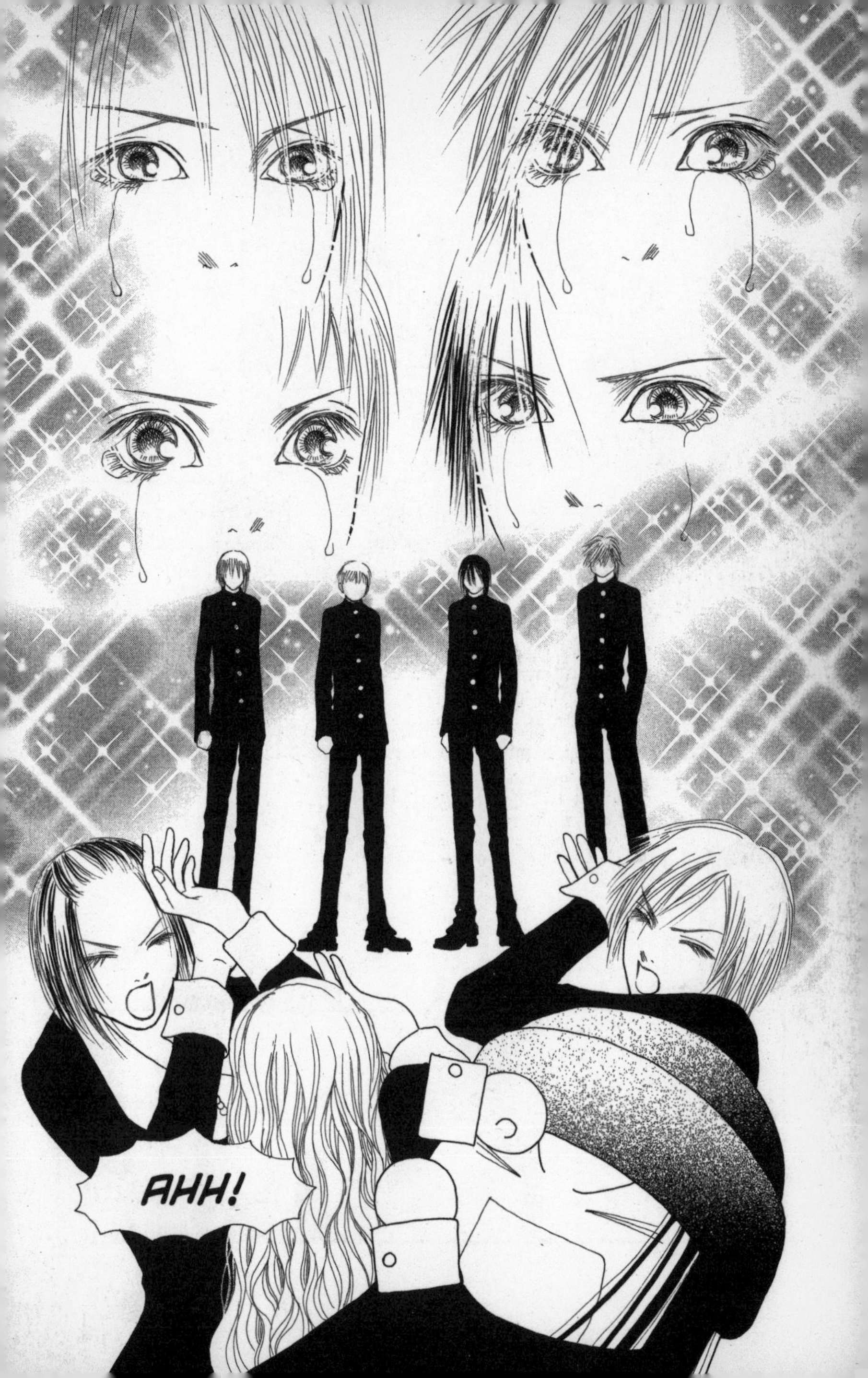
AHH!

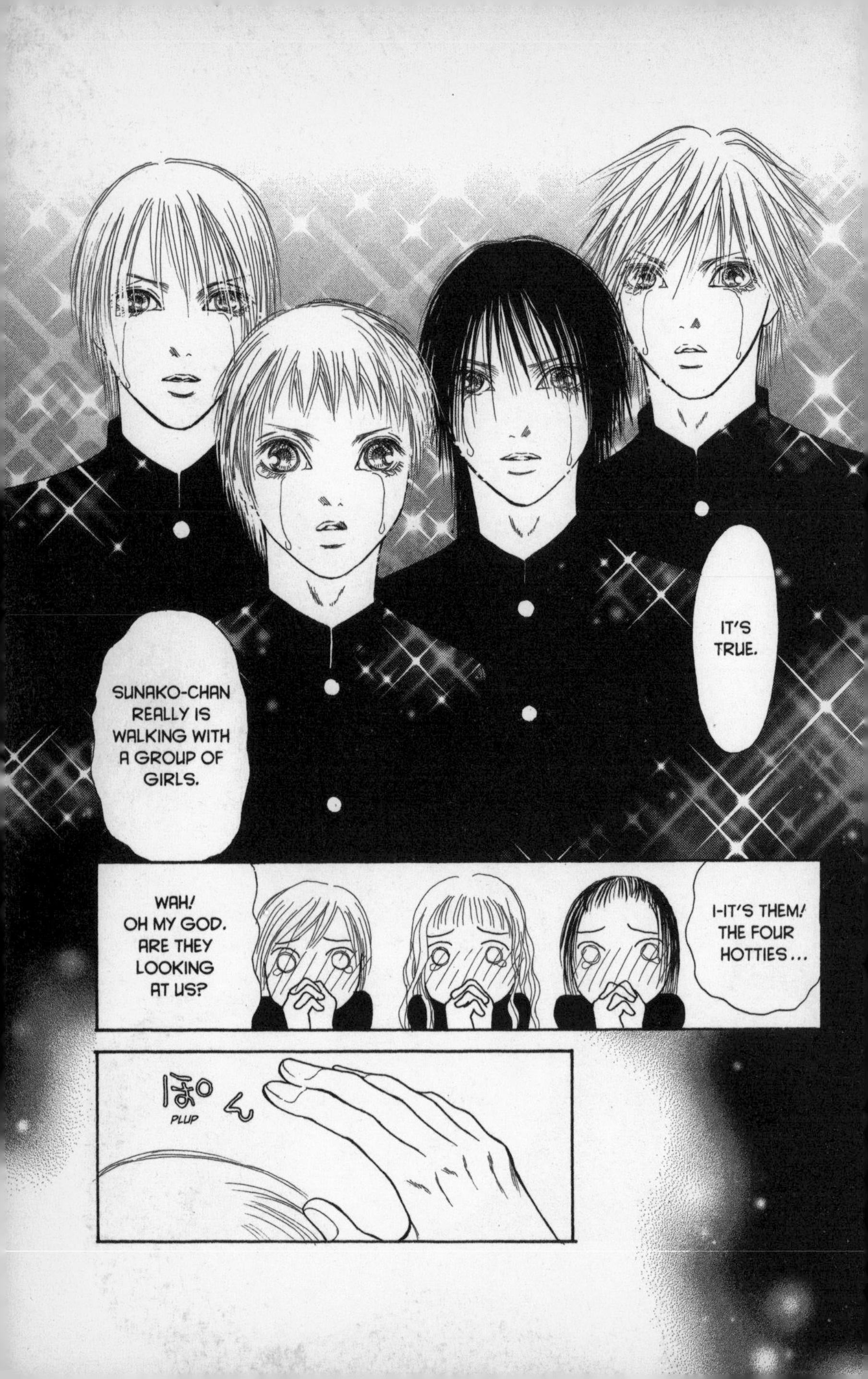
IT'S TRUE.
SUNAKO-CHAN REALLY IS WALKING WITH A GROUP OF GIRLS.
I-IT'S THEM! THE FOUR HOTTIES...
WAH! OH MY GOD. ARE THEY LOOKING AT US?
ぽん
PLUP

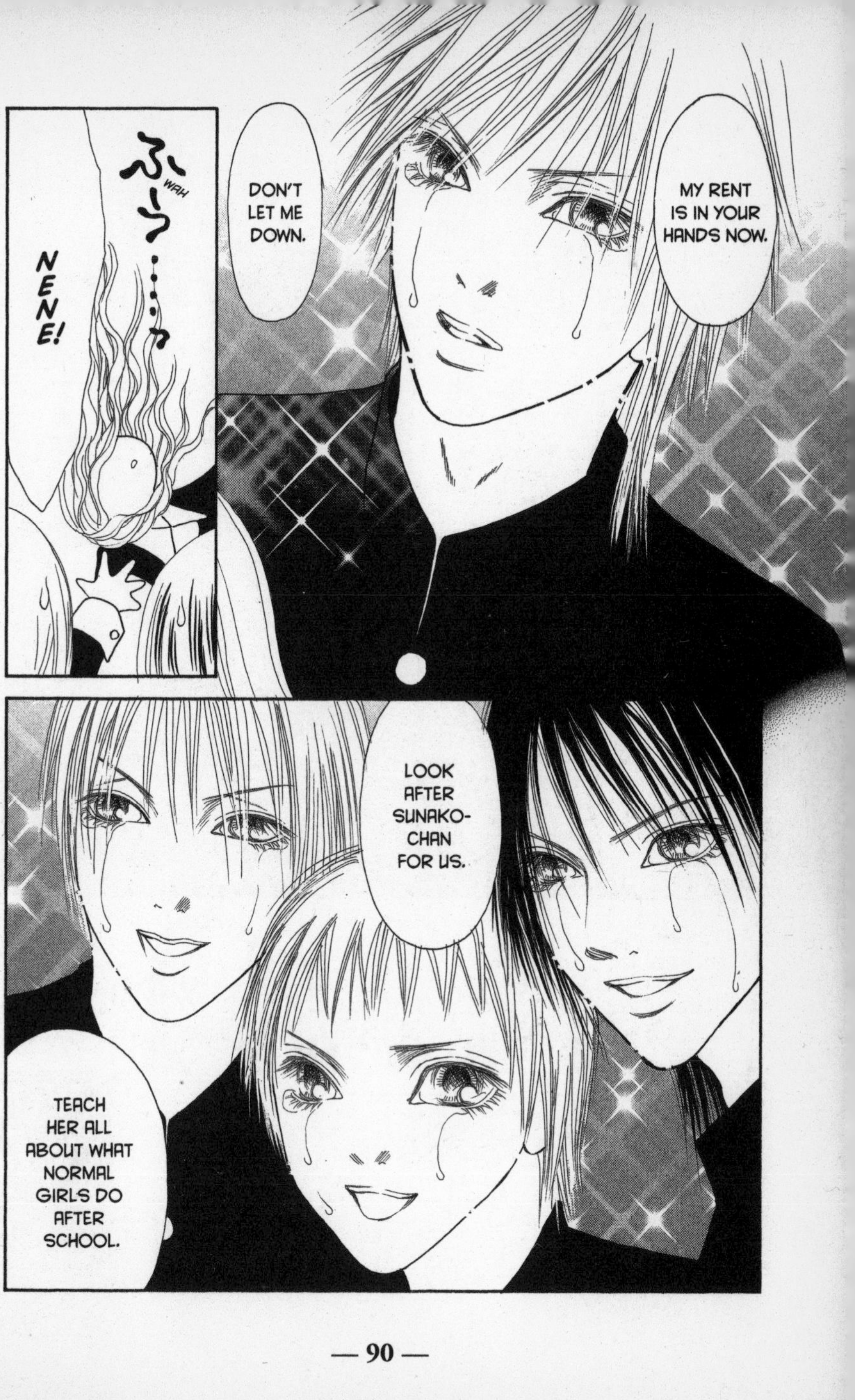
MY RENT IS IN YOUR HANDS NOW.
DON'T LET ME DOWN.
ふぅ…っ
WAH
NENE!
LOOK AFTER SUNAKO-CHAN FOR US.
TEACH HER ALL ABOUT WHAT NORMAL GIRLS DO AFTER SCHOOL.

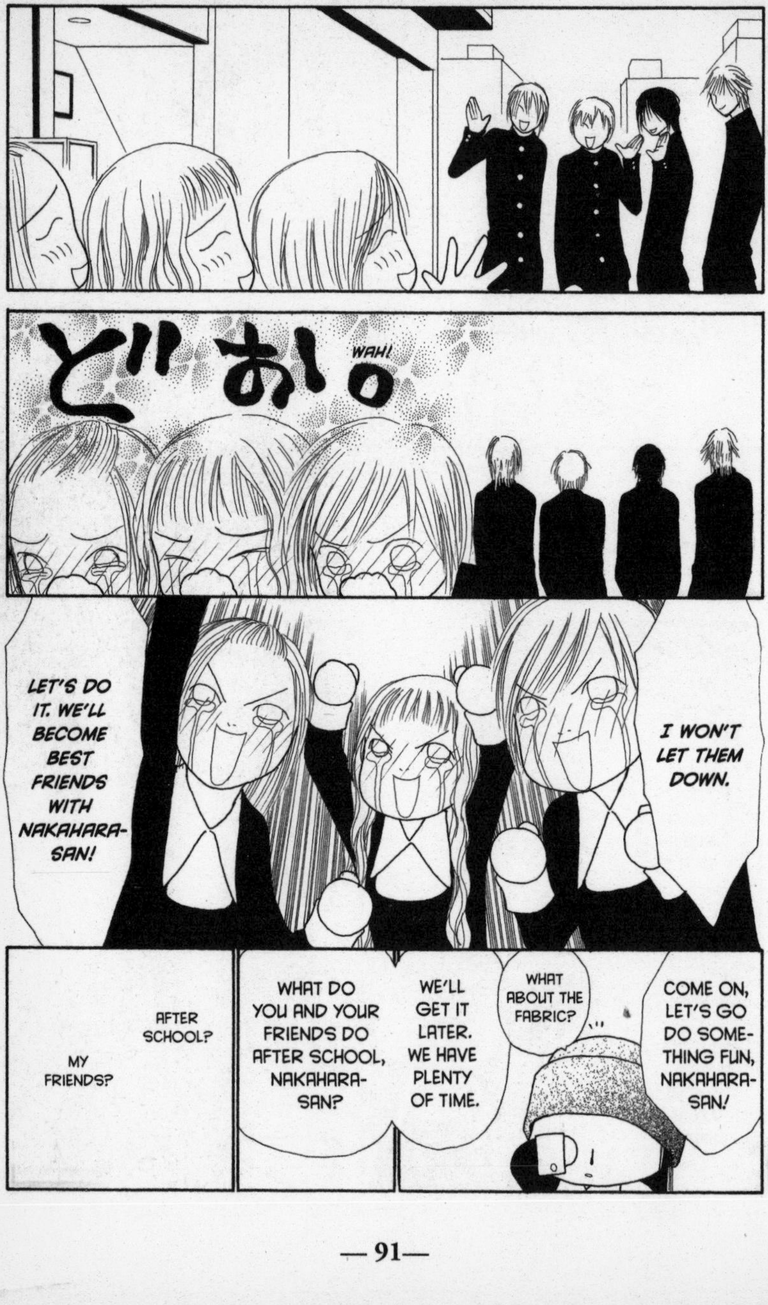
WAH!
I WON'T LET THEM DOWN.
LET'S DO IT. WE'LL BECOME BEST FRIENDS WITH NAKAHARA-SAN!
COME ON, LET'S GO DO SOME-THING FUN, NAKAHARA-SAN!
WHAT ABOUT THE FABRIC?
WE'LL GET IT LATER. WE HAVE PLENTY OF TIME.
WHAT DO YOU AND YOUR FRIENDS DO AFTER SCHOOL, NAKAHARA-SAN?
AFTER SCHOOL?
MY FRIENDS?

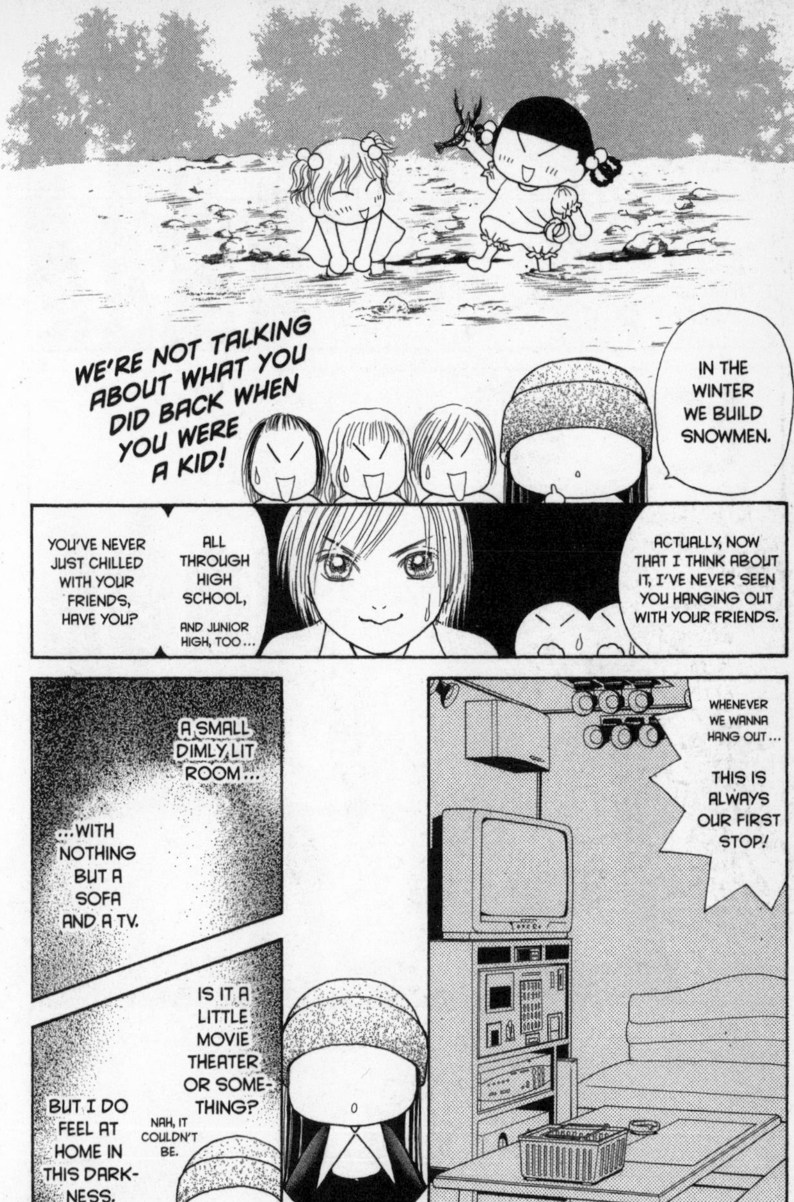
IN THE WINTER WE BUILD SNOWMEN.
WE'RE NOT TALKING ABOUT WHAT YOU DID BACK WHEN YOU WERE A KID!
ACTUALLY, NOW THAT I THINK ABOUT IT, I'VE NEVER SEEN YOU HANGING OUT WITH YOUR FRIENDS.
ALL THROUGH HIGH SCHOOL,
AND JUNIOR HIGH, TOO...
YOU'VE NEVER JUST CHILLED WITH YOUR FRIENDS, HAVE YOU?
WHENEVER WE WANNA HANG OUT...
THIS IS ALWAYS OUR FIRST STOP!
A SMALL DIMLY LIT ROOM...
...WITH NOTHING BUT A SOFA AND A TV.
IS IT A LITTLE MOVIE THEATER OR SOME-THING?
NAH, IT COULDN'T BE.
BUT I DO FEEL AT HOME IN THIS DARK-NESS.

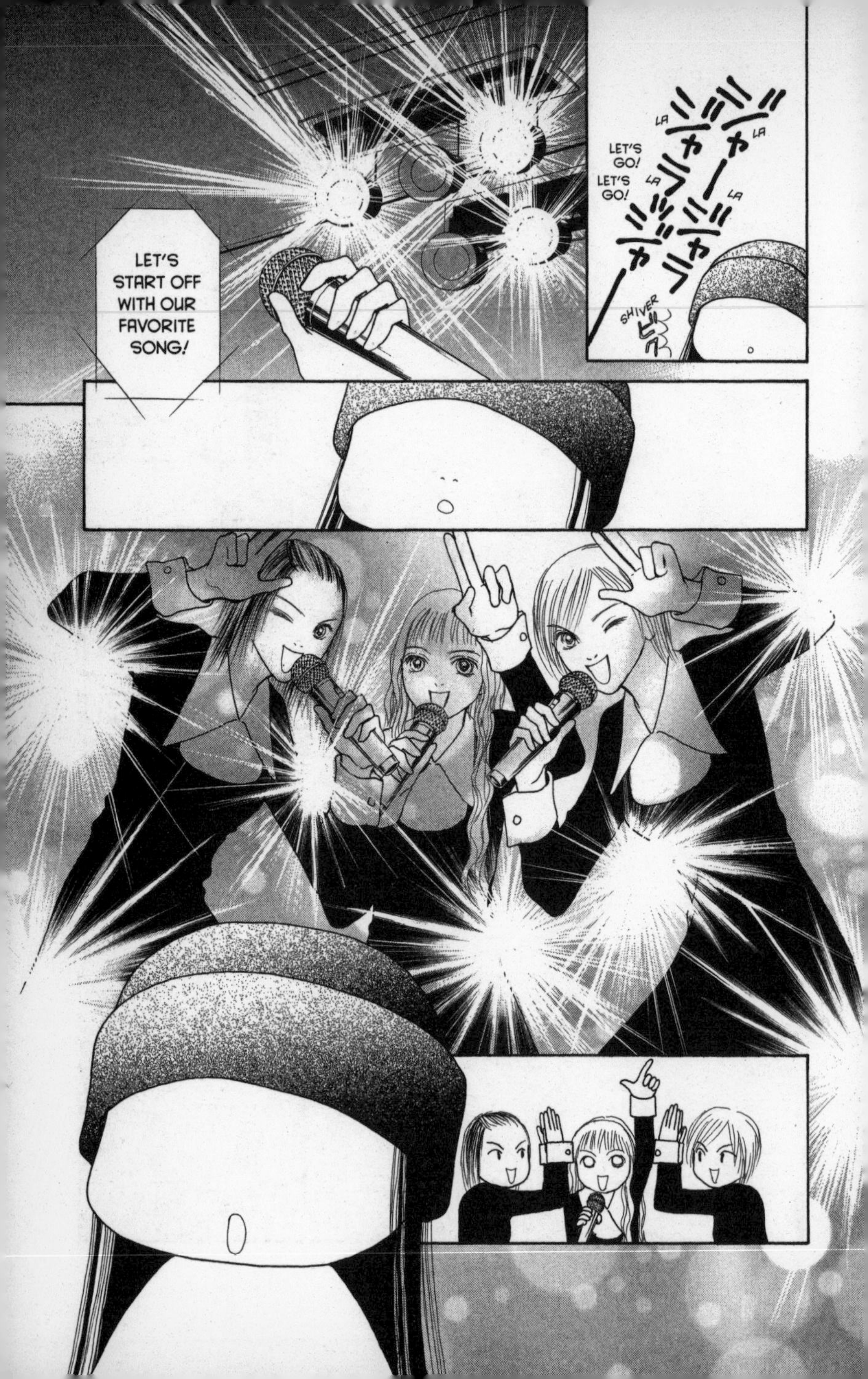

ジャーンジャラッジャーン
ジャラララ
LA
LA
LA
LA
LET'S GO! LET'S GO!
SHIVER
ビク
LET'S START OFF WITH OUR FAVORITE SONG!

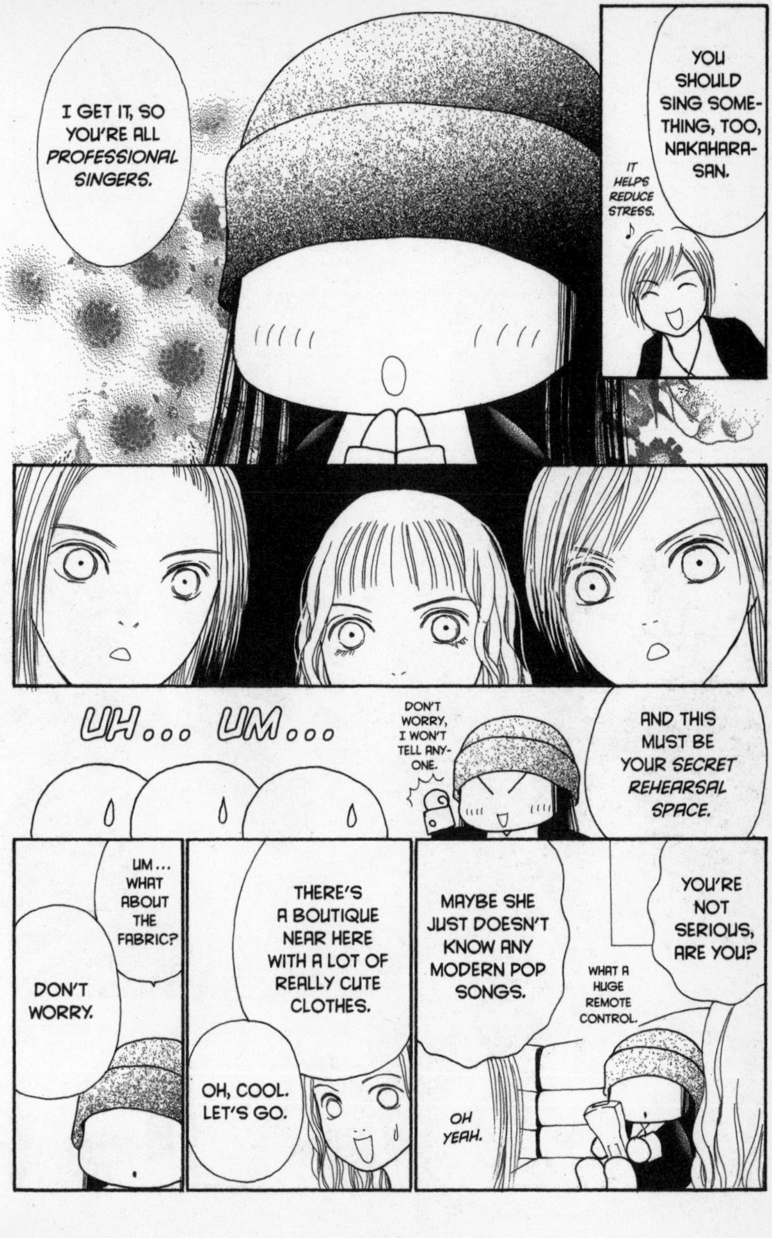
YOU SHOULD SING SOMETHING, TOO, NAKAHARA-SAN.
IT HELPS REDUCE STRESS. ♪
I GET IT, SO YOU'RE ALL PROFESSIONAL SINGERS.
AND THIS MUST BE YOUR SECRET REHEARSAL SPACE.
DON'T WORRY, I WON'T TELL ANYONE.
UH... UM...
YOU'RE NOT SERIOUS, ARE YOU?
WHAT A HUGE REMOTE CONTROL.
MAYBE SHE JUST DOESN'T KNOW ANY MODERN POP SONGS.
OH YEAH.
THERE'S A BOUTIQUE NEAR HERE WITH A LOT OF REALLY CUTE CLOTHES.
OH, COOL. LET'S GO.
UM... WHAT ABOUT THE FABRIC?
DON'T WORRY.

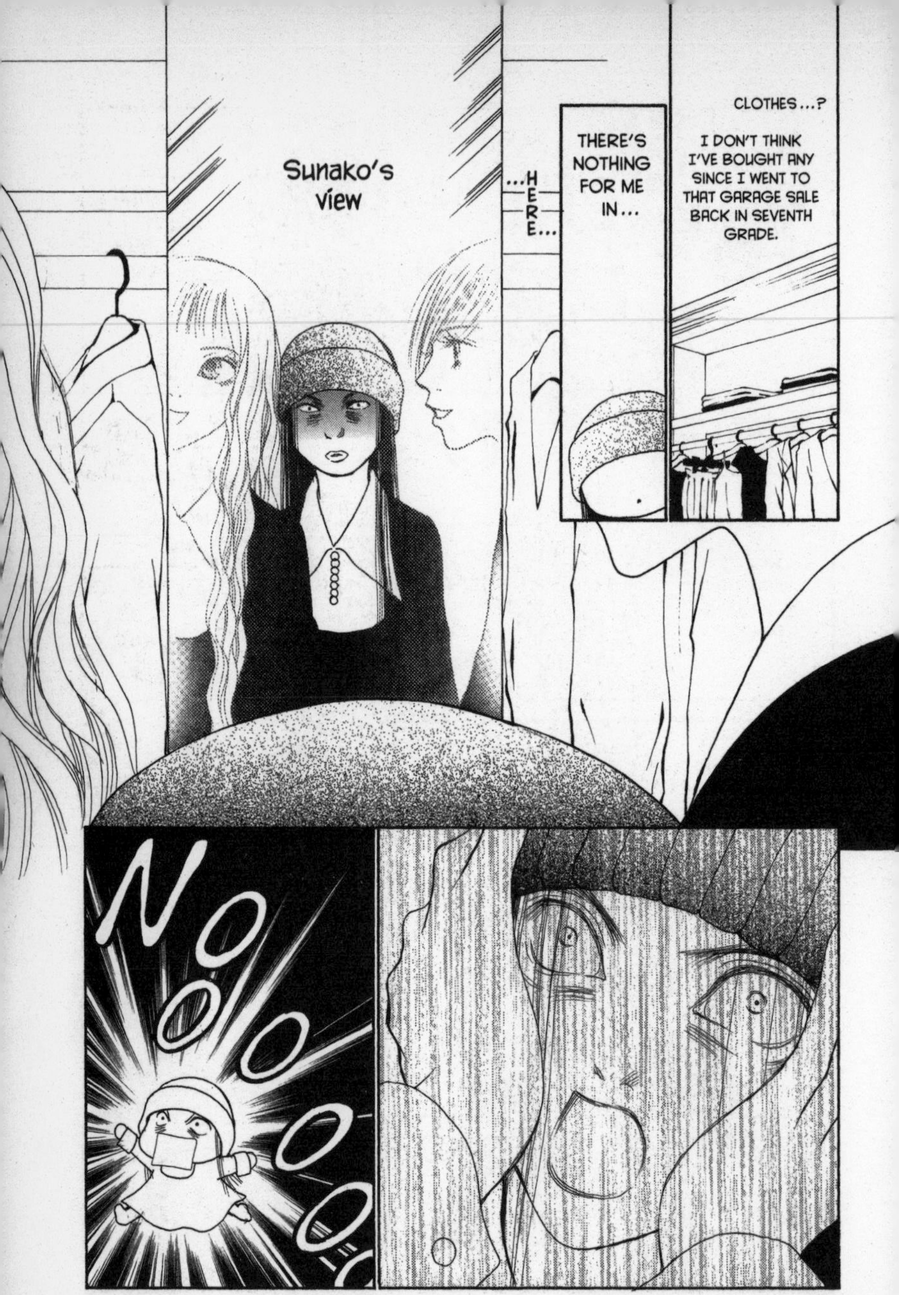
CLOTHES...?
I DON'T THINK I'VE BOUGHT ANY SINCE I WENT TO THAT GARAGE SALE BACK IN SEVENTH GRADE.
THERE'S NOTHING FOR ME IN...
...HERE...
Sunako's view
NOOOOOO

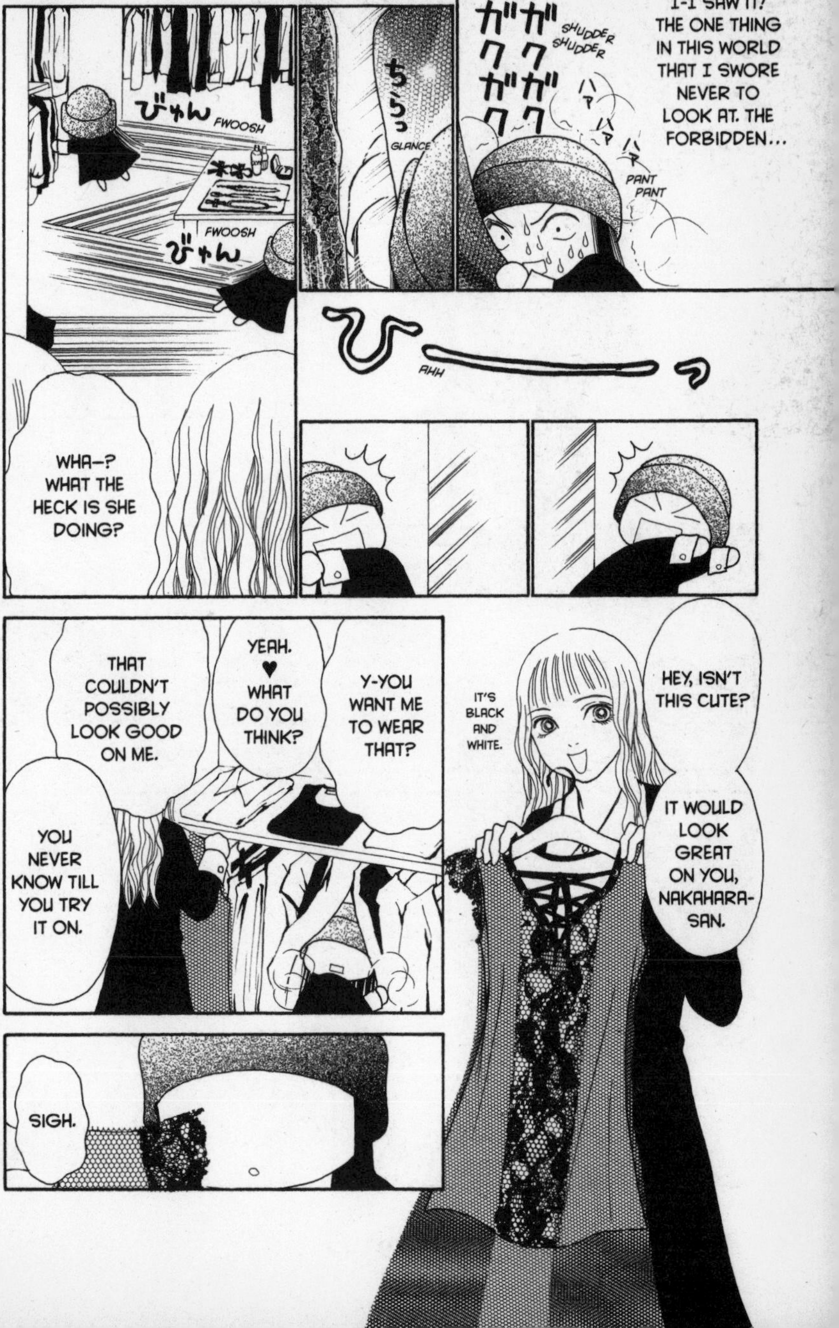
I-I SAW IT! THE ONE THING IN THIS WORLD THAT I SWORE NEVER TO LOOK AT. THE FORBIDDEN...
ガクガクガクガク
SHUDDER SHUDDER
ハァハァハァ
PANT PANT
ちらっ
GLANCE
ひーっ
AHH
びゅん
FWOOSH
びゅん
FWOOSH
WHA-? WHAT THE HECK IS SHE DOING?
HEY, ISN'T THIS CUTE?
IT'S BLACK AND WHITE.
IT WOULD LOOK GREAT ON YOU, NAKAHARA-SAN.
Y-YOU WANT ME TO WEAR THAT?
YEAH. ♥ WHAT DO YOU THINK?
THAT COULDN'T POSSIBLY LOOK GOOD ON ME.
YOU NEVER KNOW TILL YOU TRY IT ON.
SIGH.

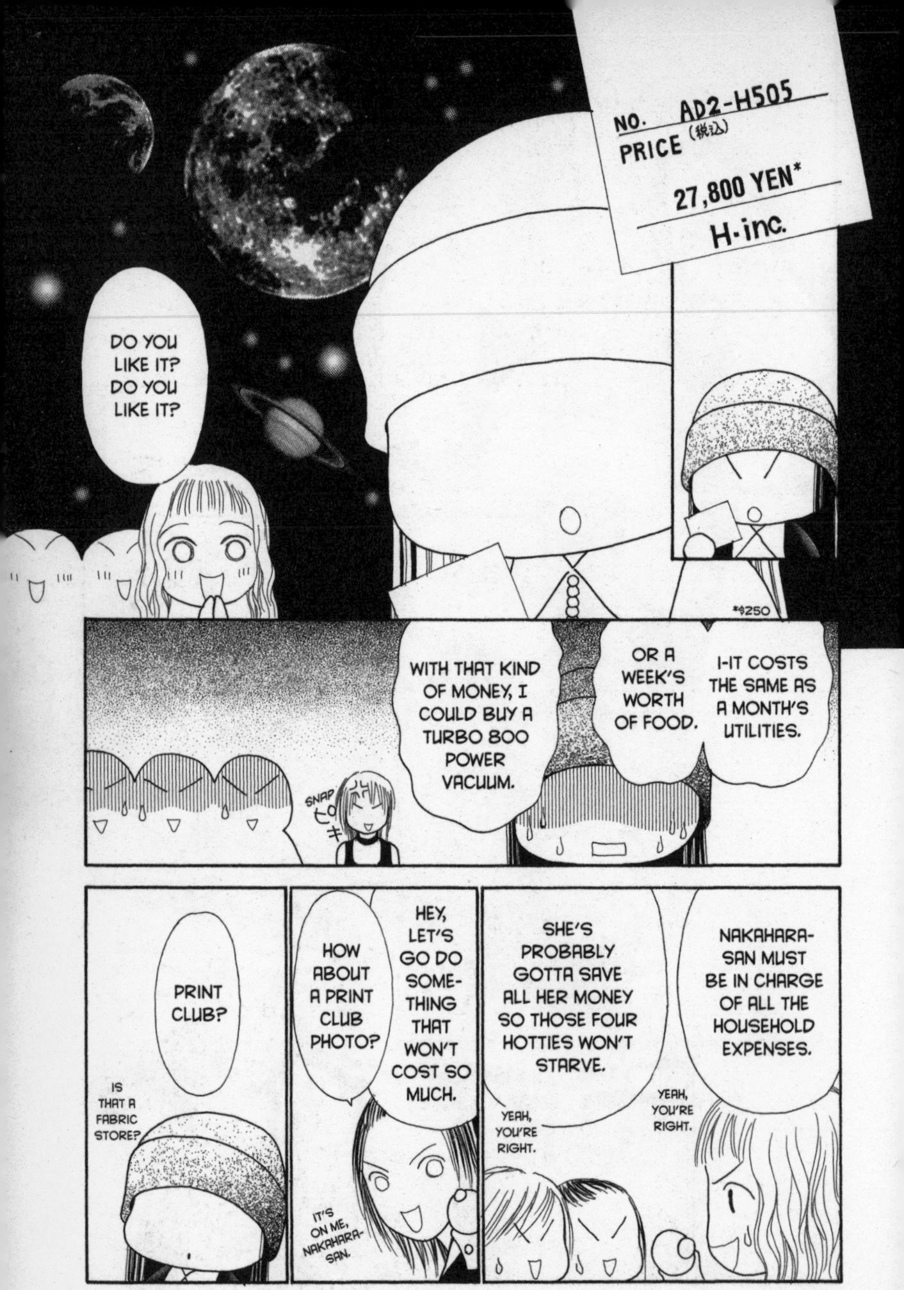
NO. AD2-H505
PRICE (税込)
27,800 YEN*
H·inc.
DO YOU LIKE IT? DO YOU LIKE IT?
*$250
I-IT COSTS THE SAME AS A MONTH'S UTILITIES.
OR A WEEK'S WORTH OF FOOD.
WITH THAT KIND OF MONEY, I COULD BUY A TURBO 800 POWER VACUUM.
SNAP
NAKAHARA-SAN MUST BE IN CHARGE OF ALL THE HOUSEHOLD EXPENSES.
YEAH, YOU'RE RIGHT.
SHE'S PROBABLY GOTTA SAVE ALL HER MONEY SO THOSE FOUR HOTTIES WON'T STARVE.
YEAH, YOU'RE RIGHT.
HEY, LET'S GO DO SOMETHING THAT WON'T COST SO MUCH.
HOW ABOUT A PRINT CLUB PHOTO?
IT'S ON ME, NAKAHARA-SAN.
PRINT CLUB?
IS THAT A FABRIC STORE?

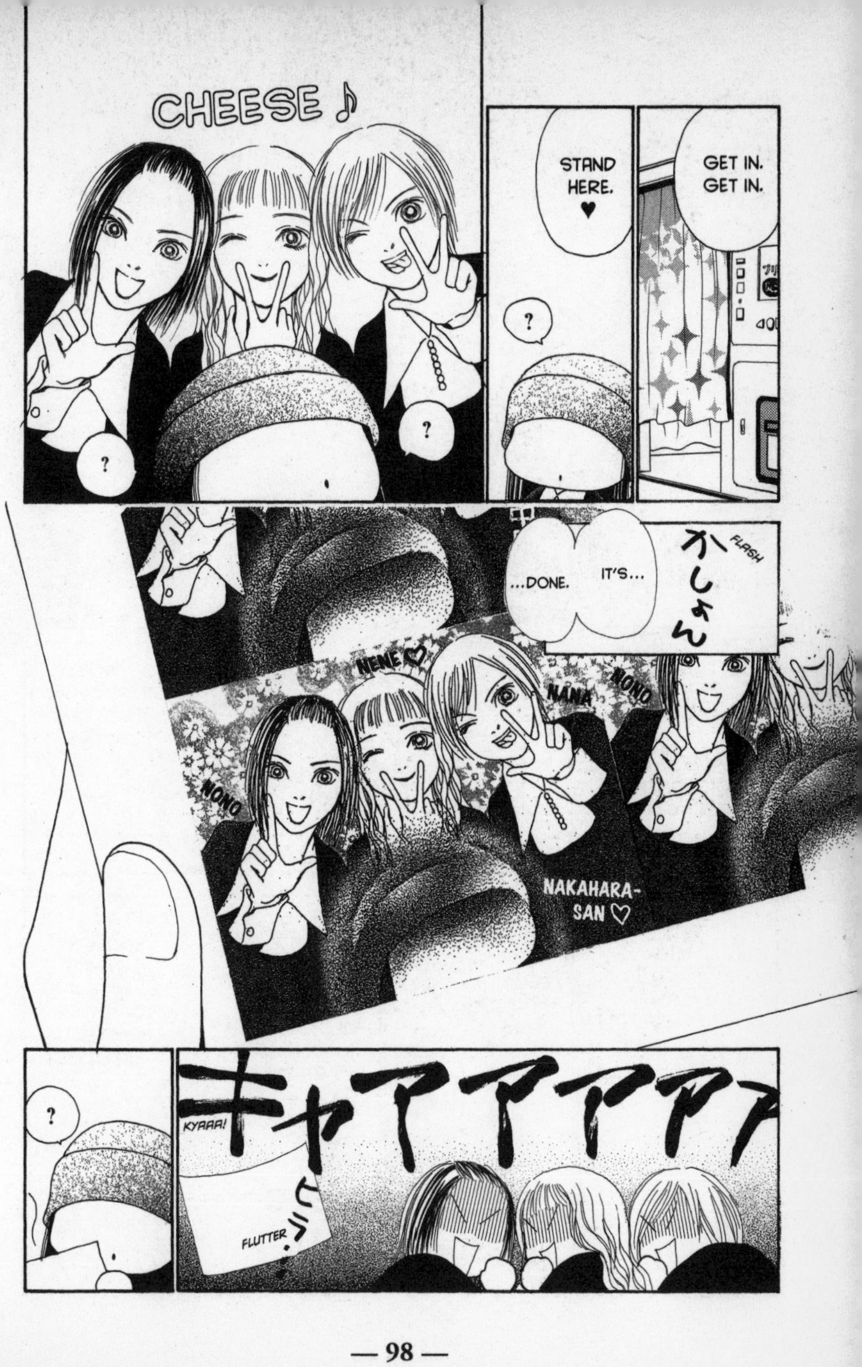
GET IN. GET IN.
STAND HERE. ♥
?
CHEESE ♪
?
?
?
かしょん
FLASH
IT'S...
...DONE.
NENE ♡
NONO
NANA
NONO
NAKAHARA-SAN ♡
キャアアアア
KYAAA!
FLUTTER
?

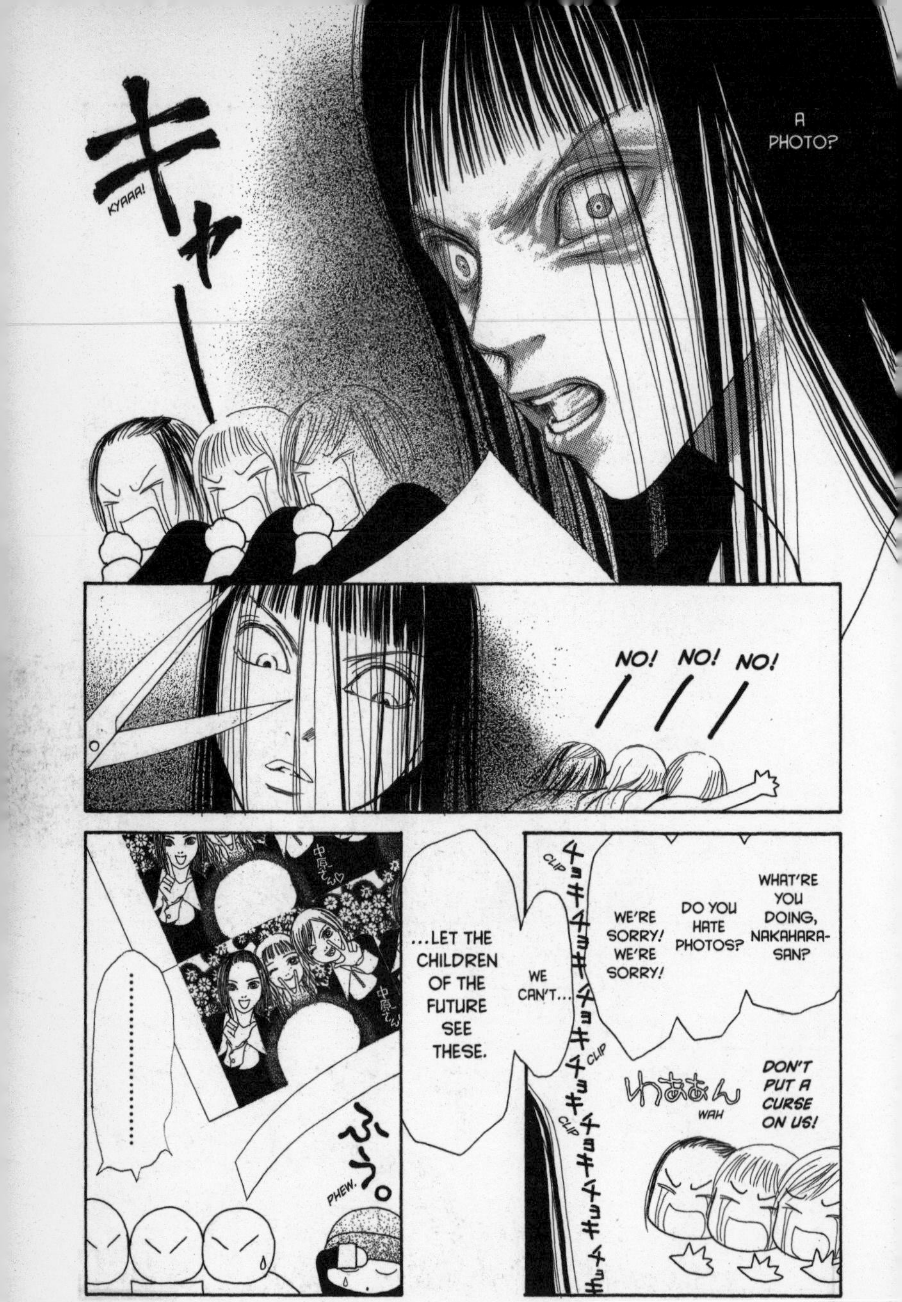
A PHOTO?
キャー
KYAAA!
NO! NO! NO!
WHAT'RE YOU DOING, NAKAHARA-SAN?
DO YOU HATE PHOTOS?
WE'RE SORRY! WE'RE SORRY!
チョキチョキチョキチョキチョキチョキチョキ
CLIP
CLIP
CLIP
DON'T PUT A CURSE ON US!
わあぁん
WAH
WE CAN'T...
...LET THE CHILDREN OF THE FUTURE SEE THESE.
......
ふう。
PHEW.

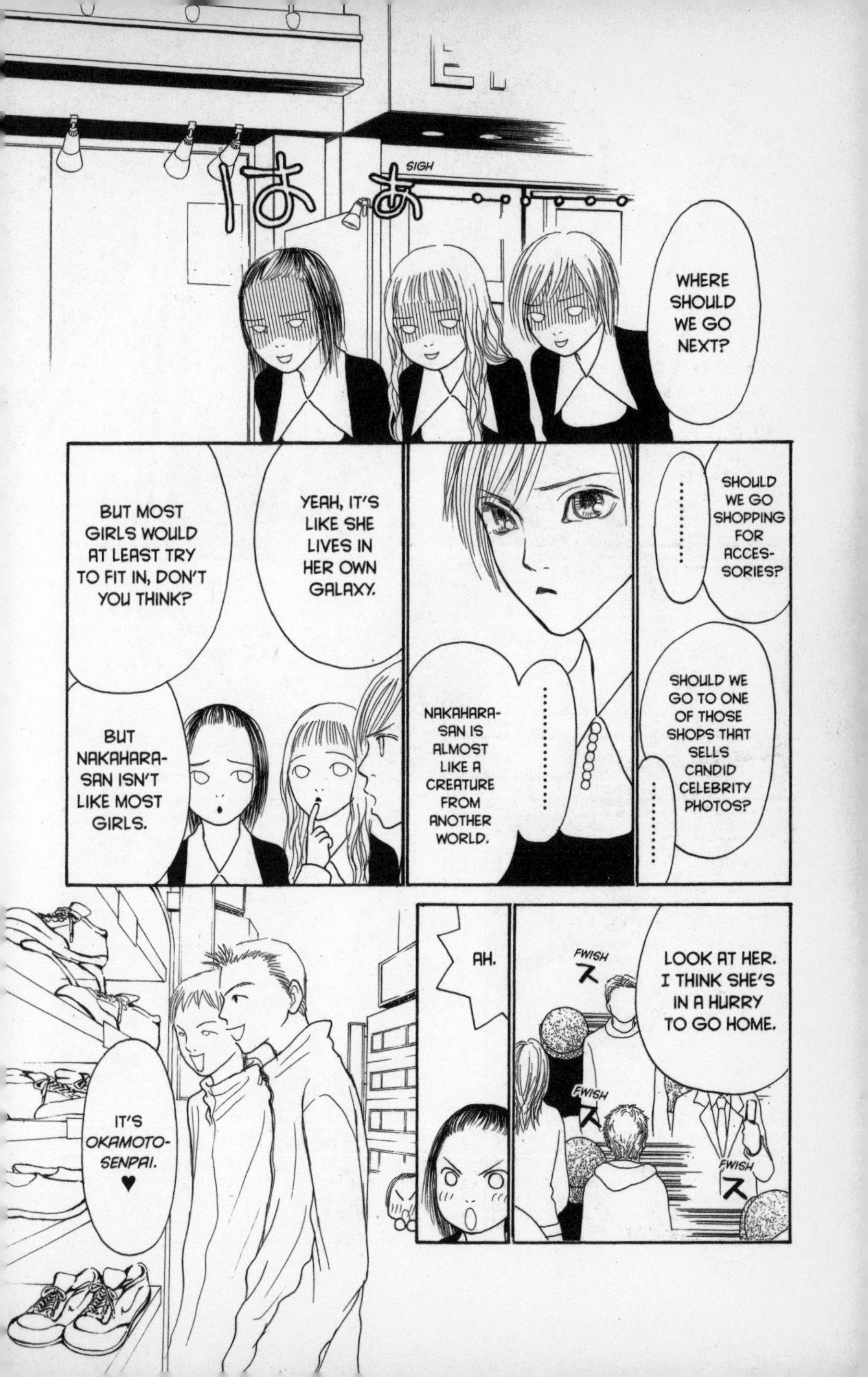
はぁ
SIGH
WHERE SHOULD WE GO NEXT?
SHOULD WE GO SHOPPING FOR ACCES-SORIES?
......
SHOULD WE GO TO ONE OF THOSE SHOPS THAT SELLS CANDID CELEBRITY PHOTOS?
......
NAKAHARA-SAN IS ALMOST LIKE A CREATURE FROM ANOTHER WORLD.
......
YEAH, IT'S LIKE SHE LIVES IN HER OWN GALAXY.
BUT MOST GIRLS WOULD AT LEAST TRY TO FIT IN, DON'T YOU THINK?
BUT NAKAHARA-SAN ISN'T LIKE MOST GIRLS.
LOOK AT HER. I THINK SHE'S IN A HURRY TO GO HOME.
FWISH ス
FWISH ス
FWISH ス
AH.
IT'S OKAMOTO-SENPAI. ♥

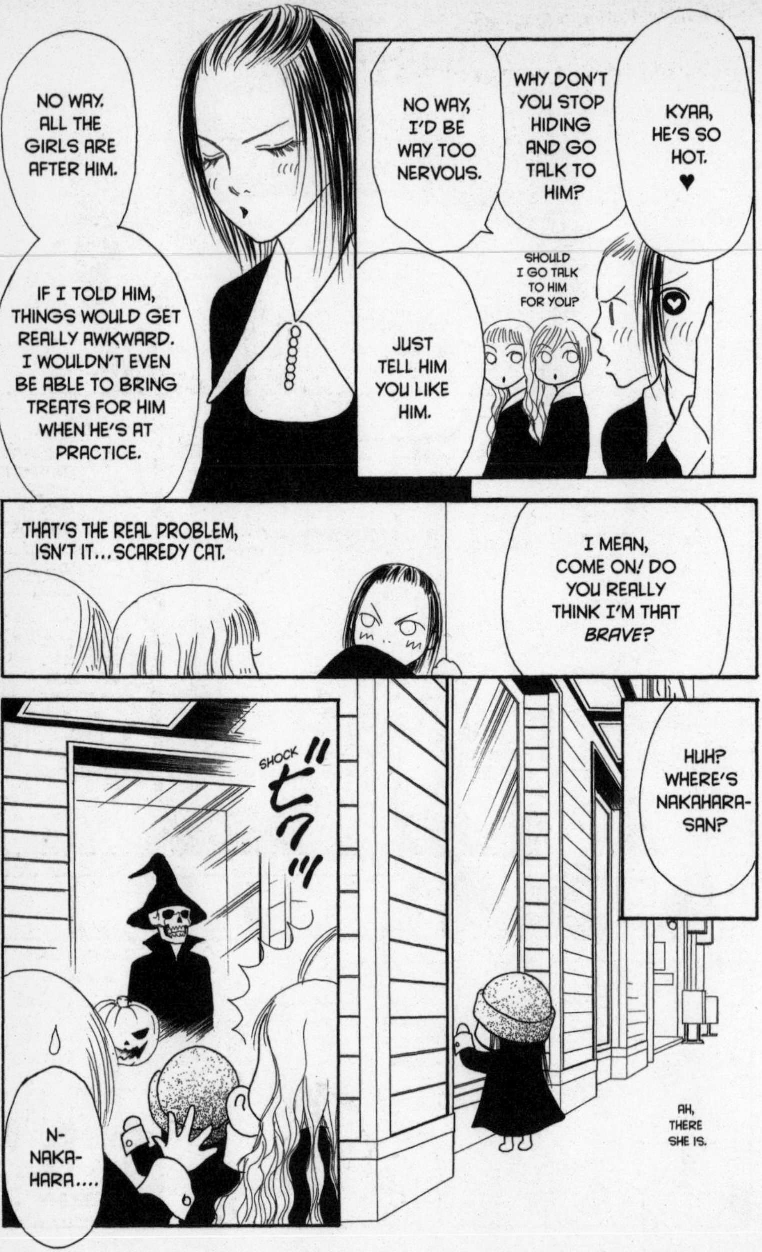
KYAA, HE'S SO HOT. ♥
WHY DON'T YOU STOP HIDING AND GO TALK TO HIM?
NO WAY, I'D BE WAY TOO NERVOUS.
SHOULD I GO TALK TO HIM FOR YOU?
JUST TELL HIM YOU LIKE HIM.
NO WAY. ALL THE GIRLS ARE AFTER HIM.
IF I TOLD HIM, THINGS WOULD GET REALLY AWKWARD. I WOULDN'T EVEN BE ABLE TO BRING TREATS FOR HIM WHEN HE'S AT PRACTICE.
I MEAN, COME ON! DO YOU REALLY THINK I'M THAT *BRAVE*?
THAT'S THE REAL PROBLEM, ISN'T IT... SCAREDY CAT.
HUH? WHERE'S NAKAHARA-SAN?
AH, THERE SHE IS.
SHOCK
N-NAKA-HARA....

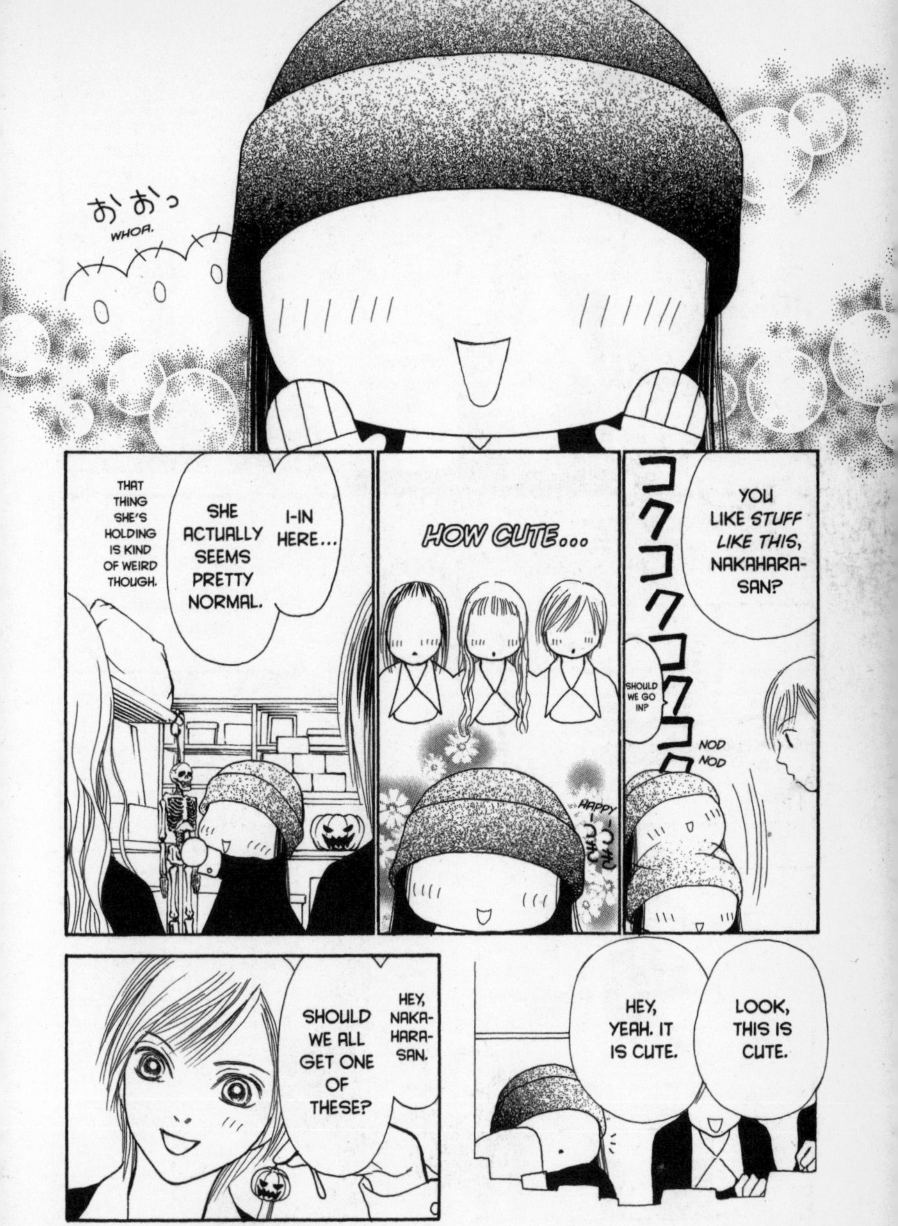
おおっ
WHOA.
コクコクコク
YOU LIKE STUFF LIKE THIS, NAKAHARA-SAN?
SHOULD WE GO IN?
NOD NOD
HOW CUTE...
HAPPY
I-IN HERE...
SHE ACTUALLY SEEMS PRETTY NORMAL.
THAT THING SHE'S HOLDING IS KIND OF WEIRD THOUGH.
LOOK, THIS IS CUTE.
HEY, YEAH. IT IS CUTE.
HEY, NAKAHARA-SAN.
SHOULD WE ALL GET ONE OF THESE?

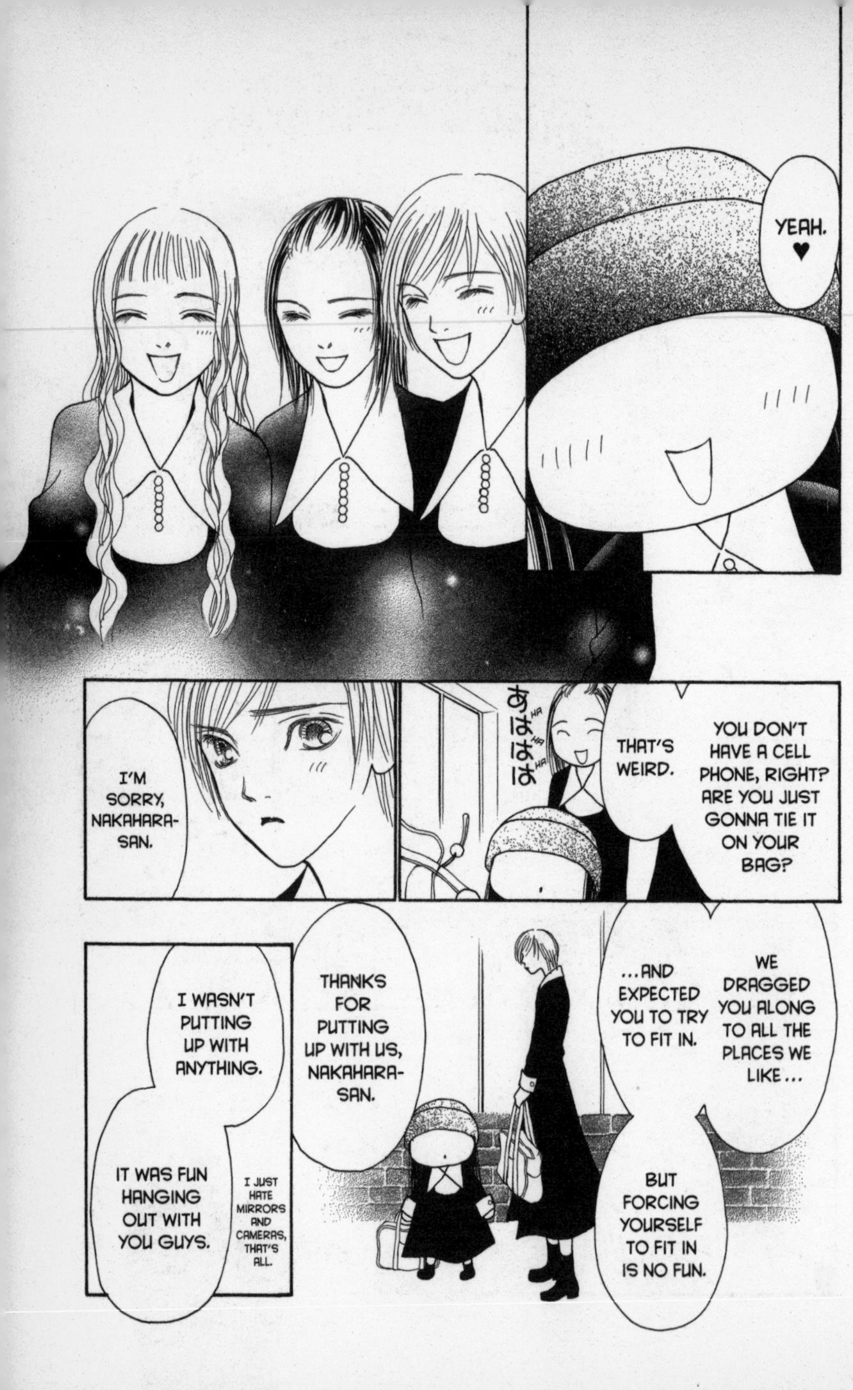
YEAH. ♥
YOU DON'T HAVE A CELL PHONE, RIGHT? ARE YOU JUST GONNA TIE IT ON YOUR BAG?
THAT'S WEIRD.
あははは HA HA HA
I'M SORRY, NAKAHARA-SAN.
WE DRAGGED YOU ALONG TO ALL THE PLACES WE LIKE...
...AND EXPECTED YOU TO TRY TO FIT IN.
BUT FORCING YOURSELF TO FIT IN IS NO FUN.
THANKS FOR PUTTING UP WITH US, NAKAHARA-SAN.
I WASN'T PUTTING UP WITH ANYTHING.
IT WAS FUN HANGING OUT WITH YOU GUYS.
I JUST HATE MIRRORS AND CAMERAS, THAT'S ALL.

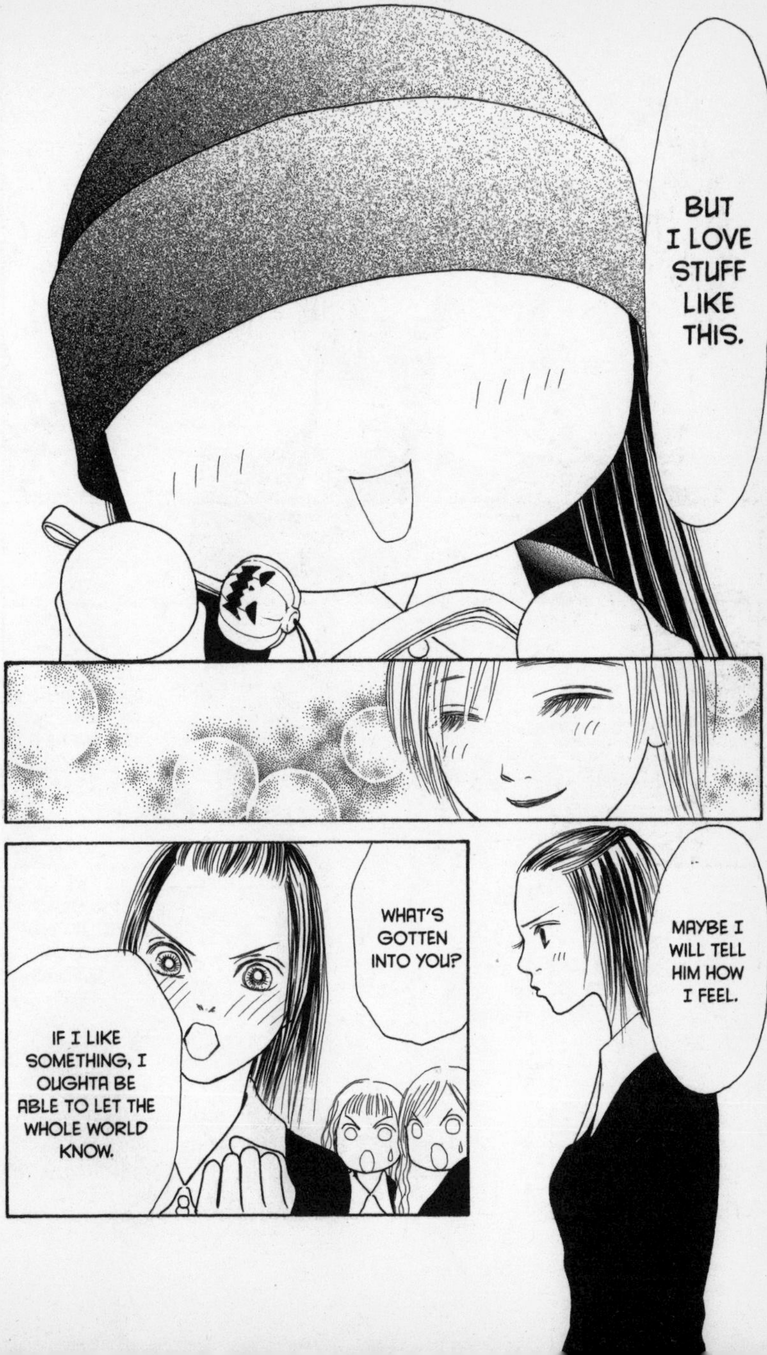
BUT I LOVE STUFF LIKE THIS.
MAYBE I WILL TELL HIM HOW I FEEL.
WHAT'S GOTTEN INTO YOU?
IF I LIKE SOMETHING, I OUGHTA BE ABLE TO LET THE WHOLE WORLD KNOW.

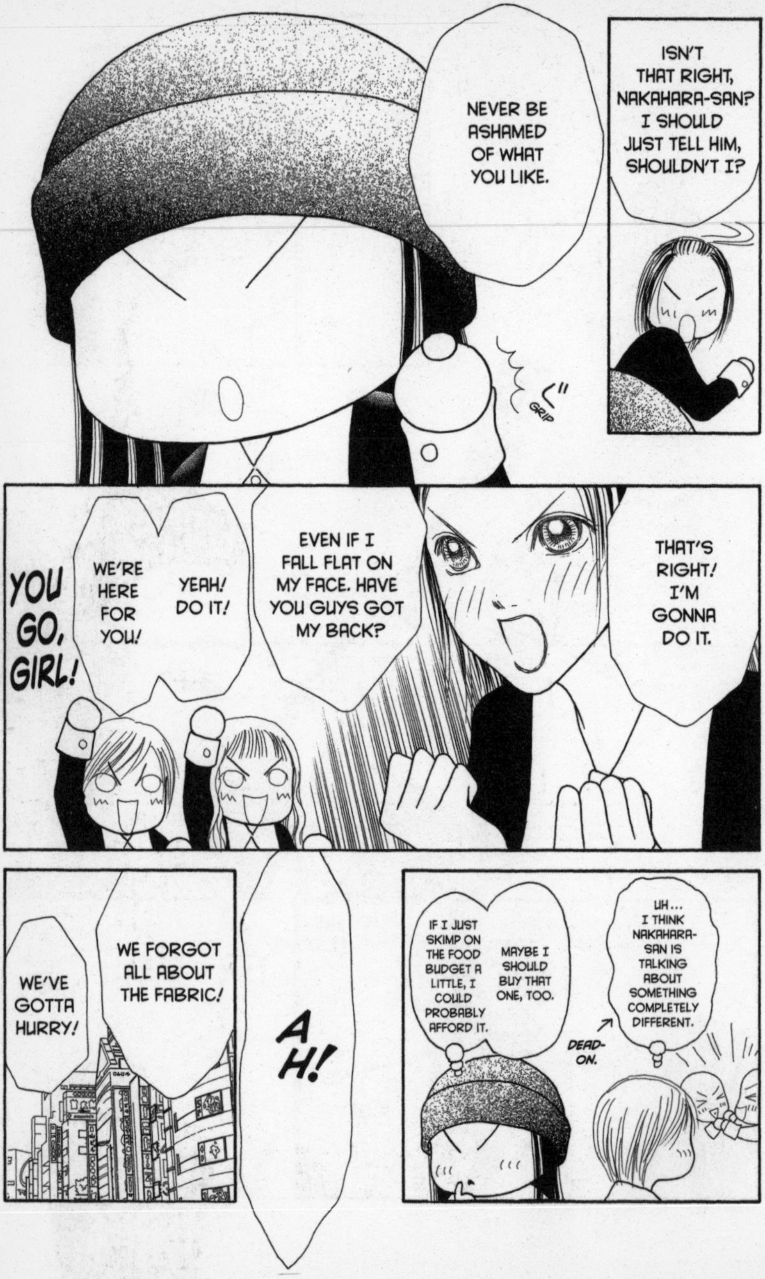
ISN'T THAT RIGHT, NAKAHARA-SAN? I SHOULD JUST TELL HIM, SHOULDN'T I?
NEVER BE ASHAMED OF WHAT YOU LIKE.
GRIP
THAT'S RIGHT! I'M GONNA DO IT.
EVEN IF I FALL FLAT ON MY FACE. HAVE YOU GUYS GOT MY BACK?
YEAH! DO IT!
WE'RE HERE FOR YOU!
YOU GO, GIRL!
UH... I THINK NAKAHARA-SAN IS TALKING ABOUT SOMETHING COMPLETELY DIFFERENT.
DEAD-ON.
MAYBE I SHOULD BUY THAT ONE, TOO.
IF I JUST SKIMP ON THE FOOD BUDGET A LITTLE, I COULD PROBABLY AFFORD IT.
AH!
WE FORGOT ALL ABOUT THE FABRIC!
WE'VE GOTTA HURRY!

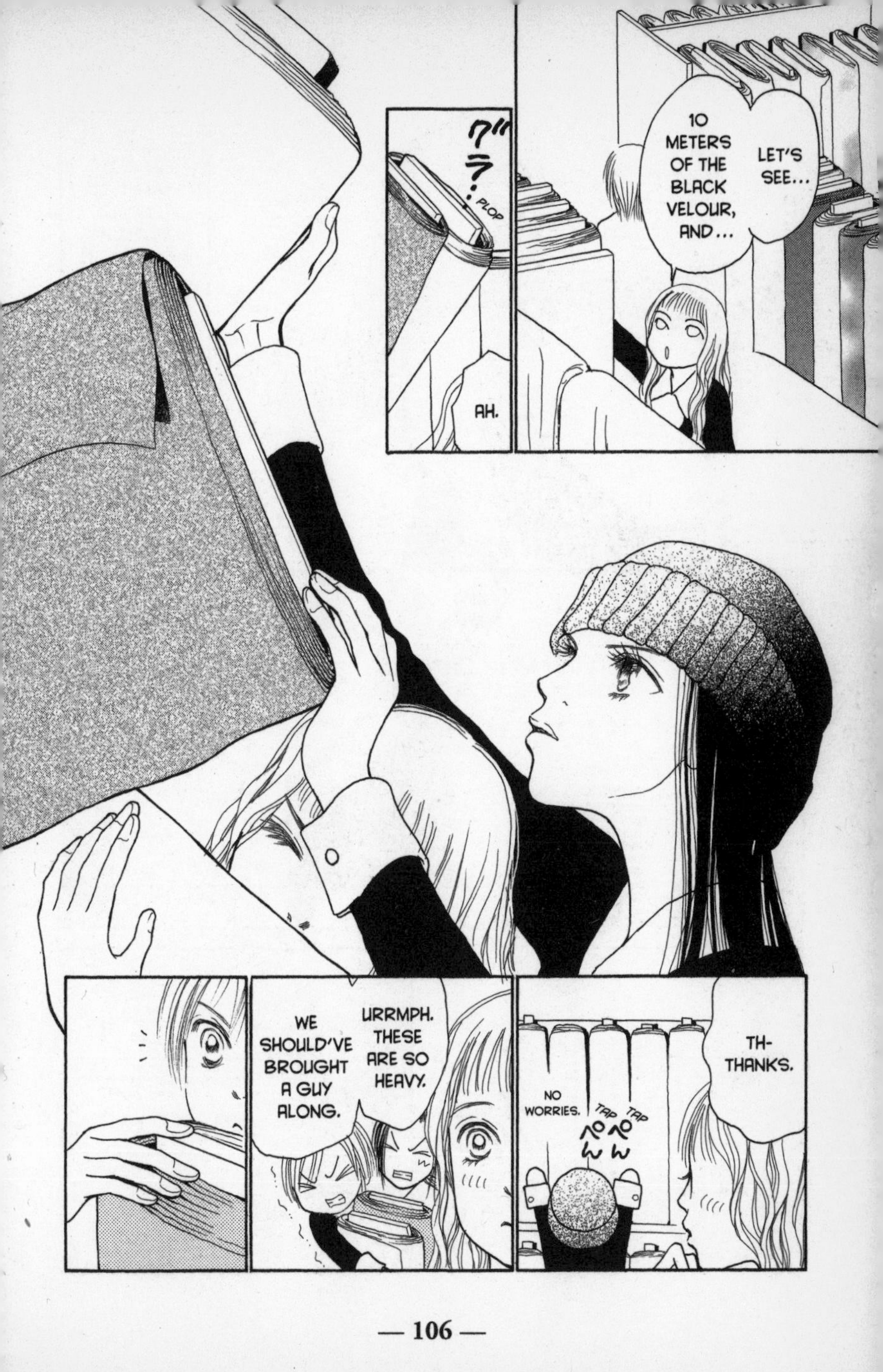
LET'S SEE...
10 METERS OF THE BLACK VELOUR, AND...
PLOP
AH.
TH- THANKS.
NO WORRIES.
TAP TAP
URRMPH. THESE ARE SO HEAVY.
WE SHOULD'VE BROUGHT A GUY ALONG.

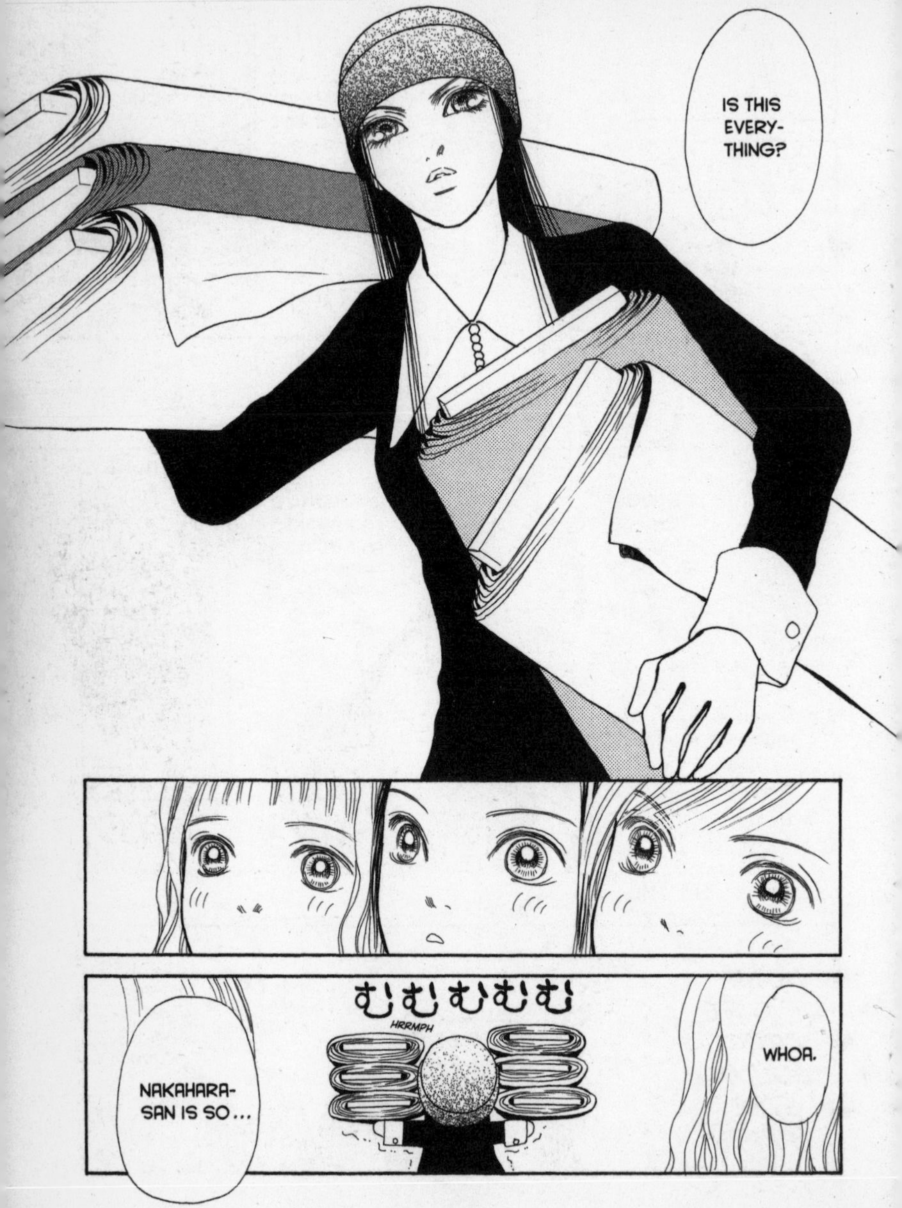
IS THIS EVERY-THING?
WHOA.
むむむむむ
HRRMPH
NAKAHARA-SAN IS SO...

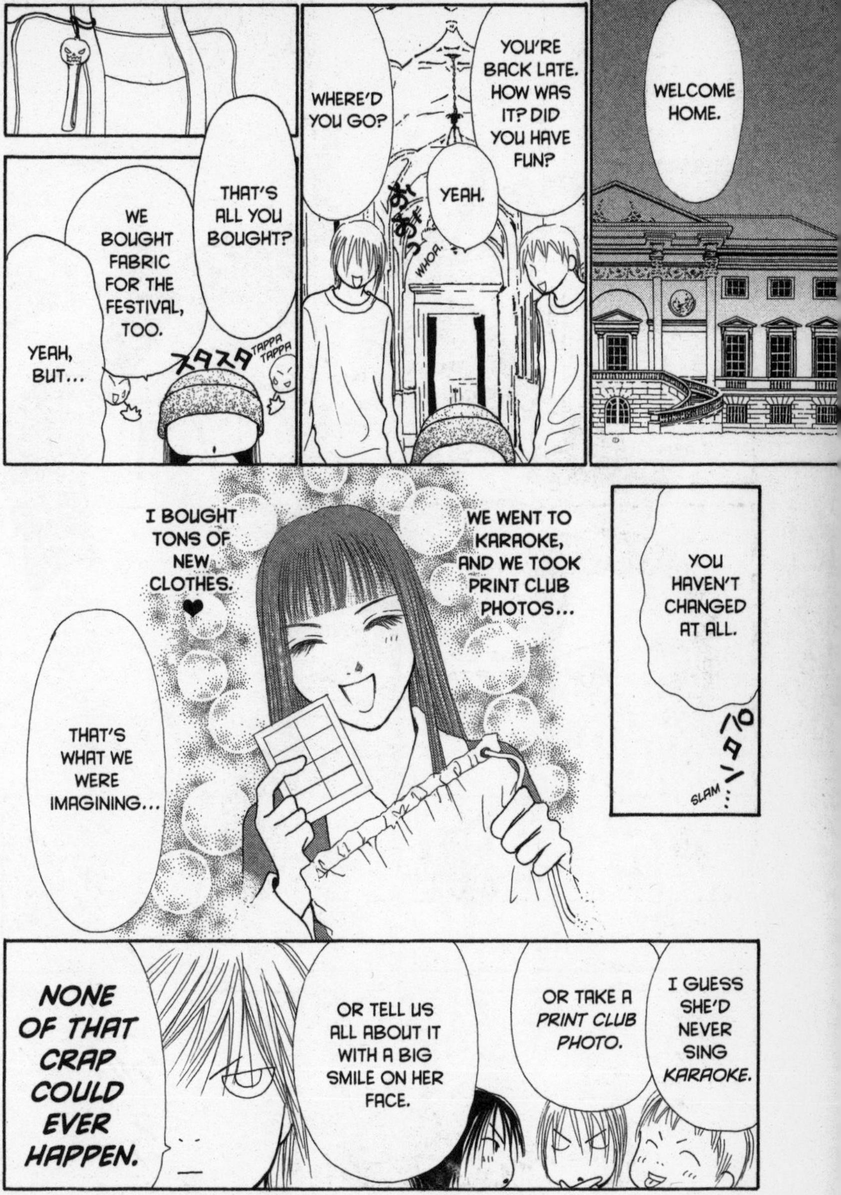
WELCOME HOME.
YOU'RE BACK LATE. HOW WAS IT? DID YOU HAVE FUN?
WHERE'D YOU GO?
YEAH.
WHOA.
THAT'S ALL YOU BOUGHT?
WE BOUGHT FABRIC FOR THE FESTIVAL, TOO.
TAPPA TAPPA
スタスタ
YEAH, BUT...
YOU HAVEN'T CHANGED AT ALL.
パタン
SLAM...
WE WENT TO KARAOKE, AND WE TOOK PRINT CLUB PHOTOS...
I BOUGHT TONS OF NEW CLOTHES. ♥
THAT'S WHAT WE WERE IMAGINING...
I GUESS SHE'D NEVER SING *KARAOKE*.
OR TAKE A *PRINT CLUB PHOTO*.
OR TELL US ALL ABOUT IT WITH A BIG SMILE ON HER FACE.
NONE OF THAT CRAP COULD EVER HAPPEN.

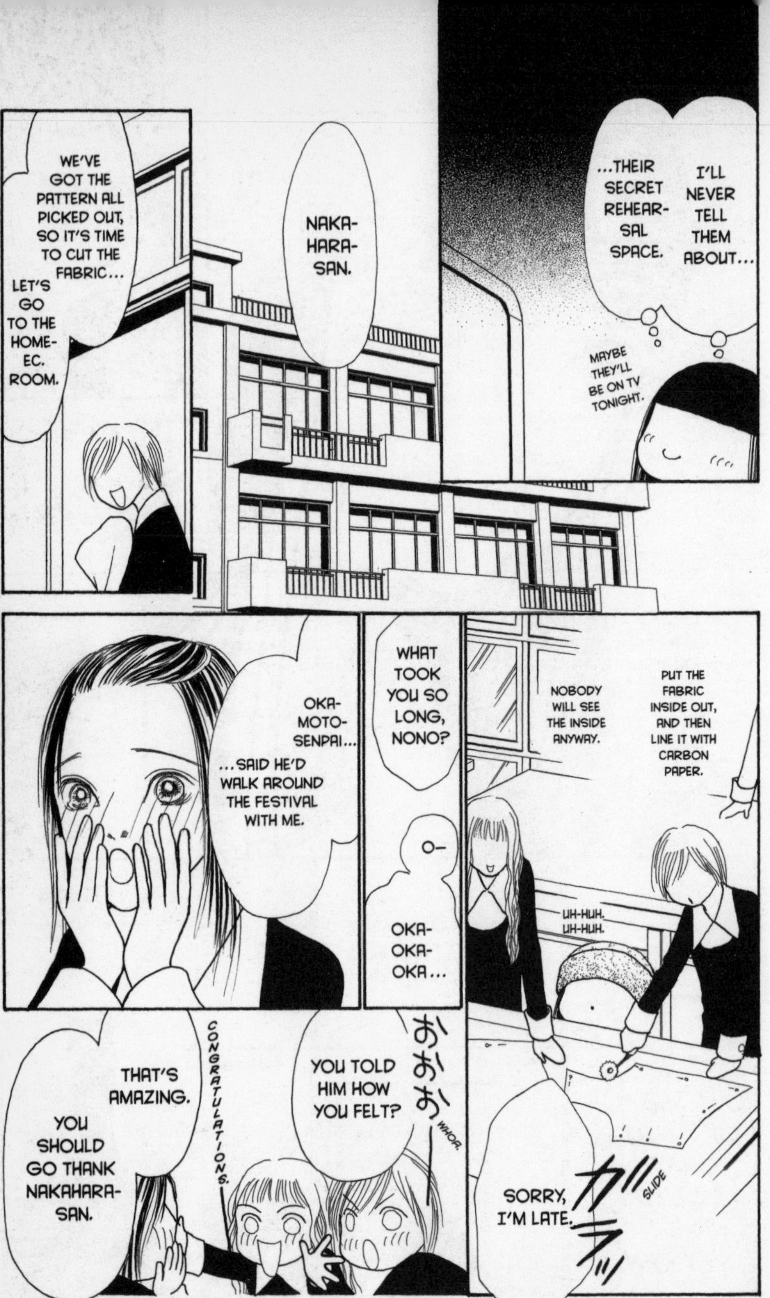
I'LL NEVER TELL THEM ABOUT...
...THEIR SECRET REHEAR-SAL SPACE.
MAYBE THEY'LL BE ON TV TONIGHT.
NAKA-HARA-SAN.
WE'VE GOT THE PATTERN ALL PICKED OUT, SO IT'S TIME TO CUT THE FABRIC...
LET'S GO TO THE HOME-EC. ROOM.
PUT THE FABRIC INSIDE OUT, AND THEN LINE IT WITH CARBON PAPER.
NOBODY WILL SEE THE INSIDE ANYWAY.
UH-HUH. UH-HUH.
SLIDE
SORRY, I'M LATE.
WHAT TOOK YOU SO LONG, NONO?
O–
OKA-OKA-OKA...
OKA-MOTO-SENPAI...
...SAID HE'D WALK AROUND THE FESTIVAL WITH ME.
おおお
WHOA.
YOU TOLD HIM HOW YOU FELT?
CONGRATULATIONS.
THAT'S AMAZING.
YOU SHOULD GO THANK NAKAHARA-SAN.

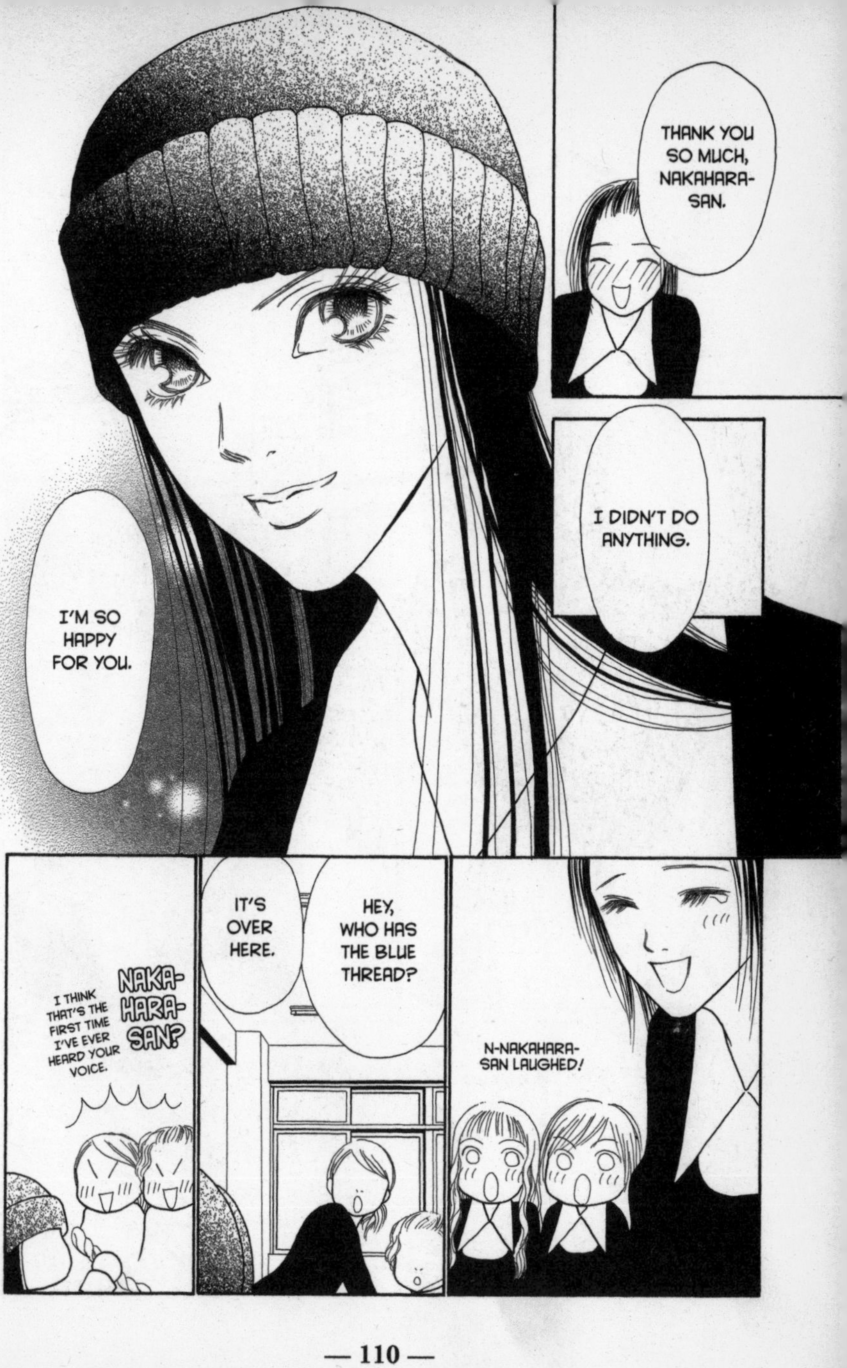
THANK YOU SO MUCH, NAKAHARA-SAN.
I DIDN'T DO ANYTHING.
I'M SO HAPPY FOR YOU.
N-NAKAHARA-SAN LAUGHED!
HEY, WHO HAS THE BLUE THREAD?
IT'S OVER HERE.
NAKA-HARA-SAN?
I THINK THAT'S THE FIRST TIME I'VE EVER HEARD YOUR VOICE.

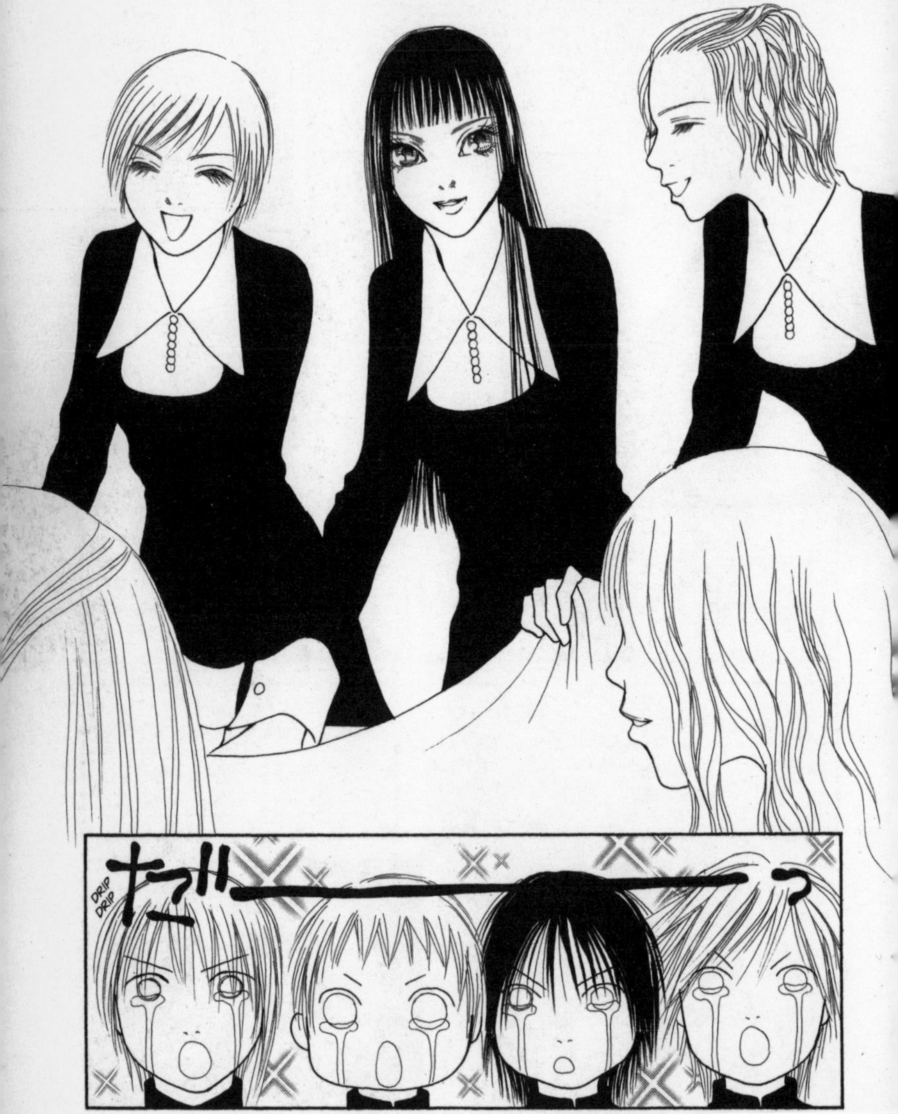
DRIP DRIP
たっ‥―――っ

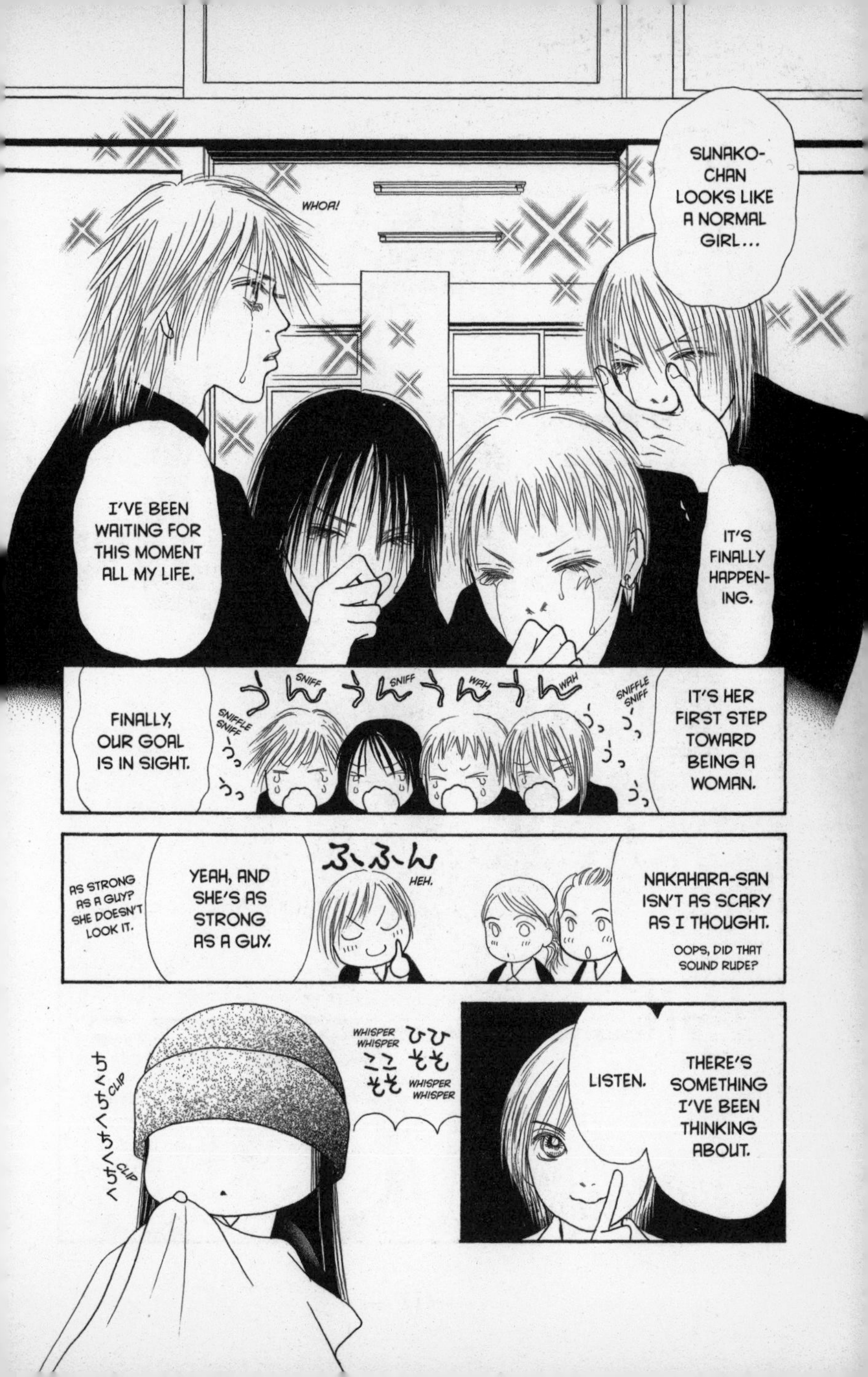
SUNAKO-CHAN LOOKS LIKE A NORMAL GIRL...
WHOA!
IT'S FINALLY HAPPENING.
I'VE BEEN WAITING FOR THIS MOMENT ALL MY LIFE.
IT'S HER FIRST STEP TOWARD BEING A WOMAN.
SNIFFLE SNIFF
うんうんうんうん
SNIFF SNIFF WAH WAH
SNIFFLE SNIFF
FINALLY, OUR GOAL IS IN SIGHT.
NAKAHARA-SAN ISN'T AS SCARY AS I THOUGHT.
OOPS, DID THAT SOUND RUDE?
ふふん
HEH.
YEAH, AND SHE'S AS STRONG AS A GUY.
AS STRONG AS A GUY? SHE DOESN'T LOOK IT.
LISTEN.
THERE'S SOMETHING I'VE BEEN THINKING ABOUT.
ひそひそ
WHISPER WHISPER
こそこそ
WHISPER WHISPER
ちくちく
CLIP
ちくちく
CLIP

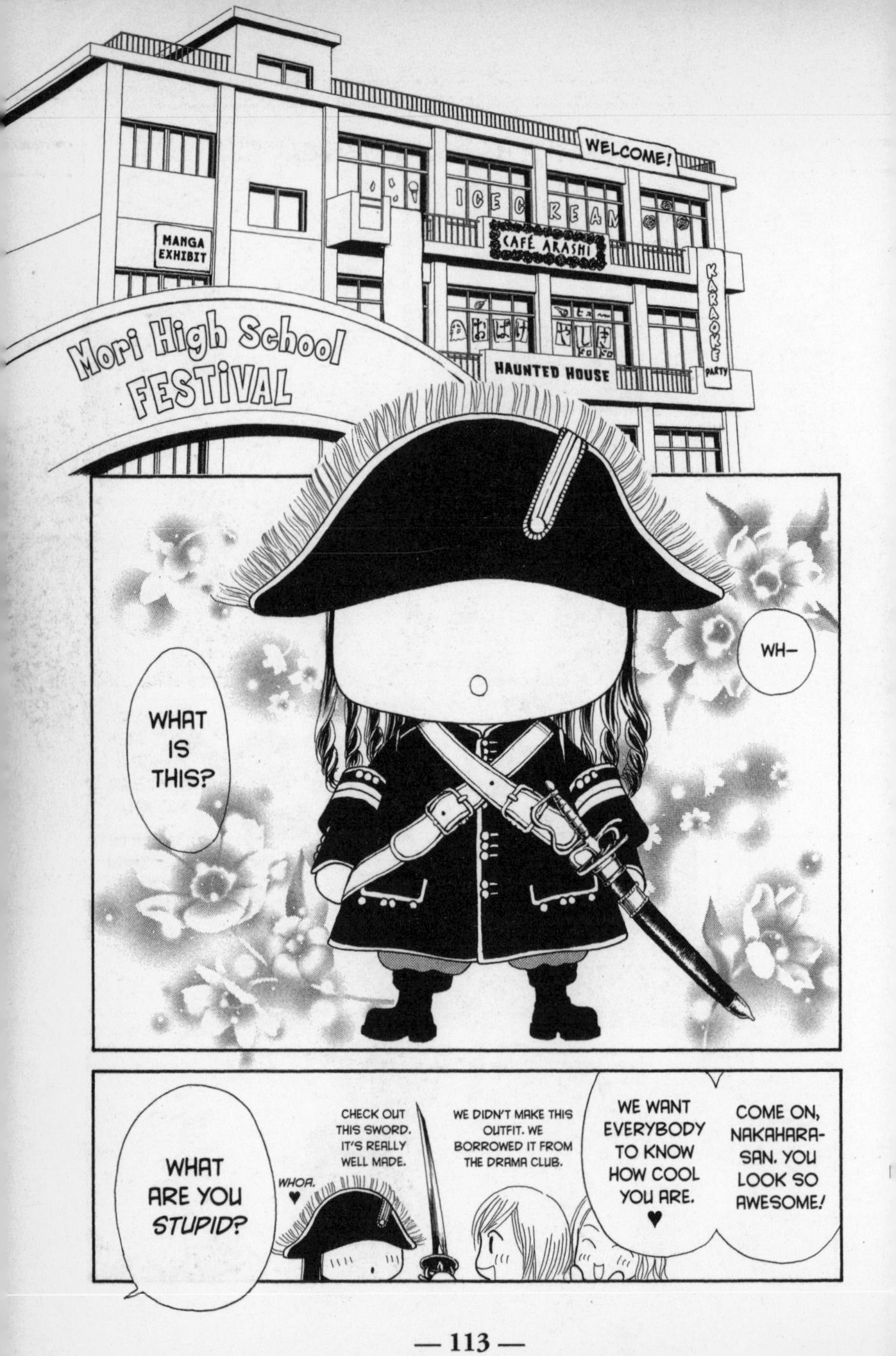
WELCOME!
ICE CREAM
CAFÉ ARASHI
KARAOKE PARTY
おばけやしき
HAUNTED HOUSE
MANGA EXHIBIT
Mori High School FESTIVAL
WH–
WHAT IS THIS?
COME ON, NAKAHARA-SAN. YOU LOOK SO AWESOME!
WE WANT EVERYBODY TO KNOW HOW COOL YOU ARE. ♥
WE DIDN'T MAKE THIS OUTFIT. WE BORROWED IT FROM THE DRAMA CLUB.
CHECK OUT THIS SWORD. IT'S REALLY WELL MADE.
WHOA. ♥
WHAT ARE YOU STUPID?

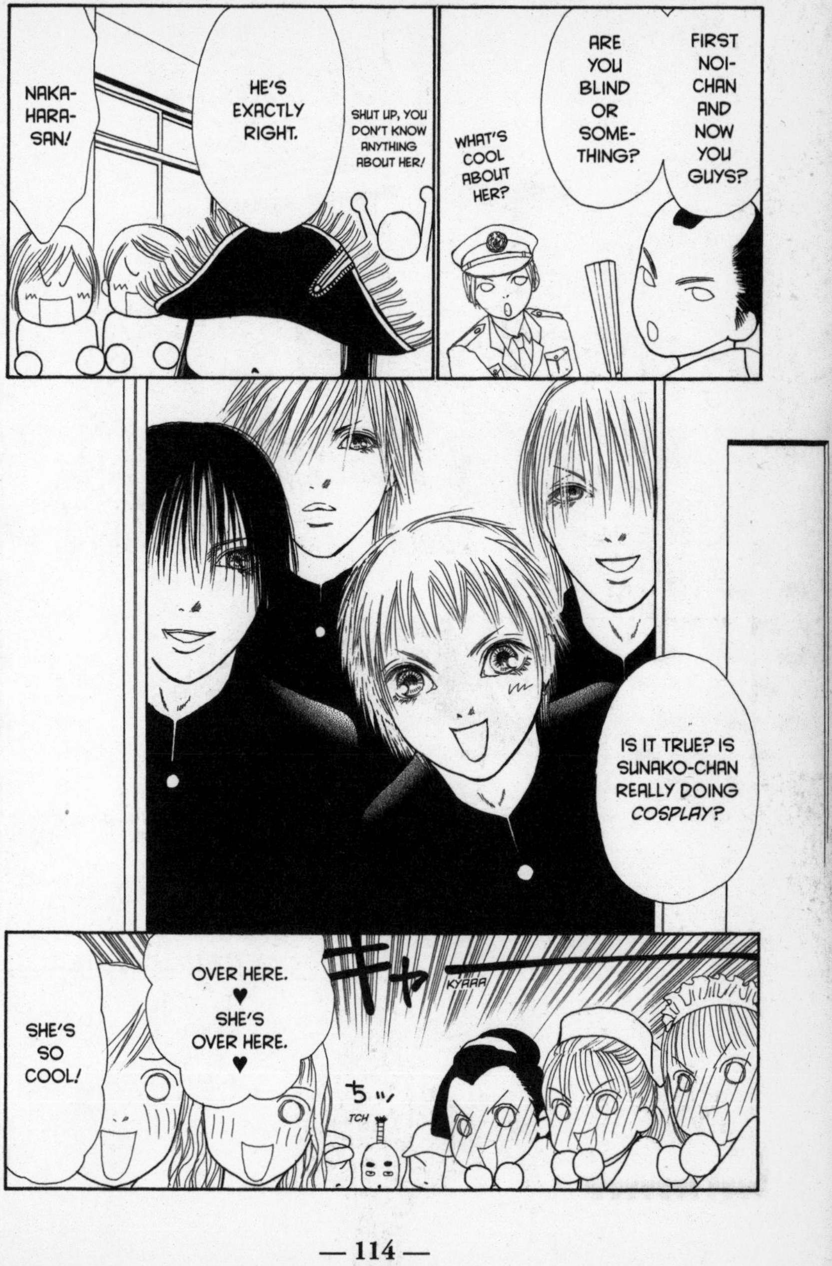
FIRST NOI-CHAN AND NOW YOU GUYS?
ARE YOU BLIND OR SOME-THING?
WHAT'S COOL ABOUT HER?
SHUT UP, YOU DON'T KNOW ANYTHING ABOUT HER!
HE'S EXACTLY RIGHT.
NAKA-HARA-SAN!
IS IT TRUE? IS SUNAKO-CHAN REALLY DOING *COSPLAY?*
キャー
KYAAA
ちッ
TCH
OVER HERE. ♥ SHE'S OVER HERE. ♥
SHE'S SO COOL!

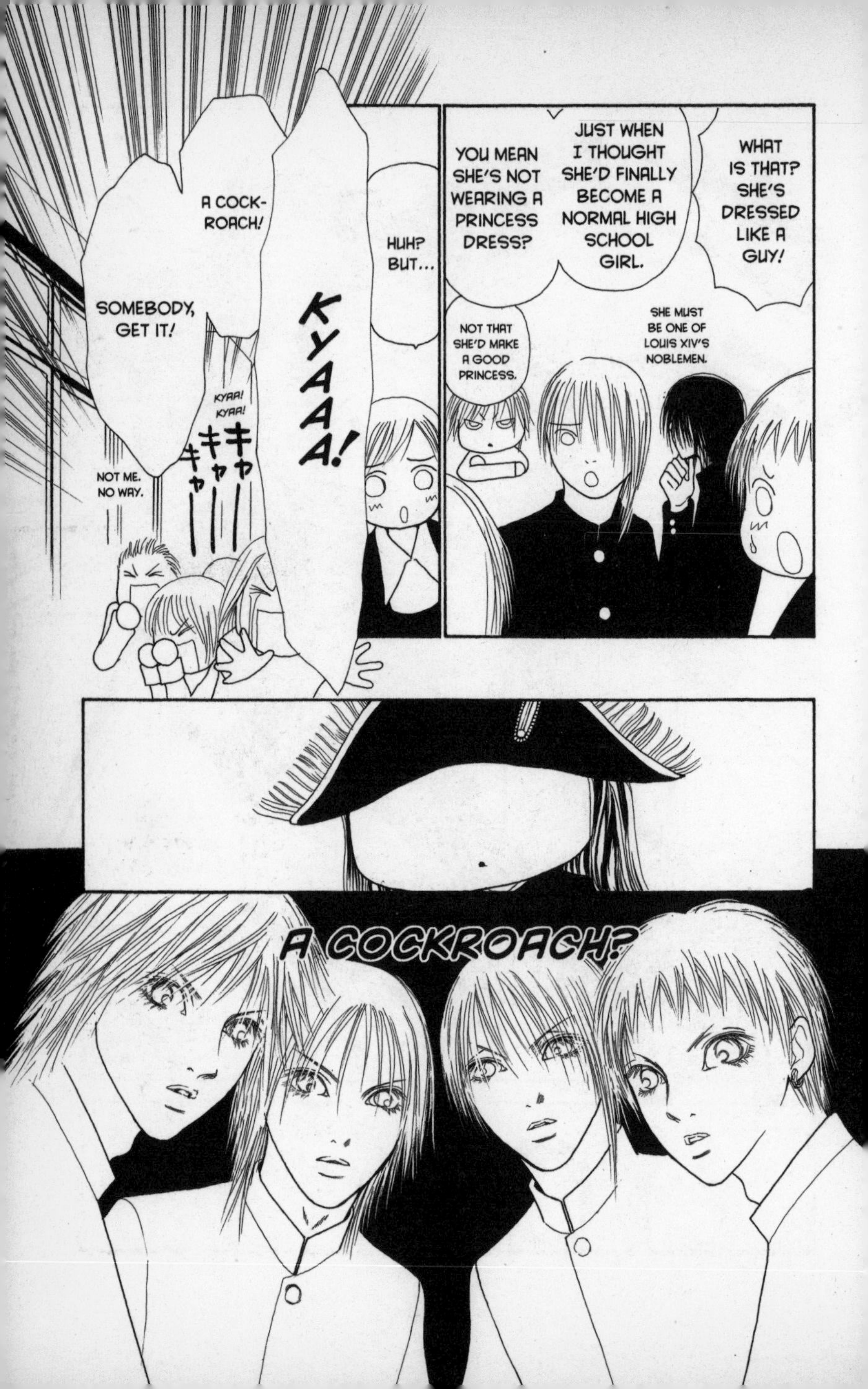
WHAT IS THAT? SHE'S DRESSED LIKE A GUY!
JUST WHEN I THOUGHT SHE'D FINALLY BECOME A NORMAL HIGH SCHOOL GIRL.
YOU MEAN SHE'S NOT WEARING A PRINCESS DRESS?
SHE MUST BE ONE OF LOUIS XIV'S NOBLEMEN.
NOT THAT SHE'D MAKE A GOOD PRINCESS.
HUH? BUT...
KYAAAA!
A COCK-ROACH!
SOMEBODY, GET IT!
KYAA! KYAA!
キャー キャー
NOT ME. NO WAY.
A COCKROACH?

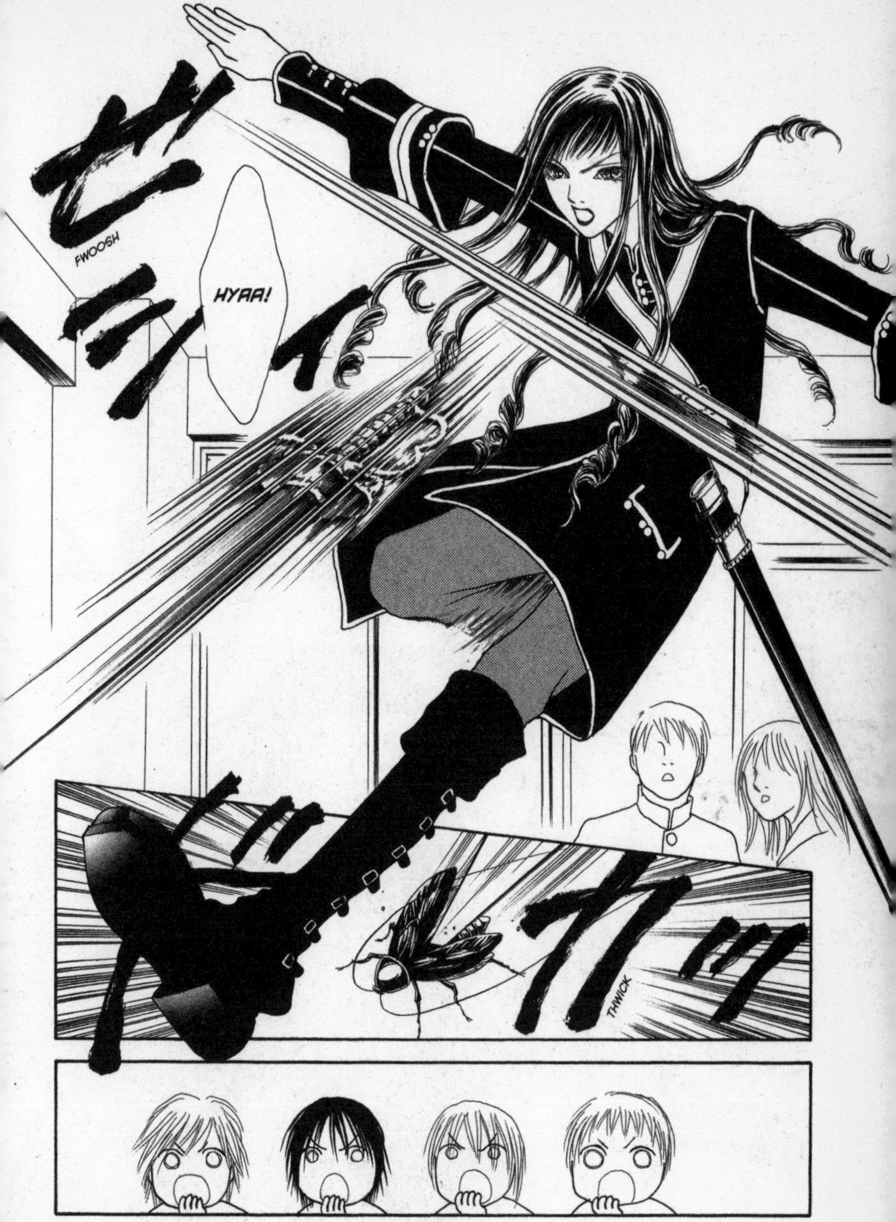
HYAA!
FWOOSH
THWICK

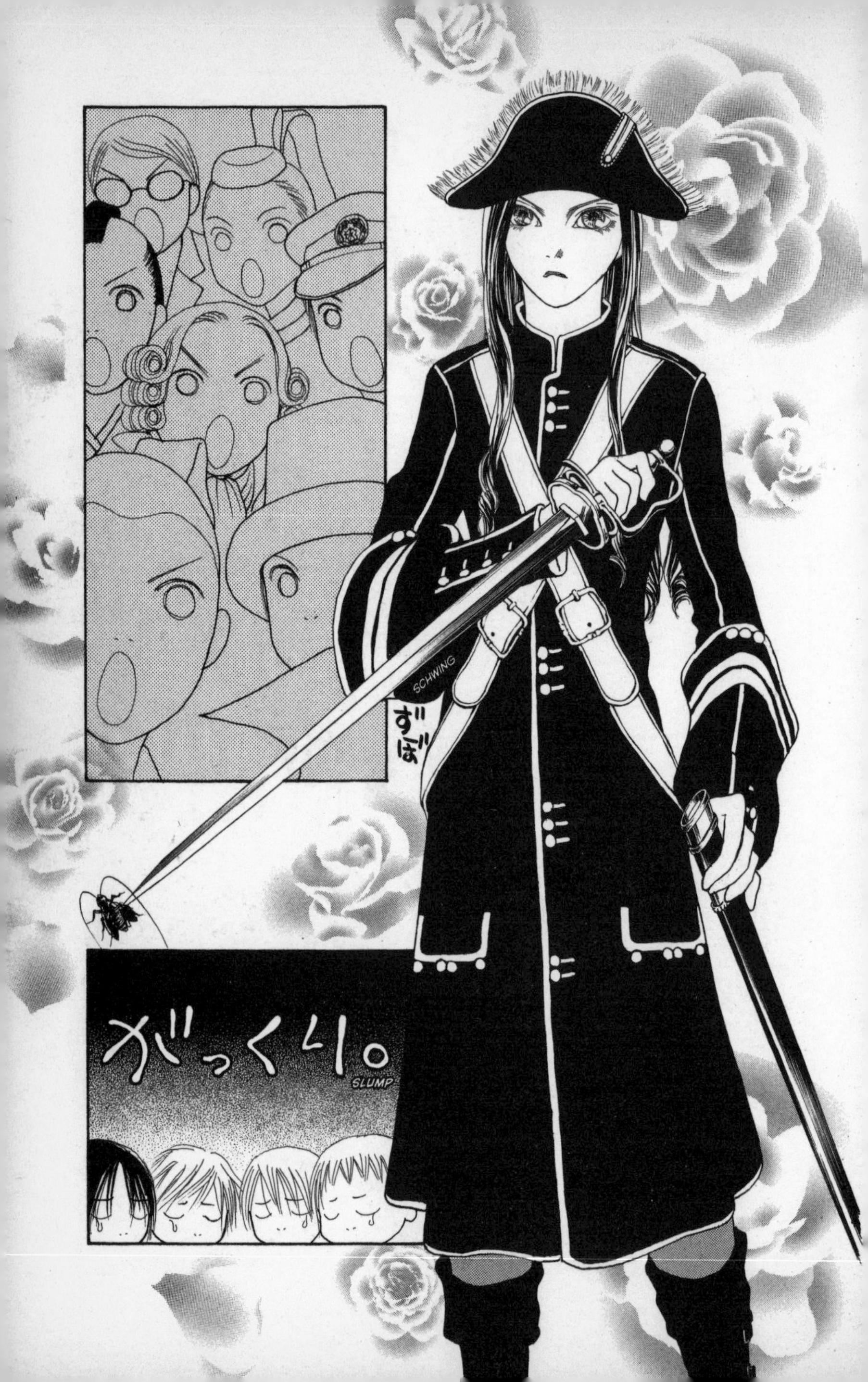
SCHWING
ずぼ
がっくり。
SLUMP

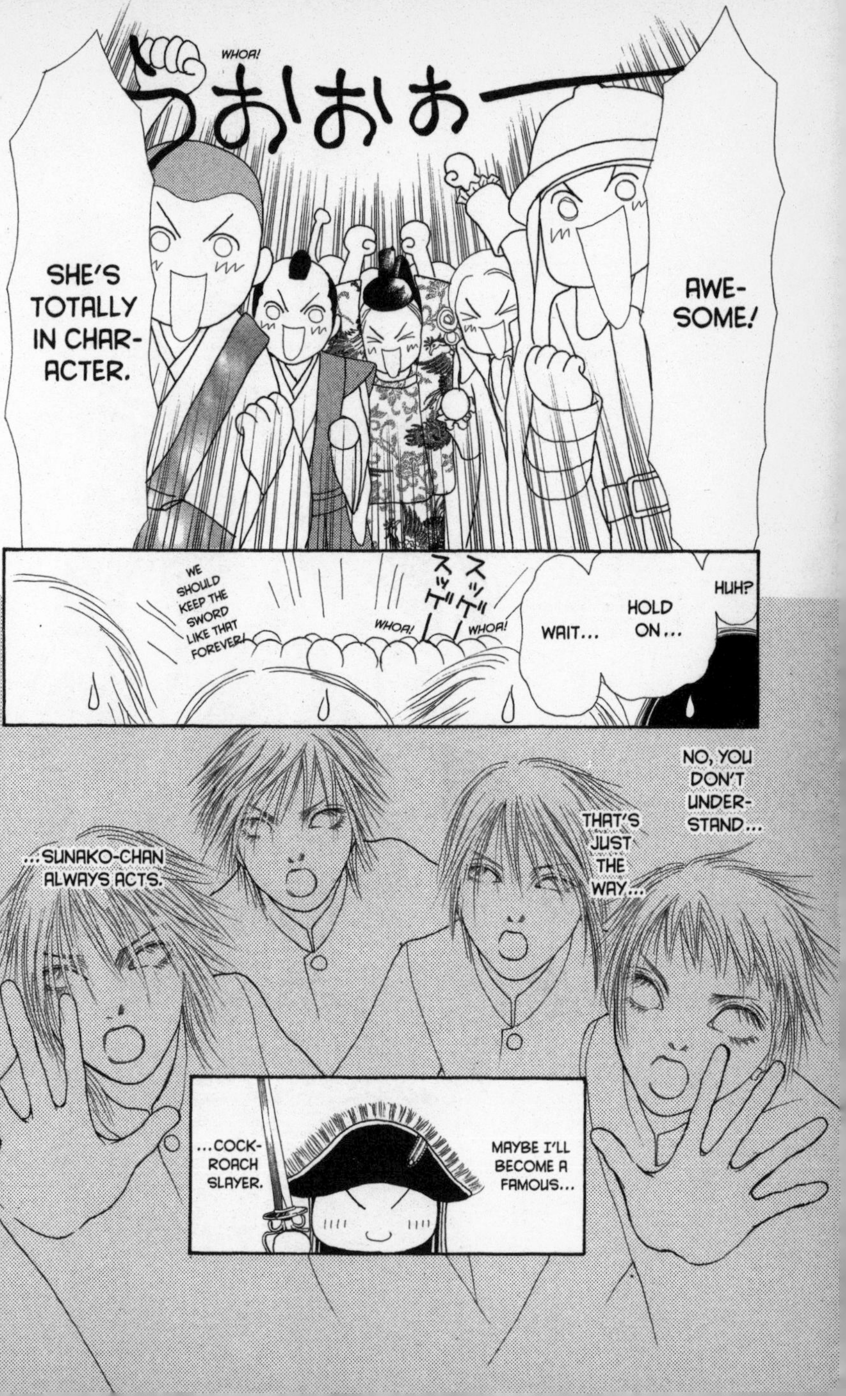
WHOA!
うお!お!ぉー
AWE-SOME!
SHE'S TOTALLY IN CHAR-ACTER.
HUH?
HOLD ON...
WAIT...
スッゲ
WHOA!
スッゲ
WHOA!
WE SHOULD KEEP THE SWORD LIKE THAT FOREVER!
NO, YOU DON'T UNDER-STAND...
THAT'S JUST THE WAY...
...SUNAKO-CHAN ALWAYS ACTS.
MAYBE I'LL BECOME A FAMOUS...
...COCK-ROACH SLAYER.

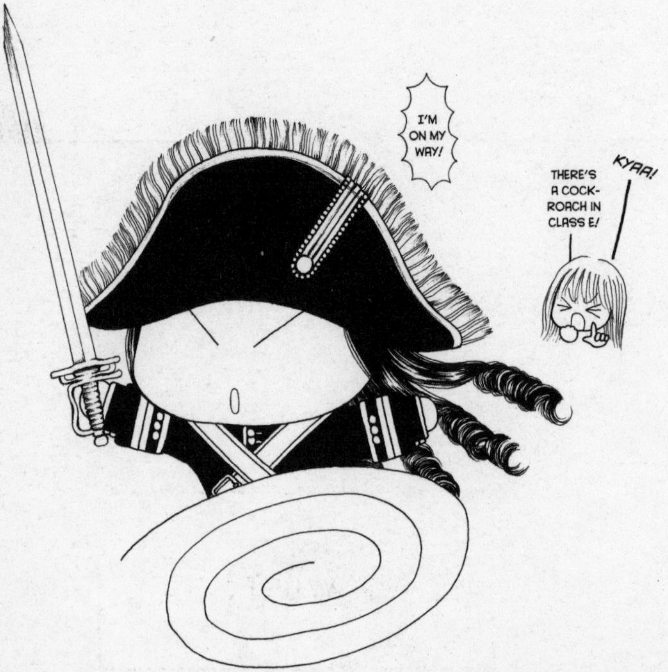
KYAA!
THERE'S A COCK-ROACH IN CLASS E!
I'M ON MY WAY!

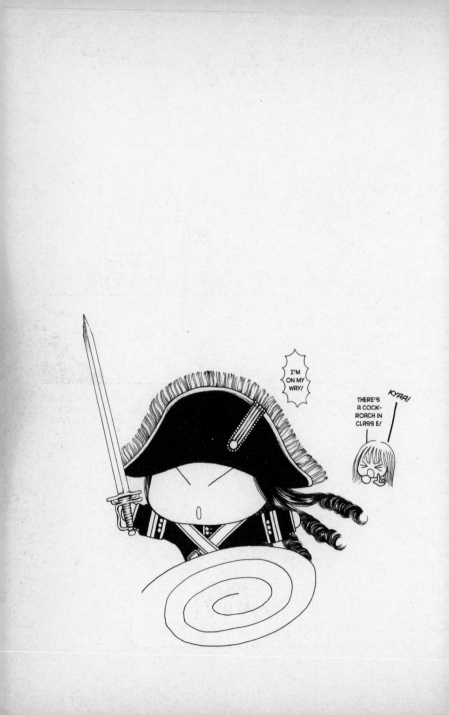

Chapter 50
Do It for the Fried Shrimp

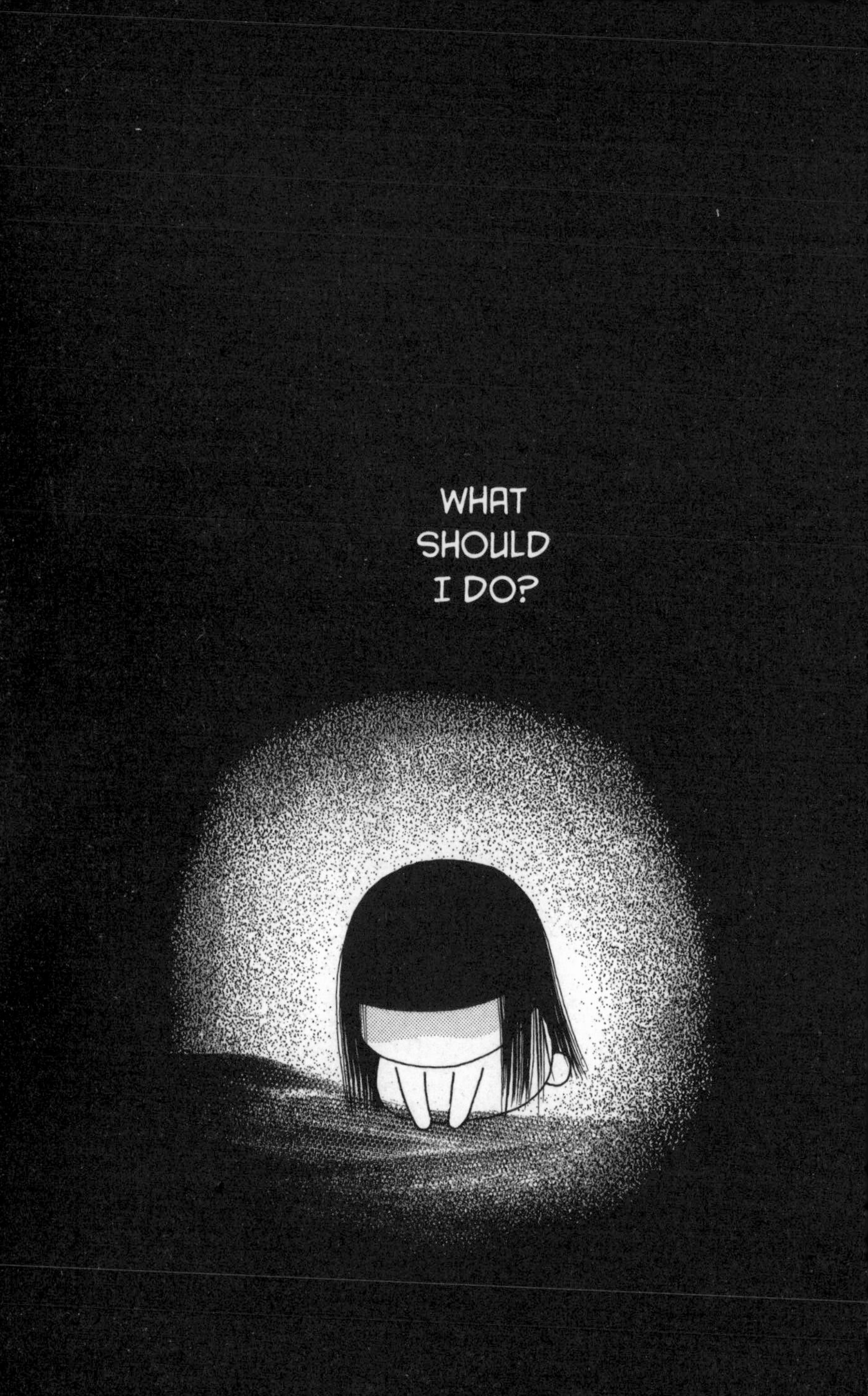
WHAT SHOULD I DO?

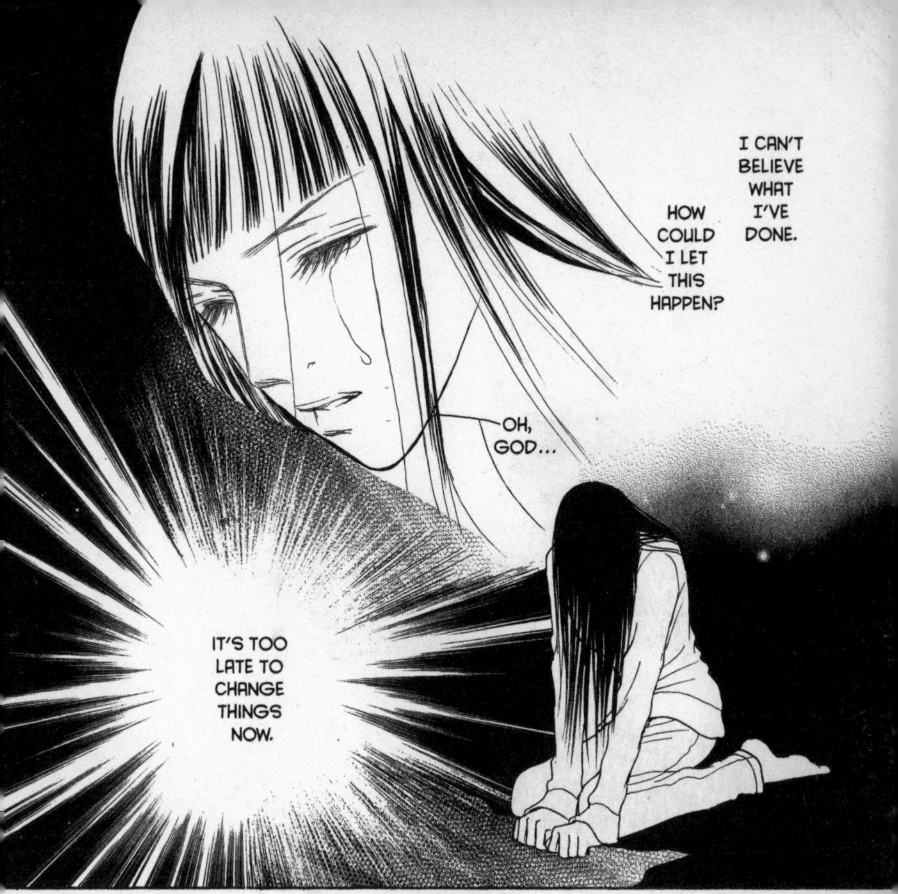
I CAN'T BELIEVE WHAT I'VE DONE.
HOW COULD I LET THIS HAPPEN?
OH, GOD...
IT'S TOO LATE TO CHANGE THINGS NOW.

BEHIND THE SCENES

WHILE I WAS WORKING ON THE STORYBOARDS FOR THIS STORY... SOMETHING TRAGICALLY SAD HAPPENED AND SOMETHING AMAZINGLY JOYOUS HAPPENED AS WELL.

THE TRAGIC THING WAS THAT... BAROQUE ANNOUNCED THAT THEY WERE BREAKING UP. WHENEVER I THINK ABOUT IT, I START CRYING, SO I TRY NOT TO THINK ABOUT IT... BUT THEN I THINK OF IT ANYWAY, AND BURST INTO TEARS... THAT'S WHAT MY LIFE HAS BEEN LIKE. IT LEFT ME MUCH MORE SHOCKED THAN I WOULD'VE IMAGINED, AND I BARELY HAD THE STRENGTH TO CARRY ON. I WAS LUCKY I FINISHED THE STORY.

THE JOYOUS THING WAS THAT... I SAW KIYOHARU IN CONCERT. ♥♥♥ AFTER NINE WHOLE MONTHS! (SEE VOLUME 11 FOR DETAILS) THAT DAY, I CRIED TEARS OF JOY.

I CRIED WHEN I WAS HAPPY. I CRIED WHEN I WAS SAD. IT SEEMS LIKE I CRIED EVERY SINGLE DAY.

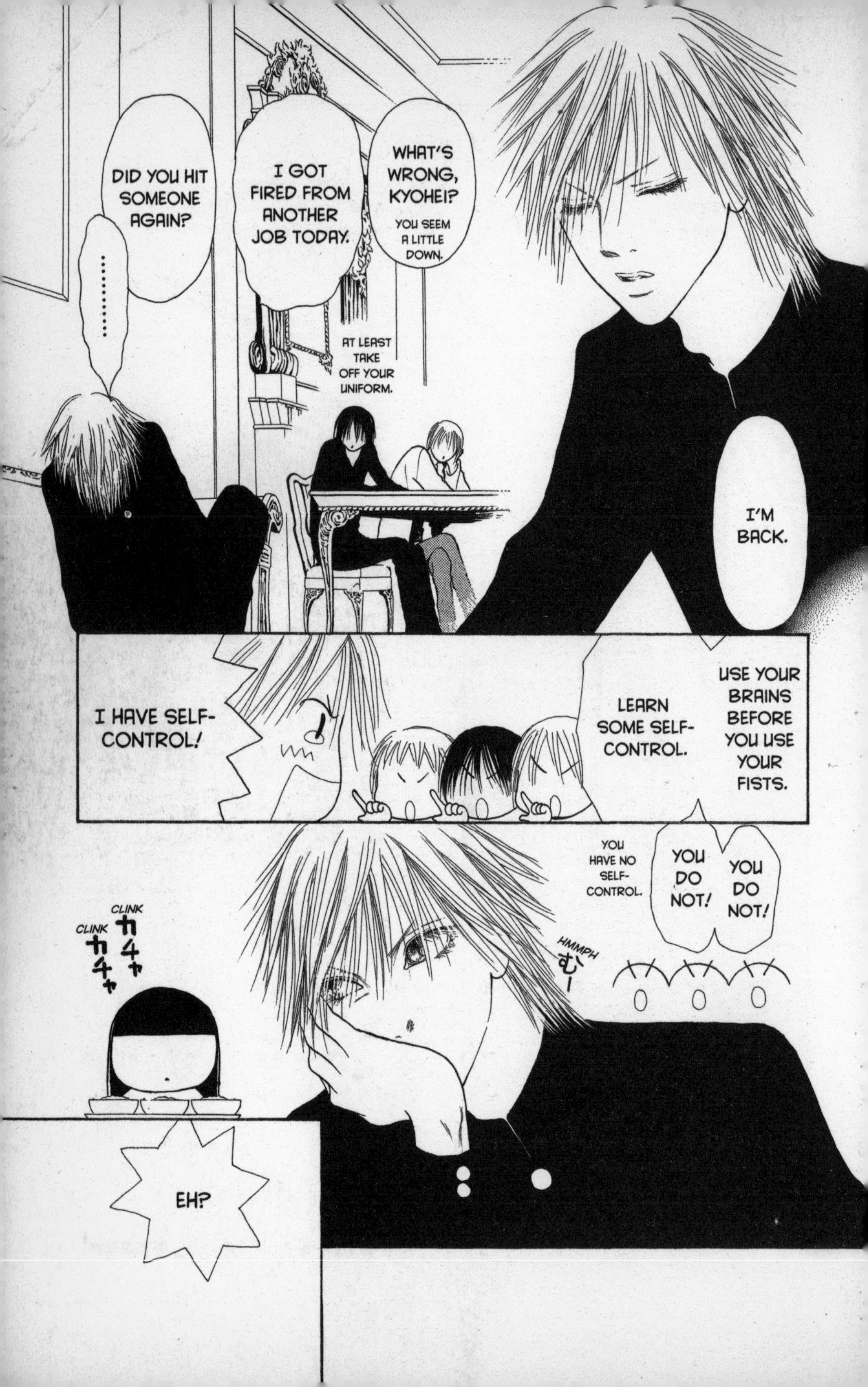
I'M BACK.
WHAT'S WRONG, KYOHEI?
YOU SEEM A LITTLE DOWN.
AT LEAST TAKE OFF YOUR UNIFORM.
I GOT FIRED FROM ANOTHER JOB TODAY.
DID YOU HIT SOMEONE AGAIN?
……
USE YOUR BRAINS BEFORE YOU USE YOUR FISTS.
LEARN SOME SELF-CONTROL.
I HAVE SELF-CONTROL!
YOU DO NOT!
YOU DO NOT!
YOU HAVE NO SELF-CONTROL.
HMMPH
むー
CLINK
カチャ
CLINK
カチャ
EH?

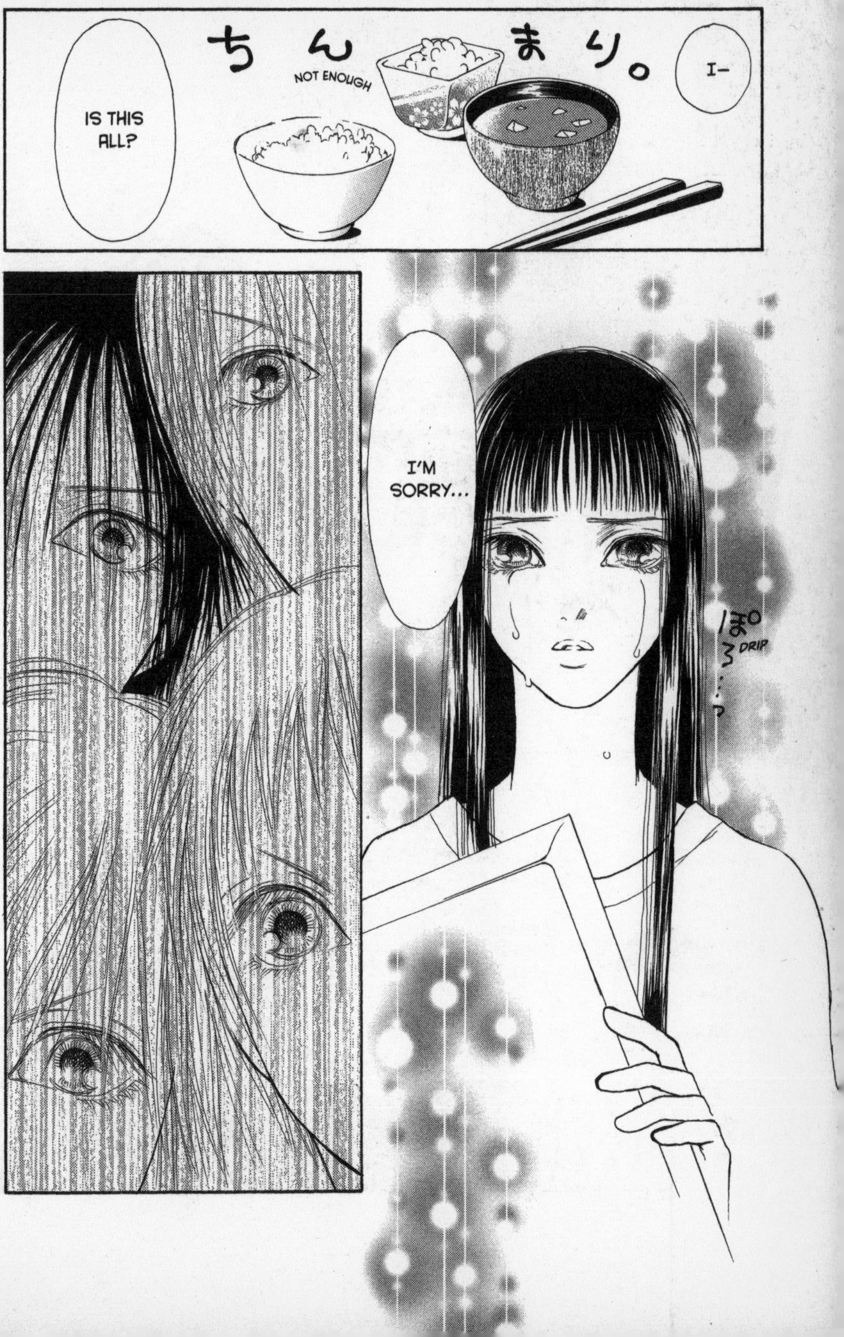
I–
ちんまり。
NOT ENOUGH
IS THIS ALL?
ぽろ…
DRIP
I'M SORRY...

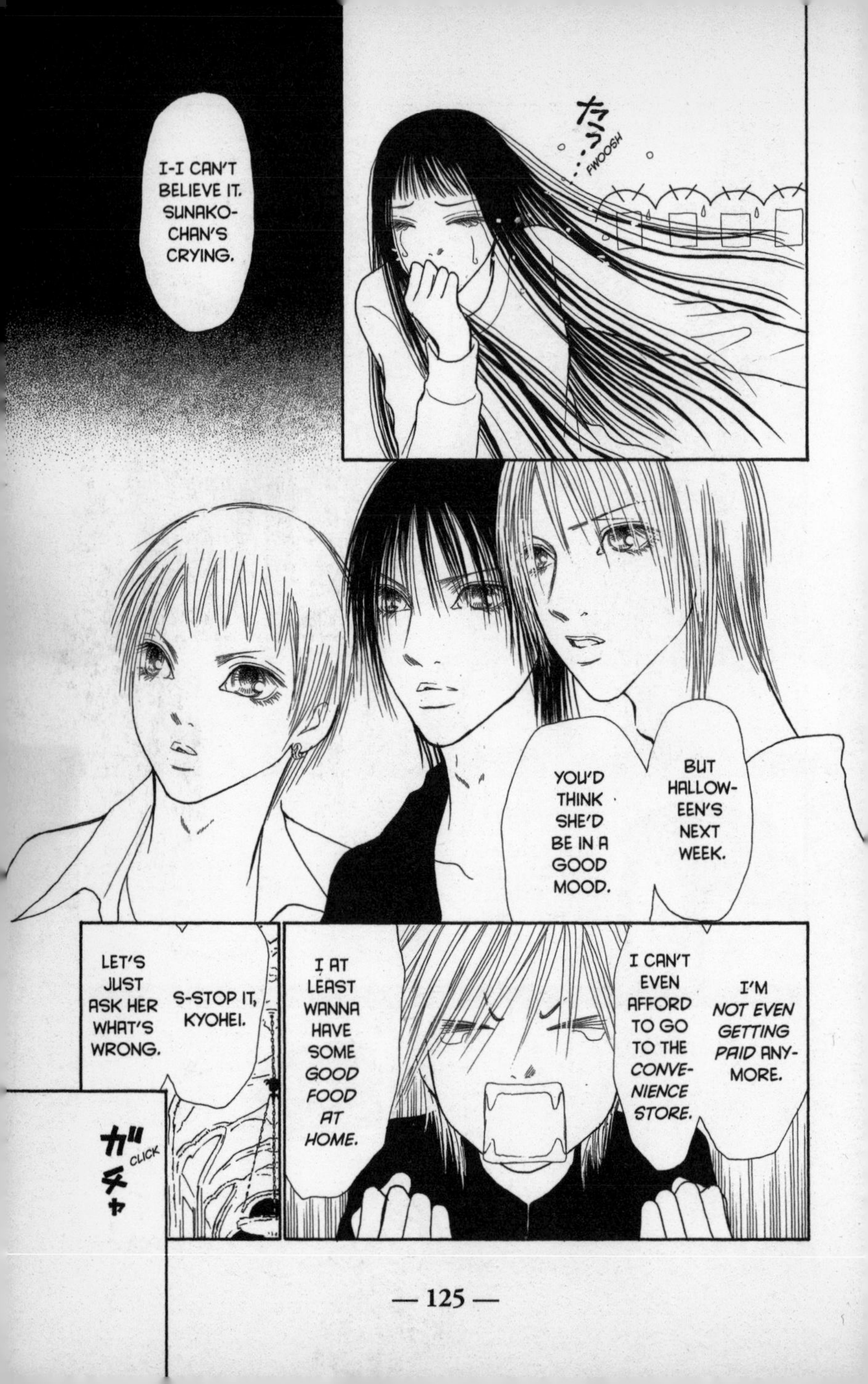
たらっ
FWOOSH
I-I CAN'T BELIEVE IT. SUNAKO-CHAN'S CRYING.
BUT HALLOWEEN'S NEXT WEEK.
YOU'D THINK SHE'D BE IN A GOOD MOOD.
I'M NOT EVEN GETTING PAID ANYMORE.
I CAN'T EVEN AFFORD TO GO TO THE CONVENIENCE STORE.
I AT LEAST WANNA HAVE SOME GOOD FOOD AT HOME.
S-STOP IT, KYOHEI.
LET'S JUST ASK HER WHAT'S WRONG.
ガチャ
CLICK

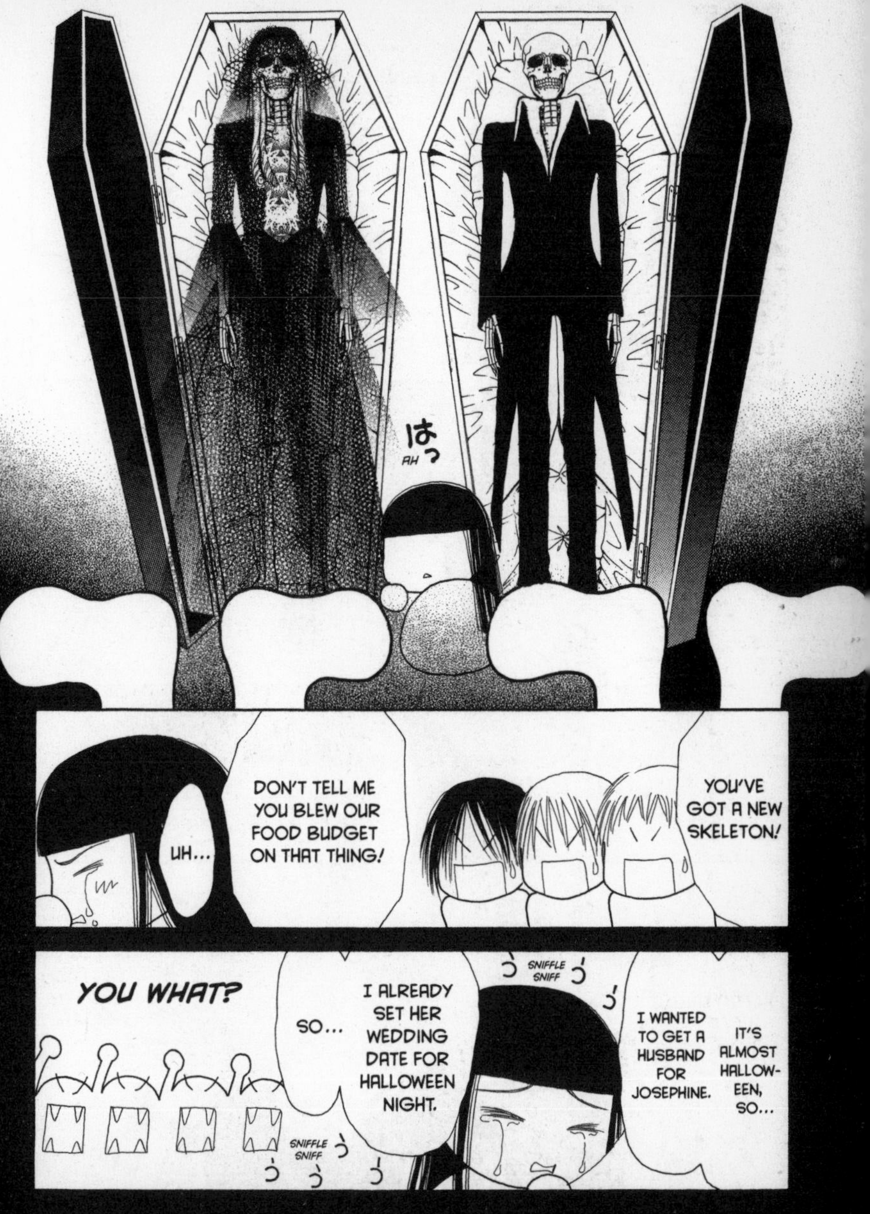
はっ
AH
YOU'VE GOT A NEW SKELETON!
DON'T TELL ME YOU BLEW OUR FOOD BUDGET ON THAT THING!
UH...
IT'S ALMOST HALLOWEEN, SO...
I WANTED TO GET A HUSBAND FOR JOSEPHINE.
SNIFFLE SNIFF
I ALREADY SET HER WEDDING DATE FOR HALLOWEEN NIGHT.
SO...
SNIFFLE SNIFF
YOU WHAT?

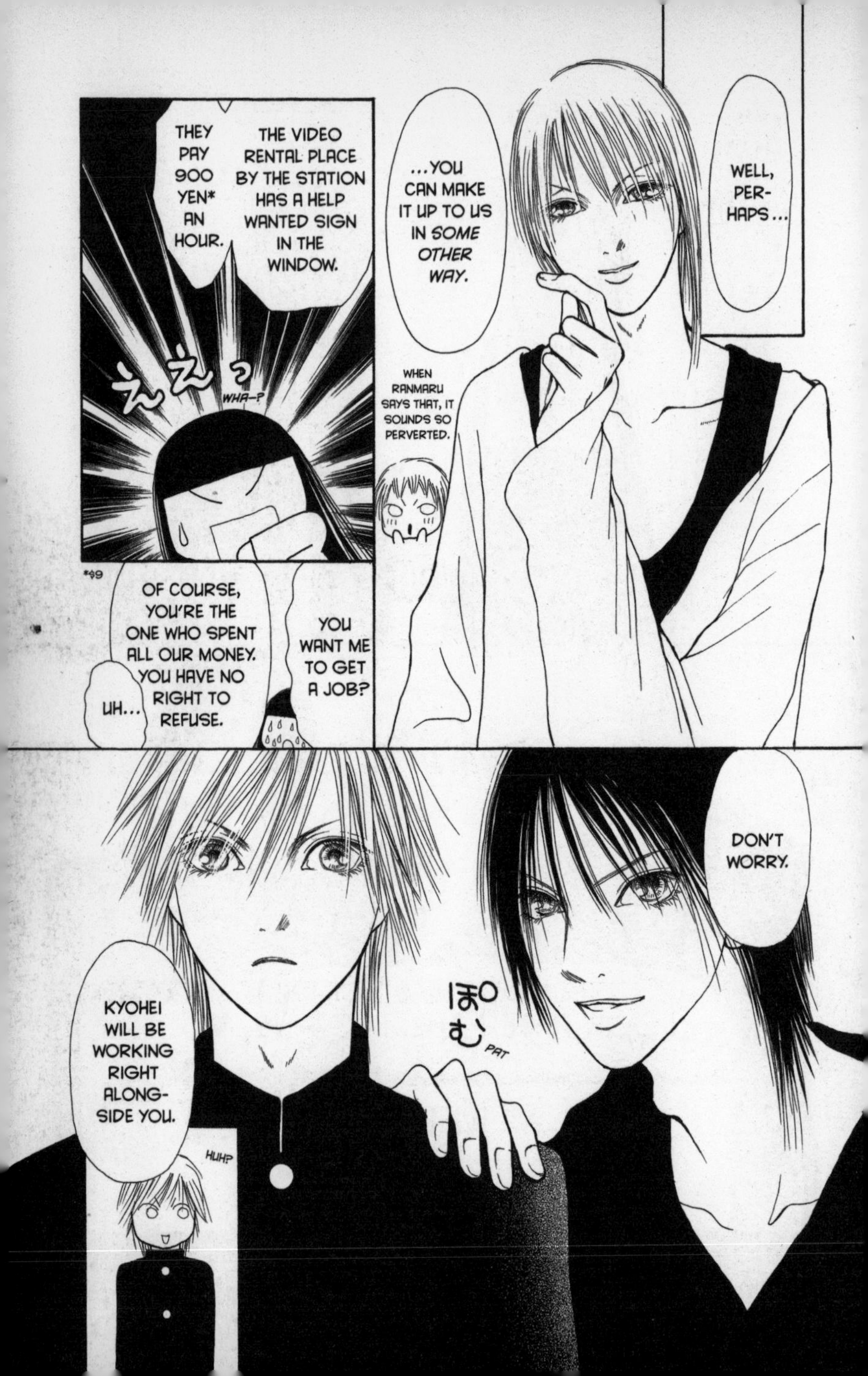
WELL, PER-HAPS...
...YOU CAN MAKE IT UP TO US IN *SOME OTHER WAY.*
WHEN RANMARU SAYS THAT, IT SOUNDS SO PERVERTED.
THE VIDEO RENTAL PLACE BY THE STATION HAS A HELP WANTED SIGN IN THE WINDOW.
THEY PAY 900 YEN* AN HOUR.
えぇっ
WHA-?
YOU WANT ME TO GET A JOB?
OF COURSE, YOU'RE THE ONE WHO SPENT ALL OUR MONEY. YOU HAVE NO RIGHT TO REFUSE.
UH...
DON'T WORRY.
KYOHEI WILL BE WORKING RIGHT ALONG-SIDE YOU.
ぽむ
PAT
HUH?
*$9

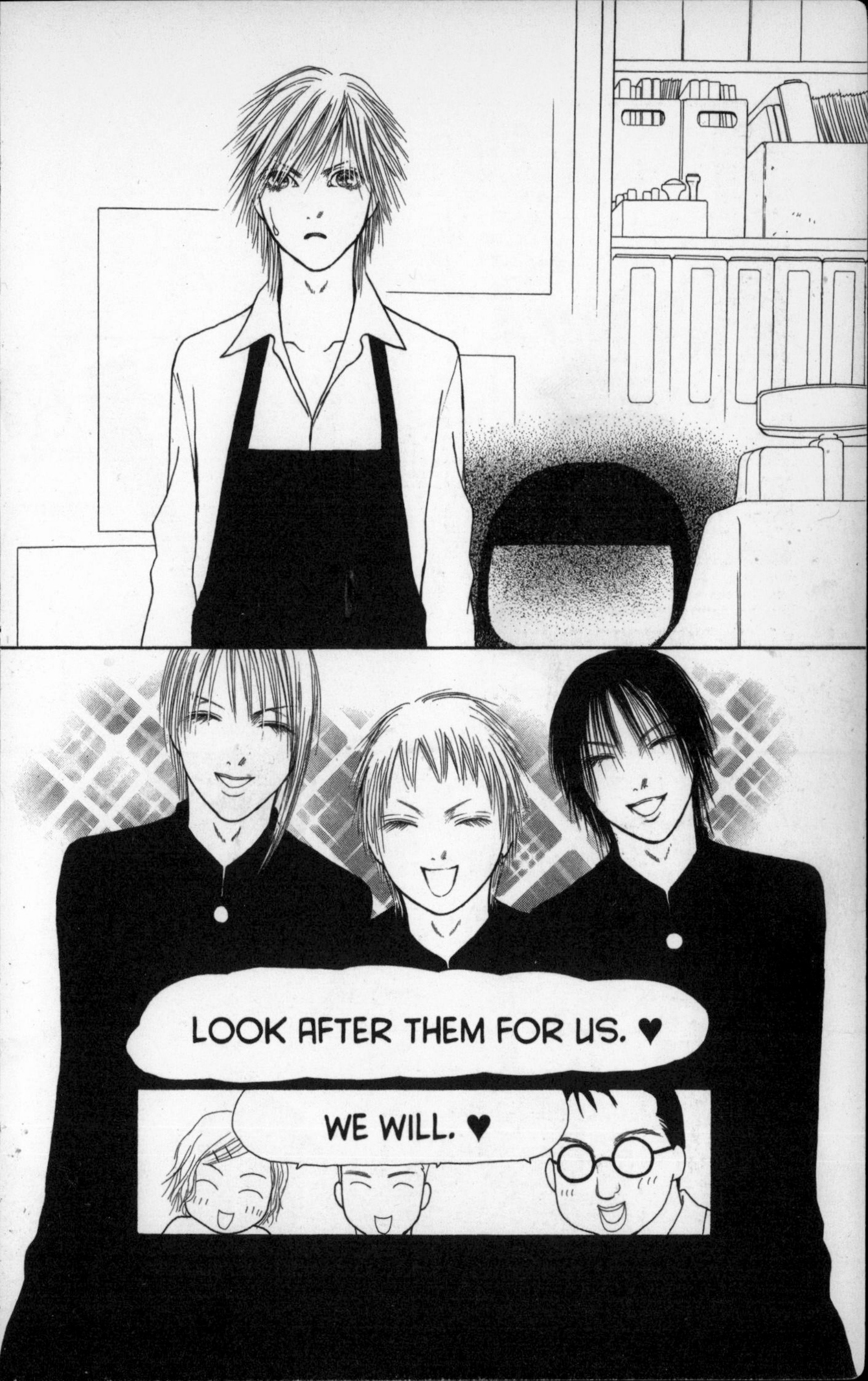
LOOK AFTER THEM FOR US. ♥
WE WILL. ♥

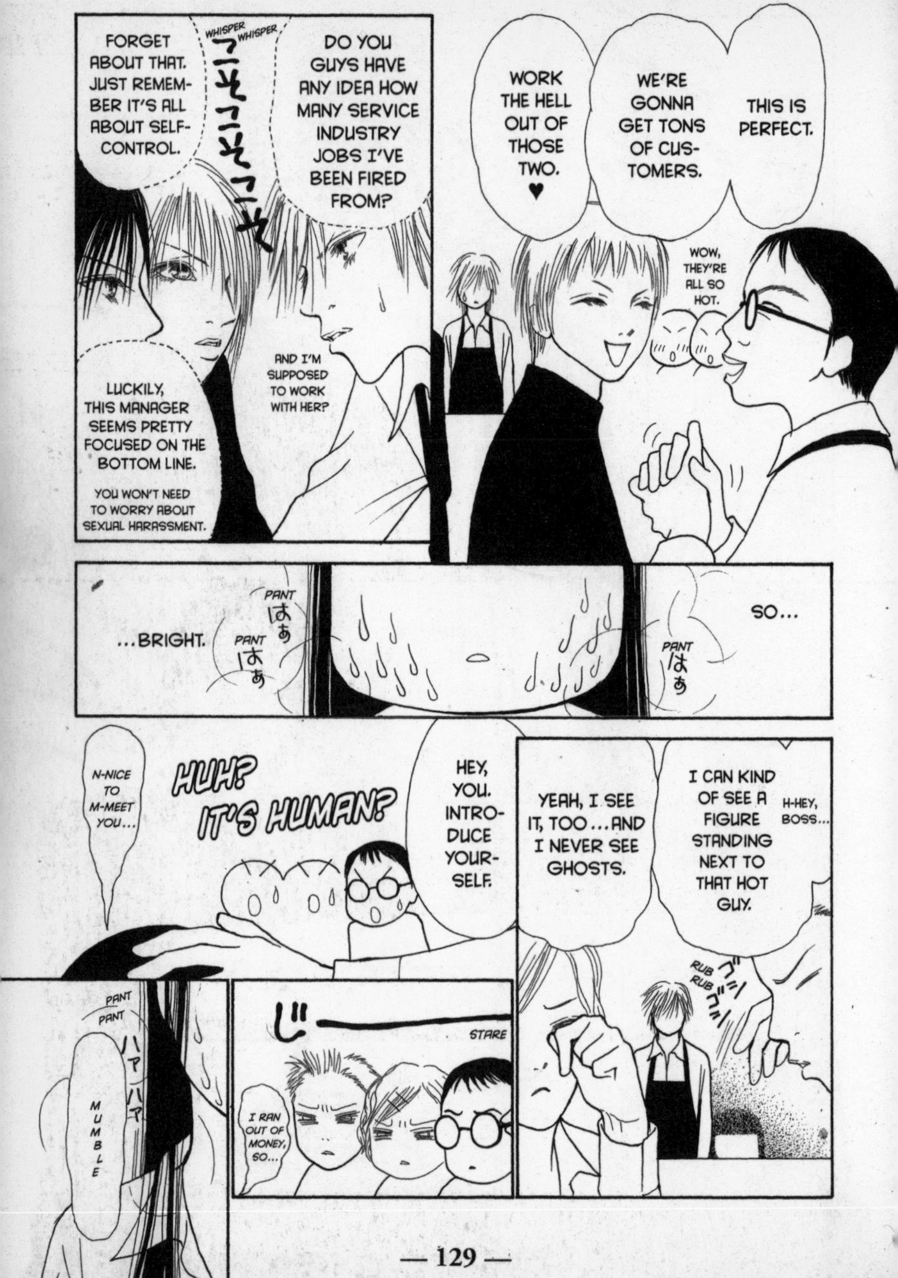
THIS IS PERFECT.
WE'RE GONNA GET TONS OF CUSTOMERS.
WORK THE HELL OUT OF THOSE TWO. ♥
WOW, THEY'RE ALL SO HOT.
DO YOU GUYS HAVE ANY IDEA HOW MANY SERVICE INDUSTRY JOBS I'VE BEEN FIRED FROM?
WHISPER WHISPER
こそこそ
FORGET ABOUT THAT. JUST REMEMBER IT'S ALL ABOUT SELF-CONTROL.
AND I'M SUPPOSED TO WORK WITH HER?
LUCKILY, THIS MANAGER SEEMS PRETTY FOCUSED ON THE BOTTOM LINE.
YOU WON'T NEED TO WORRY ABOUT SEXUAL HARASSMENT.
SO...
PANT はぁ
PANT はぁ
PANT はぁ
...BRIGHT.
H-HEY, BOSS...
I CAN KIND OF SEE A FIGURE STANDING NEXT TO THAT HOT GUY.
YEAH, I SEE IT, TOO...AND I NEVER SEE GHOSTS.
RUB RUB ゴシゴシ
HEY, YOU. INTRODUCE YOURSELF.
HUH? IT'S HUMAN?
N-NICE TO M-MEET YOU...
じー
STARE
I RAN OUT OF MONEY, SO...
PANT PANT ハァハァ
MUMBLE

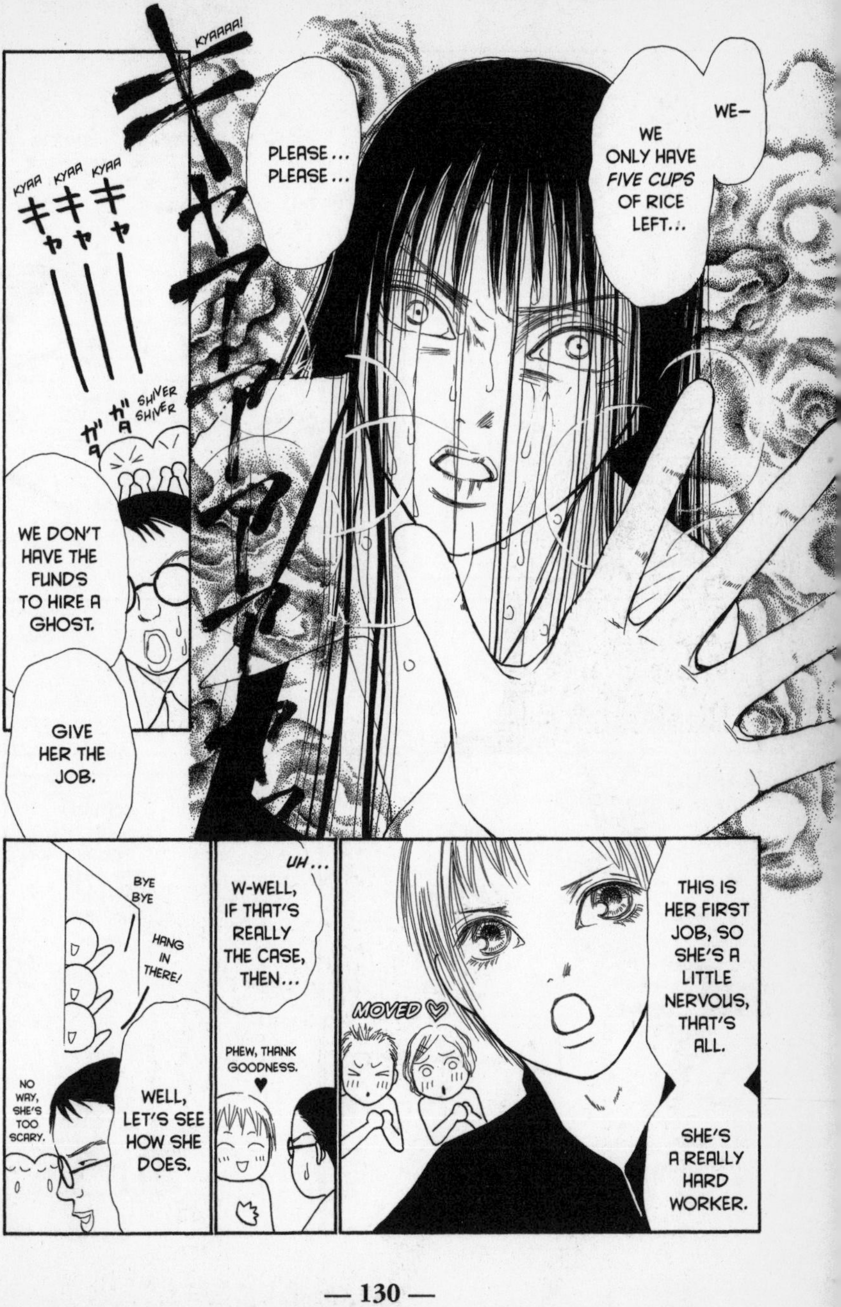
WE—
WE ONLY HAVE *FIVE CUPS* OF RICE LEFT...
PLEASE... PLEASE...
KYAAAA!
KYAA KYAA KYAA
SHIVER SHIVER
WE DON'T HAVE THE FUNDS TO HIRE A GHOST.
GIVE HER THE JOB.
THIS IS HER FIRST JOB, SO SHE'S A LITTLE NERVOUS, THAT'S ALL.
SHE'S A REALLY HARD WORKER.
MOVED ♡
UH...
W-WELL, IF THAT'S REALLY THE CASE, THEN...
PHEW, THANK GOODNESS. ♥
BYE BYE
HANG IN THERE!
WELL, LET'S SEE HOW SHE DOES.
NO WAY, SHE'S TOO SCARY.

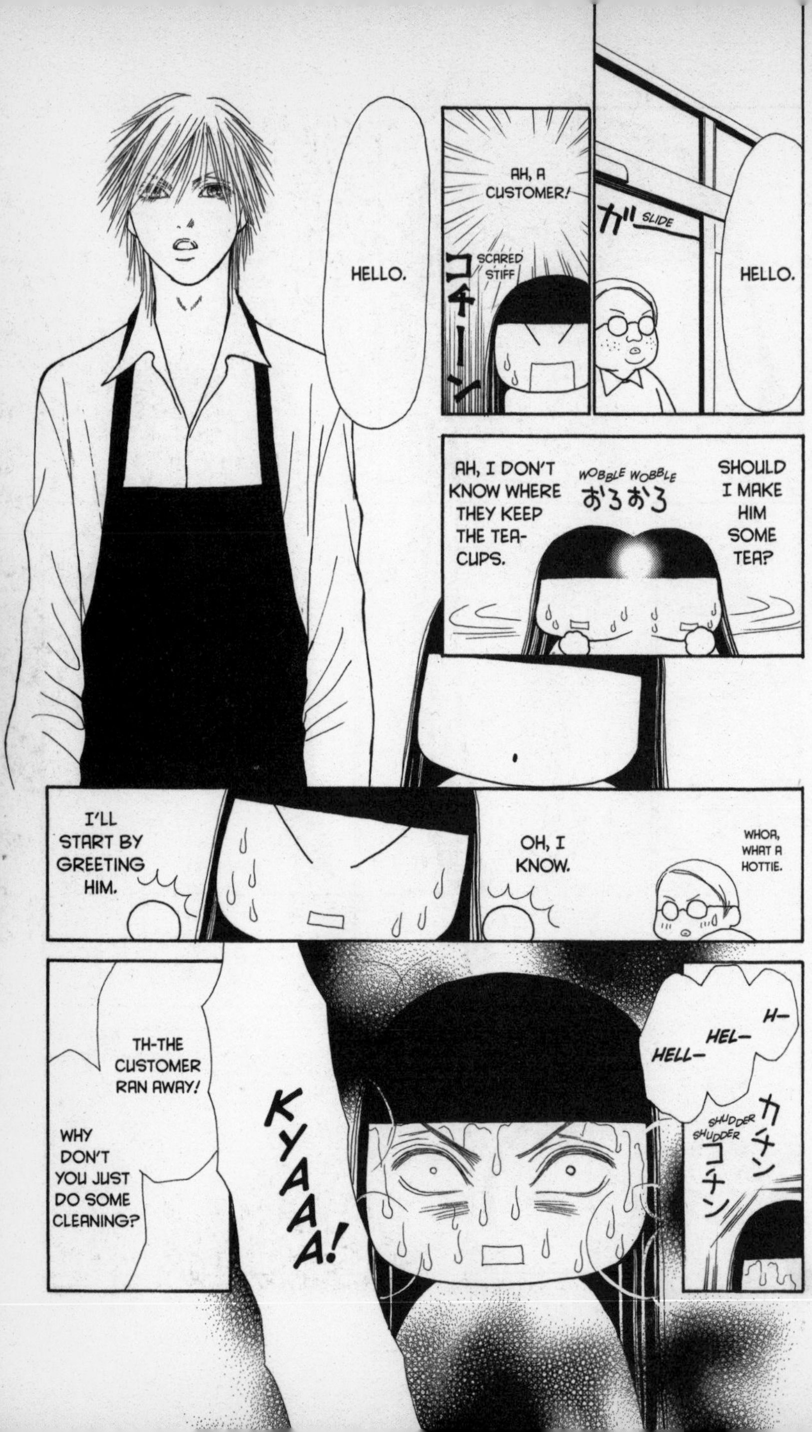
HELLO.
ガ SLIDE
AH, A CUSTOMER!
コチーン SCARED STIFF
SHOULD I MAKE HIM SOME TEA?
おろおろ WOBBLE WOBBLE
AH, I DON'T KNOW WHERE THEY KEEP THE TEA-CUPS.
HELLO.
WHOA, WHAT A HOTTIE.
OH, I KNOW.
I'LL START BY GREETING HIM.
H- HEL- HELL-
カチンコチン SHUDDER SHUDDER
KYAAAA!
TH-THE CUSTOMER RAN AWAY!
WHY DON'T YOU JUST DO SOME CLEANING?

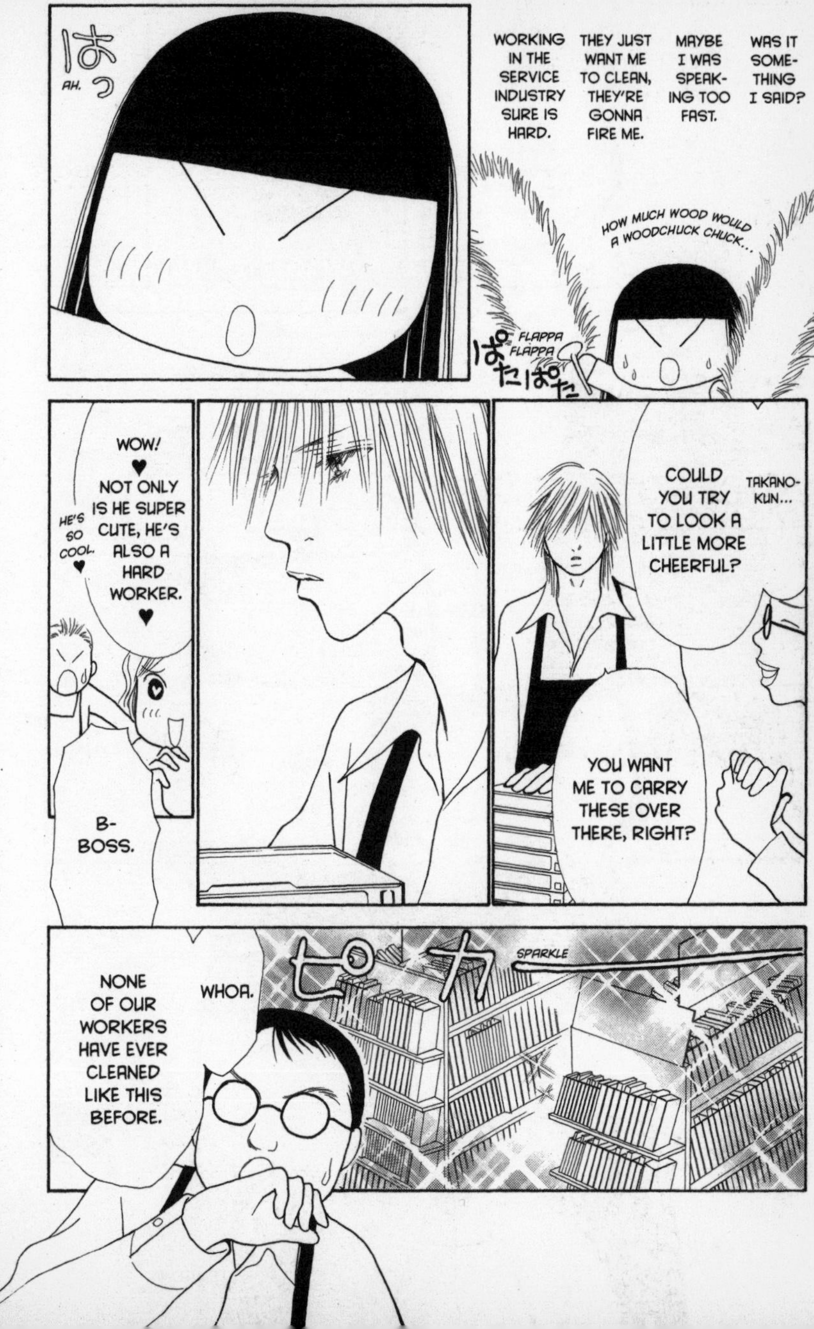
WAS IT SOMETHING I SAID?
MAYBE I WAS SPEAKING TOO FAST.
THEY JUST WANT ME TO CLEAN, THEY'RE GONNA FIRE ME.
WORKING IN THE SERVICE INDUSTRY SURE IS HARD.
HOW MUCH WOOD WOULD A WOODCHUCK CHUCK...
ぱたぱた
FLAPPA FLAPPA
はっ
AH.
TAKANO-KUN...
COULD YOU TRY TO LOOK A LITTLE MORE CHEERFUL?
YOU WANT ME TO CARRY THESE OVER THERE, RIGHT?
WOW! ♥ NOT ONLY IS HE SUPER CUTE, HE'S ALSO A HARD WORKER. ♥
HE'S SO COOL. ♥
B-BOSS.
ピカー
SPARKLE
WHOA.
NONE OF OUR WORKERS HAVE EVER CLEANED LIKE THIS BEFORE.

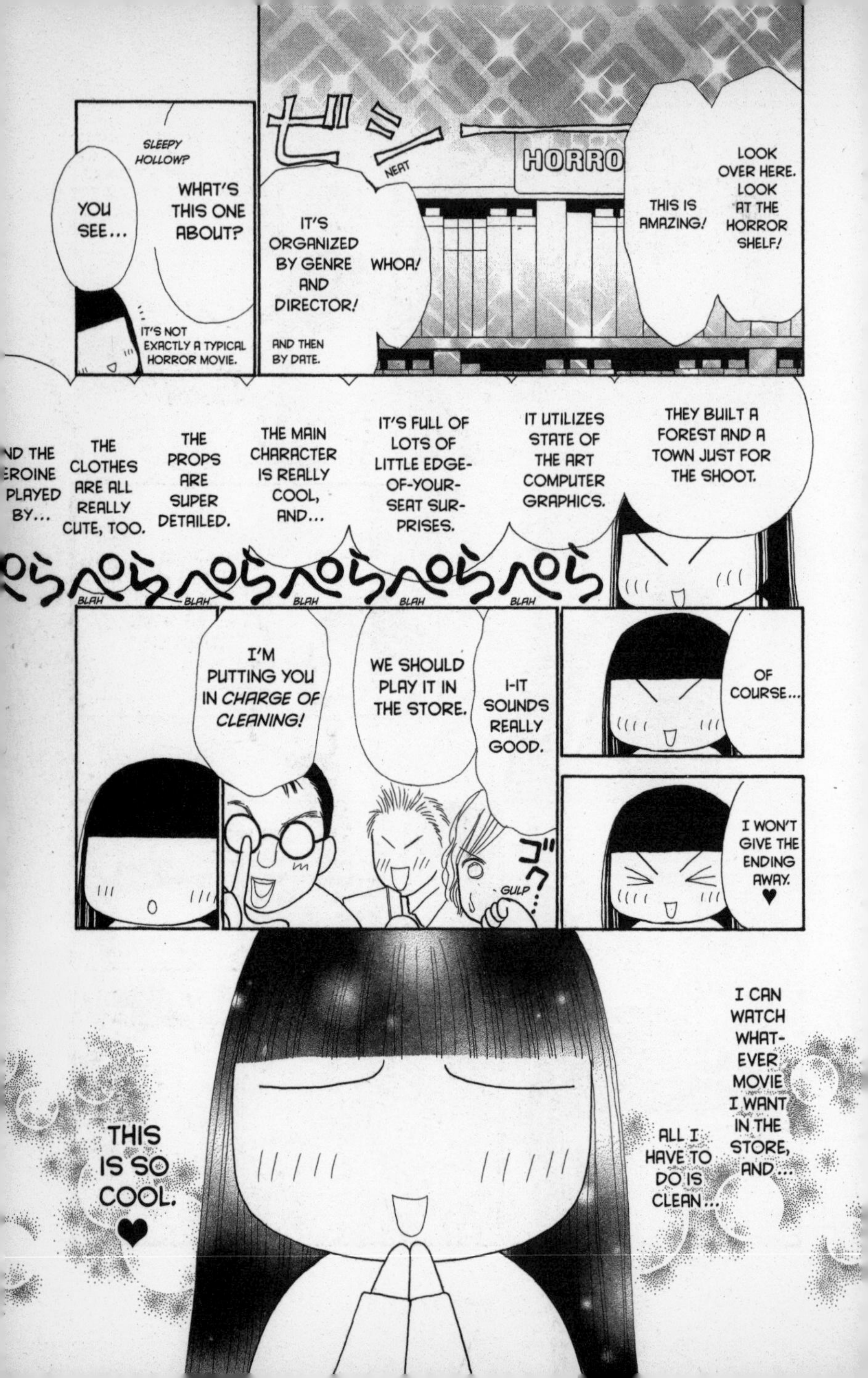
LOOK OVER HERE. LOOK AT THE HORROR SHELF!
THIS IS AMAZING!
HORRO
NEAT
WHOA!
IT'S ORGANIZED BY GENRE AND DIRECTOR!
AND THEN BY DATE.
SLEEPY HOLLOW?
WHAT'S THIS ONE ABOUT?
YOU SEE...
IT'S NOT EXACTLY A TYPICAL HORROR MOVIE.
THEY BUILT A FOREST AND A TOWN JUST FOR THE SHOOT.
IT UTILIZES STATE OF THE ART COMPUTER GRAPHICS.
IT'S FULL OF LOTS OF LITTLE EDGE-OF-YOUR-SEAT SUR-PRISES.
THE MAIN CHARACTER IS REALLY COOL, AND...
THE PROPS ARE SUPER DETAILED.
THE CLOTHES ARE ALL REALLY CUTE, TOO.
ND THE EROINE PLAYED BY...
BLAH BLAH BLAH BLAH BLAH
OF COURSE...
I WON'T GIVE THE ENDING AWAY. ♥
I-IT SOUNDS REALLY GOOD.
GULP
WE SHOULD PLAY IT IN THE STORE.
I'M PUTTING YOU IN *CHARGE OF CLEANING!*
I CAN WATCH WHATEVER MOVIE I WANT IN THE STORE, AND...
ALL I HAVE TO DO IS CLEAN...
THIS IS SO COOL. ♥

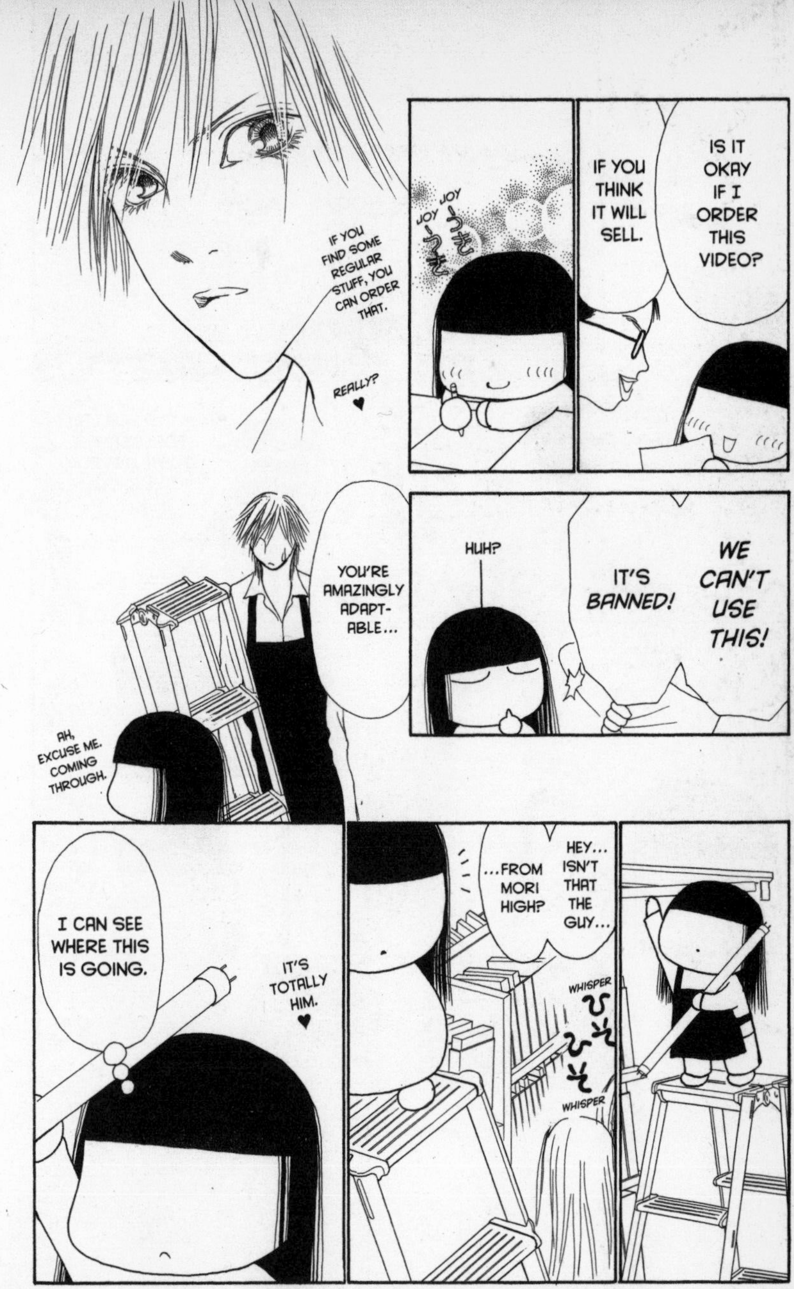
IS IT OKAY IF I ORDER THIS VIDEO?
IF YOU THINK IT WILL SELL.
JOY JOY
IF YOU FIND SOME REGULAR STUFF, YOU CAN ORDER THAT.
REALLY? ♥
WE CAN'T USE THIS!
IT'S BANNED!
HUH?
YOU'RE AMAZINGLY ADAPT-ABLE...
AH, EXCUSE ME. COMING THROUGH.
HEY... ISN'T THAT THE GUY...
...FROM MORI HIGH?
WHISPER
WHISPER
IT'S TOTALLY HIM. ♥
I CAN SEE WHERE THIS IS GOING.

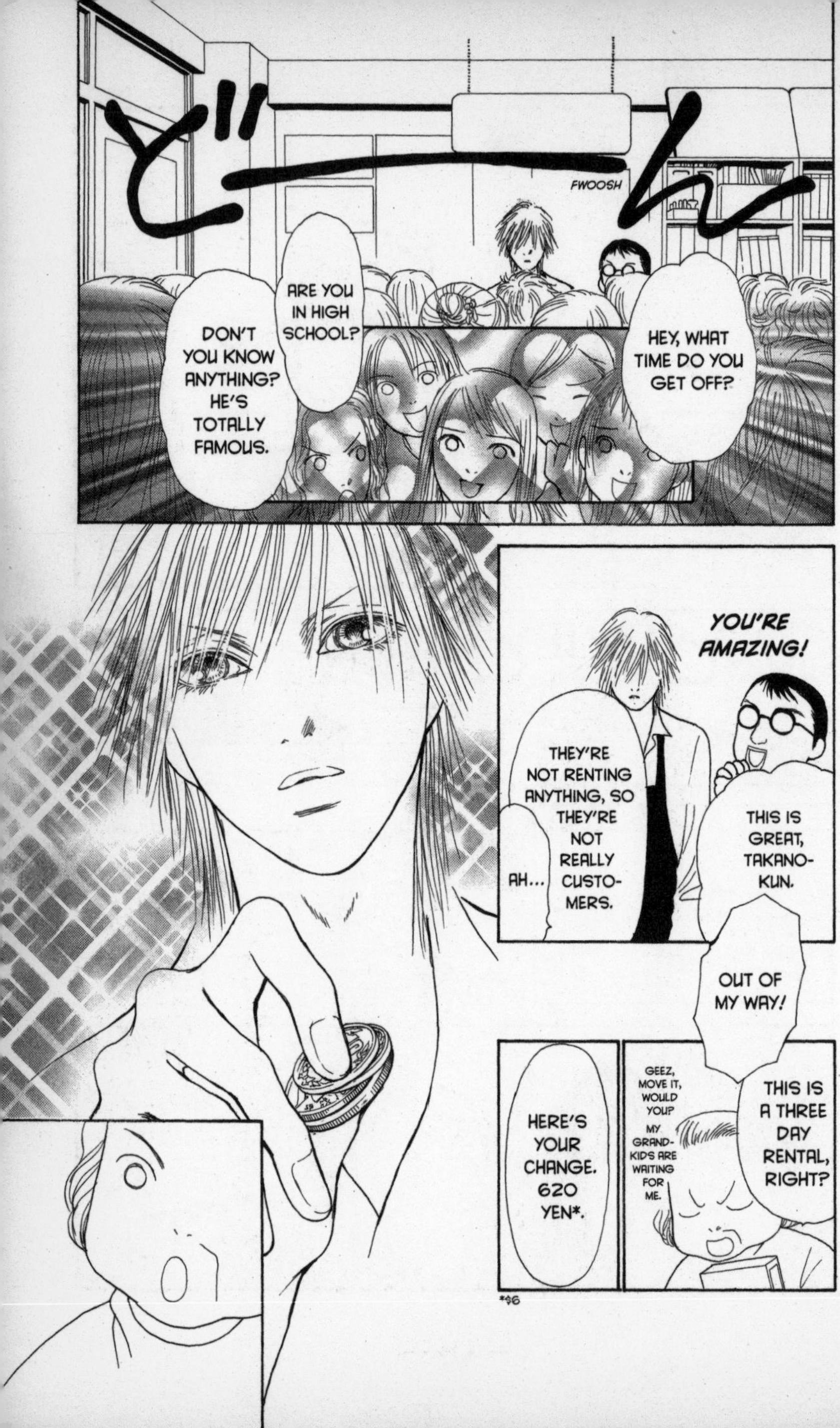
どーん
FWOOSH
HEY, WHAT TIME DO YOU GET OFF?
ARE YOU IN HIGH SCHOOL?
DON'T YOU KNOW ANYTHING? HE'S TOTALLY FAMOUS.
YOU'RE AMAZING!
THIS IS GREAT, TAKANO-KUN.
THEY'RE NOT RENTING ANYTHING, SO THEY'RE NOT REALLY CUSTOMERS.
AH...
OUT OF MY WAY!
THIS IS A THREE DAY RENTAL, RIGHT?
GEEZ, MOVE IT, WOULD YOU? MY GRAND-KIDS ARE WAITING FOR ME.
HERE'S YOUR CHANGE. 620 YEN*.

*$6

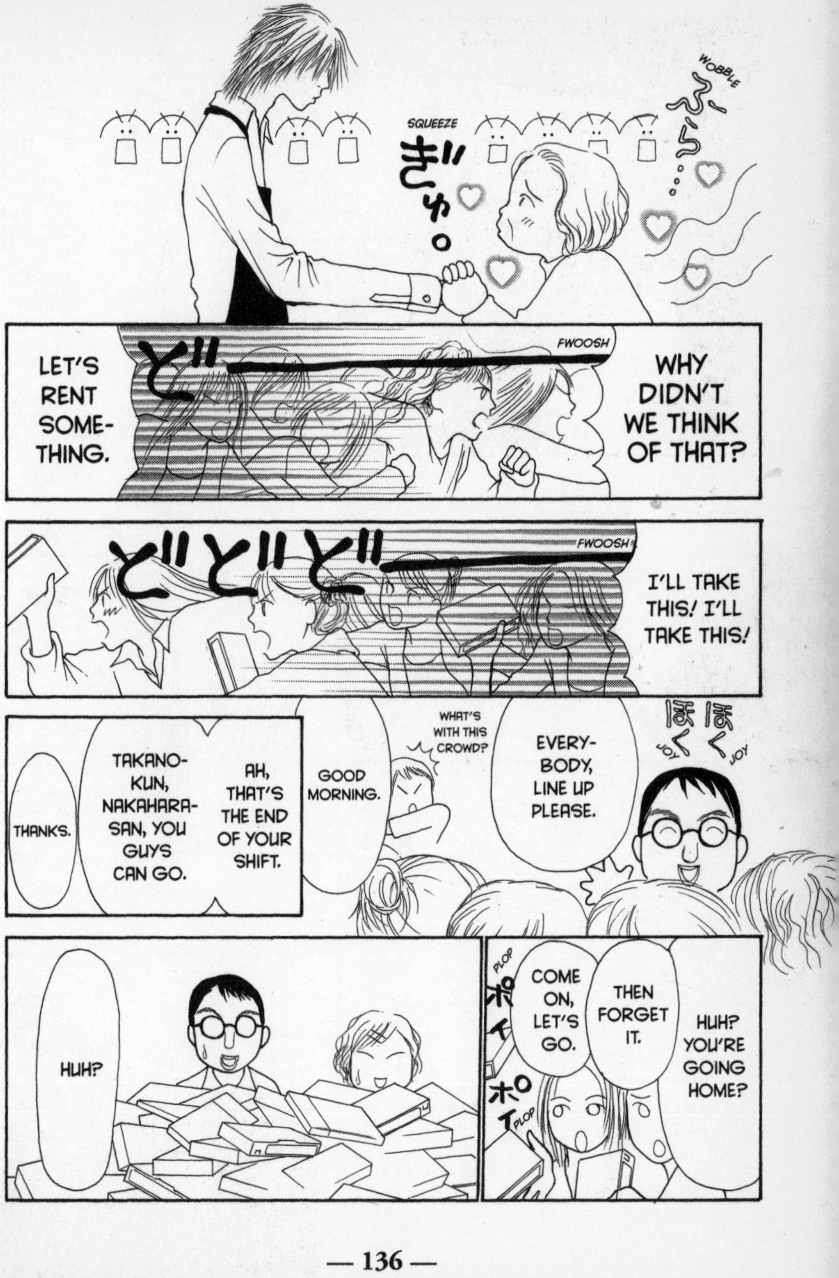
WOBBLE
ふら~…
SQUEEZE
ぎゅ。
WHY DIDN'T WE THINK OF THAT?
FWOOSH
ど"
LET'S RENT SOME-THING.
I'LL TAKE THIS! I'LL TAKE THIS!
FWOOSH
ど"ど"ど"
ほくほく
JOY JOY
EVERY-BODY, LINE UP PLEASE.
WHAT'S WITH THIS CROWD?
GOOD MORNING.
AH, THAT'S THE END OF YOUR SHIFT.
TAKANO-KUN, NAKAHARA-SAN, YOU GUYS CAN GO.
THANKS.
HUH? YOU'RE GOING HOME?
THEN FORGET IT.
COME ON, LET'S GO.
PLOP
ポイ
ポイ
PLOP
HUH?

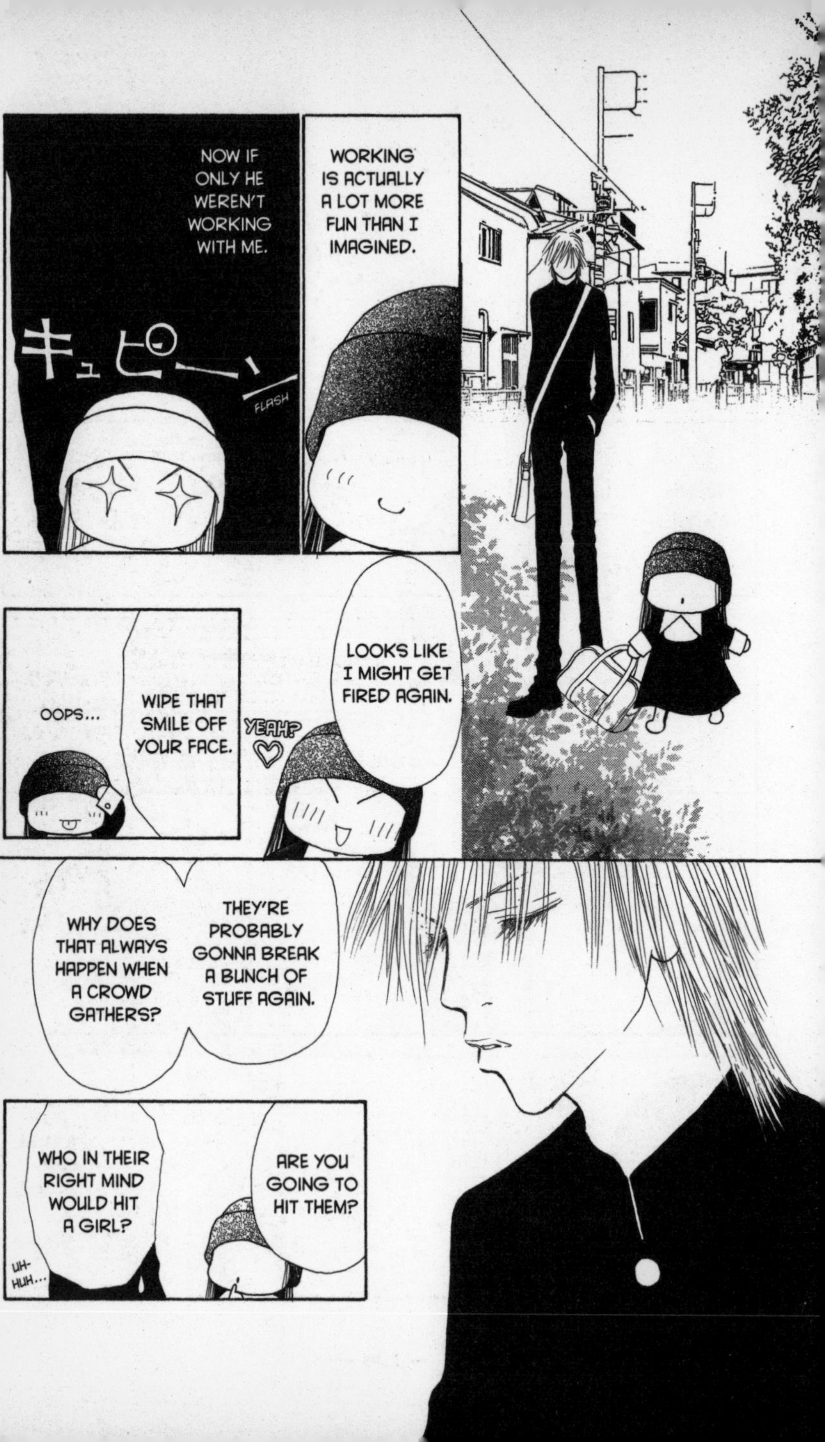
WORKING IS ACTUALLY A LOT MORE FUN THAN I IMAGINED.
NOW IF ONLY HE WEREN'T WORKING WITH ME.
キュピーン
FLASH
LOOKS LIKE I MIGHT GET FIRED AGAIN.
YEAH? ♡
WIPE THAT SMILE OFF YOUR FACE.
OOPS...
THEY'RE PROBABLY GONNA BREAK A BUNCH OF STUFF AGAIN.
WHY DOES THAT ALWAYS HAPPEN WHEN A CROWD GATHERS?
ARE YOU GOING TO HIT THEM?
WHO IN THEIR RIGHT MIND WOULD HIT A GIRL?
UH-HUH...

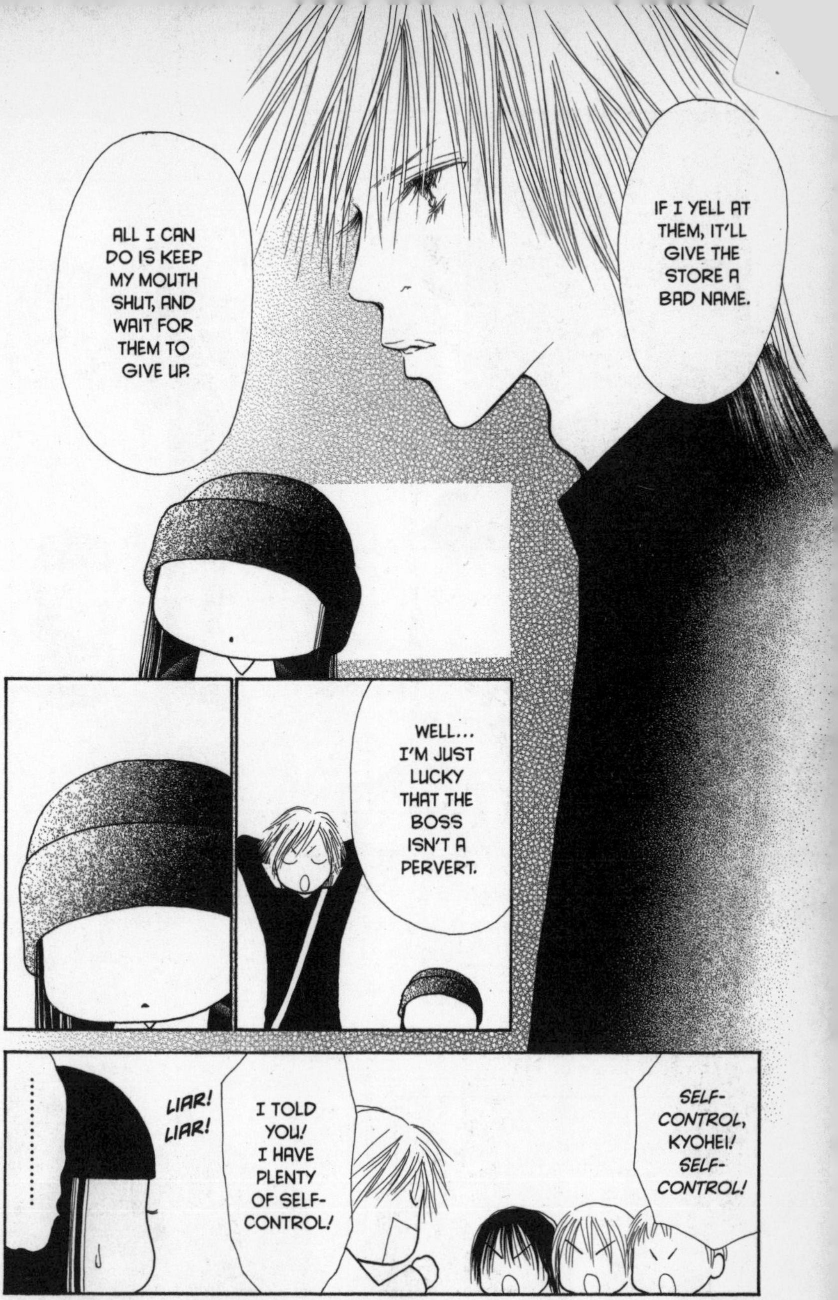
IF I YELL AT THEM, IT'LL GIVE THE STORE A BAD NAME.
ALL I CAN DO IS KEEP MY MOUTH SHUT, AND WAIT FOR THEM TO GIVE UP.
WELL... I'M JUST LUCKY THAT THE BOSS ISN'T A PERVERT.
SELF-CONTROL, KYOHEI! SELF-CONTROL!
I TOLD YOU! I HAVE PLENTY OF SELF-CONTROL!
LIAR! LIAR!
......

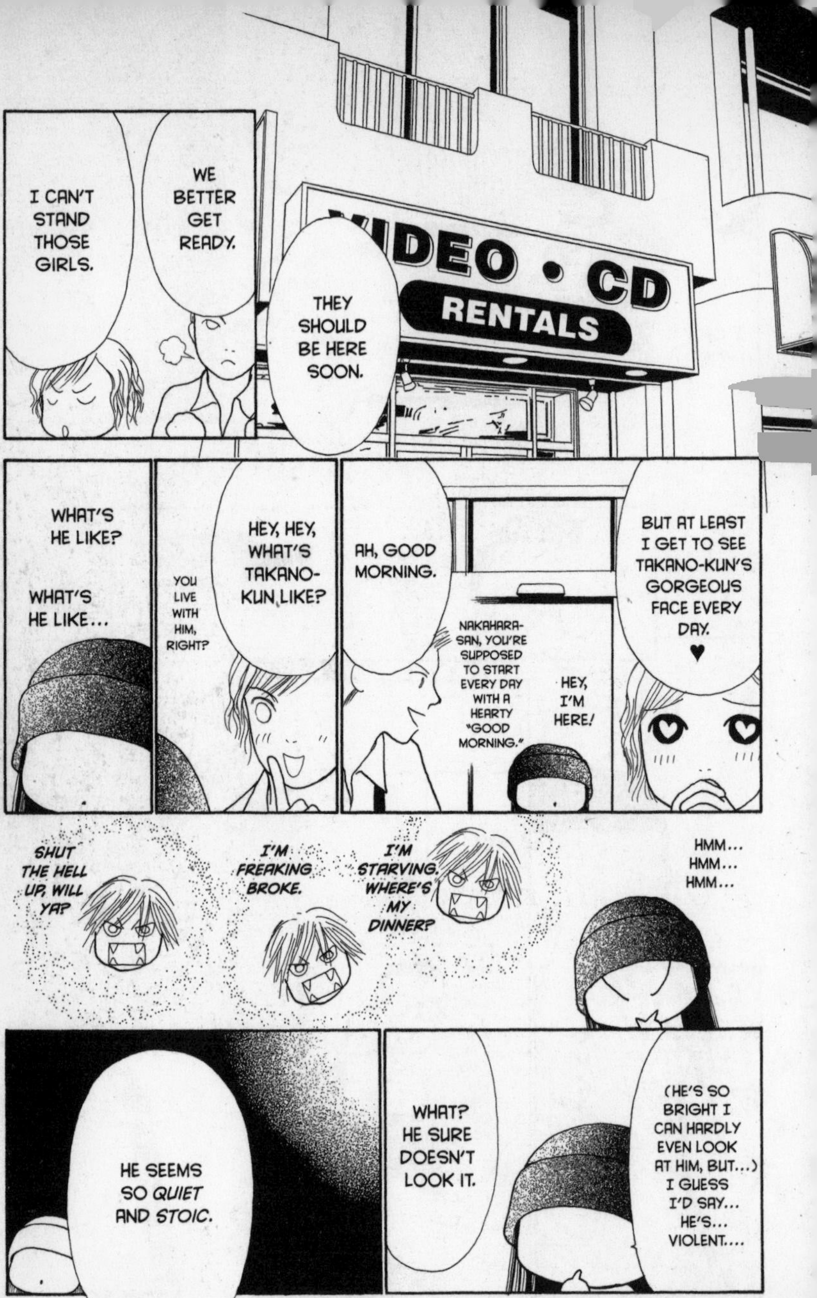
VIDEO • CD
RENTALS
THEY SHOULD BE HERE SOON.
WE BETTER GET READY.
I CAN'T STAND THOSE GIRLS.
BUT AT LEAST I GET TO SEE TAKANO-KUN'S GORGEOUS FACE EVERY DAY. ♥
AH, GOOD MORNING.
NAKAHARA-SAN, YOU'RE SUPPOSED TO START EVERY DAY WITH A HEARTY "GOOD MORNING."
HEY, I'M HERE!
HEY, HEY, WHAT'S TAKANO-KUN LIKE?
YOU LIVE WITH HIM, RIGHT?
WHAT'S HE LIKE?
WHAT'S HE LIKE...
HMM... HMM... HMM...
I'M STARVING. WHERE'S MY DINNER?
I'M FREAKING BROKE.
SHUT THE HELL UP, WILL YA?
(HE'S SO BRIGHT I CAN HARDLY EVEN LOOK AT HIM, BUT...) I GUESS I'D SAY... HE'S... VIOLENT....
WHAT? HE SURE DOESN'T LOOK IT.
HE SEEMS SO *QUIET* AND *STOIC*.

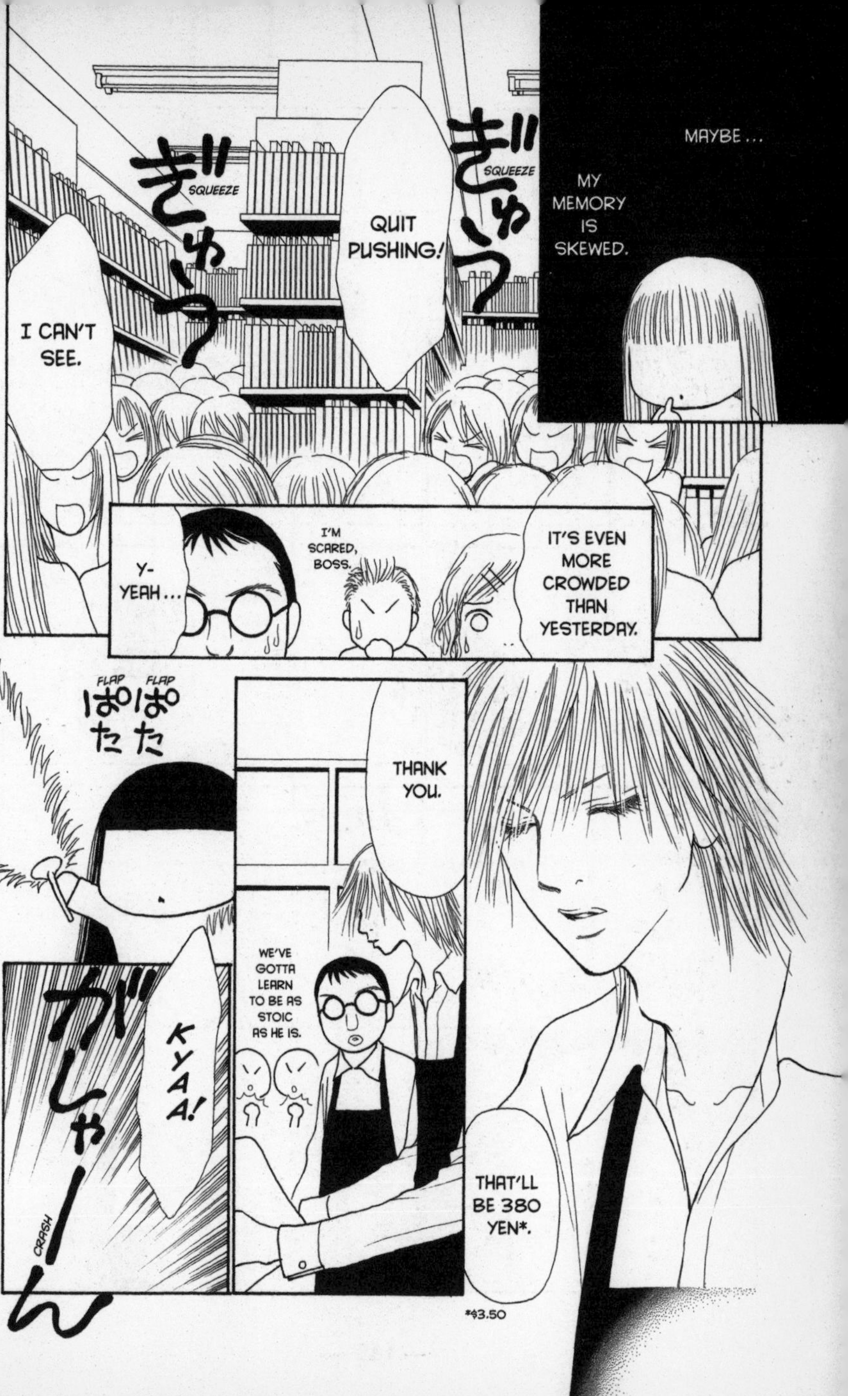
MAYBE...
MY MEMORY IS SKEWED.
ぎゅう
SQUEEZE
QUIT PUSHING!
ぎゅう
SQUEEZE
I CAN'T SEE.
IT'S EVEN MORE CROWDED THAN YESTERDAY.
I'M SCARED, BOSS.
Y-YEAH...
THAT'LL BE 380 YEN*.
THANK YOU.
WE'VE GOTTA LEARN TO BE AS STOIC AS HE IS.
ぱたぱた
FLAP FLAP
KYAA!
がしゃーん
CRASH

*$3.50

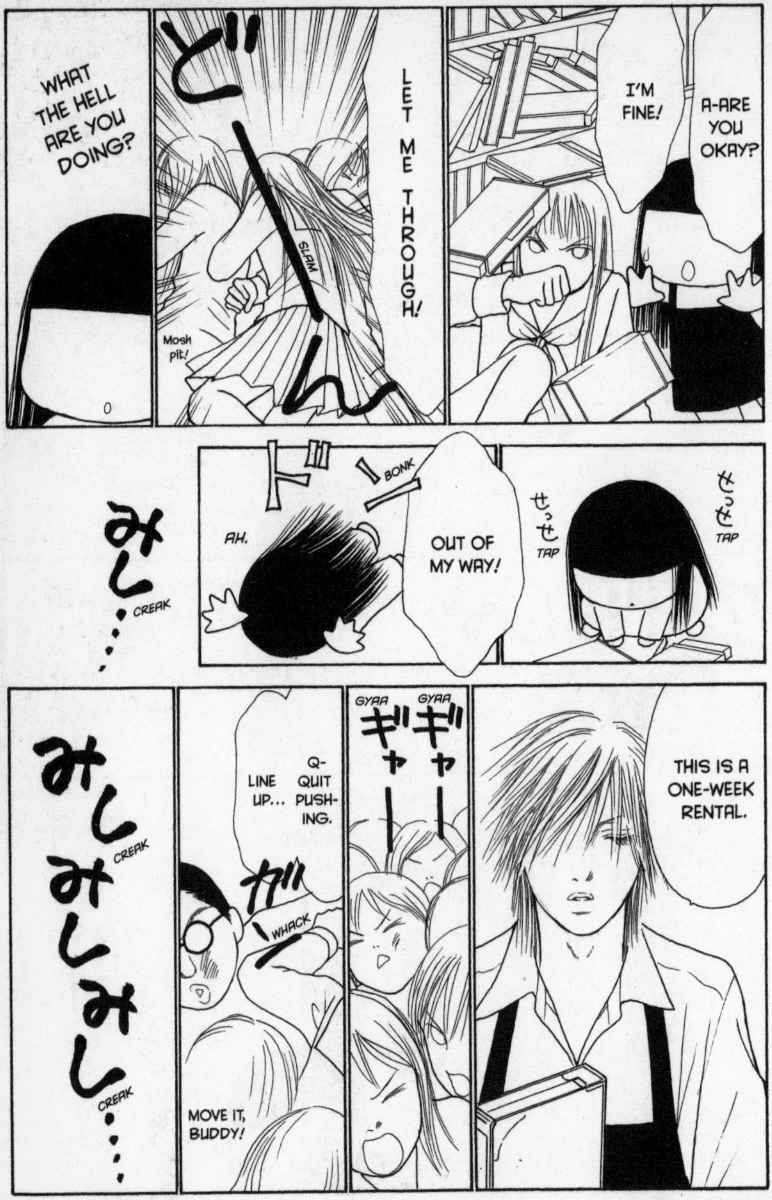
A-ARE YOU OKAY?
I'M FINE!
LET ME THROUGH!
どーん
SLAM
Mosh pit!
WHAT THE HELL ARE YOU DOING?
せっせ
TAP
せっせ
TAP
OUT OF MY WAY!
ドン
BONK
AH.
みし…
CREAK
THIS IS A ONE-WEEK RENTAL.
ギャー
GYAA
ギャー
GYAA
Q-QUIT PUSHING.
LINE UP...
ガッ
WHACK
MOVE IT, BUDDY!
みしみしみし…
CREAK
CREAK

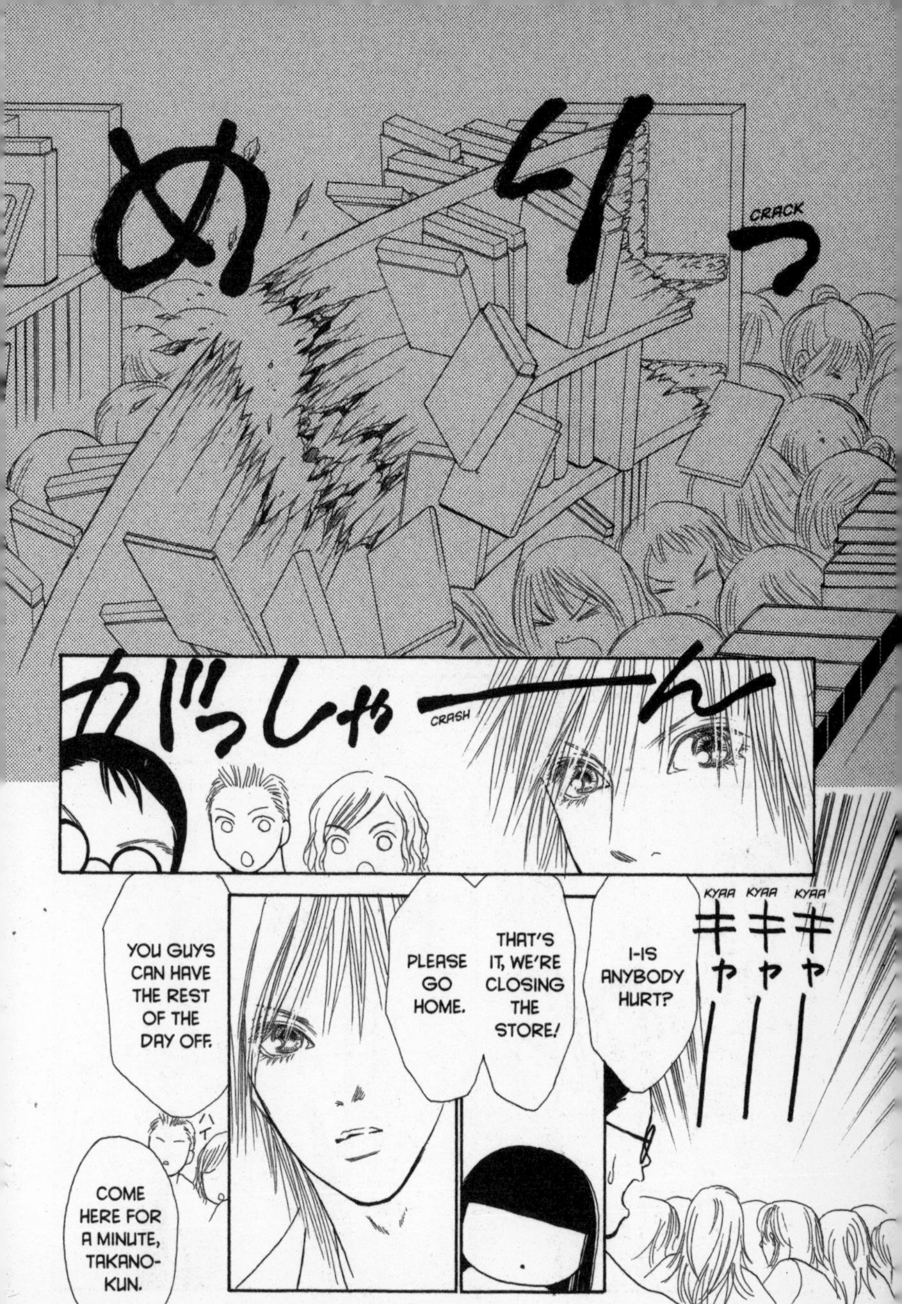
めりっ
CRACK
がっしゃーん
CRASH
KYAA KYAA KYAA
キャー キャー キャー
I-IS ANYBODY HURT?
THAT'S IT, WE'RE CLOSING THE STORE!
PLEASE GO HOME.
YOU GUYS CAN HAVE THE REST OF THE DAY OFF.
ハイ
COME HERE FOR A MINUTE, TAKANO-KUN.

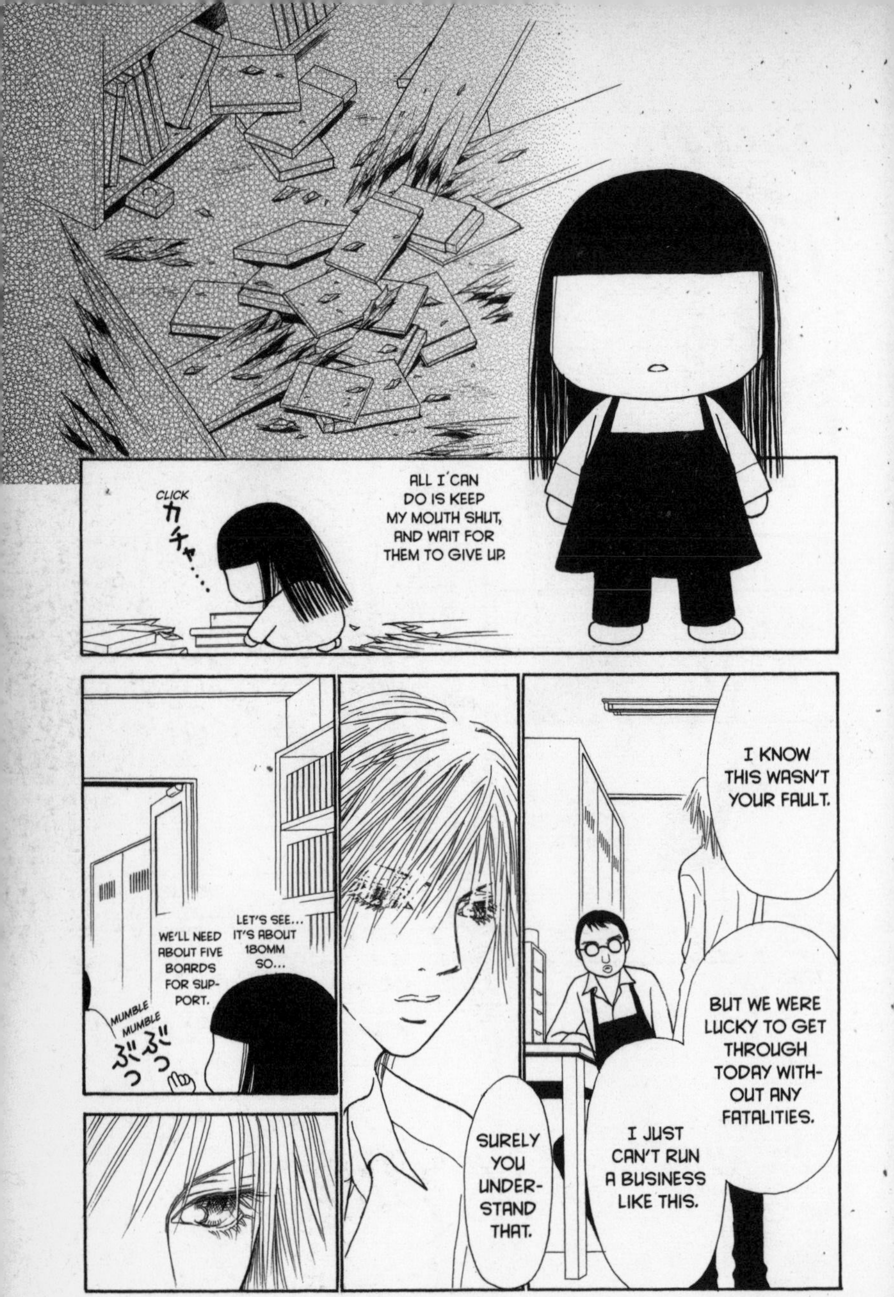
ALL I CAN DO IS KEEP MY MOUTH SHUT, AND WAIT FOR THEM TO GIVE UP.
CLICK
カチャ…
I KNOW THIS WASN'T YOUR FAULT.
BUT WE WERE LUCKY TO GET THROUGH TODAY WITHOUT ANY FATALITIES.
I JUST CAN'T RUN A BUSINESS LIKE THIS.
SURELY YOU UNDERSTAND THAT.
LET'S SEE… IT'S ABOUT 180MM SO…
WE'LL NEED ABOUT FIVE BOARDS FOR SUPPORT.
MUMBLE MUMBLE
ぶつぶつ

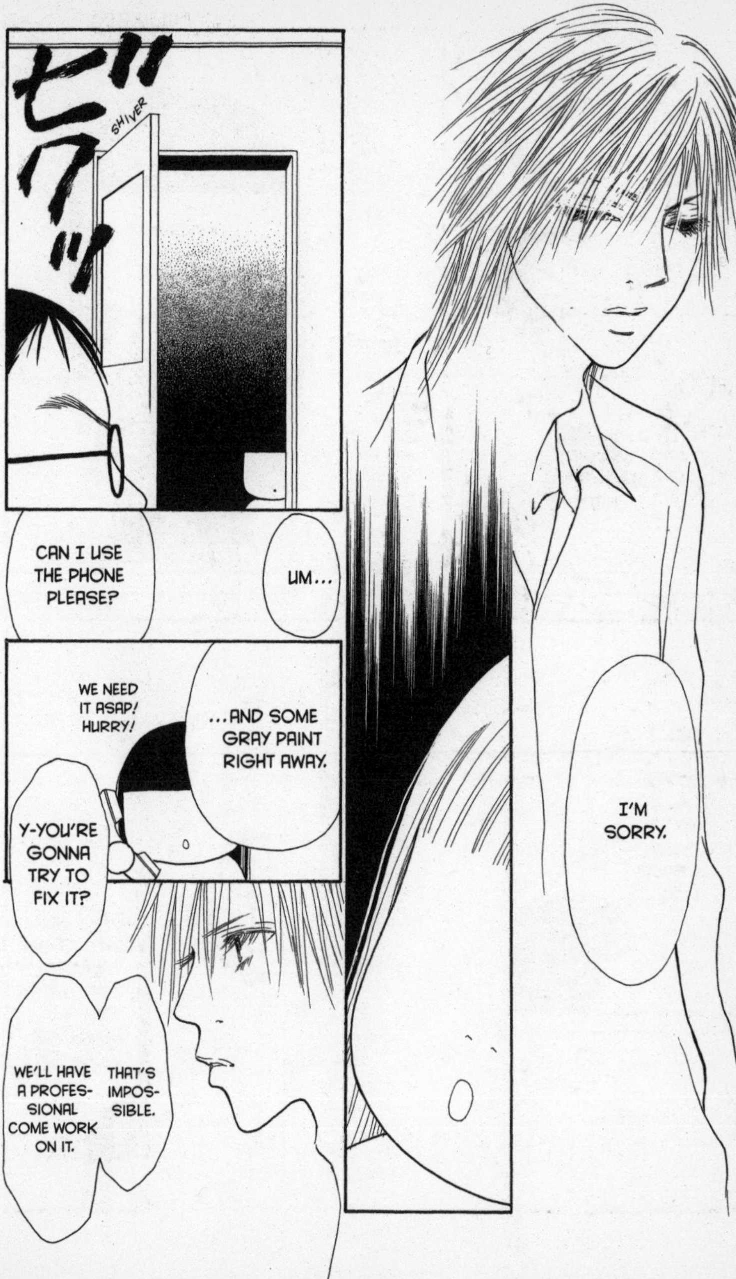
I'M SORRY.
ビクッ
SHIVER
UM...
CAN I USE THE PHONE PLEASE?
...AND SOME GRAY PAINT RIGHT AWAY.
WE NEED IT ASAP! HURRY!
Y-YOU'RE GONNA TRY TO FIX IT?
THAT'S IMPOSSIBLE.
WE'LL HAVE A PROFESSIONAL COME WORK ON IT.

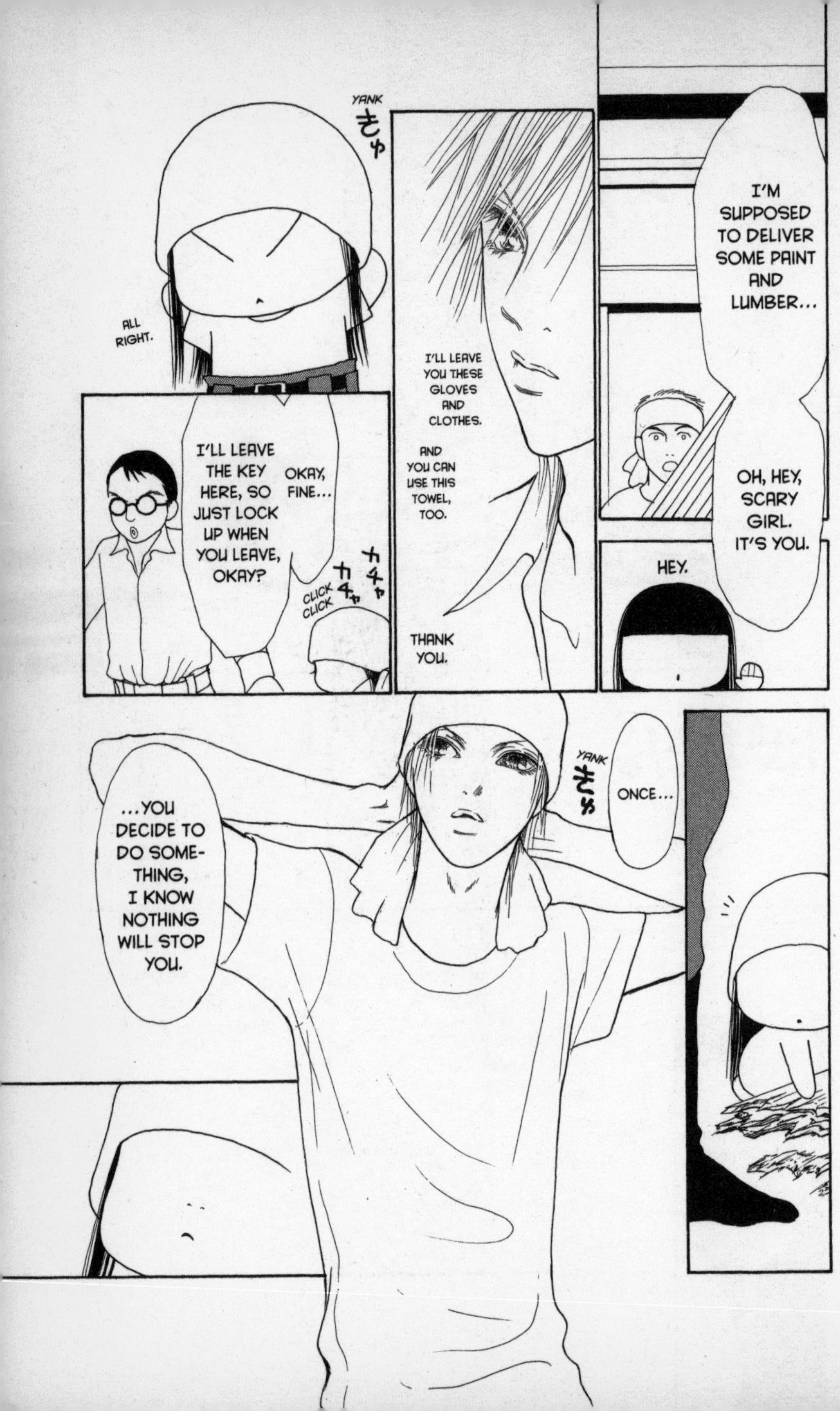
I'M SUPPOSED TO DELIVER SOME PAINT AND LUMBER...
OH, HEY, SCARY GIRL. IT'S YOU.
HEY.
I'LL LEAVE YOU THESE GLOVES AND CLOTHES.
AND YOU CAN USE THIS TOWEL, TOO.
THANK YOU.
YANK
ALL RIGHT.
I'LL LEAVE THE KEY HERE, SO JUST LOCK UP WHEN YOU LEAVE, OKAY?
OKAY, FINE...
カチャ カチャ
CLICK CLICK
ONCE...
YANK
...YOU DECIDE TO DO SOMETHING, I KNOW NOTHING WILL STOP YOU.

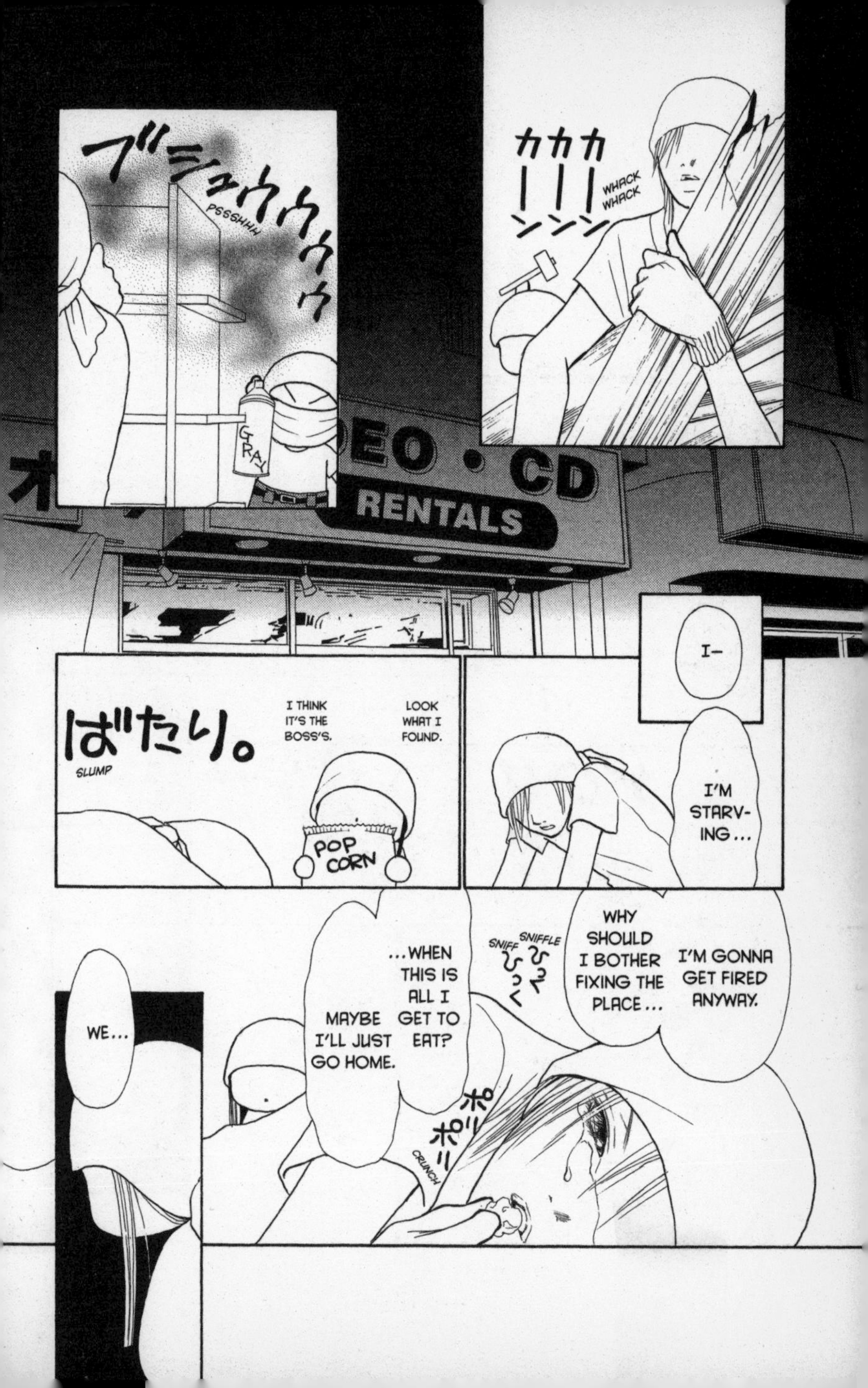
カーン カーン カーン
WHACK WHACK
ブシュウウウウ
PSSSHHH
GRAY
EO · CD
RENTALS
I—
I'M STARVING...
LOOK WHAT I FOUND.
I THINK IT'S THE BOSS'S.
ばたり。
SLUMP
POP CORN
I'M GONNA GET FIRED ANYWAY.
WHY SHOULD I BOTHER FIXING THE PLACE...
ひっく ひっく
SNIFF SNIFFLE
...WHEN THIS IS ALL I GET TO EAT?
MAYBE I'LL JUST GO HOME.
ポリポリ
CRUNCH
WE...

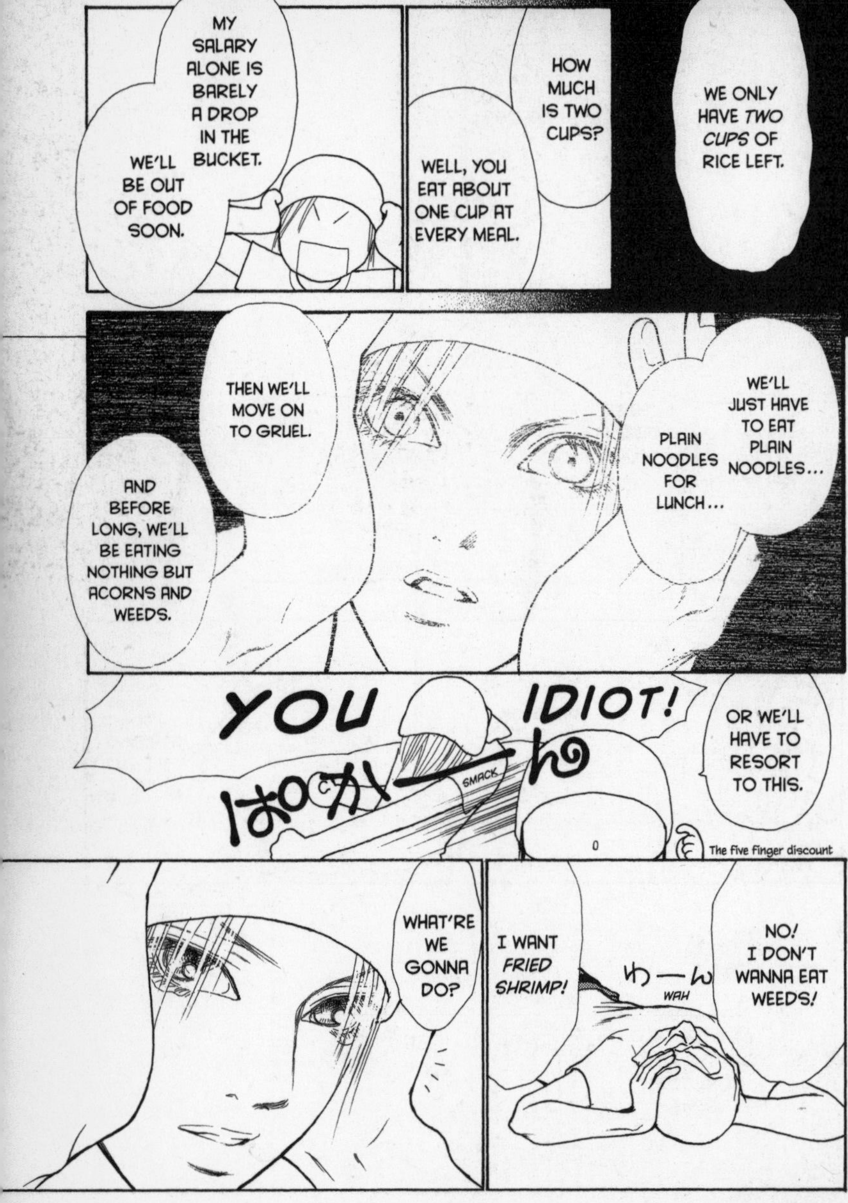
WE ONLY HAVE *TWO CUPS* OF RICE LEFT.
HOW MUCH IS TWO CUPS?
WELL, YOU EAT ABOUT ONE CUP AT EVERY MEAL.
MY SALARY ALONE IS BARELY A DROP IN THE BUCKET.
WE'LL BE OUT OF FOOD SOON.
WE'LL JUST HAVE TO EAT PLAIN NOODLES...
PLAIN NOODLES FOR LUNCH...
THEN WE'LL MOVE ON TO GRUEL.
AND BEFORE LONG, WE'LL BE EATING NOTHING BUT ACORNS AND WEEDS.
OR WE'LL HAVE TO RESORT TO THIS.
The five finger discount
YOU IDIOT!
ばかーん
SMACK
NO! I DON'T WANNA EAT WEEDS!
わーん
WAH
I WANT *FRIED SHRIMP!*
WHAT'RE WE GONNA DO?

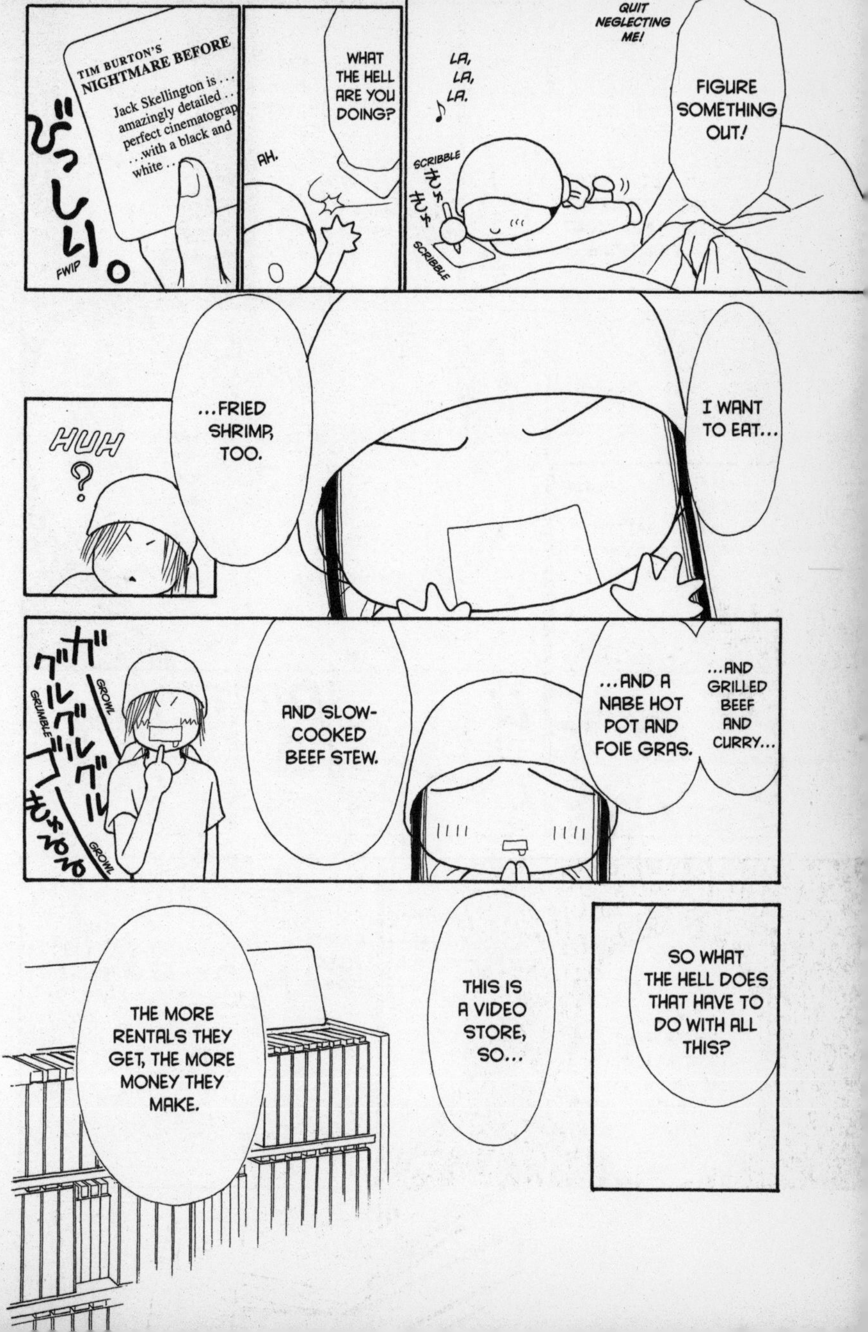
QUIT NEGLECTING ME!
FIGURE SOMETHING OUT!
LA, LA, LA.
SCRIBBLE
SCRIBBLE
WHAT THE HELL ARE YOU DOING?
AH.
TIM BURTON'S NIGHTMARE BEFORE
Jack Skellington is . . . amazingly detailed . . . perfect cinematograp . . . with a black and white . . .
びっしり。
FWIP
I WANT TO EAT...
...FRIED SHRIMP, TOO.
HUH
?
...AND GRILLED BEEF AND CURRY...
...AND A NABE HOT POT AND FOIE GRAS.
AND SLOW-COOKED BEEF STEW.
GROWL
GRUMBLE
GROWL
SO WHAT THE HELL DOES THAT HAVE TO DO WITH ALL THIS?
THIS IS A VIDEO STORE, SO...
THE MORE RENTALS THEY GET, THE MORE MONEY THEY MAKE.

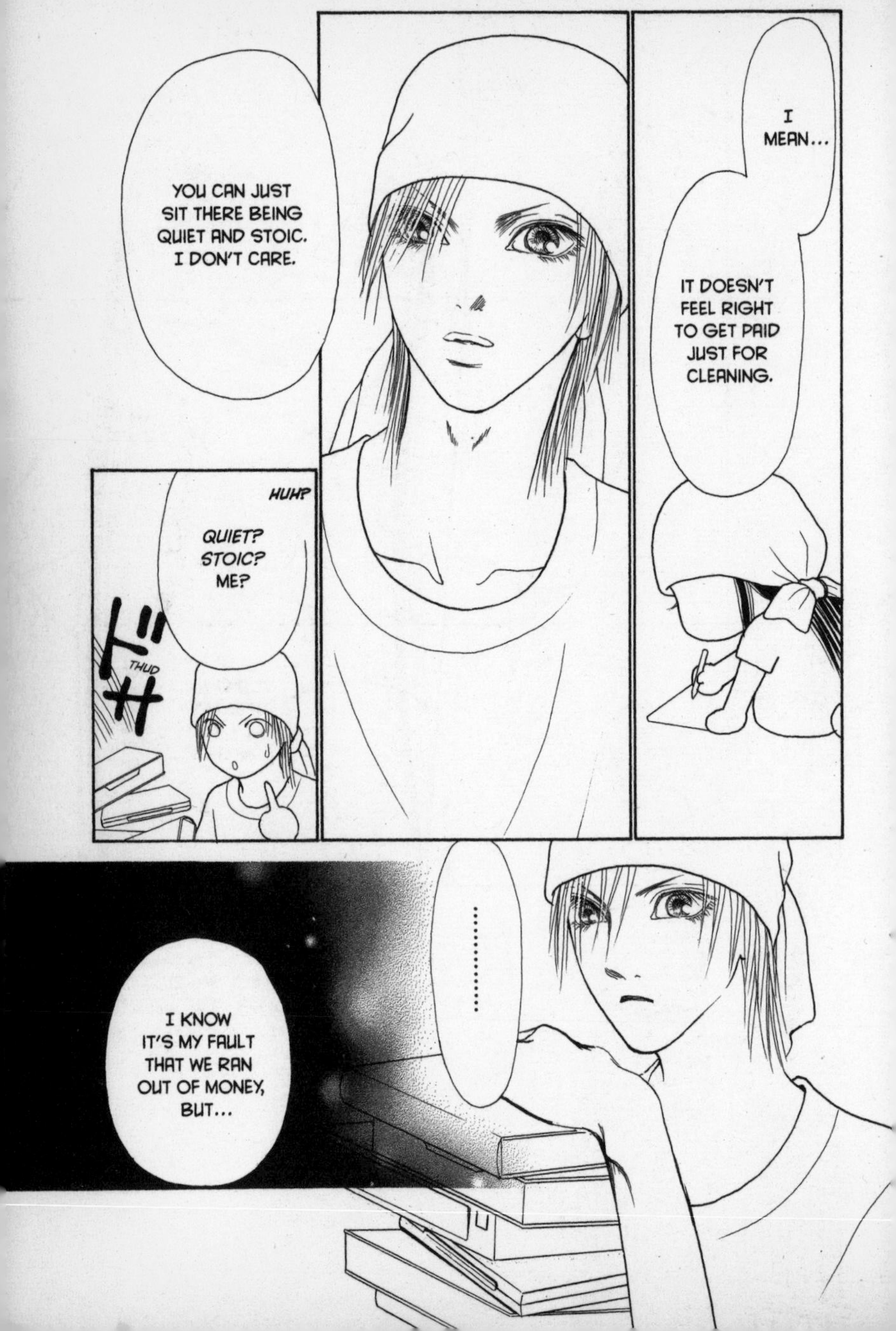
I MEAN...
IT DOESN'T FEEL RIGHT TO GET PAID JUST FOR CLEANING.
YOU CAN JUST SIT THERE BEING QUIET AND STOIC. I DON'T CARE.
HUH?
QUIET? STOIC? ME?
ドサ
THUD
......
I KNOW IT'S MY FAULT THAT WE RAN OUT OF MONEY, BUT...

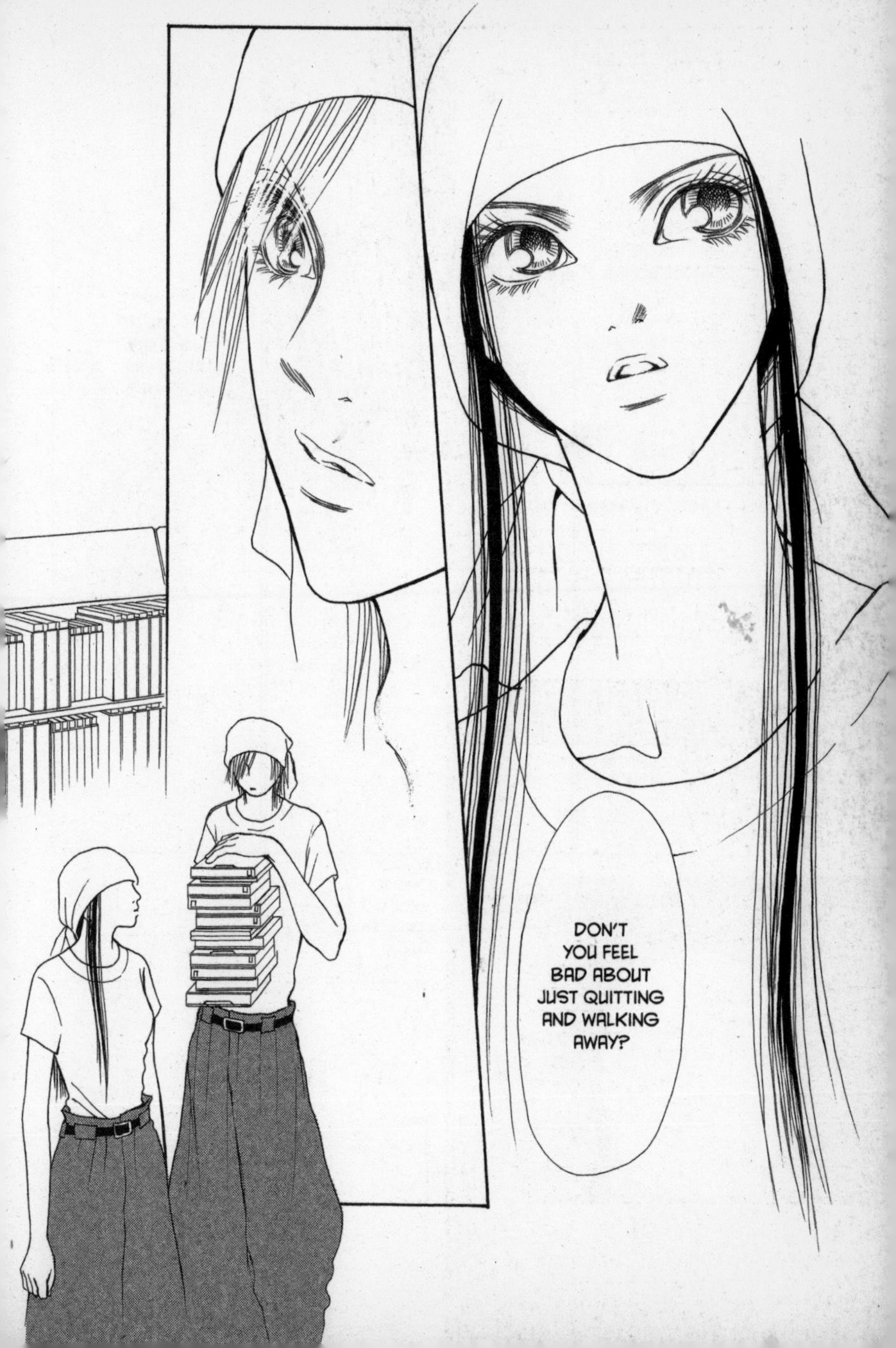
DON'T YOU FEEL BAD ABOUT JUST QUITTING AND WALKING AWAY?

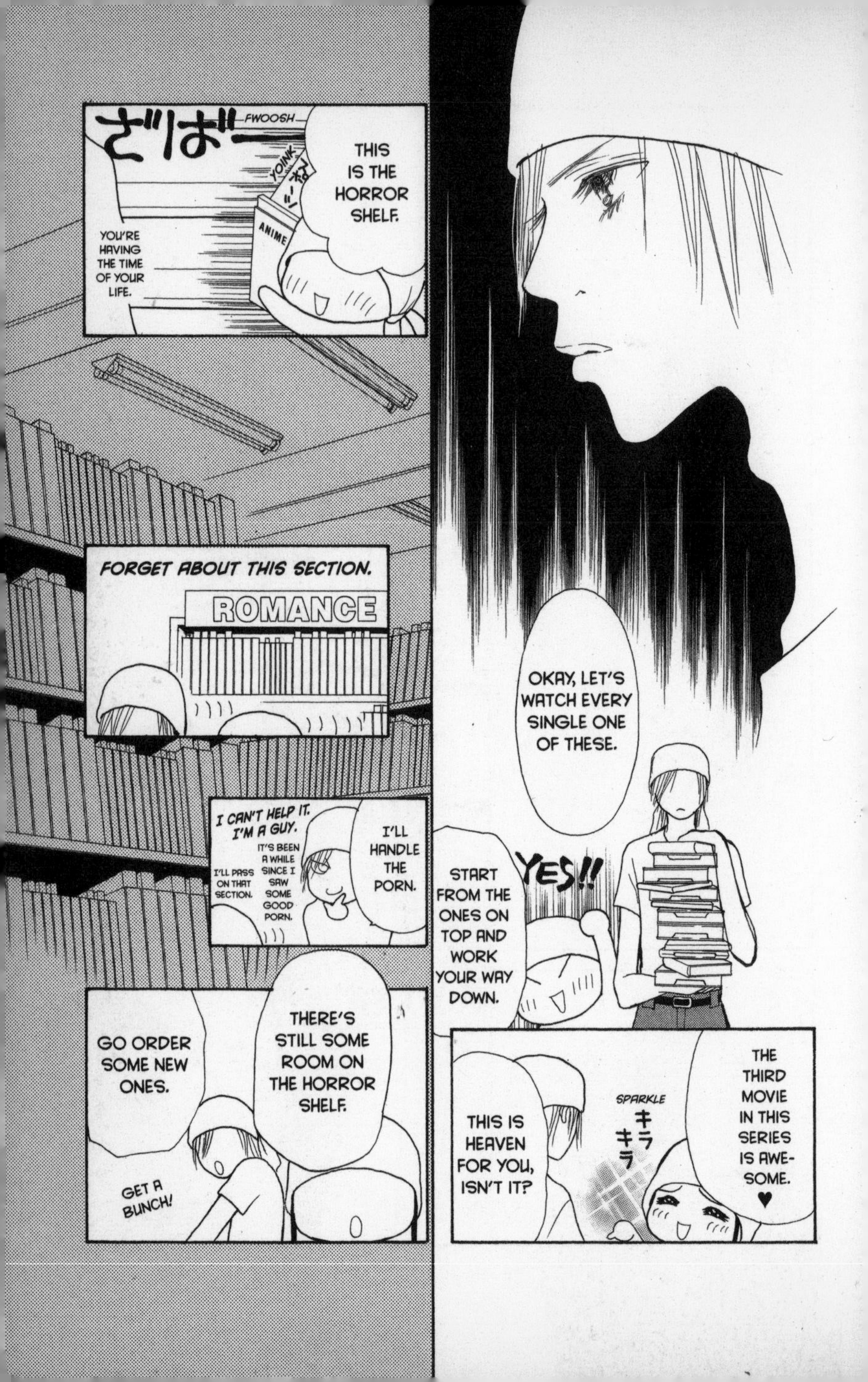

OKAY, LET'S WATCH EVERY SINGLE ONE OF THESE.
YES!!
START FROM THE ONES ON TOP AND WORK YOUR WAY DOWN.
THE THIRD MOVIE IN THIS SERIES IS AWE-SOME. ♥
SPARKLE
キラキラ
THIS IS HEAVEN FOR YOU, ISN'T IT?
THIS IS THE HORROR SHELF.
ざばー
FWOOSH
YOINK
ANIME
YOU'RE HAVING THE TIME OF YOUR LIFE.
FORGET ABOUT THIS SECTION.
ROMANCE
I'LL HANDLE THE PORN.
I CAN'T HELP IT. I'M A GUY.
IT'S BEEN A WHILE SINCE I SAW SOME GOOD PORN.
I'LL PASS ON THAT SECTION.
THERE'S STILL SOME ROOM ON THE HORROR SHELF.
GO ORDER SOME NEW ONES.
GET A BUNCH!

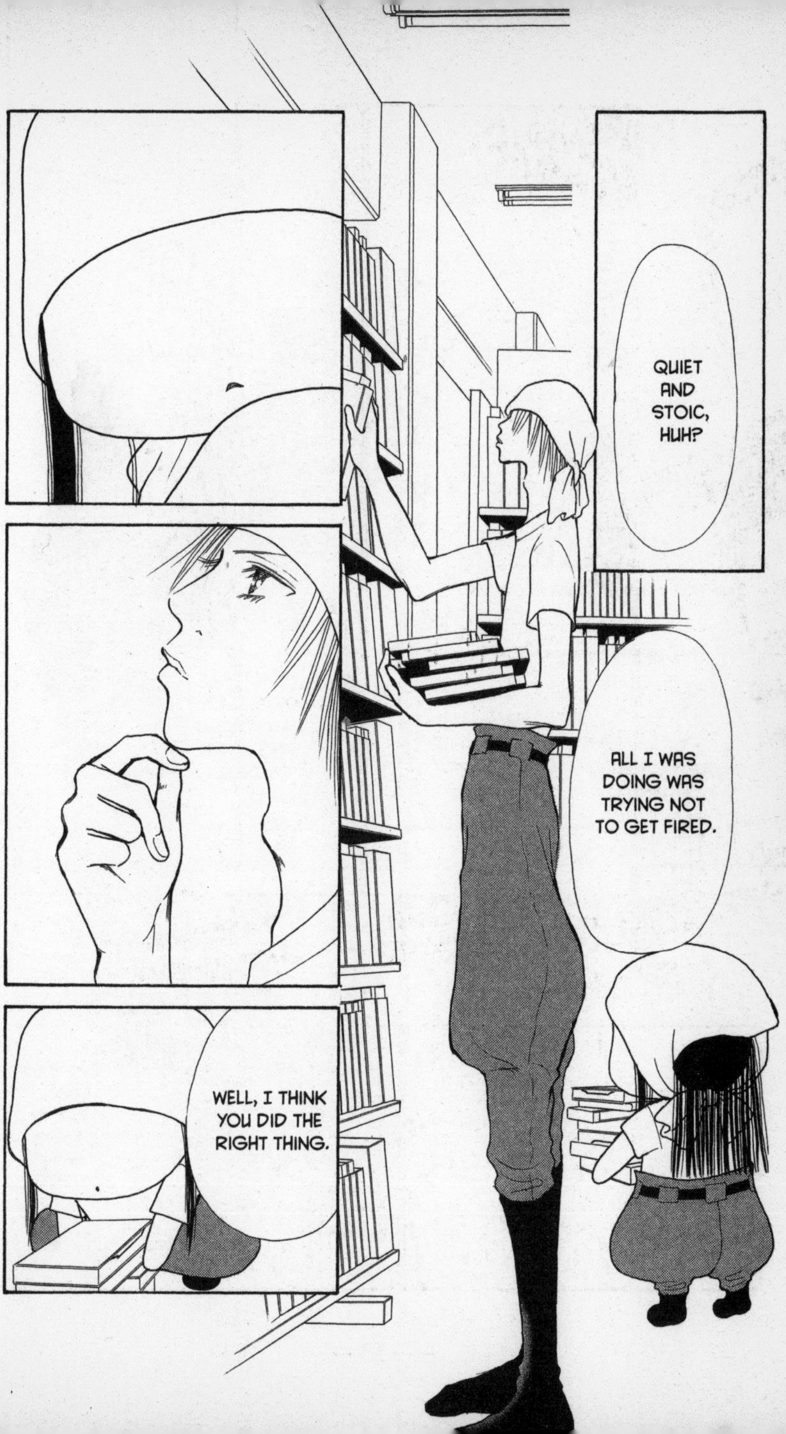
QUIET AND STOIC, HUH?
ALL I WAS DOING WAS TRYING NOT TO GET FIRED.
WELL, I THINK YOU DID THE RIGHT THING.

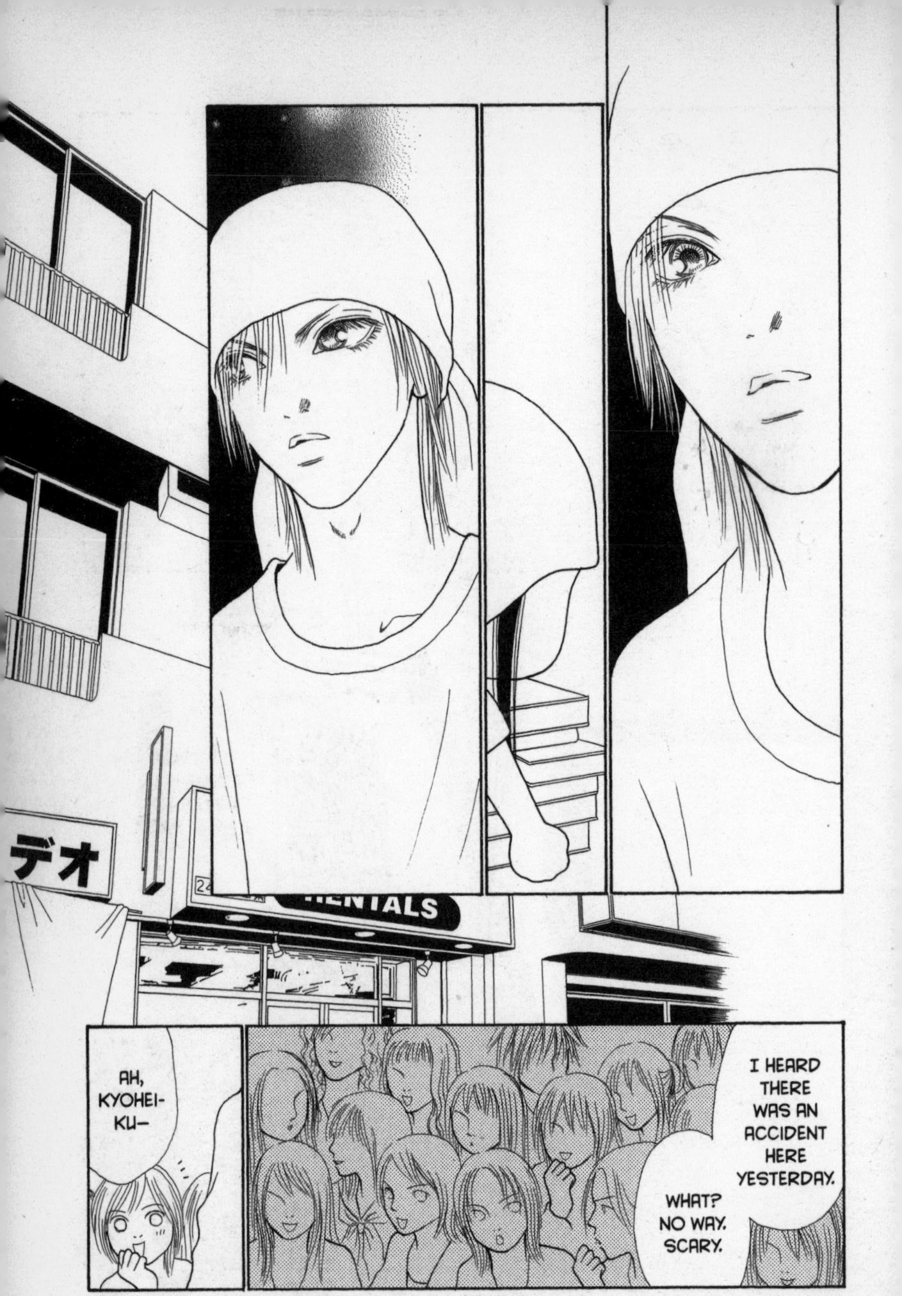
デオ
ENTALS
I HEARD THERE WAS AN ACCIDENT HERE YESTERDAY.
WHAT? NO WAY. SCARY.
AH, KYOHEI-KU–

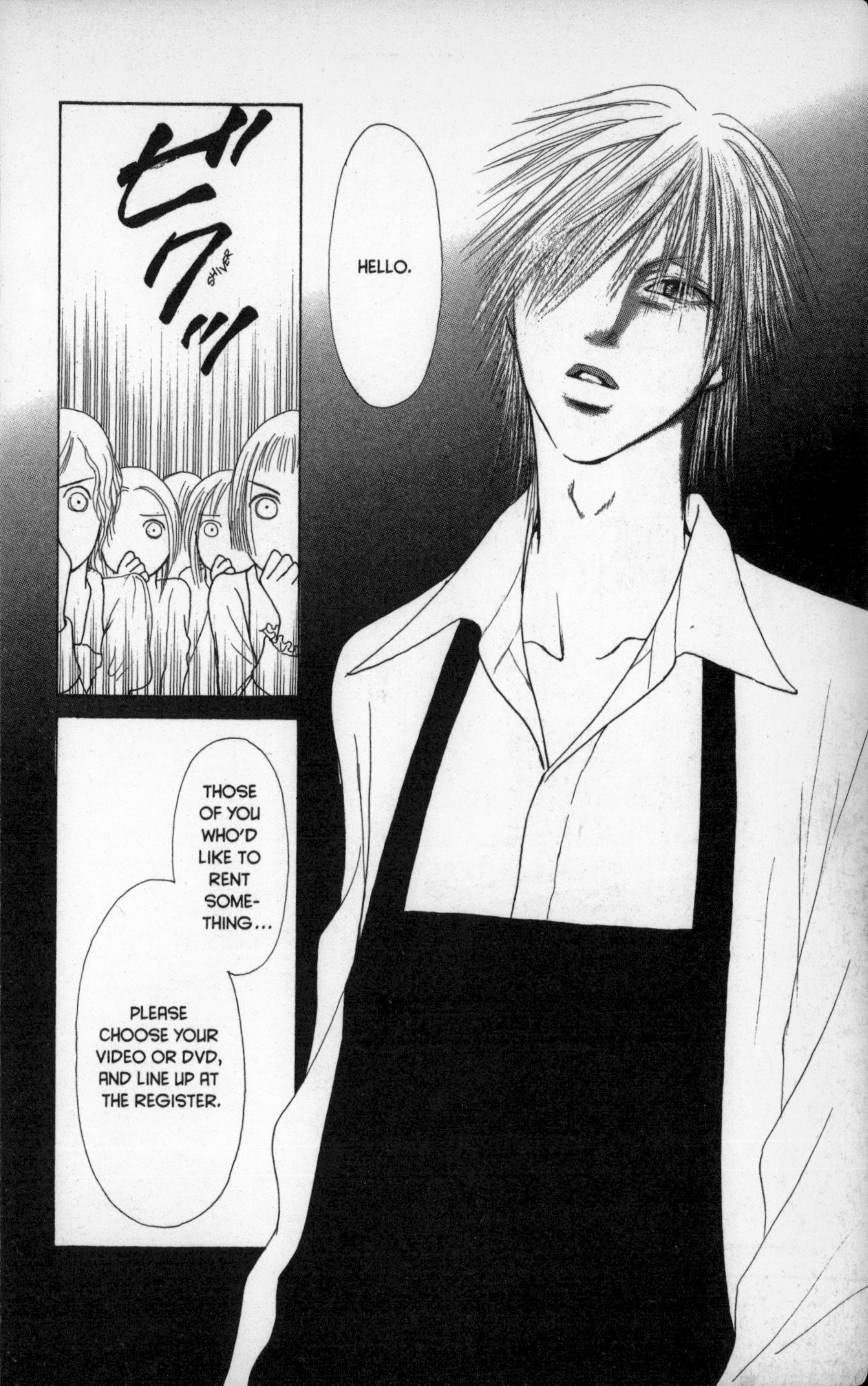
HELLO.
ビクッ
SHIVER
THOSE OF YOU WHO'D LIKE TO RENT SOME-THING...
PLEASE CHOOSE YOUR VIDEO OR DVD, AND LINE UP AT THE REGISTER.

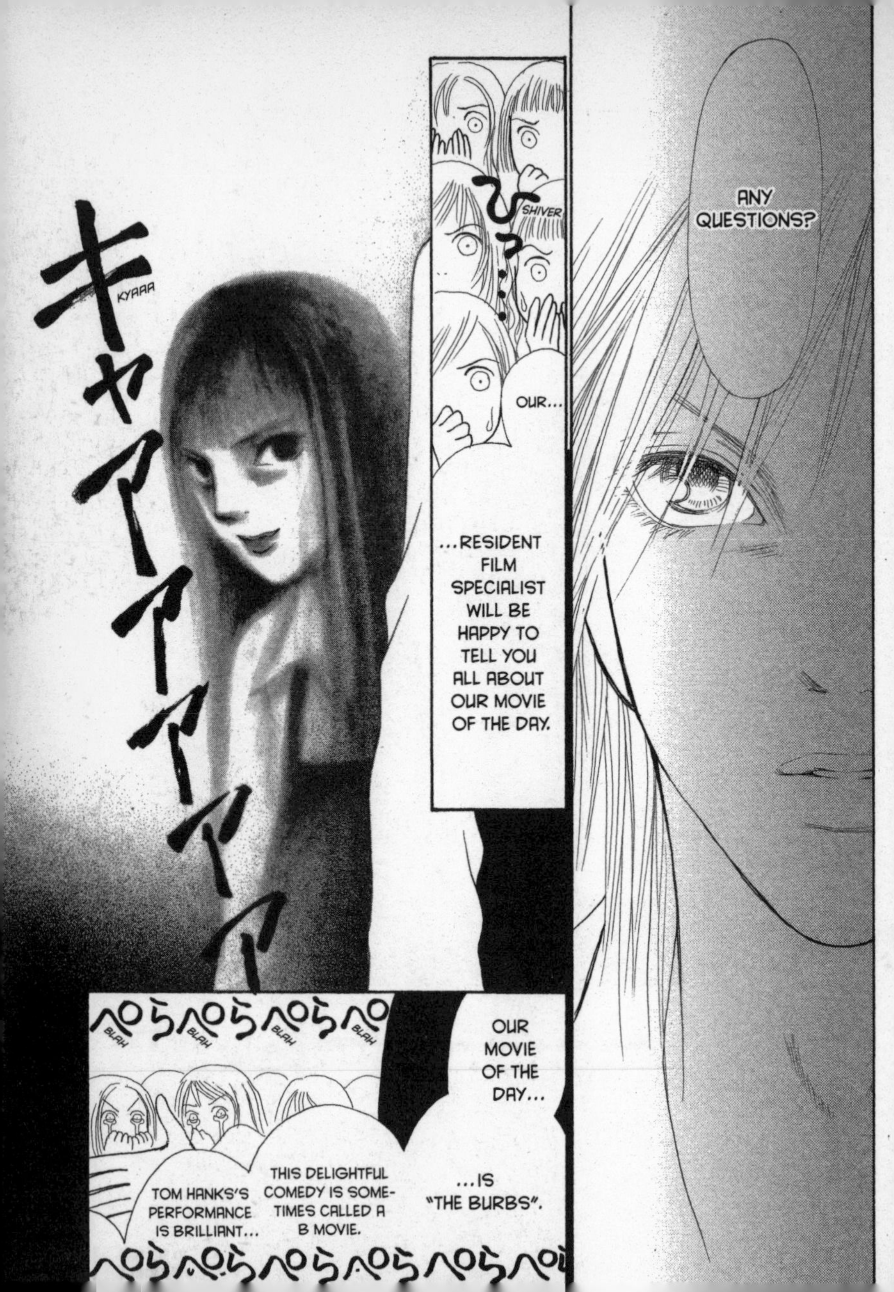
ANY QUESTIONS?
ひっ…
SHIVER
OUR...
...RESIDENT FILM SPECIALIST WILL BE HAPPY TO TELL YOU ALL ABOUT OUR MOVIE OF THE DAY.
キャアアアアア
KYAAA
へらへらへらへらへらへらへ
BLAH BLAH BLAH BLAH
OUR MOVIE OF THE DAY...
...IS "THE BURBS".
THIS DELIGHTFUL COMEDY IS SOME-TIMES CALLED A B MOVIE.
TOM HANKS'S PERFORMANCE IS BRILLIANT...
へらへらへらへらへらへらへらへらへらへらへ

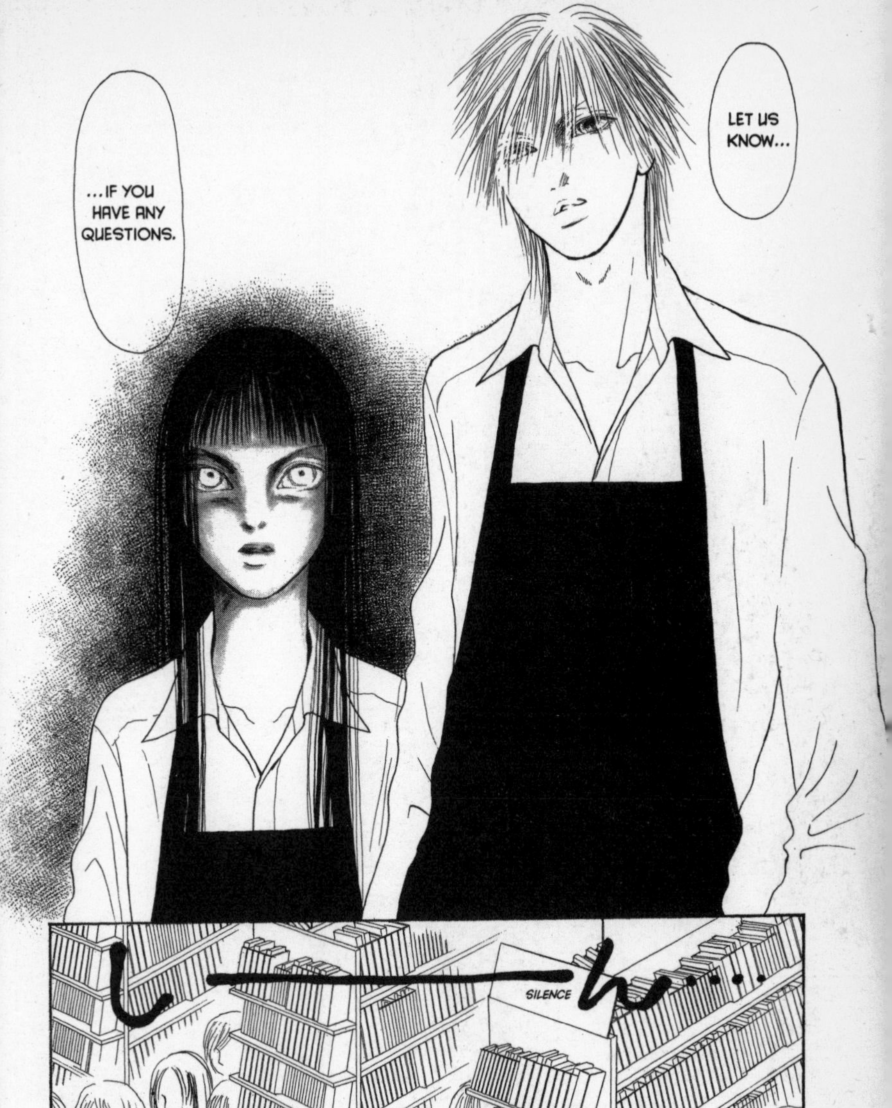
LET US KNOW...
...IF YOU HAVE ANY QUESTIONS.
SILENCE

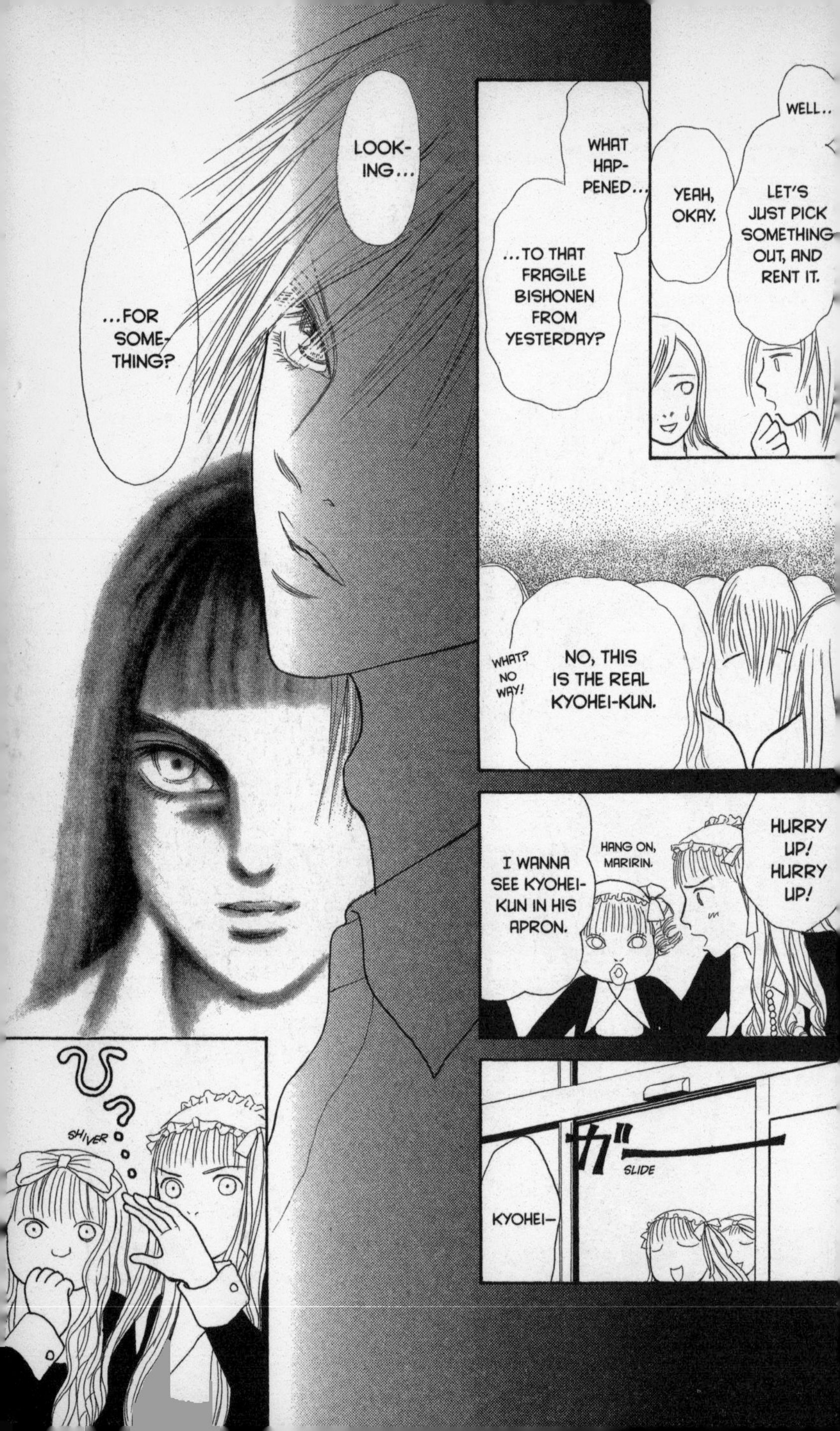
WELL..
LET'S JUST PICK SOMETHING OUT, AND RENT IT.
YEAH, OKAY.
WHAT HAP-PENED...
...TO THAT FRAGILE BISHONEN FROM YESTERDAY?
NO, THIS IS THE REAL KYOHEI-KUN.
WHAT? NO WAY!
HURRY UP! HURRY UP!
HANG ON, MARIRIN.
I WANNA SEE KYOHEI-KUN IN HIS APRON.
ガー
SLIDE
KYOHEI—
LOOK-ING...
...FOR SOME-THING?
SHIVER

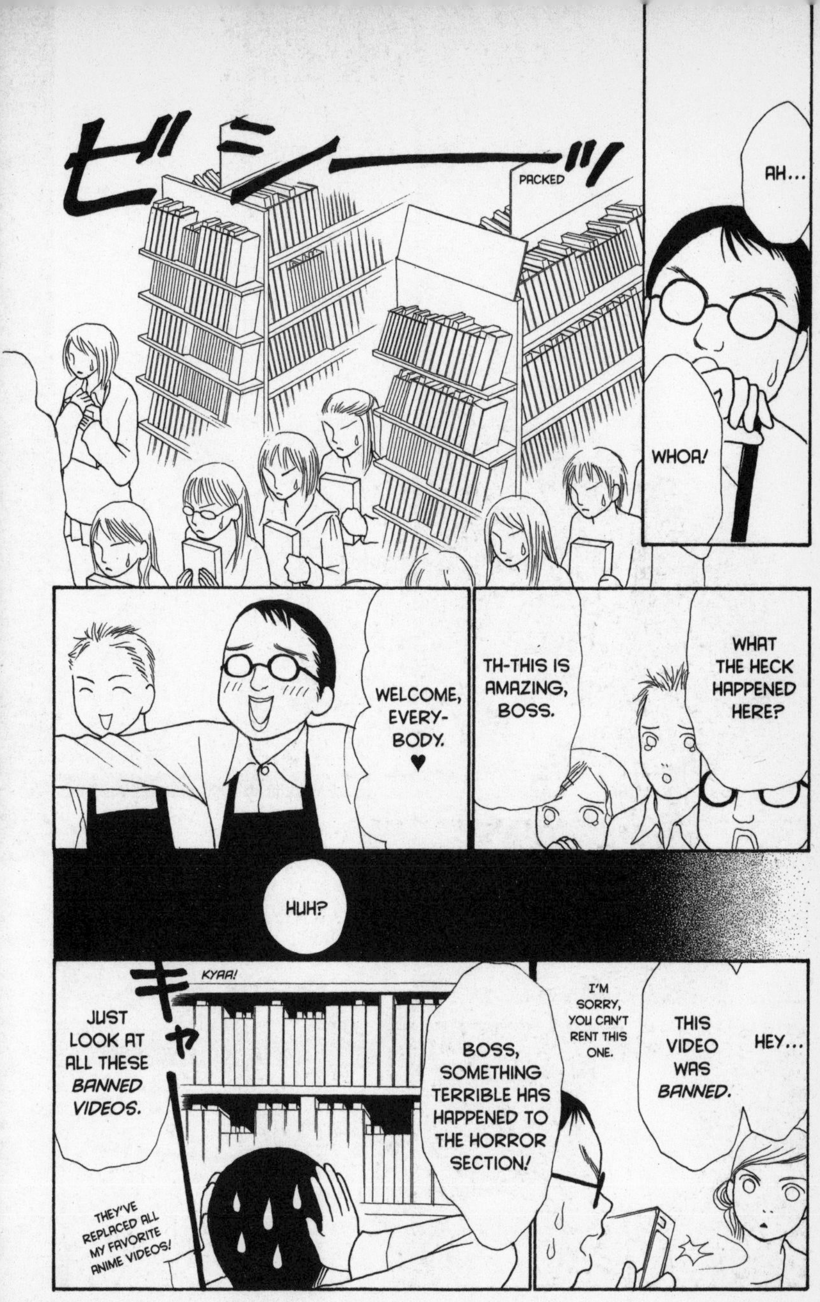
AH...
WHOA!
PACKED
WHAT THE HECK HAPPENED HERE?
TH-THIS IS AMAZING, BOSS.
WELCOME, EVERY-BODY. ♥
HUH?
HEY...
THIS VIDEO WAS *BANNED*.
I'M SORRY, YOU CAN'T RENT THIS ONE.
BOSS, SOMETHING TERRIBLE HAS HAPPENED TO THE HORROR SECTION!
KYAA!
キャ
JUST LOOK AT ALL THESE *BANNED VIDEOS*.
THEY'VE REPLACED ALL MY FAVORITE ANIME VIDEOS!

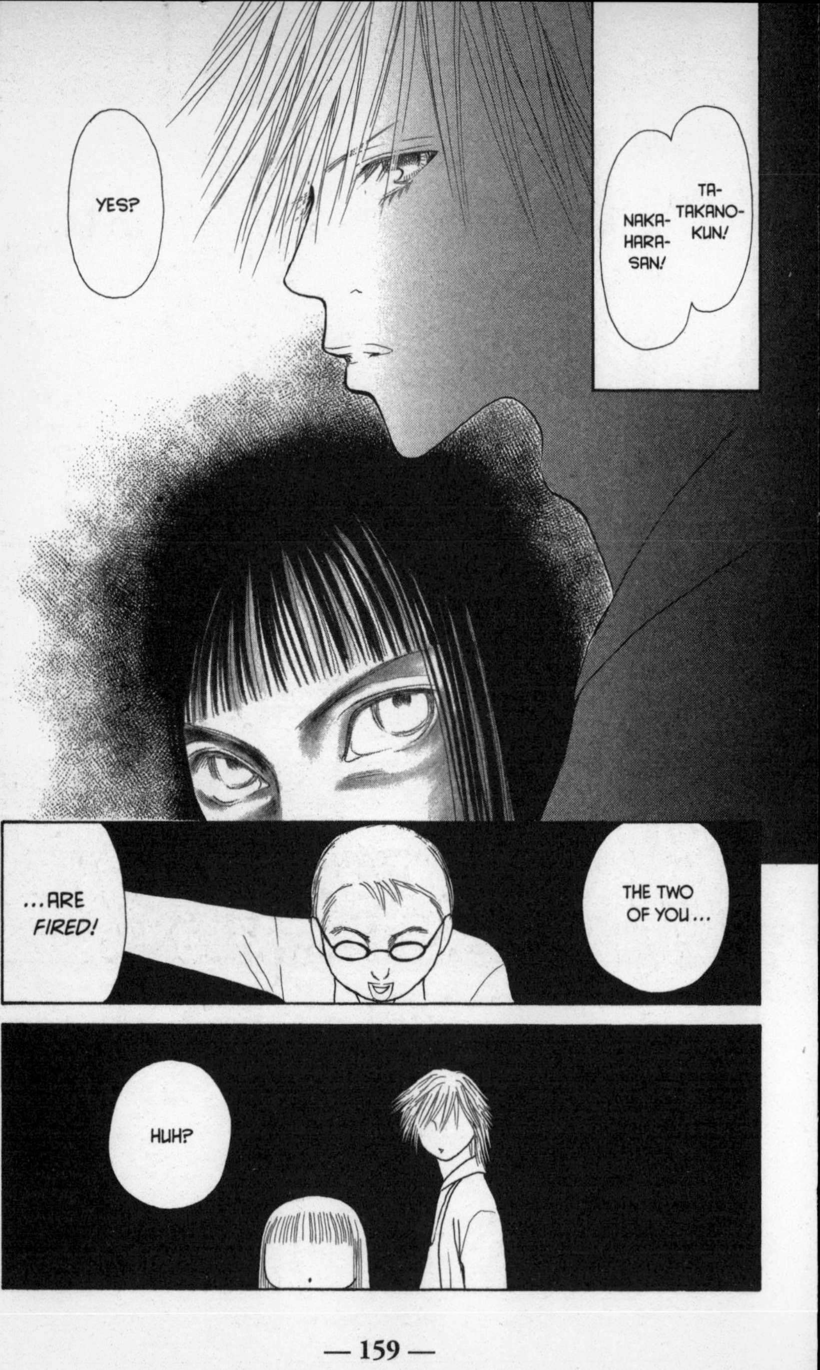
TA- TAKANO-KUN! NAKA-HARA-SAN!
YES?
THE TWO OF YOU...
...ARE FIRED!
HUH?

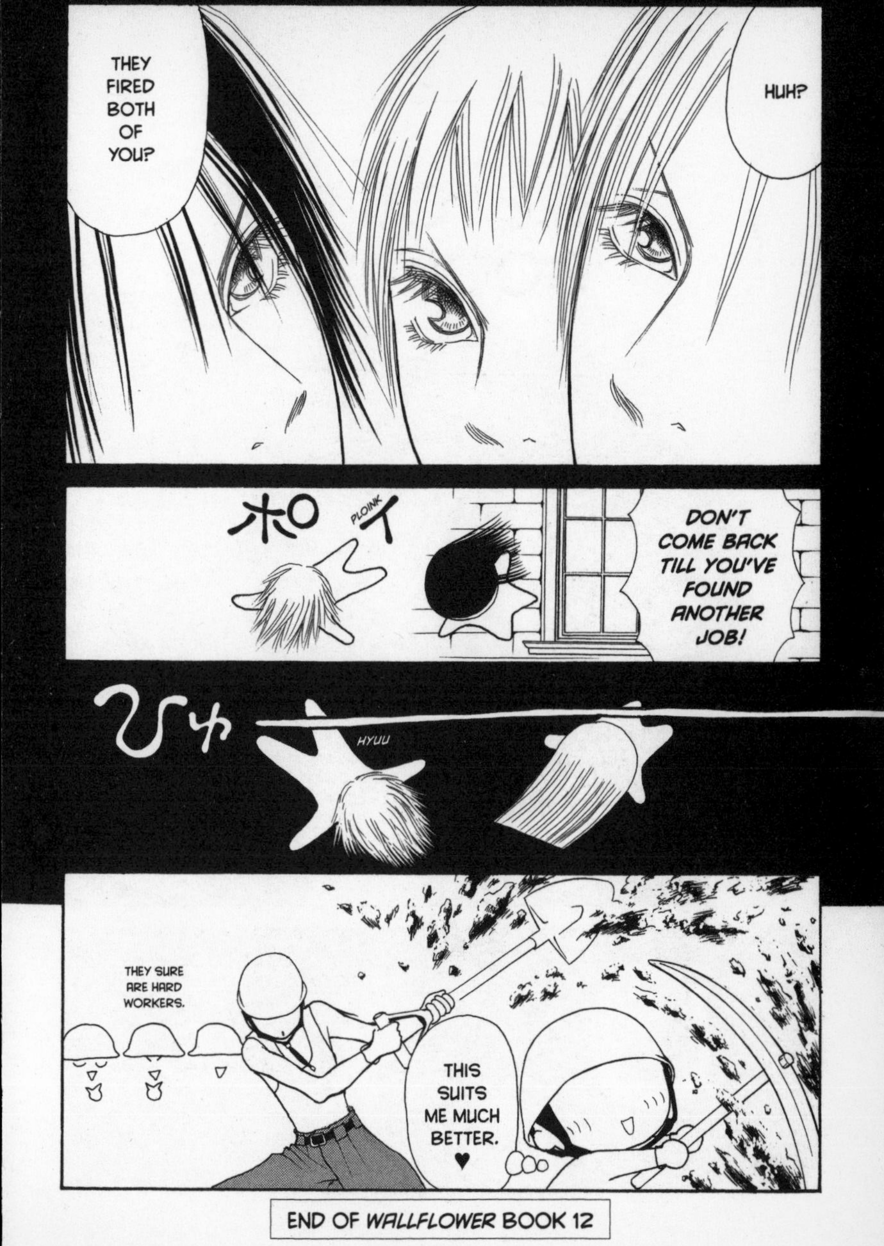
HUH?
THEY FIRED BOTH OF YOU?
DON'T COME BACK TILL YOU'VE FOUND ANOTHER JOB!
ホイ
PLOINK
ひゅ
HYUU
THIS SUITS ME MUCH BETTER. ♥
THEY SURE ARE HARD WORKERS.

END OF *WALLFLOWER* BOOK 12

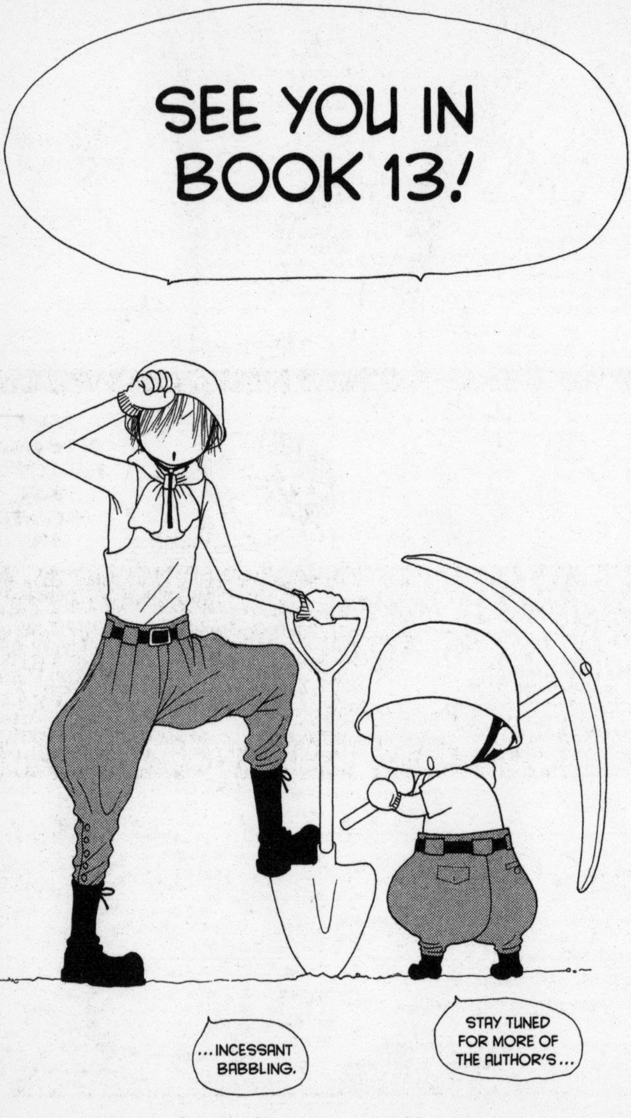
SEE YOU IN BOOK 13!
STAY TUNED FOR MORE OF THE AUTHOR'S...
...INCESSANT BABBLING.

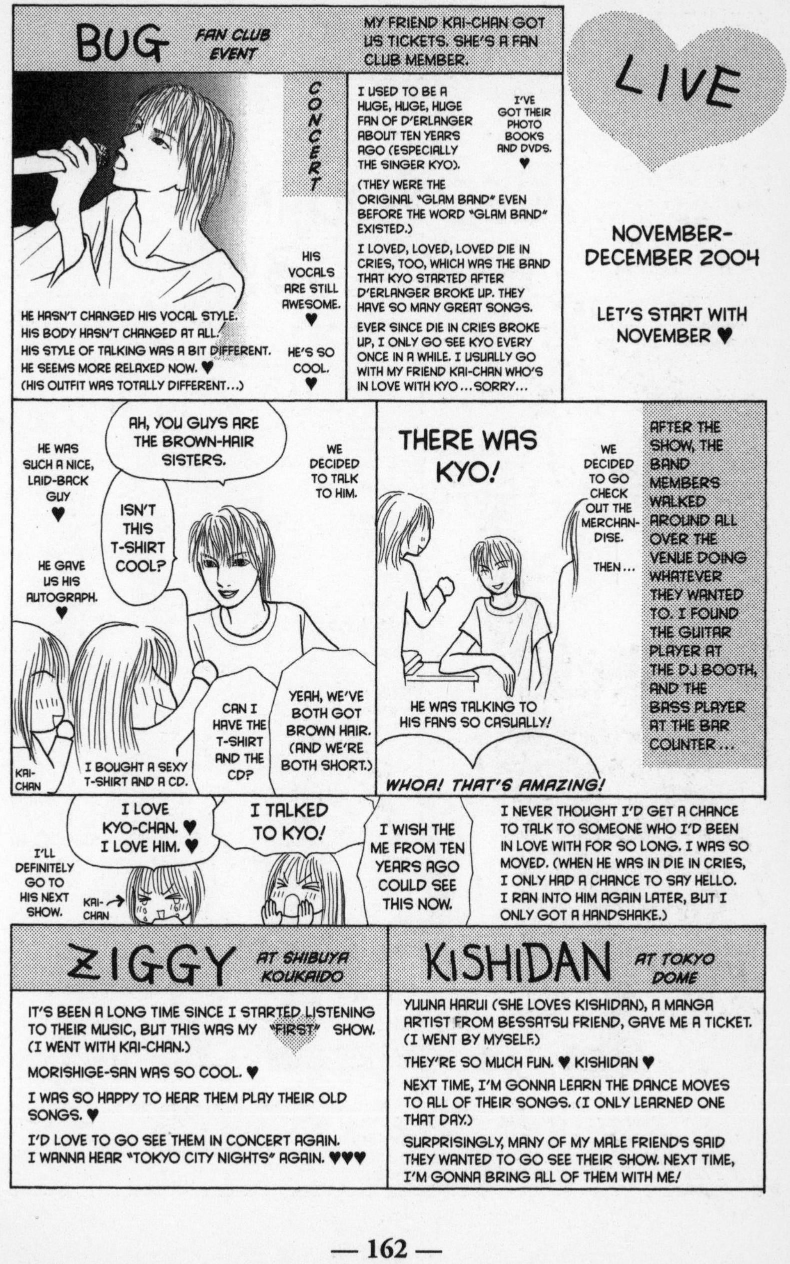
LIVE
NOVEMBER-DECEMBER 2004
LET'S START WITH NOVEMBER ♥
BUG FAN CLUB EVENT
MY FRIEND KAI-CHAN GOT US TICKETS. SHE'S A FAN CLUB MEMBER.
I USED TO BE A HUGE, HUGE, HUGE FAN OF D'ERLANGER ABOUT TEN YEARS AGO (ESPECIALLY THE SINGER KYO).
I'VE GOT THEIR PHOTO BOOKS AND DVDS. ♥
(THEY WERE THE ORIGINAL "GLAM BAND" EVEN BEFORE THE WORD "GLAM BAND" EXISTED.)
I LOVED, LOVED, LOVED DIE IN CRIES, TOO, WHICH WAS THE BAND THAT KYO STARTED AFTER D'ERLANGER BROKE UP. THEY HAVE SO MANY GREAT SONGS.
EVER SINCE DIE IN CRIES BROKE UP, I ONLY GO SEE KYO EVERY ONCE IN A WHILE. I USUALLY GO WITH MY FRIEND KAI-CHAN WHO'S IN LOVE WITH KYO... SORRY...
CONCERT
HIS VOCALS ARE STILL AWESOME. ♥
HE'S SO COOL. ♥
HE HASN'T CHANGED HIS VOCAL STYLE. HIS BODY HASN'T CHANGED AT ALL. HIS STYLE OF TALKING WAS A BIT DIFFERENT. HE SEEMS MORE RELAXED NOW. ♥ (HIS OUTFIT WAS TOTALLY DIFFERENT...)
AFTER THE SHOW, THE BAND MEMBERS WALKED AROUND ALL OVER THE VENUE DOING WHATEVER THEY WANTED TO. I FOUND THE GUITAR PLAYER AT THE DJ BOOTH, AND THE BASS PLAYER AT THE BAR COUNTER...
WE DECIDED TO GO CHECK OUT THE MERCHANDISE.
THEN...
THERE WAS KYO!
HE WAS TALKING TO HIS FANS SO CASUALLY!
WHOA! THAT'S AMAZING!
WE DECIDED TO TALK TO HIM.
AH, YOU GUYS ARE THE BROWN-HAIR SISTERS.
HE WAS SUCH A NICE, LAID-BACK GUY ♥
ISN'T THIS T-SHIRT COOL?
HE GAVE US HIS AUTOGRAPH. ♥
YEAH, WE'VE BOTH GOT BROWN HAIR. (AND WE'RE BOTH SHORT.)
CAN I HAVE THE T-SHIRT AND THE CD?
I BOUGHT A SEXY T-SHIRT AND A CD.
KAI-CHAN
I NEVER THOUGHT I'D GET A CHANCE TO TALK TO SOMEONE WHO I'D BEEN IN LOVE WITH FOR SO LONG. I WAS SO MOVED. (WHEN HE WAS IN DIE IN CRIES, I ONLY HAD A CHANCE TO SAY HELLO. I RAN INTO HIM AGAIN LATER, BUT I ONLY GOT A HANDSHAKE.)
I WISH THE ME FROM TEN YEARS AGO COULD SEE THIS NOW.
I TALKED TO KYO!
I LOVE KYO-CHAN. ♥ I LOVE HIM. ♥
I'LL DEFINITELY GO TO HIS NEXT SHOW.
KAI-CHAN
KISHIDAN AT TOKYO DOME
YUUNA HARUI (SHE LOVES KISHIDAN), A MANGA ARTIST FROM BESSATSU FRIEND, GAVE ME A TICKET. (I WENT BY MYSELF.)
THEY'RE SO MUCH FUN. ♥ KISHIDAN ♥
NEXT TIME, I'M GONNA LEARN THE DANCE MOVES TO ALL OF THEIR SONGS. (I ONLY LEARNED ONE THAT DAY.)
SURPRISINGLY, MANY OF MY MALE FRIENDS SAID THEY WANTED TO GO SEE THEIR SHOW. NEXT TIME, I'M GONNA BRING ALL OF THEM WITH ME!
ZIGGY AT SHIBUYA KOUKAIDO
IT'S BEEN A LONG TIME SINCE I STARTED LISTENING TO THEIR MUSIC, BUT THIS WAS MY "FIRST" SHOW. (I WENT WITH KAI-CHAN.)
MORISHIGE-SAN WAS SO COOL. ♥
I WAS SO HAPPY TO HEAR THEM PLAY THEIR OLD SONGS. ♥
I'D LOVE TO GO SEE THEM IN CONCERT AGAIN. I WANNA HEAR "TOKYO CITY NIGHTS" AGAIN. ♥♥♥

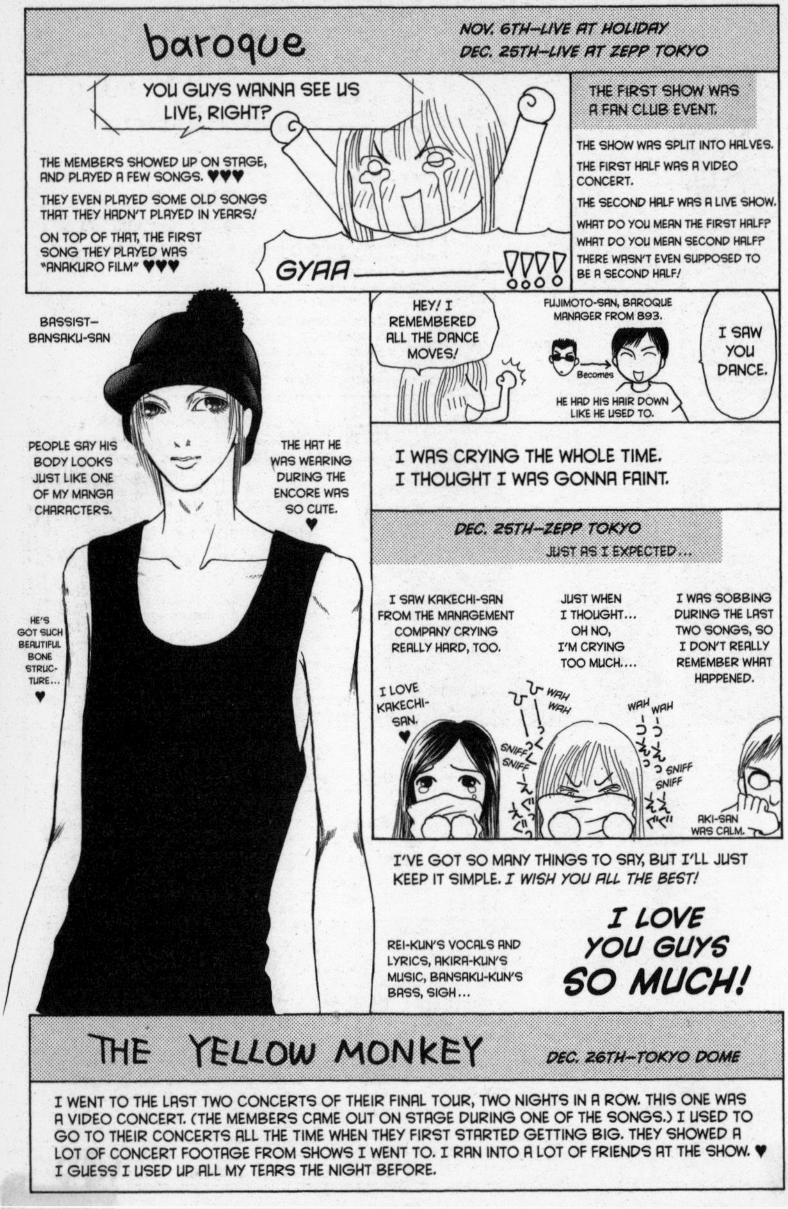

baroque
NOV. 6TH—LIVE AT HOLIDAY
DEC. 25TH—LIVE AT ZEPP TOKYO
THE FIRST SHOW WAS A FAN CLUB EVENT.
THE SHOW WAS SPLIT INTO HALVES.
THE FIRST HALF WAS A VIDEO CONCERT.
THE SECOND HALF WAS A LIVE SHOW.
WHAT DO YOU MEAN THE FIRST HALF?
WHAT DO YOU MEAN SECOND HALF?
THERE WASN'T EVEN SUPPOSED TO BE A SECOND HALF!
YOU GUYS WANNA SEE US LIVE, RIGHT?
THE MEMBERS SHOWED UP ON STAGE, AND PLAYED A FEW SONGS. ♥♥♥
THEY EVEN PLAYED SOME OLD SONGS THAT THEY HADN'T PLAYED IN YEARS!
ON TOP OF THAT, THE FIRST SONG THEY PLAYED WAS "ANAKURO FILM" ♥♥♥
GYAA——————!!!!!
I SAW YOU DANCE.
FUJIMOTO-SAN, BAROQUE MANAGER FROM 893.
Becomes
HE HAD HIS HAIR DOWN LIKE HE USED TO.
HEY! I REMEMBERED ALL THE DANCE MOVES!
I WAS CRYING THE WHOLE TIME. I THOUGHT I WAS GONNA FAINT.
DEC. 25TH—ZEPP TOKYO
JUST AS I EXPECTED...
I WAS SOBBING DURING THE LAST TWO SONGS, SO I DON'T REALLY REMEMBER WHAT HAPPENED.
JUST WHEN I THOUGHT... OH NO, I'M CRYING TOO MUCH....
I SAW KAKECHI-SAN FROM THE MANAGEMENT COMPANY CRYING REALLY HARD, TOO.
AKI-SAN WAS CALM.
WAH WAH
SNIFF SNIFF
WAH WAH
SNIFF SNIFF
I LOVE KAKECHI-SAN. ♥
I'VE GOT SO MANY THINGS TO SAY, BUT I'LL JUST KEEP IT SIMPLE. I WISH YOU ALL THE BEST!
I LOVE YOU GUYS SO MUCH!
REI-KUN'S VOCALS AND LYRICS, AKIRA-KUN'S MUSIC, BANSAKU-KUN'S BASS, SIGH...
BASSIST—BANSAKU-SAN
THE HAT HE WAS WEARING DURING THE ENCORE WAS SO CUTE. ♥
PEOPLE SAY HIS BODY LOOKS JUST LIKE ONE OF MY MANGA CHARACTERS.
HE'S GOT SUCH BEAUTIFUL BONE STRUCTURE... ♥
THE YELLOW MONKEY
DEC. 26TH—TOKYO DOME
I WENT TO THE LAST TWO CONCERTS OF THEIR FINAL TOUR, TWO NIGHTS IN A ROW. THIS ONE WAS A VIDEO CONCERT. (THE MEMBERS CAME OUT ON STAGE DURING ONE OF THE SONGS.) I USED TO GO TO THEIR CONCERTS ALL THE TIME WHEN THEY FIRST STARTED GETTING BIG. THEY SHOWED A LOT OF CONCERT FOOTAGE FROM SHOWS I WENT TO. I RAN INTO A LOT OF FRIENDS AT THE SHOW. ♥
I GUESS I USED UP ALL MY TEARS THE NIGHT BEFORE.

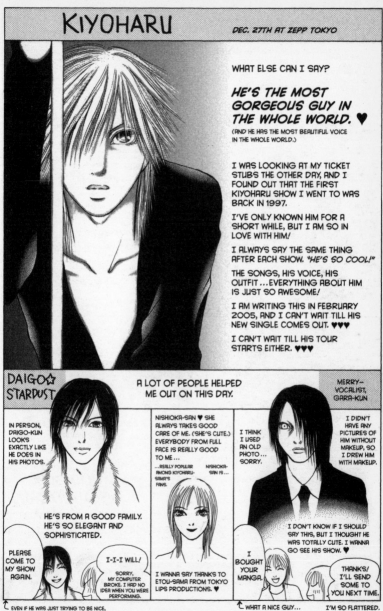

KIYOHARU

DEC. 27TH AT ZEPP TOKYO

WHAT ELSE CAN I SAY?

HE'S THE MOST GORGEOUS GUY IN THE WHOLE WORLD. ♥

(AND HE HAS THE MOST BEAUTIFUL VOICE IN THE WHOLE WORLD.)

I WAS LOOKING AT MY TICKET STUBS THE OTHER DAY, AND I FOUND OUT THAT THE FIRST KIYOHARU SHOW I WENT TO WAS BACK IN 1997.

I'VE ONLY KNOWN HIM FOR A SHORT WHILE, BUT I AM SO IN LOVE WITH HIM!

I ALWAYS SAY THE SAME THING AFTER EACH SHOW. *"HE'S SO COOL!"*

THE SONGS, HIS VOICE, HIS OUTFIT... EVERYTHING ABOUT HIM IS JUST SO AWESOME!

I AM WRITING THIS IN FEBRUARY 2005, AND I CAN'T WAIT TILL HIS NEW SINGLE COMES OUT. ♥♥♥

I CAN'T WAIT TILL HIS TOUR STARTS EITHER. ♥♥♥

MERRY—VOCALIST, GARA-KUN
A LOT OF PEOPLE HELPED ME OUT ON THIS DAY.
DAIGO☆STARDUST
I DIDN'T HAVE ANY PICTURES OF HIM WITHOUT MAKEUP, SO I DREW HIM WITH MAKEUP.
I THINK I USED AN OLD PHOTO... SORRY.
I DON'T KNOW IF I SHOULD SAY THIS, BUT I THOUGHT HE WAS TOTALLY CUTE. I WANNA GO SEE HIS SHOW. ♥
THANKS! I'LL SEND SOME TO YOU NEXT TIME.
I BOUGHT YOUR MANGA.
I'M SO FLATTERED.
WHAT A NICE GUY...
NISHIOKA-SAN ♥ SHE ALWAYS TAKES GOOD CARE OF ME. (SHE'S CUTE.) EVERYBODY FROM FULL FACE IS REALLY GOOD TO ME...
NISHIOKA-SAN IS...
...REALLY POPULAR AMONG KIYOHARU-SAMA'S FANS.
I WANNA SAY THANKS TO ETOU-SAMA FROM TOKYO LIPS PRODUCTIONS. ♥
IN PERSON, DAIGO-KUN LOOKS EXACTLY LIKE HE DOES IN HIS PHOTOS.
HE'S FROM A GOOD FAMILY. HE'S SO ELEGANT AND SOPHISTICATED.
I-I-I WILL!
SORRY, MY COMPUTER BROKE. I HAD NO IDEA WHEN YOU WERE PERFORMING.
PLEASE COME TO MY SHOW AGAIN.
EVEN IF HE WAS JUST TRYING TO BE NICE, I WAS REALLY HAPPY HE SAID THAT. ♥

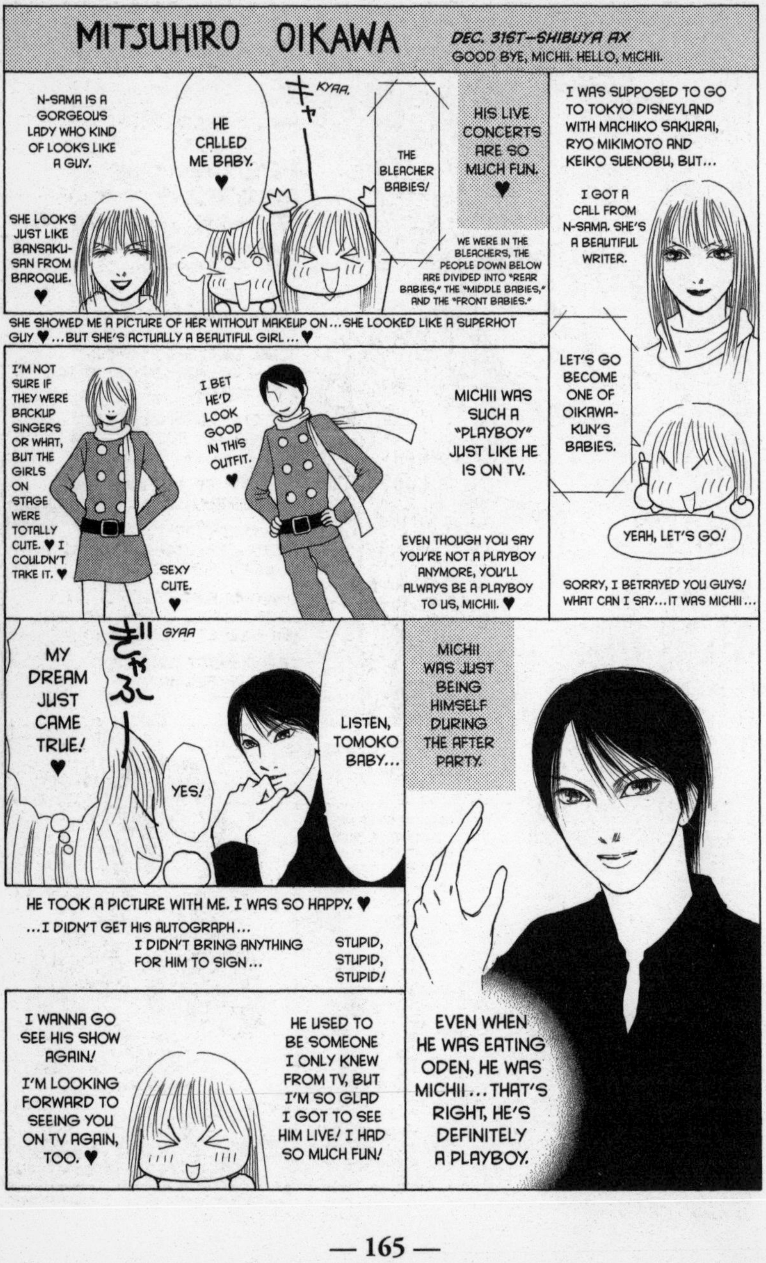
MITSUHIRO OIKAWA
DEC. 31ST—SHIBUYA AX
GOOD BYE, MICHII. HELLO, MICHII.
I WAS SUPPOSED TO GO TO TOKYO DISNEYLAND WITH MACHIKO SAKURAI, RYO MIKIMOTO AND KEIKO SUENOBU, BUT...
I GOT A CALL FROM N-SAMA. SHE'S A BEAUTIFUL WRITER.
LET'S GO BECOME ONE OF OIKAWA-KUN'S BABIES.
YEAH, LET'S GO!
SORRY, I BETRAYED YOU GUYS! WHAT CAN I SAY... IT WAS MICHII...
HIS LIVE CONCERTS ARE SO MUCH FUN. ♥
WE WERE IN THE BLEACHERS, THE PEOPLE DOWN BELOW ARE DIVIDED INTO "REAR BABIES," THE "MIDDLE BABIES," AND THE "FRONT BABIES."
THE BLEACHER BABIES!
KYAA.
HE CALLED ME BABY. ♥
N-SAMA IS A GORGEOUS LADY WHO KIND OF LOOKS LIKE A GUY.
SHE LOOKS JUST LIKE BANSAKU-SAN FROM BAROQUE. ♥
SHE SHOWED ME A PICTURE OF HER WITHOUT MAKEUP ON... SHE LOOKED LIKE A SUPERHOT GUY ♥... BUT SHE'S ACTUALLY A BEAUTIFUL GIRL... ♥
MICHII WAS SUCH A "PLAYBOY" JUST LIKE HE IS ON TV.
EVEN THOUGH YOU SAY YOU'RE NOT A PLAYBOY ANYMORE, YOU'LL ALWAYS BE A PLAYBOY TO US, MICHII. ♥
I BET HE'D LOOK GOOD IN THIS OUTFIT. ♥
I'M NOT SURE IF THEY WERE BACKUP SINGERS OR WHAT, BUT THE GIRLS ON STAGE WERE TOTALLY CUTE. ♥ I COULDN'T TAKE IT. ♥
SEXY CUTE. ♥
MICHII WAS JUST BEING HIMSELF DURING THE AFTER PARTY.
EVEN WHEN HE WAS EATING ODEN, HE WAS MICHII... THAT'S RIGHT, HE'S DEFINITELY A PLAYBOY.
LISTEN, TOMOKO BABY...
GYAA
MY DREAM JUST CAME TRUE! ♥
YES!
HE TOOK A PICTURE WITH ME. I WAS SO HAPPY. ♥
...I DIDN'T GET HIS AUTOGRAPH...
I DIDN'T BRING ANYTHING FOR HIM TO SIGN...
STUPID, STUPID, STUPID!
HE USED TO BE SOMEONE I ONLY KNEW FROM TV, BUT I'M SO GLAD I GOT TO SEE HIM LIVE! I HAD SO MUCH FUN!
I WANNA GO SEE HIS SHOW AGAIN!
I'M LOOKING FORWARD TO SEEING YOU ON TV AGAIN, TOO. ♥

THIS IS
TENNOSUKE HAYAKAWA.

I SUCK AT DRAWING CATS, AND I SUCK AT TAKING PICTURES, TOO...
I CAN ONLY USE ONE OUT OF EVERY THIRTY SHOTS I TAKE...

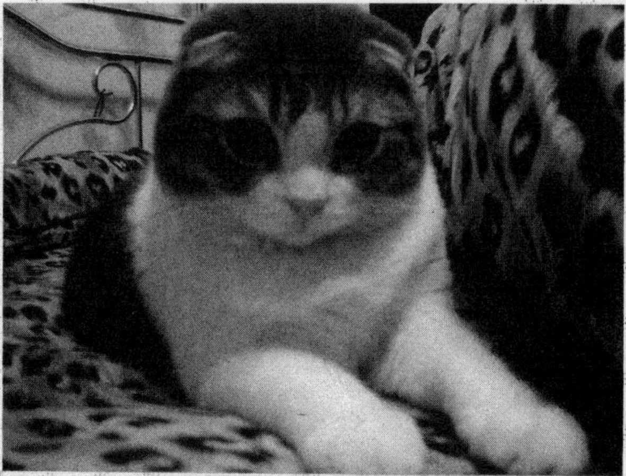

HE'S A SUPER CUTE, WILD BOY. ♥

♥ *TEN'S FAVORITE POSES* ♥

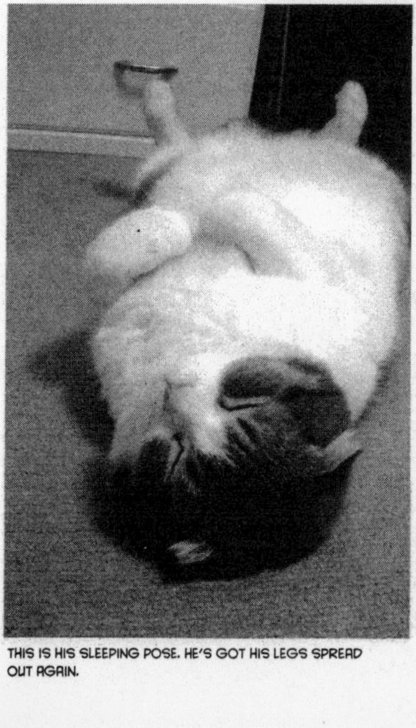

THIS IS HIS SLEEPING POSE. HE'S GOT HIS LEGS SPREAD OUT AGAIN.

THIS PICTURE SHOWS HOW HUGE TEN IS.

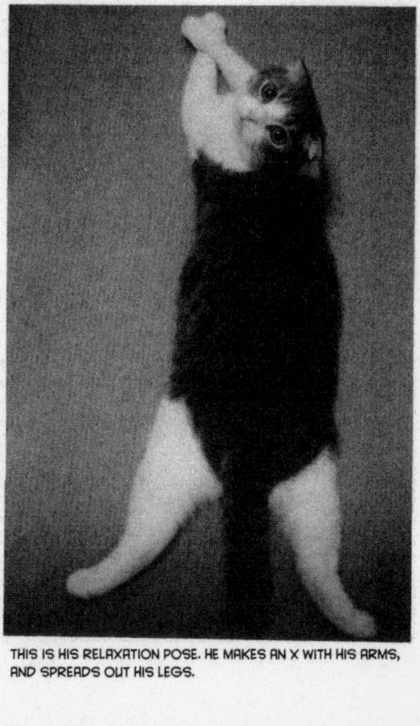

THIS IS HIS RELAXATION POSE. HE MAKES AN X WITH HIS ARMS, AND SPREADS OUT HIS LEGS.

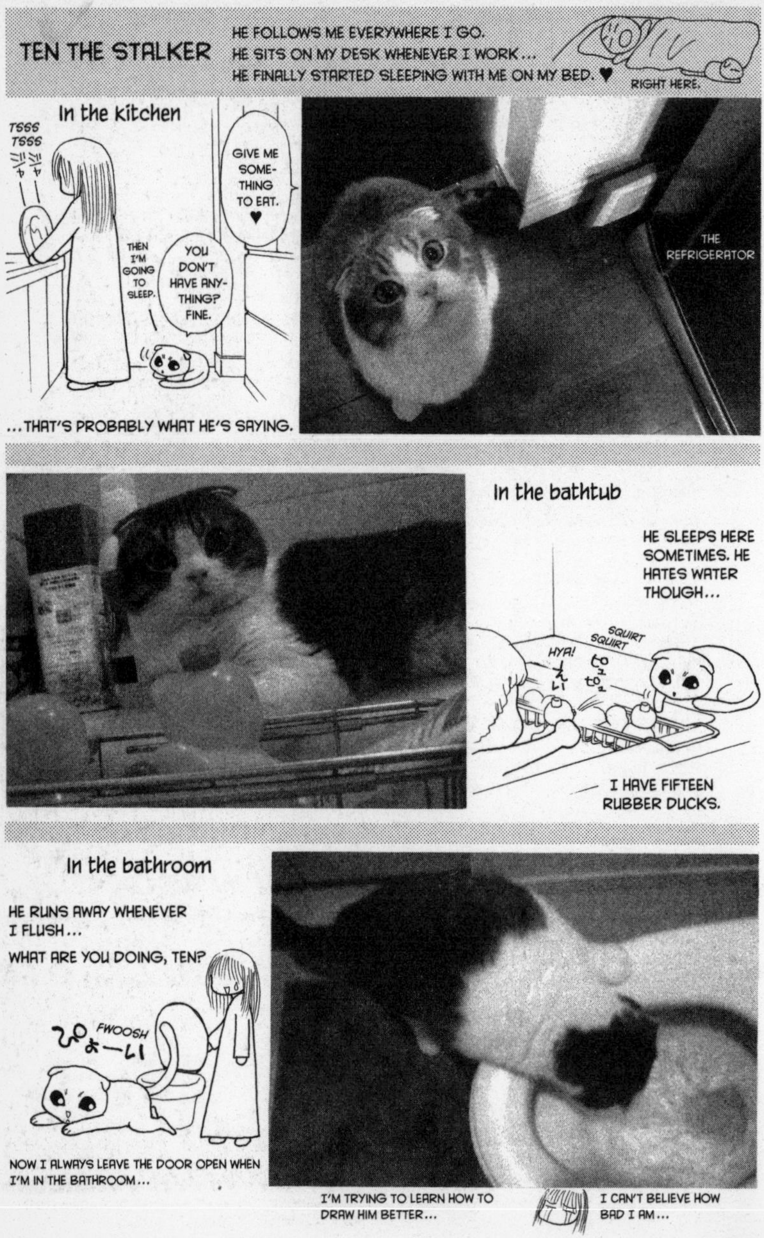

TEN THE STALKER
HE FOLLOWS ME EVERYWHERE I GO.
HE SITS ON MY DESK WHENEVER I WORK...
HE FINALLY STARTED SLEEPING WITH ME ON MY BED. ♥
RIGHT HERE.
THE REFRIGERATOR
In the kitchen
GIVE ME SOMETHING TO EAT. ♥
YOU DON'T HAVE ANYTHING? FINE.
THEN I'M GOING TO SLEEP.
TSSS TSSS
ジャー ジャー
...THAT'S PROBABLY WHAT HE'S SAYING.
In the bathtub
HE SLEEPS HERE SOMETIMES. HE HATES WATER THOUGH...
SQUIRT SQUIRT
HYA!
I HAVE FIFTEEN RUBBER DUCKS.
In the bathroom
HE RUNS AWAY WHENEVER I FLUSH...
WHAT ARE YOU DOING, TEN?
FWOOSH
ぴょーい
NOW I ALWAYS LEAVE THE DOOR OPEN WHEN I'M IN THE BATHROOM...
I'M TRYING TO LEARN HOW TO DRAW HIM BETTER...
I CAN'T BELIEVE HOW BAD I AM...

THANKS FOR BUYING DEL REY MANGA.

I HAD SOME EXTRA BONUS PAGES THIS TIME, SO I HAD LOTS OF FUN. ♥
TEN GOT TWO PAGES ALL TO HIMSELF ... HEH, HEH!

THANKS FOR SENDING ME ALL YOUR FAN MAIL. ♥
WHEN I'M DEPRESSED, I READ THEM OVER AND OVER AGAIN. YOUR LETTERS ARE A CONSTANT SOURCE OF ENERGY FOR ME. THEY MAKE ME FEEL A MILLION TIMES BETTER. ♥ I CRY A LOT WHEN I READ YOUR LETTERS ... ♥ I MEAN IT.

I WROTE IN BOOK 11 THAT I WANTED TO MAKE AN ANNOUNCEMENT ABOUT MY WEIGHT LOSS, BUT... *I'M NOT THERE YET*. I'M STILL WORKING ON IT. ♥
I'M TRYING REALLY HARD ♥... SIGH... PLEASE WAIT TILL BOOK 13 ... BY THE TIME BOOK 13 COMES OUT, I WANT MY WEIGHT TO BE 38 KG ... ♥ ← THAT'S NEVER GONNA HAPPEN.
THANKS FOR GIVING ME TIPS. I'M IMPRESSED BY HOW MUCH YOU GUYS KNOW ABOUT DIETING. ♥ I'M USING SOME OF YOUR SUGGESTIONS. THEY'RE REALLY HELPFUL. ♥♥♥
I'M REALLY HOPING TO SEE SOME RESULTS!

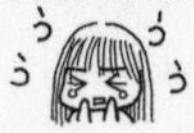

THANKS FOR SENDING "PET PHOTOS" AND "PET STORIES." ♥
WHEN WE LIVE WITH ANIMALS, WE ALL TURN INTO LOVEY-DOVEY PARENTS, RIGHT? ♥ RIGHT? ♥ RIGHT? ♥

THANKS FOR SENDING ME CLIPPINGS, POSTERS, AND FAN CLUB ZINES. WOW!
THANK YOU SOOOO MUCH. PLEASE DON'T FEEL ANY PRESSURE THOUGH, OKAY?

THANKS FOR SENDING ME *NIGHTMARE BEFORE CHRISTMAS* STUFF AND LOTS OF SKULL STUFF. I'M GLAD THERE'RE SO MANY PEOPLE OUT THERE WHO ARE INTO MY FAVORITE STUFF. ♥

THANKS FOR SENDING ME MINI DISCS. ♥ IT'S INTERESTING TO LISTEN TO MUSICIANS I'VE NEVER HEARD OF, OR I NEVER HAD A CHANCE TO LISTEN TO. SOMETIMES I COME ACROSS SONGS THAT I LIKE. SOME OF YOU SEEM TO HAVE THE SAME MUSICAL TASTE AS ME. ♥

THANK YOU SOOOOOO MUCH. ♥ I TREASURE ALL THE GIFTS FROM YOU. ♥

OKAY, THANKS FOR STICKING AROUND.

♥ SEE YOU IN BOOK 13. ♥

SPECIAL THANKS

HANA-CHAN,
YOSHII,
KIMURA-SAN,
NAKAZAWA-SAN,
HITOSHI HAYAKAWA (LITTLE BROTHER),
TAKEKO HAYAKAWA (MOM)

RYO NARUMI-SAMA,
YUUKA KITAGAWA-SAMA

MINE-SAMA,
INO-SAMA,
IZAWA-SAMA,
EVERYBODY FROM THE EDITING DEPARTMENT.

EVERYBODY WHO SENT ME LETTERS,
EVERYBODY WHO'S READING THIS RIGHT NOW.

EXTRA BONUS

HOW TO DRAW SUNAKO

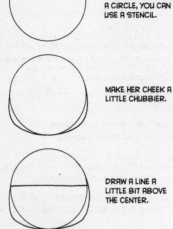

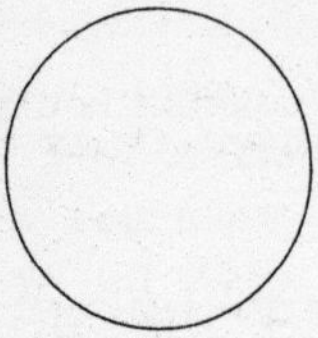

IF YOU'RE NOT GOOD AT DRAWING A CIRCLE, YOU CAN USE A STENCIL.

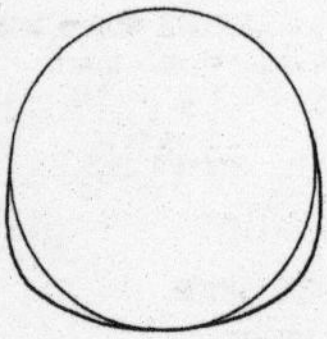

MAKE HER CHEEK A LITTLE CHUBBIER.

DRAW A LINE A LITTLE BIT ABOVE THE CENTER.

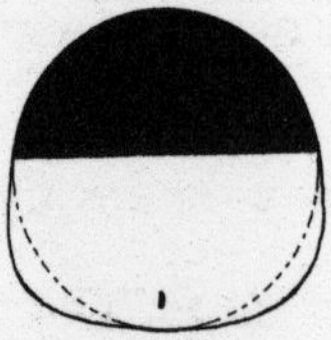

DRAW A SLIGHTLY LONG DOT.

ADD SOME HAIR, AND THERE SHE IS!

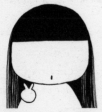

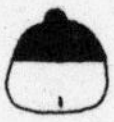

THIS STYLE IS EVEN EASIER.

About the Creator

Tomoko Hayakawa was born on March 4.

Since her debut as a manga creator, Tomoko Hayakawa has worked on many shojo titles with the theme of romantic love—only to realize that she could write about other subjects as well. She decided to pack her newest story with the things she likes most, which led to her current, enormously popular series, *The Wallflower*.

Her favorite things are: Tim Burton's *The Nightmare Before Christmas*, Jean-Paul Gaultier, and samurai dramas on TV. Her hobbies are collecting items with skull designs and watching *bishonen* (beautiful boys). Her dream is to build a mansion like the one the Addams family lives in. Her favorite pastime is to lie around at home with her cat, Ten (whose full name is Tennosuke).

Her zodiac sign is Pisces, and her blood group is AB.

Translation Notes

Japanese is a tricky language for most Westerners, and translation is often more art than science. For your edification and reading pleasure, here are notes on some of the places where we could have gone in a different direction in our translation of the work, or where a Japanese cultural reference is used.

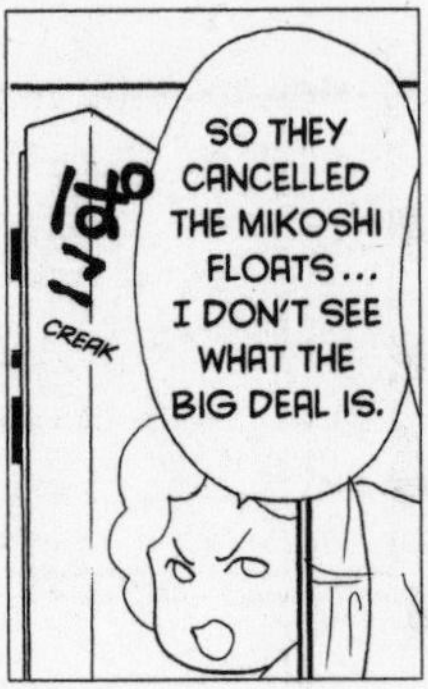

SO THEY CANCELLED THE MIKOSHI FLOATS... I DON'T SEE WHAT THE BIG DEAL IS.
ギィ
CREAK

***Mikoshi*, page 10**
A *mikoshi* is a kind of float used in Japanese festivals. They're generally carried on the shoulders of dozens of festival participants.

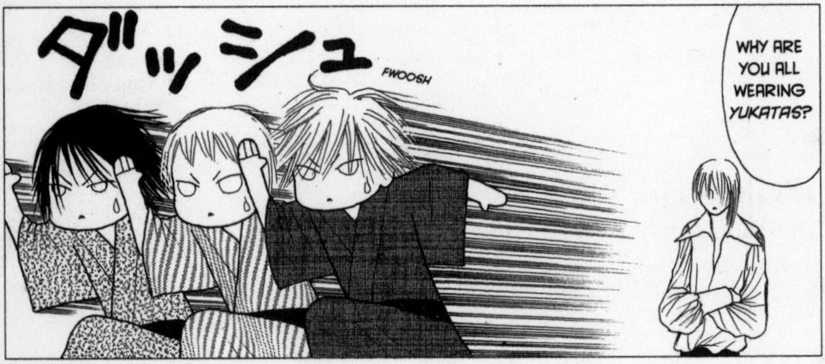

WHY ARE YOU ALL WEARING *YUKATAS*?
ダッシュ
FWOOSH

***Yukata*, page 11**
Yukata are lightweight kimonos that are often worn to summer festivals.

Goldfish scooping, page 11

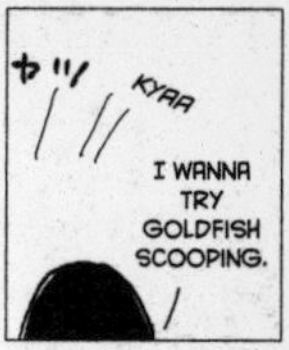
KYAA
I WANNA TRY GOLDFISH SCOOPING.

Just like American carnivals, Japanese festivals are full of games. "Goldfish scooping" is a game in which you try to scoop up a goldfish with a paper spoon before the spoon breaks.

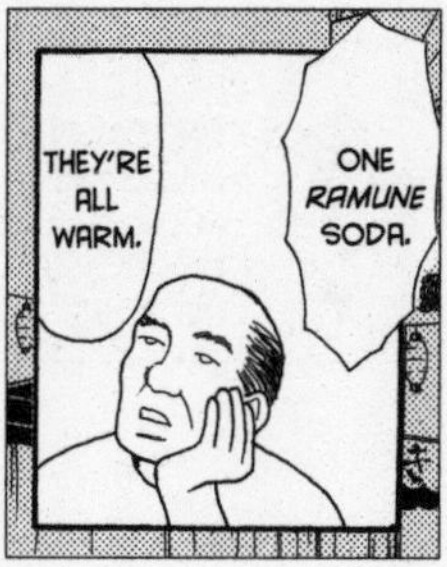
ONE *RAMUNE* SODA.
THEY'RE ALL WARM.

Ramune, page 17

Ramune is a popular lemon-flavored Japanese soda. It comes in a glass bottle with a little marble for a stopper. The pressure from the carbon dioxide holds the stopper in place. When you open the bottle, the marble comes loose but stays inside the neck of the bottle, and jiggles around as you enjoy your soda.

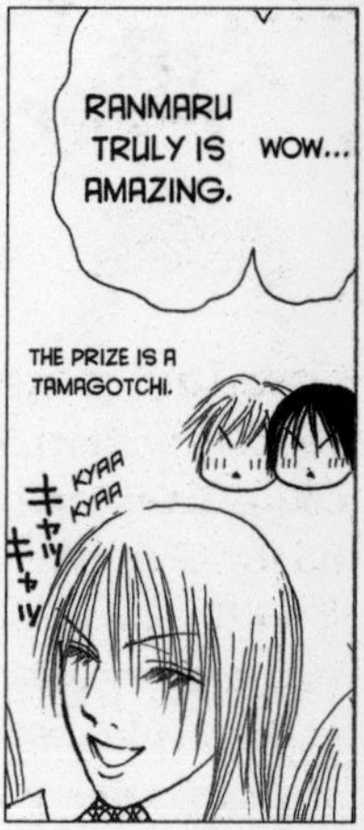
WOW...
RANMARU TRULY IS AMAZING.
THE PRIZE IS A TAMAGOTCHI.
KYAA KYAA

Tamagotchi, page 24

The Tamagotchi was a virtual reality toy popular in the late 90s.

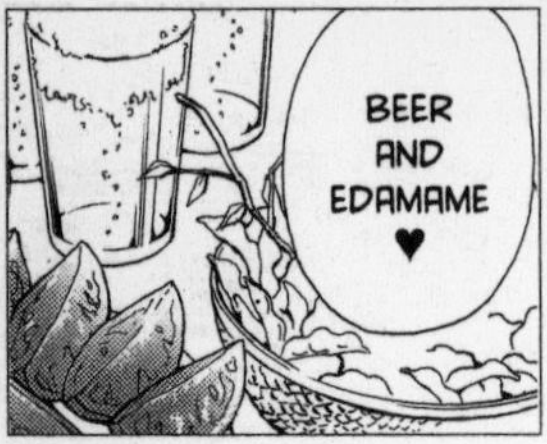
BEER AND EDAMAME ♥

Edamame, page 40

Edamame are soybeans still in their pods. They're a popular snack in Japan and are often served with beer.

Tsurikichi Sanpei, page 44

Tsurikichi Sanpei was a popular anime about fishing.

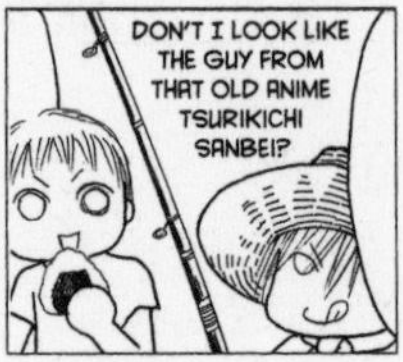
DON'T I LOOK LIKE THE GUY FROM THAT OLD ANIME TSURIKICHI SANBEI?

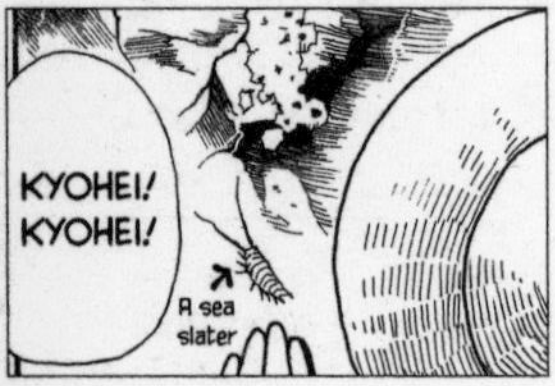
KYOHEI! KYOHEI!
A sea slater

Sea slaters, page 58

Sea slaters are little cockroach-like critters that scurry around the sand and rocks of Japan's beaches.

Cosplay, page 85

Cosplay is short for "costume play." Cosplay generally refers to the hobby of dressing up as one's favorite manga or anime character. At a cosplay café, the waiters dress up in cosplay as they serve their anxious *otaku* guests.

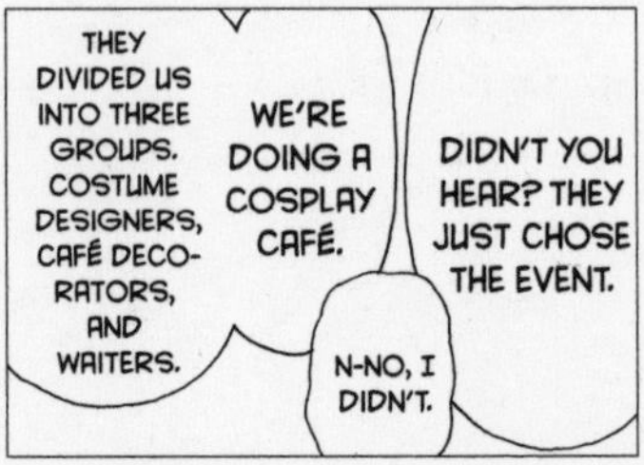
DIDN'T YOU HEAR? THEY JUST CHOSE THE EVENT.
N-NO, I DIDN'T.
WE'RE DOING A COSPLAY CAFÉ.
THEY DIVIDED US INTO THREE GROUPS. COSTUME DESIGNERS, CAFÉ DECORATORS, AND WAITERS.

Print Club, page 97
Print Club, usually abbreviated as "Purikura" in Japanese, are photo booths that produce cute little photo stickers. You step inside the booth with your friends, take a few photos, and out pops a little sheet of stickers like those shown on page 98.

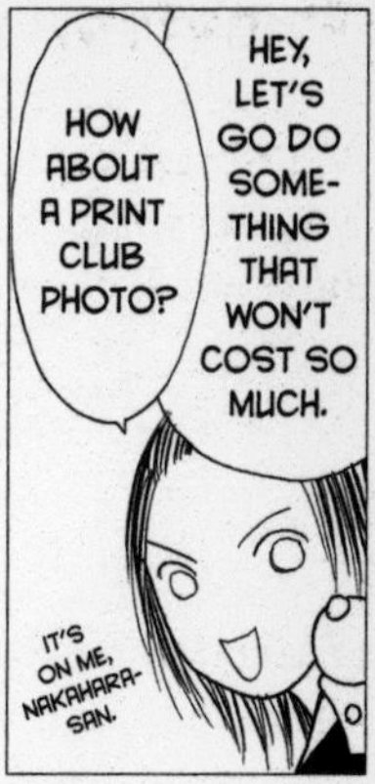
HEY, LET'S GO DO SOME-THING THAT WON'T COST SO MUCH.
HOW ABOUT A PRINT CLUB PHOTO?
IT'S ON ME, NAKAHARA-SAN.

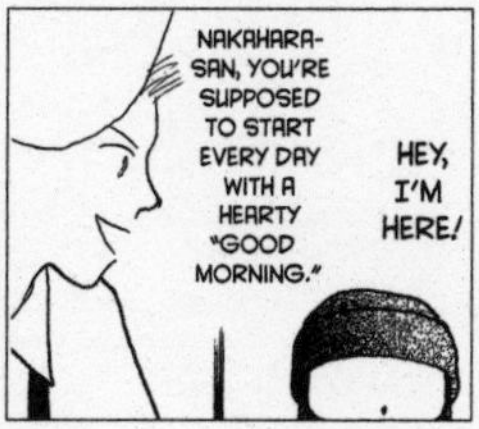
HEY, I'M HERE!
NAKAHARA-SAN, YOU'RE SUPPOSED TO START EVERY DAY WITH A HEARTY "GOOD MORNING."

"Hey, I'm here," page 139
Some Japanese companies require their employees to start and end the day with certain greetings. Here Sunako is warned for saying "Hey, I'm here!" instead of "Good morning."

Preview of volume 13

We're pleased to present you with a preview from volume 13. This volume will be available in English on September 25, 2007, but for now you'll have to make do with Japanese!

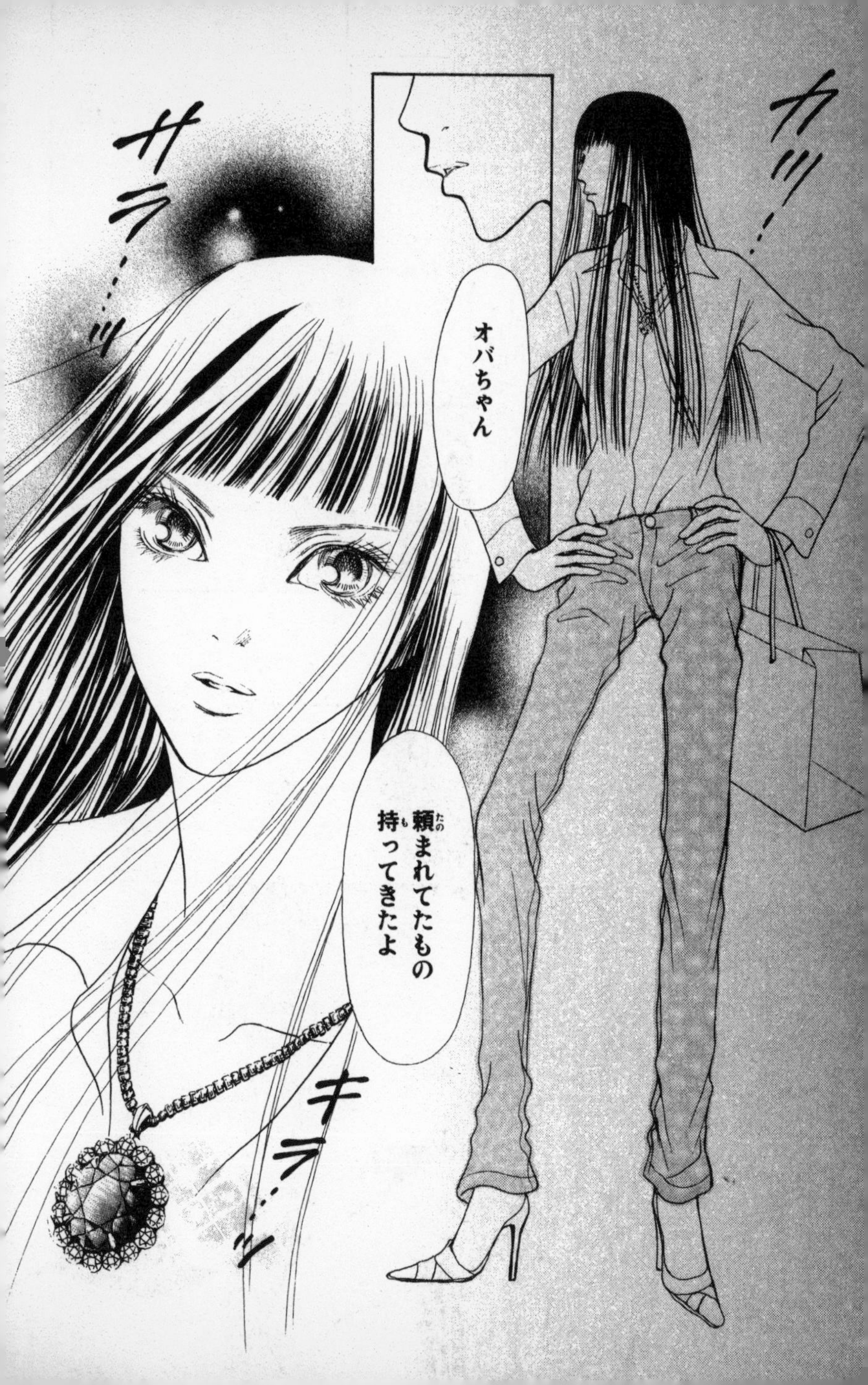
カツ…
オバちゃん
サラ…ッ
頼まれてたもの持ってきたよ
キラ…ッ

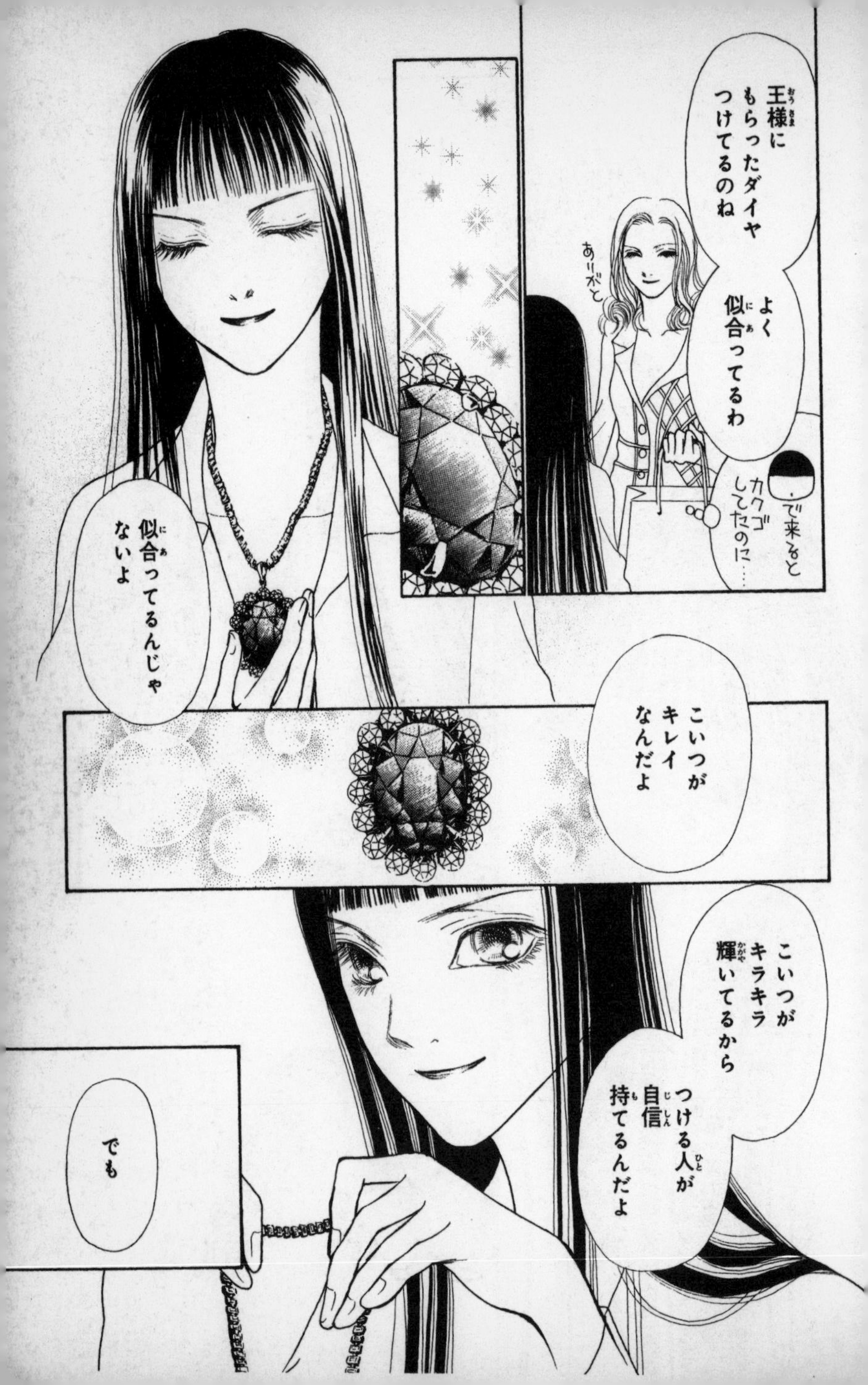
王様にもらったダイヤつけてるのね
よく似合ってるわ
ありがと
で来るとカクゴしてたのに……
似合ってるんじゃないよ
こいつがキレイなんだよ
こいつがキラキラ輝いてるから
つける人が自信持てるんだよ
でも

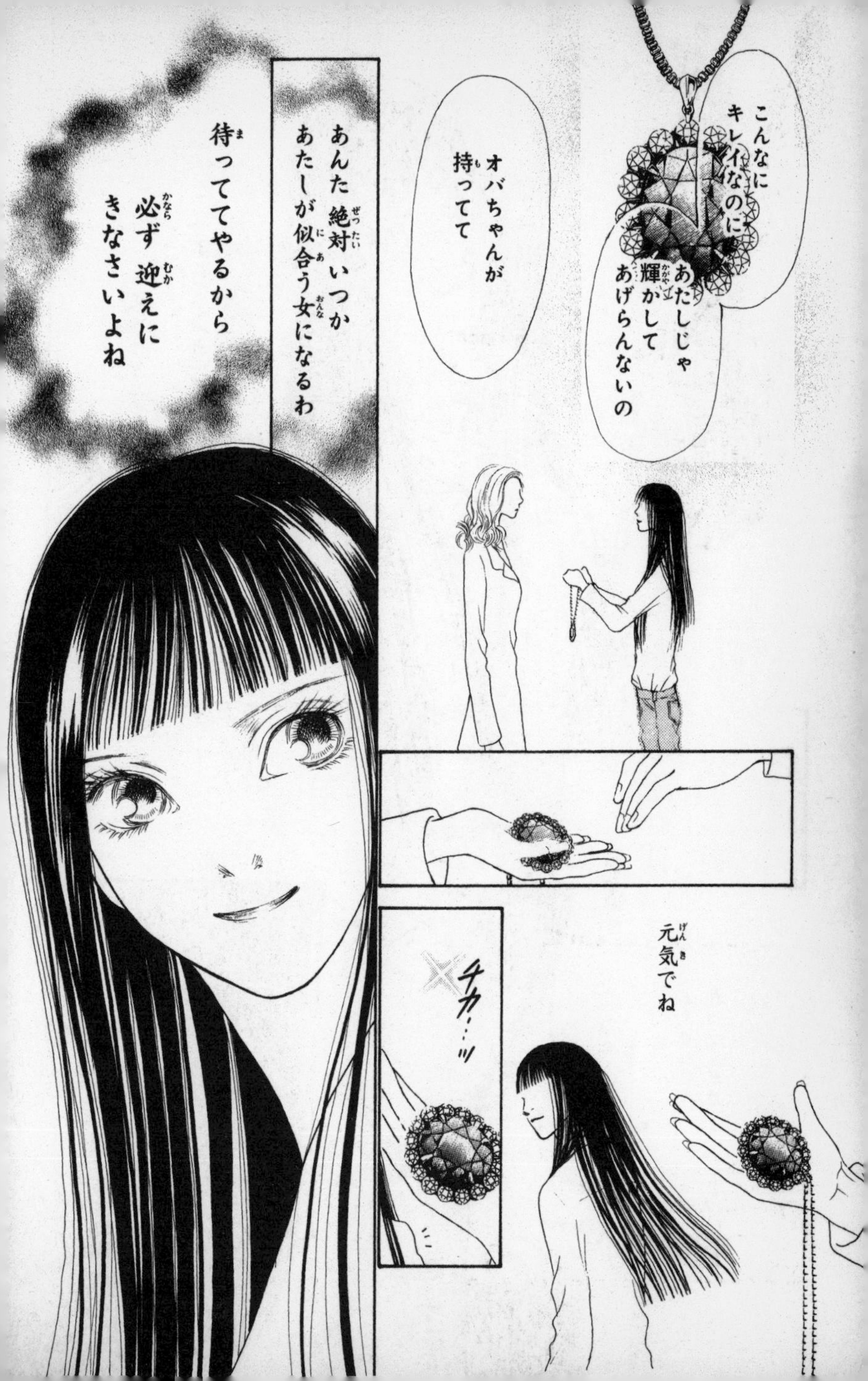
こんなにキレイなのにあたしじゃ輝かしてあげらんないの
オバちゃんが持ってて
元気でね
チカ…ッ
あんた絶対いつかあたしが似合う女になるわ
待っててやるから必ず迎えにきなさいよね

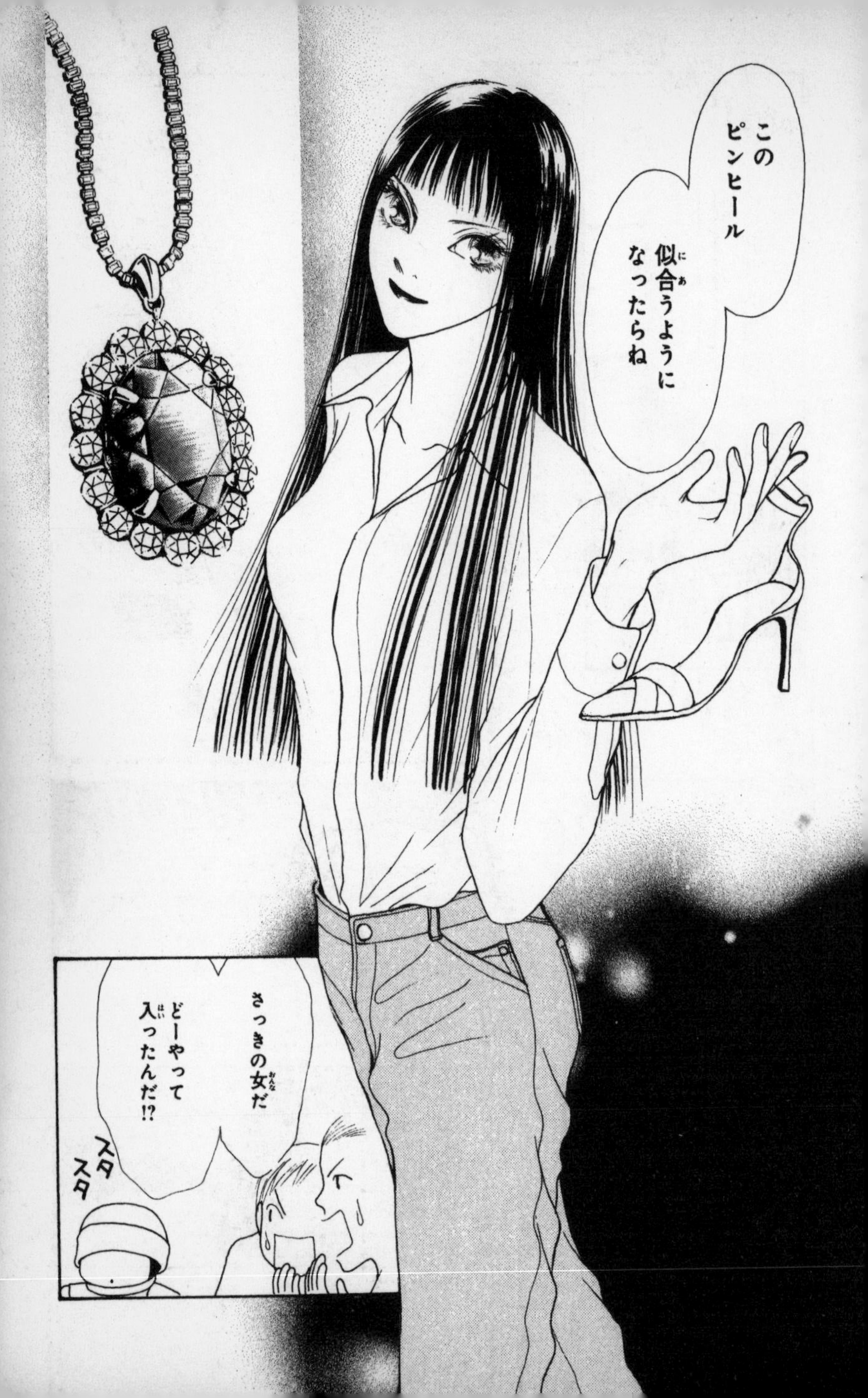
このピンヒール似合うようになったらね
さっきの女だ
どーやって入ったんだ!?
スタスタ

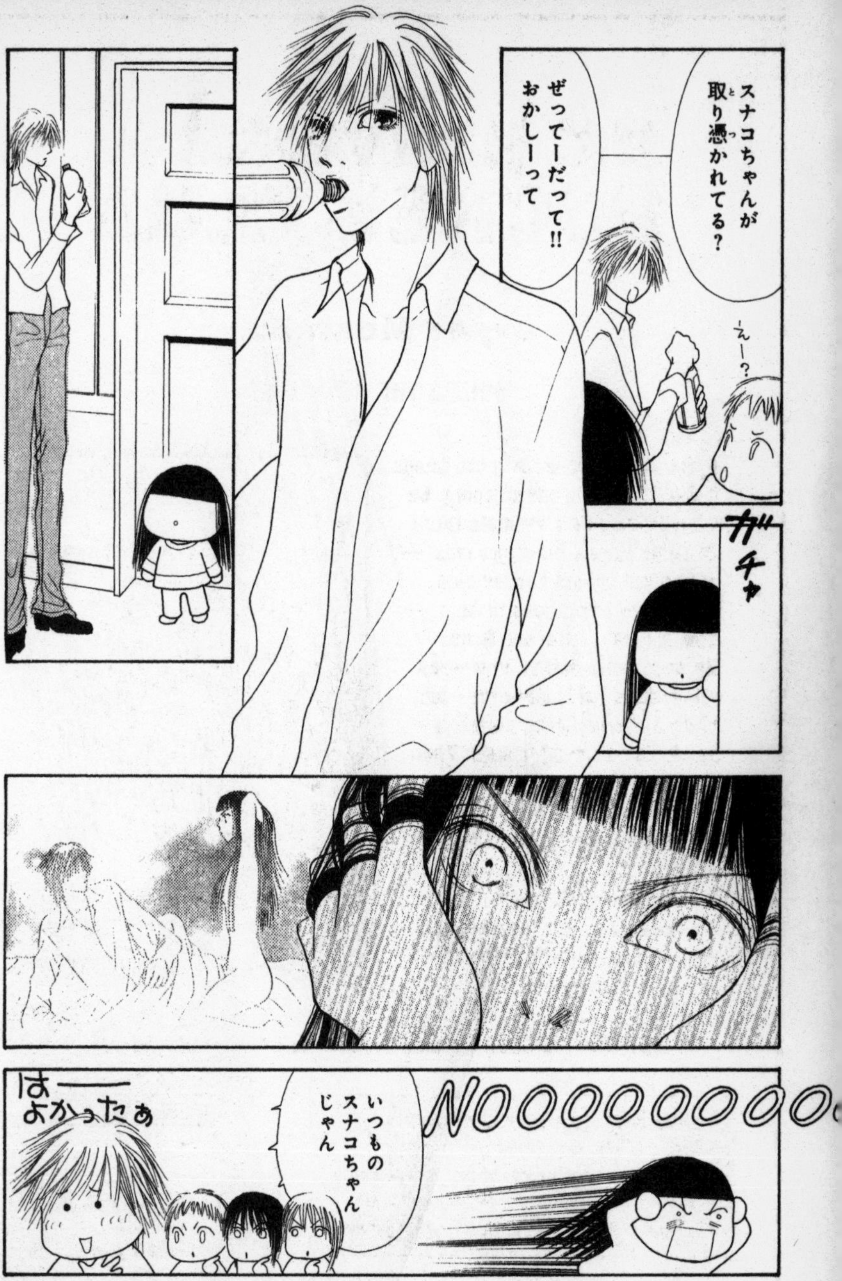
スナコちゃんが取り憑かれてる？
ぜってーだって!!おかしーって
えー？
ガチャ
NOOOOOOOOO
いつものスナコちゃんじゃん
はーーよかったぁ

MY HEAVENLY HOCKEY CLUB

BY AI MORINAGA

WHERE THE BOYS ARE!

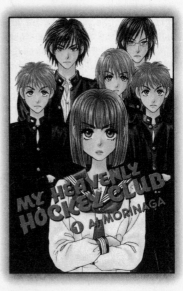

Hana Suzuki loves only two things in life: eating and sleeping. So when handsome classmate Izumi Oda asks Hana—his major crush—to join the school hockey club, convincing her proves to be a difficult task. True, the Grand Hockey Club is full of boys—and all the boys are super-cute—but, given a choice, Hana prefers a sizzling steak to a hot date. Then Izumi mentions the field trips to fancy resorts. Now Hana can't wait for the first away game, with its promise of delicious food and luxurious linens. Of course there's the getting up early, working hard, and playing well with others. How will Hana survive?

MY HEAVENLY HOCKEY CLUB
1 AI MORINAGA

Special extras in each volume! Read them all!

VISIT WWW.DELREYMANGA.COM TO:
- Read sample pages
- View release date calendars for upcoming volumes
- Sign up for Del Rey's free manga e-newsletter
- Find out the latest about new Del Rey Manga series

RATING AGES T 13+

DEL REY DEL REY MANGA デルレイ
The Otaku's Choice™

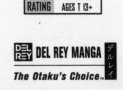

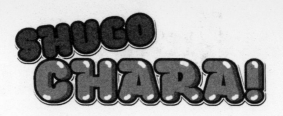

SHUGO CHARA!

PEACH-PIT

Creators of *Dears* and *Rozen Maiden*

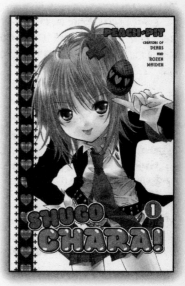

Everybody at Seiyo Elementary thinks that stylish and super-cool Amu has it all. But nobody knows the *real* Amu, a shy girl who wishes she had the courage to truly be herself. Changing Amu's life is going to take more than wishes and dreams—it's going to take a little magic! One morning, Amu finds a surprise in her bed: three strange little eggs. Each egg contains a Guardian Character, an angel-like being who can give her the power to be someone new. With the help of her Guardian Characters, Amu is about to discover that her true self is even more amazing than she ever dreamed.

PEACH-PIT
CREATORS OF
DEARS
AND
ROZEN
MAIDEN
SHUGO
CHARA!
1

Special extras in each volume! Read them all!

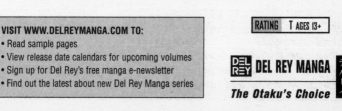

VISIT WWW.DELREYMANGA.COM TO:

- Read sample pages
- View release date calendars for upcoming volumes
- Sign up for Del Rey's free manga e-newsletter
- Find out the latest about new Del Rey Manga series

RATING T AGES 13+

DEL REY MANGA デルレイ

The Otaku's Choice

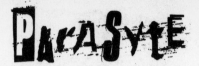

PARASYTE

BY HITOSHI IWAAKI

THEY DESCEND FROM THE SKIES.
THEY HAVE A HUNGER FOR HUMAN FLESH.

They are parasites and they are everywhere. They must take control of a human host to survive, and once they do, they can assume any deadly form they choose.

But they haven't taken over everyone! High school student Shin is resisting the invasion—battling for control of his own body against an alien parasite committed to thwart his plans to warn humanity of the horrors to come.

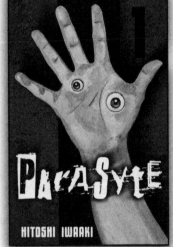

- *Now published in authentic right-to-left format!*
- *Featuring an all-new translation!*

Special extras in each volume! Read them all!

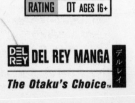

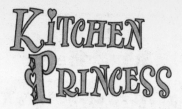

KITCHEN PRINCESS

STORY BY MIYUKI KOBAYASHI
MANGA BY NATSUMI ANDO
CREATOR OF ZODIAC P.I.

HUNGRY HEART

Kitchen Princess
1
custard pudding
rainbow colored jelly
christmas cookie
onion gratin soup
Story by
MIYUKI KOBAYASHI
Manga by
NATSUMI ANDO
Creator of Zodiac P.I.

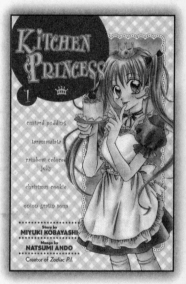

Najika is a great cook and likes to make meals for the people she loves. But something is missing from her life. When she was a child, she met a boy who touched her heart—and now Najika is determined to find him. The only clue she has is a silver spoon that leads her to the prestigious Seika Academy.

Attending Seika will be a challenge. Every kid at the school has a special talent, and the girls in Najika's class think she doesn't deserve to be there. But Sora and Daichi, two popular brothers who barely speak to each other, recognize Najika's cooking for what it is—magical. Could one of the boys be Najika's mysterious prince?

Special extras in each volume! Read them all!

VISIT WWW.DELREYMANGA.COM TO:
- Read sample pages
- View release date calendars for upcoming volumes
- Sign up for Del Rey's free manga e-newsletter
- Find out the latest about new Del Rey Manga series

RATING | T AGES 13+

DEL REY MANGA デルレイ
The Otaku's Choice

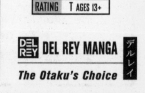

TOMARE!

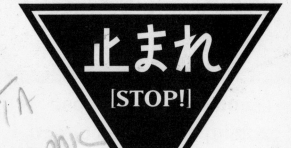

止まれ

[STOP!]

You're going the wrong way!

Manga is a completely different type of reading experience.

To start at the *beginning*, go to the *end*!

That's right! Authentic manga is read the traditional Japanese way—from right to left. Exactly the *opposite* of how American books are read. It's easy to follow: Just go to the other end of the book, and read each page—and each panel—from right side to left side, starting at the top right. Now you're experiencing manga as it was meant to be!